Reclaiming Indigenous
Voice and Vision

Edited by Marie Battiste

Reclaiming Indigenous
Voice and Vision

UBC Press · Vancouver · Toronto

09 08 07 06 05 04   5 4 3

Printed in Canada on acid-free paper ∞

National Library of Canada Cataloguing in Publication

Main entry under title:
  Reclaiming indigenous voice and vision

  Includes bibliographical references and index.
  ISBN 0-7748-0745-8 (bound); ISBN 0-7748-0746-6 (pbk)

  1. Indigenous peoples. 2. Decolonization. I. Battiste, Marie, 1949-

GV380.R42 2000   306'.08   C99-911286-4

Canadä

UBC Press gratefully acknowledges the financial support for our publishing program of the Government of Canada through the Book Publishing Industry Development Program (BPIDP), and of the Canada Council for the Arts, and the British Columbia Arts Council.

This book has been published with the help of a grant from the Canadian Federation for the Humanities and Social Sciences, through the Aid to Scholarly Publications Programme, using funds provided by the Social Sciences and Humanities Research Council of Canada

Set in Stone Serif by Brenda and Neil West, BN Typographics West
Printed and bound in Canada by Friesens
Copy editor: Dallas Harrison
Indexer: Christine Jacobs

UBC Press
The University of British Columbia
2029 West Mall
Vancouver, BC V6T 1Z2
604-822-5959 / Fax: 604-822-6083
www.ubcpress.ca

Contents

Foreword

L.M. Findlay

> I bring to you
> these Voices I will not name. Voices
> filled with bird calls, snorting buffalo,
> kicking bears, mountain goats.
> I do not recognize who speaks.
>
> ....
>
> Listen to the bones.
>
> – Louise Halfe, from "Listen to the Bones," in *Blue Marrow*

But what's in it for me? The apparent crassness of this question may startle the reader attracted by the title of this book and moved by my epigraph from Louise Halfe's most recent book of poems. Is this not a collection of essays specifically directed *beyond* narrow self-interest and the human and planetary costs of its pursuit by colonial powers? This is indeed the case, but to disapprove of or argue against narrow self-interest is not, alas, to eliminate it from the considerations and practices of individuals, communities, nations, and cartels. There is a need for at least a double strategy to combat such an entrenched orthodoxy, linked as it is to the fundamentals of modernity expressed in an increasingly globalizing economic and political ideology. One must vigorously protest the reduction of important and complex questions to the calculation of narrow self-interest, and the folly and dangers of such a reduction are eloquently documented in the main body of this text. But there is also a need, I think, to work within power structures that claim and compromise all of us whether we want them to or not. There is no escaping, for instance, the economic and military consequences of satellite surveillance or the appropriation of all forms of communities everywhere as markets to be penetrated or obstacles to be eliminated in one way or another. All the world's a stage – but too often and too simply a stage in the accelerating history of transnational capitalism. And once China comes to its senses, many say, we can all play the same consuming game with equal zeal, until, on the surface of an Earth made massively unproductive in the name of productivity, we are forced literally to cannibalize each other, just as they said (and say) those early "savages" did.

The task of opposing the dominant orthodoxies of modernity from a position at their ever-extending margins, or from a strategically primitivist place outside, is crucial and dangerous work. But perhaps the greater challenge, at least for non-Aboriginal academics, is for them to admit to their own inescapable self-interest and to discover its compatibility with the agenda of the Aboriginal "Other." Significant numbers of Euro-Canadian scholars have become remarkably good at critiquing the pretensions and practices of modernity and defending marginalized groups, but they do so within institutions among whose faculties Aboriginal people are minimally represented. And so the university, that unrivalled engine of what is called progress, can point only to meagre internal self-representation by Aboriginal scholars and to the growing industry of speaking for the Indigene, explaining Aboriginal people to themselves, to governments, to the general public of whom they form an important part, and justifying doing so in the name of a kinder, gentler academic "truth" than those that were and are still used across the world by states and their functionary institutions to legitimate betrayal, theft, and genocide.

Culture, underpinned as usual by faith, law, and revisionary history, has proven only too capable of doing what main force could not, which was to make the colonizer capable of sleeping at night or reaching across the dinner or communion table without recoiling from the sense of the blood of the "Other" on his hands. In the name of culture, colonialism does its work and dignifies its meaning as duty and improvement and the exhilarating march of progress. And so there is the need, so urgent and ubiquitous today, for cultural restoration of the colonized. There is the further need, for those who have the most say about what counts as culture, to *use* their knowledge and professional and institutional status to *help change* the dominant definition and understanding of Aboriginal knowledge. And in order that such scholars assist in effecting change far greater than their current liberal complacency requires, each needs to know what's in it for him or her.

So, as a Euro-Canadian, tenured full professor in a university English department, what's in the cultural restoration of Aboriginal peoples for me? The short answer for a foreword like this is an education such as I have never had and cannot otherwise acquire. And this education must come in part from the appointment of Aboriginal scholars to positions of leadership within universities. But such a development is hard to achieve, not only because of the variety and urgency of the demands on the time and energy of such people, but also because of Eurocentric reactions within universities to such possibilities. And this is true of my "own" university, the very institution that in 1996 hosted an international summer institute on the cultural restoration of Aboriginal peoples and hosted a special, unforgettable convocation to honour Chief Ted Moses, Dr. Erika-Irene Daes, and Rigoberta Menchu Tum. Like other universities across

Canada and around the world, the University of Saskatchewan is still influenced to a significant degree by faculty who find much to paternalistically pity or high-mindedly deplore in the "uncivilized" histories and "subcultural" practices of Aboriginal peoples. These self-styled guardians of academic "excellence" feel obliged to exclude or depreciate the possibility of Aboriginal knowledge, Aboriginal understanding of power, accountability, and leadership. For these guardians, who are found in all disciplines as well as in the ranks of senior administrators and remain key to the ongoing marginalization and/or assimilation of Aboriginal students and scholars, to think otherwise would be *to bring thinking itself into question*. It would be tantamount to seeing academic rationality as in part a Euro-imperial, historically specific construct and therefore not a neutral, "human" universal.

To do otherwise than resist or pay the most reluctant lip service to the claims of Aboriginal leadership is, it would seem, to lower academic standards while conceiving power, status, autonomy, and accountability outside the Euro-imperial mix of hierarchy and careerism. And still today, for some academics, that would never do. So we are still faced with the regrettable but surmountable barrier of academic analysis, policy, and resource distribution accommodating prejudice in the name of knowledge. We are also faced with the depressing but remediable truth that universities remain massively complicit with neocolonial forces in society. Universities are in great need of Aboriginal leadership because it will benefit everyone, even those who resist it. Alas, universities are still run for the most part by an academic managerial cadre more at home schmoozing with corporate donors (many of whom dominate university boards of governors) than really putting their minds to the task of indigenizing knowledge in those institutions where legitimacy is established and opportunity enhanced. These academic managers too often choose to plead "helplessness" in the face of fiercely territorial faculty and the alleged insolubility and invasiveness of "Aboriginal politics." Fashioned as they are as chief executive officers, in fact or in the making, within the increasingly corporatized university, non-Aboriginal administrators are under considerable pressure to appear genteel, collegial, clubbable, while acting in a supine, prudent, or paternalistic way. Their selective "helplessness" serves as code for a more broadly sanctioned reluctance to act boldly and decisively on behalf of Aboriginal knowledge within universities and social elites. There is therefore a great deal for me in the possibility of following Aboriginal academic leadership as I endeavour to function as a socially just and appropriately informed cultural worker within but also beyond and against the Western canon.

What's in it for me includes not only education through generous and inspiring leadership but also the education that Aboriginal colleagues and students can give one, and not only in areas narrowly conceived as cultural. In fact, the project of Aboriginal self-legitimization within the academy, which has had prominent expressions in the area of law and education, with creeping presences in literary studies, history, anthropology, nursing, and business studies, and in Native studies in recent decades, needs to demystify "research," contesting the supremacy of science and technology and the professional bastions of medicine and engineering. As a humanist whose teaching and research are frequently trivialized by colleagues in the sciences and professions, though often with the best of intentions, I can benefit directly and indirectly from the vigorous promotion of Aboriginal pedagogy and knowledge across the academic disciplines. If leading-edge medicine, mining, fishing, forestry, or agriculture are ever to become truly ethical and sustainable, in short to *better* themselves, then it is hard to see how they can do so without gaining access to Aboriginal knowledge; and they will only get close to that priceless living archive in a climate of social and economic justice and trust. The obligations and opportunities are obvious enough, but old colonial habits die hard, and Aboriginal suspicions derive from a heinous experience of colonial encounter. Yet there is reason for hope. At the appointment to the Provincial Court of Saskatchewan of Dr. Mary Ellen Turpel-Lafond, a leading Aboriginal lawyer, teacher, and scholar, in a ceremony held in the wonderfully apt and ancient Cree setting of Wanuskewin, on the banks of the South Saskatchewan River, Sákéj Henderson described the new judge's location in the legal system as an in-between lodge. If she had instead, as she well might have, joined the academy as, say, dean of arts and science or law, then Henderson's description would have been no less resonant and suggestive. Perhaps the university as a whole ought to accept the in-between lodge as its institutional identity, offering hope and responsibility in a space where staff, students, faculty, and administrators invoke and respect all their interrelations. That change of identity might encourage us not only to think the hitherto unthinkable but also to do what many deem impossible or undesirable or both.

Culture – as the university community and society know it – would undoubtedly be changed by the cultural restoration of Aboriginal peoples, but that change would benefit everyone, encouraging those who have much to offer while moderating the pretensions and increasing the receptivity of those who too often think and act as if they know it all. Anyone who has taught classes including Aboriginal students knows not only the challenges that those students face but also the remarkable contributions that they can make if they think that the learning environment recognizes them as a resource rather than a liability. Anyone who has had the opportunity to work with Aboriginal colleagues in a university setting will know the subtlety of their thinking and the generosity of their scholarly practice. By such a claim, I mean neither to patronize nor to sentimentalize or exoticize individuals with very different temperaments and aptitudes but only to point to the rights of various communities to promote group practices and values based on their collective histories and strengths. Aboriginal peoples have had to wait centuries for settler societies and waves of immigrants to catch up with them in dealing respectfully with all life forms, especially the ones on which our very survival depends. Unfortunately, far too many non-Aboriginals have been educated to see dependency as an insult or an embarrassment or something to be managed hierarchically within the ultra-competitive structures of a corporate or government team.

We need to *learn*, then, that not all our limits are there to be transcended. We need to *learn* that much more in life is inevitable than death and taxes. And this *learning* may best occur in and beyond institutions directed by a new politics of difference and an indigenized understanding of sustainability. This will in turn require the rethinking and radical transformation of the colonizing encounter that remains the predominant experience of the Aboriginal student or scholar interacting with elite institutions such as universities. And the present collection of essays, graced and essentially empowered as it is by Aboriginal voices, will surely help readers individually and collectively to advance along the pathway to acknowledged and fruitful interdependency and a new respect for the Earth. Admittedly, there will always be a question hanging over or eating away at us. However, the broadly restorative valuing of Indigenous knowledge may change that question from "But what's in it for me?" to "What's in us for it?" Let us all listen to the bones and listen also to the living. Let us help whenever, wherever, and however we can in restoring Aboriginal cultures, and we will all be the wiser and better for that.

Acknowledgments

The editor gratefully acknowledges all those who have made this book possible. I am especially grateful to the participants of the 1996 International Summer Institute and to the authors whose oral and written texts have been revised as the basis for this book. While the texts went through extensive editing, some of the orality is retained in keeping with a valued tradition of Indigenous peoples. Their visions and continuing quest for a new order, despite great challenges, honour Indigenous peoples everywhere.

Thank you to the Social Sciences and Humanities Research Council of Canada (SSHRCC), which provided generous support for the 1996 International Summer Institute held at the University of Saskatchewan, Saskatoon, from which these essays emerged. Many persons and units within the University of Saskatchewan also provided abundant support, including President George Ivany; Dr. Asit Sarkar, Director of U of S International; Dr. Michael Owen, former Director of Research Services and current Director of Research Services at Ryerson Polytechnical University, Ontario; Marge St. Denis, former assistant to the president; Don Cochrane, Department Head of Educational Foundations; the Colleges of Education, Law, Arts and Sciences, Medicine, Pharmacy, Graduate Studies and Research, and Agriculture; the Native Law Centre, the Humanities Research Unit (HRU) within the Department of English, the Extension Division, and the Department of Educational Foundations.

Very special thanks are extended to Sákéj (James Youngblood) Henderson, Director of the Native Law Centre, and Professor Len Findlay for their partnership and mentorship in initiating and developing the institute and for their astute appraisal, valued suggestions, and continuous and generous support during the many stages of this book; to Dr. Danny Musqua, Saulteaux Elder, and Eric Tootoosis, Cree Elder, whose knowledge, guidance, and support during the institute were most valued and appreciated; to Dr. Isobel Findlay for her insightful and extensive editing of earlier drafts and for her constant encouragement and friendship; to Jane Billinghurst of Pagewood Publishing for her copious editing of the initial manuscript; to Alex Taylor Cid and Helga Lomosits, whose energy and caring engineered the institute; to Ginny Brown, graduate secretary in the Department of Educational Foundations, and graduate student Elizabeth Maier for their work on various stages of production; to our extended community, which shared its support, advice, and laughter during many needed times; and to my children, Jaime, Mariah, and Annie, whose understanding and support are always needed and valued.

Portions of this book have appeared elsewhere in different forms. I am thankful for the permission to reprint several excerpts from books and for the timely consideration for their use in this book. The excerpt of Louise Halfe's poem "Listen to the Bones" first appeared in *Blue Marrow* (Toronto: McClelland and Stewart, 1998). Chief Lindsay Marshall of Chapel Island Reserve, Nova Scotia, graciously provided permission to reprint "Clay Pots and Bones" and "The Nation World," both of which first appeared in *Clay Pots and Bones Pka'woqq aq Waqntal* (Sydney, NS: Sydney Printers, 1997). The poem "The Rose of Hope" first appeared in *Kelusultiek Original Women's Voices* (1994) with the permission of poet Shirley Kiju Kawi (Shirley Christmas). Chapter 6 is an abridged version reprinted from *Native American Post-Colonial Psychology* by Eduardo Duran and Bonnie Duran, by permission of the State University of New York Press © 1995, State University of New York. All rights reserved. Chapter 4 relies heavily on several authors, including Roberto Mangabeira Unger, *Law in Modern Society: Toward a Criticism of Social Theory* (p. 1; © 1976 by Roberto Mangabeira Unger, reprinted with permission of the Free Press, a Division of Simon & Schuster) and *Passion: An Essay on Personality* (p. 10; © 1984 by Roberto Mangabeira Unger, reprinted with permission of The Free Press, a Division of Simon & Schuster); J.M. Blaut, *The Colonizer's Model of the World: Geographical Diffusionism and Eurocentric History* (New York: Guilford Press, 1993); Albert Memmi, *The Colonizer and the Colonized* and *Dominated Man: Notes Toward a Portrait* (used by permission of Viking Penguin, a division of Penguin Putnam Inc.); and Lise Noël, *Intolerance: A General Survey* (Montreal: McGill-Queen's University Press, 1994). *Intolerance* is an English translation of *L'Intolérance: Une problématique générale*, first published by Les Éditions du Boréal in 1989. Viking Penguin, a division of Penguin Putnam Inc., provided permission for the use of an excerpt from Leslie Silko's book *Ceremony* (© 1977 by Leslie Silko). Chapter 8, "A Different Yield," by Linda Hogan, is reprinted from *Dwellings: A Spiritual History of the Living World* (New York: W.W. Norton, 1995) with permission of the author. Chapter 9 draws on the works of several authors. Excerpts from the 1969 Boyer Lectures entitled 'After the Dreaming' reproduced by kind permission of Mrs. P. Stanner and the Australian Broadcasting Corporation. I also thank Farrar, Straus and Giroux for verses of Derek Walcott's poem "Forest of Europe" from the book *Collected Poems 1948-1984* by Derek Walcott (© 1986 by Derek Walcott). And last but not least, I thank Donna Banks of Saskatoon, Saskatchewan for the cover photo of 3 tipis taken at Wanuskewin Heritage Park in Saskatoon.

Introduction: Unfolding the Lessons of Colonization

Marie Battiste

As the twentieth century unfolds to a new millennium, many voices and forums are converging to form a new perspective on knowledge. Many of these voices belong to the Indigenous peoples who have survived European colonization and cognitive imperialism. They represent the thoughts and experiences of the people of the Earth whom Europeans have characterized as primitive, backward, and inferior – the colonized and dominated people of the last five centuries. The voices of these victims of empire, once predominantly silenced in the social sciences, have been not only resisting colonialization in thought and actions but also attempting to restore Indigenous knowledge and heritage. By harmonizing Indigenous knowledge with Eurocentric knowledge, they are attempting to heal their people, restore their inherent dignity, and apply fundamental human rights to their communities. They are ready to imagine and unfold post-colonial orders and society.

This book reveals some of these voices of commitment. They emerged from the meetings of the delegates of the United Nations Working Group on Indigenous Populations, held every year in Geneva, that converged in debates and drafting sessions on Indigenous rights. In 1996, many of these committed voices gathered at the University of Saskatchewan in Saskatoon, Canada, to honour Rigaberto Menchu Tum, Chief Ted Moses, and Erica-Irene Daes, "organic" leaders in Indigenous human rights initiatives. In the intense summer days and nights of 1996, delegates from many lands – lands that colonizers called Australia, New Zealand, South America, Europe, and North America – assembled for an unprecedented honouring ceremony and a focused talking circle to seek remedies for the colonization of the minds and souls of their peoples. The participants were Indigenous teachers and scholars and non-Aboriginal "friends" or allies. In the following collection of essays, the voices of commitment and action articulate their teachings, stories, perspectives, and reflections in many different styles – passionate, scholarly, poetic, painful, practical – all of them visionary.

A significant starting point for discussing these themes was the story of the elder's box as told by Eber Hampton, a Chickasaw educator and the president of the Saskatchewan Indian Federated College, the national post-secondary educational institute of the First Nations of Canada. He told of an elder who asked him to carry a box. Thinking well of his own youthful stature, he felt proud to be chosen and agreed willingly. The elder then thrust forward what appeared to be an empty box, which puzzled him:

> His question came from behind the box, "How many sides do you see?"
> "One," I said.
> He pulled the box towards his chest and turned it so one corner faced me. "Now how many do you see?"
> "Now I see three sides."
> He stepped back and extended the box, one corner towards him and one towards me. "You and I together can see six sides of this box," he told me. (Hampton 1995, 42)

Just as the elder revealed that there is more than one perspective required to view a box holistically, the gathering revealed many perspectives on how to map and diagnose colonization, how to heal the colonized, and how to imagine and invoke a new society. In group sittings and stories told in many dialogues and related in many texts, the gathering found multiple layers of experience and knowledge about colonization that profoundly challenged us to find remedies. We began to see the many sides of our confinement, our box.

Through our sharing, listening, feeling, and analyzing, we engaged in a critique of the trauma of colonization. We examined the frameworks of meaning behind it, we acknowledged the destructiveness that it authorized, and we imagined a postcolonial society that embraced and honoured our diversity. We shared many sides of a box that we came to know more fully. We came to see colonization as a system of oppression rather than as personal or local prejudice. We came to understand that it is the systemic nature of colonization that creates cognitive imperialism, our cognitive prisons (Battiste 1996).

Over the course of those ten days, the voices in the gathering converged to address strategies for neutralizing the systemic nature of our oppression, identifying its viral sources, and understanding how it imprisons our thoughts. Together we sought to find ways of healing and rebuilding our nations, peoples, communities, and selves by restoring Indigenous ecologies, consciousnesses, and languages and by creating bridges between Indigenous and Eurocentric knowledge. We discovered that we could not be the cure if we were the disease. Discovering the cures that will heal and restore our heritage and knowledge is an urgent agenda occupying the daily and intellectual lives of Indigenous peoples. It will be the most significant problem facing Indigenous peoples in the Decade of the World's Indigenous Peoples, 1995-2004, as Indigenous peoples around the world continue to struggle against oppression. Understanding the processes that we detected in the course of our gathering will help to unravel ethnic tensions and wars and allow humanity to rebuild society based on diversity rather than on an ancient quest for singularity.

The participants were unique representatives of their peoples who brought to the meeting diverse ecological consciousnesses, languages, and cultures, as well as similar expressions of caring and kindness. They were the first generation of Indigenous scholars accomplished in both Eurocentric and Indigenous thought, thus providing a bridge that allowed us to enter into a dialogue and translate Indigenous knowledge and heritage. Each had walked in the colonizers' moccasins, learned to speak their languages and know their methodologies, thus earning their critiques and their respect as valued leaders and resources to protect the heritages of their nations, peoples, and communities.

Led by Leroy Little Bear, an eminent Blackfoot philosopher and scholar, now retired from the University of Lethbridge and the American Indian Programs at Harvard University, we worked together to solve the mystery of the box. He enriched our analyses and imagined the possibility of a postcolonial society that would enable us to create our own sustaining and nourishing realities. He gently urged us to respect the process of developing ourselves in healing and renewing ways and to dream for those equitable and shared benefits that we felt were necessary. He led our dialogues to sharpen our insights gained from our experiences, and he helped us to confirm our commitment to forms of inquiry both timely and exacting, as we developed new networks of solidarity.

Under the Medicine Wheel processes of the northern Plains, the sessions were organized around four related themes: mapping colonialism, diagnosing colonialism, healing colonized Indigenous peoples, and imagining postcolonial visions. As we shared our thoughts in our group dialogues, we sought to address some of the essential questions of colonization. What is it in the nature of European cultures that has resulted in the oppression of so many peoples worldwide? What is it in the nature of Indigenous peoples' culture that has allowed colonization to happen? What can we do now, and what principles can we bring forward to achieve these visions from those ten days together?

The participants shared their personal and collective pain, anguish, and analyses of their experiences with colonialism. Each had experienced most or some aspects of colonization and was enmeshed in reforming colonial governments, laws, education, economies, and institutions that sought to erase their identities, languages, and cultures, creating new colonized identities that would be impoverished in the wake of violence and destruction. Each had experienced a side of the box that others had not experienced; for some of us, there were parts of the box that we could not fully access but we still felt their presence.

These sharing sessions and dialogues are enfolded within these essays, which represent modern Indigenous voices and syntheses of the experience of colonization and Indigenous thought in many styles and from many different points of view. Many of the essays contain the "orality" of Indigenous traditions, aspects that could not be changed without destroying these voices. These essays declare an Indigenous framework of meaning and of what has been destructive that is rarely shared. They provide new frameworks for understanding how and why colonization has been so pervasive among Indigenous peoples, as well as what Indigenous peoples desire and imagine as a better life in a postcolonial context. They also offer existing and new methodologies, conceptual designs, and approaches for implementing the healing and cultural restoration of Indigenous peoples across disciplines.

The writings seek to move beyond the existing Indigenous experience of colonization by liberating Indigenous thought, practices, and discourses rather than by relying on existing Eurocentric or colonial theory. Indigenous thinkers use the term "postcolonial" to describe a symbolic strategy for shaping a desirable future, not an existing reality. The term is an aspirational practice, goal, or idea that the delegates used to imagine a new form of society that they desired to create. Yet we recognized that postcolonial societies do not exist. Rather, we acknowledged the colonial mentality and structures that still exist in all societies and nations and the neocolonial tendencies that resist decolonization in the contemporary world. Such structures and tendencies can only be resisted and healed by reliance on Indigenous knowledge and its imaginative processes.

Postcolonial Indigenous thought should not be confused with postcolonial theory in literature. Although they are related endeavours, postcolonial Indigenous thought also emerges from the inability of Eurocentric theory to deal with the complexities of colonialism and its assumptions. Postcolonial Indigenous thought is based on our pain and our experiences, and it refuses to allow others to appropriate this pain and these experiences. It rejects the use of any Eurocentric theory or its categories.

The writings in this book firmly embed the fundamental concept that Indigenous knowledge exists and is a legitimate research issue. Many parts of the existing Eurocentric academy have not fully accepted this principle, arguing that there is no such thing as an Indigenous perspective. Post-colonial, Aboriginal, and postmodern scholars have had to confront this position, as they have had to confront the institutions in which they function. Most delegates from university communities were having trouble articulating the differences between these two systems of knowledge, but through the shared dialogues they became aware of the singularity of Eurocentric thought – even if some of the issues around the diversity of approaches to life and nature remained unresolved. They came to understand the prevailing authority of Eurocentric discourses and how the unreflective dominance of these discourses in academia has led to the historical and contemporary immunity to understanding and tolerating Indigenous knowledge.

Indigenous knowledge, including its oral modes of transmission, is a vital, integral, and significant process for Indigenous educators and scholars. It has been upheld by the Supreme Court of Canada as a legitimate form for understanding and transmitting Indigenous knowledge, history, and consciousness. The Supreme Court of Canada has ordered the legal profession, in *Delgamuukw* v. *The Queen* (1997), to include and respect Indigenous oral traditions in standards of evidence, overruling centuries of development of the British rules of evidence. The justices of the Supreme Court held that Indigenous oral traditions are legitimate sources of evidence and ordered the courts to modify rules of evidence and procedures to acknowledge and value these traditions. This decision offers a powerful analogy for the interpretive monopoly of existing standards of research scholarship. If the courts are required to consider oral traditions, then all other decision makers should likewise consider the validity of oral traditions, including oral dissemination within Aboriginal and non-Aboriginal communities, as significant sources for the distribution and dissemination of Aboriginal knowledge and scholarship.

The necessity of bringing forward Aboriginal knowledge, perspectives, and research is being increasingly felt at all levels of scholarship. In a speech to the university community, the president of the Social Sciences and Humanities Research Council of Canada aptly pointed out that the traditions of the university to "publish or perish" have been globally tested and that the new agenda for universities will need to be "go public or perish" (Marc Renaud, Sorokin Lecture, University of Saskatchewan, Saskatoon, February 4, 1999).

Indigenous scholarship, along with research that requires moral dialogue with and the participation of Indigenous communities, is the foundation for postcolonial transformation. This scholarship evolves from a need to comprehend, resist, and transform the crises related to the dual concerns of the effect that colonization has had on Indigenous peoples and the ongoing erosion of Indigenous languages, knowledge, and culture as a result of colonization. It has involved clarifying the contested interests that occur in the many disciplines and fields of thought.

Much of the focus of Indigenous scholarship in the early years was on liberal solutions that attempted to make modal adjustments to existing institutions and their modes of delivery. There has been a growing awareness of late that we need a more systemic analysis of the complex and subtle ideologies that continue to shape postcolonial Indigenous educational policy and pedagogy. The writings in this book document action-oriented research practices. These practices identify sites of oppression and emancipation. They also support the agenda of Indigenous scholarship, which is to transform Eurocentric theory so that it will not only include and properly value Indigenous knowledge, thought, and heritage in all levels of education, curriculum, and professional practice but also develop a cooperative and dignified strategy that will invigorate and animate Indigenous languages, cultures, knowledge, and vision in academic structures.

This book offers a complex arrangement of conscientization, resistance, and transformative praxis that seeks to transform the dual crises related to colonization and culture. It is constructed on the multidisciplinary foundation essential to remedying the acknowledged failure of the current Eurocentric system in addressing educational equity for Indigenous peoples, in particular the diverse groups of disempowered peoples around the world. Similarly, it recognizes that Indigenous education is not one site of struggle but multiple struggles in multiple sites. Thus, these diverse struggles cannot simply be reduced to singular, one-dimensional solutions. Interventions and transformative strategies must be correspondingly complex, and they must be able to engage with and react to the multiple circumstances and shapes of oppression, exploitation, assimilation, colonization, racism, genderism, ageism, and the many other strategies of marginalization. This collection seeks not to resolve all tensions or their complex interfaces but to acknowledge and expose their existence and to take account of the factors as they appear in multiple sites, including epistemology, curriculum, schools, and teacher education (Smith 1997).

This book seeks to clarify postcolonial Indigenous thought at the end of the twentieth century. It is not a definitive work, but it is a good reflection. It represents the voices of the first generation of Indigenous scholars and seeks to bring those voices, their analyses, and their dreams of a decolonized context further into the academic arena. It urges an agenda of restoration within a multidisciplinary context for human dignity and the collective dignity of Indigenous peoples. It recognizes the existing right of self-determination, and it urges Indigenous peoples to promote, develop, exercise, and maintain their orders and laws and to determine their political status and pursue freely their cultural destiny within supportive social and economic development.

One Indigenous educator, Nata Inn ni Maki–Sacred Hawk Woman (Rose von Thater), has written about the knowledge and experience that she gained at the gathering:

> We were bringing to conscious recognition those elements foreign to our knowing that had entwined themselves within us, sapping us of our natural strength. We were seeing the experiences that had defined our lives with new eyes. We were looking at our history, accounting for its impact, taking ourselves to the doorways of understanding, discovering new possibilities, other strategies, watching as sources of power and strength emerged to reveal themselves in a new light. From this place and from these days together we were selecting, like artists, the elements that would tell a new story, taking from the past, re-ordering the present, envisioning a future that felt very much like a vision that had been held for us until we could reach out and hold it for ourselves. (Personal communication, June 27, 1997)

Indigenous peoples worldwide are still undergoing trauma and stress from genocide and the destruction of their lives by colonization. Their stories are often silenced as they are made to endure other atrocities. Many of these Indigenous peoples were unable to attend the institute to share their stories, despite their efforts. For them and for all Indigenous peoples worldwide, we seek to initiate dialogue, advance a postcolonial discourse, and work actively for a transformation of colonial thought. It becomes our greatest challenge and our honour to move beyond the analysis of naming the site of our oppression to act in individual and collective ways to effect change at many levels and to live in a good way. These writers are actively seeking to reject the categories assigned to them and to make a difference in creating sustainable communities. Our efforts are to reveal the inconsistencies, challenge the assumptions and the taken for granted, expose the ills, and search from within ourselves and our Indigenous heritages for the principles that will guide our children's future in a dignified life. Our efforts are enfolded within the deep meaning of poet Antonio Machado's beautiful thought: "Caminante, no hay camino, se hace camino al andar" ("Traveller, there are no roads. The road is created as we walk it [together]") (as cited in Macedo 1994, 183).

Using the Medicine Wheel to guide and illustrate the interconnectedness and continuous flux of ideas, I have used the four directions of the Sacred Circle Wheel (the winds of West, North, East, and South) to characterize the divisions of this interrelated dialogue. The Medicine Wheel illustrates symbolically that all things are interconnected and related, spiritual, complex, and powerful. Indigenous writers have explained elsewhere about the teachings of the Sacred Directions (Battiste 1995; Calliou 1995; Hampton 1995). I start with the Western Door, an unlikely place for most Aboriginal people to begin their journeys, as most Aboriginal people begin their ceremonies with the East. However, my friend Eber Hampton, in "Redefinition of Indian Education" (1995), has offered his understandings of the meanings of the directions taken from within traditional ceremonies, and for me the Western Door is appropriate for the theme of *mapping colonialism* because the west is the direction of "Autumn, the end of summer, and the precursor of winter. On the great plains, thunderstorms roll in from the west. In Lakota cosmology, the good red road of life runs north and south and the road of death runs east and west. The coming of Western civilization (meaning western European), with its Western forms of education, to this continent was the autumn of traditional Indian education" (31). The Western Door thus begins with mapping the contours of the ideas that have shaped the last era of domination underpinning modern society and the varied faces of colonization as it is maintained in the present era. It is introduced in the prologue by Erica-Irene Daes and developed in subsequent essays.

The Northern Door is the "home of winter." Long nights of darkness evoke feelings of struggle and cold; long winters are when our very survival is challenged. Indigenous peoples are challenged by winter, but from their experience they learn endurance and wisdom. The north, as Eber has pointed out, is cold and dark, with just a hint of light that makes it possible for us to hope and dream. This direction represents the theme of *diagnosing colonialism*. Whenever I teach my course Decolonizing Aboriginal Education, I find that my graduate students are enriched by the diagnosis of colonialism and by their own unravelling of their experience, whether they are the colonizers or the colonized. The Northern Door is the direction from which the diagnosis of colonialism emanates. It goes beyond the practice of colonial oppression to explore the unquestioned and conflicting assumptions that underpin oppressive relationships.

The Eastern Door is the direction of spring, of the sun rising. "The east is, through its association with the sunrise, a place of beginnings and enlightenment, and a place where new knowledge can be created or received to bring about harmony or right relations" (Calliou 1995, 67). In the morning, as we turn to the east, we pray for our children, our nations, and our future generations. We are conscious of how so many of our peoples have suffered through the winter, and now we look to find new ways to warm, nourish, and heal our fragile spirits. We can turn to the Earth, as Linda Hogan suggests, to find a different yield or to invoke new understandings from the collective efforts of Indigenous peoples, whether they come from political thought, constitutional reform, or international law. The Eastern Door of *healing colonized indigenous peoples* presents the intellectual and practical challenges to current ways of pursuing humane relationships. It is a process of healing ourselves, our collective identities, our communities, and the spirit that sustains us.

Finally, the Southern Door is "the direction of summer, the home of the sun, and the time of fullest growth" (Hampton 1995, 28). The summer resounds with the healthy sounds of our peoples as we convene to honour our teachings, our elders, and our ancestors in ceremonies and gatherings. It calls to mind long summer days and nights in dialogue and laughter and sharing around campfires, at feasts, pow wows, potlatches, and multiple ceremonies. Our traditions, as Eber has pointed out, preserve and sustain us. Thus, the final section of this book resounds with hope and anticipation as we turn to our traditions to preserve our communities, our education, our governance, and our future through focusing on the integrity of Aboriginal knowledge, systems, and their applications. It offers the foundation for reclaiming ourselves and our voice, as we *vision the Indigenous renaissance* based on Indigenous knowledge and heritage.

Raising consciousness of the struggles of oppressed Indigenous peoples throughout the world has been an intensely challenging objective but one that Erica-Irene Daes has achieved quietly and laboriously in her role as chairperson of the United Nations Working Group on Indigenous Populations. In her essay, "The Experience of Colonization Around the World," Erica introduces the theme of mapping colonization. She acknowledges that the anguished and urgent voices that she hears persistently are linked inextricably with aggression, violence, repression, and domination. These acts of oppression tear at the very spirit of individuals, denigrating the relevance and meaningfulness of their individual human lives. But being oppressed and marginalized, they are also, she notes, closest to an understanding of their oppression and to the sources of their healing and renewal. She outlines the social and psychological process of self-discovery in an emerging postcolonial world and the concomitant need for rebuilding alliances, making commitments, and holding nations accountable for their peoples. Her note of optimism is a fresh breeze on a still, hot summer day.

Western Door

Domination and oppression cannot be altered without the dominated and the dominators confronting the knowledge and thought processes that frame their thinking, their complacency, and their resistance. In "The Context of the State of Nature," James Youngblood (a.k.a. Sákéj) Henderson maps the contours of the false context that has shaped the recent era of domination that underpins modern society. He describes the foundational constructs of an artificial social contract and the laws and institutions that sustain it. The modern liberal state in Canada is the outcome of historic events. Sákéj suggests, however, that the liberal state was and is by no means the only alternative for developing a social contract for society. Treaty commonwealth is a social and legal alternative to colonization that challenges the current artificial context of the liberal state. As Sákéj explains, it is a viable alternative that represents rules of negotiation, consent, and remedies that embrace a more equitable relationship among people in a natural society.

Robert Yazzie, Chief Justice of the Navajo Supreme Court, contextualizes colonization among the Navajo, describing a series of laws, practices, and schemes that sought to control and dominate Native Americans in the United States. In "Indigenous Peoples and Postcolonial Colonialism," he chronicles the historical destruction of the Navajo and the consequences of this destruction for their worldview, traditions, and beliefs. He explains how historical clashes between Navajo and Eurocentric worldviews are manifested in legal and social discontinuity today. He offers a model of Navajo restoration of justice that is reemerging as a foundation for decolonized forms of justice and peacemaking within the Navajo Nation and that yields programs of recovery, reconciliation, and healing.

Poka Laenui (a.k.a. Hayden F. Burgess), a leading Indigenous lawyer, provides the voice of resistance of the Indigenous peoples of Hawaii. In his essay, "Hawaiian Statehood Revisited," he relates the cost of statehood to self-determination and raises vital questions for the future of the Indigenous people of Hawaii. The annexation of the islands that were called Hawaii to the United States was characterized as a glorious moment of celebration, a seemingly win-win liaison of positive value and merit to both Hawaii and the United States. However, a decade later the Indigenous voices of opposition began to be heard amid the large-scale destruction of Indigenous lands, rights, and sovereignty. Fraud rooted in colonial attitudes and policies led to Indigenous lands being "ceded" to the United States. The call for self-governance in the territories, a process meant to break the chains of colonization, ultimately led to an intentional perverting of the alternatives to statehood for Indigenous Hawaiians, which led to their further colonization.

Northern Door

Dismantling colonization to create a postcolonial state is an unfolding vision for Indigenous peoples worldwide. Sákéj Henderson, in "Postcolonial Ghost Dancing: Diagnosing European Colonialism," continues his analysis of colonization by examining the strategies, techniques, and competing components that constitute the system of colonialism. The theory of universality and the strategy of difference that underpin Eurocentric thought serve colonial domination by universalizing negative caricatures of Indigenous peoples to justify aggression, control, and domination. In the late nineteenth century, in their desperate longing to restore their past, the Plains Indians danced the Ghost Dance. The Ghost Dance that Indigenous peoples are dancing today is for the restoration of their worldviews in all areas of scholarship and professional practice.

Leroy Little Bear, the animator of the ten-day summer institute, provided ongoing analysis of the clashing worldviews of Aboriginal people and Canadian immigrants. His mapping of the Plains Indian worldview, culture, socialization, and methods of social control in "Jagged Worldviews Colliding" explains the jagged edge of empire that the Blackfoot encountered. It also explains how colonization results in overlapping, contentious, and competing cultures in modern society. Recognizing how these differences create discontinuity, division, and dissent among oppressed Indigenous peoples, including areas of law and education, Leroy seeks a new global order built on respect for diversity.

The psychological consequences of colonization for the oppressed have been largely characterized by Western psychology's attempt to achieve a state of "normalcy," an identity projected onto Indigenous peoples from European origins and images. In "Applied Postcolonial Clinical and Research Strategies," Bonnie and Eduardo Duran investigate cross-cultural psychology and seek a recognition of the sociohistoric reality that created the psychology of the oppressed – their acute and chronic reaction to genocide and colonization. They seek a decolonized analysis that includes giving credence to Native American history, identities, traditions, dreams, and visions, as well as utilizing Native people's own theories and methods for restoring the self and the nation. This essay, drawn from their book *Native American Post-Colonial Psychology*, seeks to reconceptualize cross-cultural psychology and to build bridges between Western therapy and Native American healing methods.

The psychology of the oppressor and the psychology of the oppressed are different faces of the same coin, dependent on each other for their value. Ian Hingley, a Saskatchewan teacher, chronicles his personal journey as dominator in "Transforming the Realities of Colonialism: Voyage of Self-Discovery," an introspective narrative that brings him to the awareness of his own privilege. He outlines his growing awareness of a systematically internalized mind-set that benefited from the subjugation and oppression of others. His journey to aspire to social justice, he acknowledges, must come with an awareness of his own privileges, often gained at the cost of others. He describes his awakening realization of his personal responsibility to make a conscious choice for change, a change that will result in a postcolonial world where privilege is not an inherent ingredient of oppression and self-honesty can lead to a collaboratively structured society.

Eastern Door

Our visions and dreams of a postcolonial world are not just emerging from a cognitive realm, and thus subject to the great or small minds of humanity, but they are also evolving from the whole Earth, which has its own yield. "A Different Yield," by Linda Hogan, is excerpted from her book *Dwellings: A Spiritual History of the Living World*. In it she offers a view, taken from an Aboriginal awareness, of the Earth as alive – thinking, creating, cautioning, and offering a new and humane alternative. She reminds us that the Earth responds to kindness, respect, prayers, and songs in the same way that humans do. She urges humanity to listen to the underground language in us. Its currents pass between us and nature to reveal a new clarity and reverence for life found in an ecology of the mind, a yield that returns us to our own sacredness, self-love, and a respect that will extend to others.

People speak their languages and relate their stories not just to tell of subsistence or sovereignty but also to tell of all that is meaningful for understanding ourselves, individually and collectively, as human beings. In "From Hand to Mouth: The Postcolonial Politics of Oral and Written Traditions," J. Edward Chamberlin reminds us how the world of reality and the world of imagination are sites of struggle for authenticity and authority. These worlds are manifested in languages, which are instruments of both survival and power. Chamberlin draws on language to examine the parameters of postcolonial theory, as one way but not the only way of looking at the lands, livelihoods, and languages of Indigenous peoples. He anticipates that postcolonial theory can open new understandings of the situation faced by peoples involved in the challenge of decolonization.

Asha Varadharajan provides a critical examination of the Western intellectual tradition that has institutionalized racial and cultural differences, thereby excluding "Others," and she urges a dialogue about the ideological conflicts in the Western intellectual tradition. In her essay, "The 'Repressive Tolerance' of Cultural Peripheries," she argues that it is not particularly useful to find or declare who is guilty in Western culture for colonialization, or to substitute one culture for another, but it is vital for modern society to explore the paradigmatic power of Western conceptions and to interrogate their function as normative categories in colonization. Her essay relates how race, sex, and class configure the critical discourse of Western thought from what is essentially a position of difference and how race, sex, and class subsequently inform anticolonial dissent and a vision of an antiracist future.

In "Processes of Decolonization," Poka Laenui again brings forward the Hawaiian example to illustrate the processes of colonization and decolonization and to describe what the processes of rediscovery, recovery,

mourning, dreaming, commitment, and action mean in the context of
Hawaii's quest for sovereignty.

This book raises some essential questions for Indigenous peoples. How
do we create a postcolonial society? How do we create a just society and an
innovative consciousness? How do we heal people who continue to suffer?
Recognizing the role that society and its institutions have played in
imposing their script on Indigenous peoples, Sákéj Henderson examines
the legal system of jurisprudence. In "Postcolonial Ledger Drawing: Legal
Reform," he points out both the cognitive and ideological prisons of
modern legal thought and the postcolonial dreams and processes that can
in practice empower peoples. Restoring rights to the diverse worldviews,
languages, identities, and treaty orders of Indigenous peoples in the
supreme law of Canada is not just a dream; it has been achieved in the
Constitution of Canada in sections 35 and 25, which affirm and protect
the rights of Aboriginal people. Aboriginal orders, visions, and dreams are
entrenched in the Constitution. These constitutional rights offer one layer
of restoration for Indigenous peoples; the next layer is one for each of us
to undertake, to implement restoration in responsible and reciprocal ways.

Aboriginal peoples have been invisible. Their rights have been trampled
on by nation-states that protect themselves behind domestic and international laws that simultaneously speak out against standards of injustice,
while they routinely normalize the genocide and torture of Indigenous
peoples. The principle of non-interference in the internal affairs of states
has led to massive human rights violations. The Indigenous peoples of
Canada in small but vocal groups have made their way to the international forums to find people of like mind who have had to endure similar
treatment worldwide and who are ready to stand together in solidarity
against these oppressions. In "Invoking International Law," Ted Moses,
Ambassador to the United Nations for the Cree Nation, describes the
efforts made in bringing Indigenous issues to the international community and the struggles that continue in multiple layers of diplomatic activity as Indigenous peoples persist in their efforts to protect their Indigenous
right for self-determination.

Southern Door

Seeking a postcolonial education begins with Indigenous peoples exploring their own symbols, expressions, and philosophy of Indigenous education and creating the context that they need, not only to make sense of
who they are but also to assert that sensibility in all aspects of their lives.
It begins with Indigenous peoples knowing their languages, their metaphors, their symbols, their characters, their stories, their teachers, and their
teachings. In "Indigenous Knowledge: The Pueblo Metaphor of Indigenous Education," Gregory Cajete offers some Pueblo teachings embedded

in the symbols of his people as a way to reflect on how we can use the tools of education in the process of redefining and reinventing the contemporary philosophy of Indigenous education. These teachings reverberate in Indigenous societies throughout North America in many different forms and practices and serve as a model for reconnecting with what was once hidden or suppressed, to find ourselves whole, balanced, open, and responsive, ready to assume the map that we have inherited and enfolded within each of us.

Given the persistent travesty of trust of Indigenous children in federal and public schools in Canada, the challenge for postcolonial educators is to transform education from its cognitive imperialistic roots to an enlightened and decolonized process that embraces and accepts diversity as normative. In the essay "Maintaining Aboriginal Identity, Languages, and Culture in Modern Society," I have sought to unravel and challenge the assumptions of modern society and to seek alternatives and processes that acknowledge the rights outlined in the Canadian Constitution and United Nations conventions and declarations. Legislation and policies that advance equitable education and respect for distinctive perspectives and understandings and ways of knowing are offered as a means of achieving these goals. Modern Western society has much to gain by learning about and from Indigenous peoples, but without a structural framework to achieve these ends the goals of decolonization will fall short of being actualized.

In the course of seeking a postcolonial vision, Indigenous peoples find many sites of struggle where they must actively assert themselves, their visions, and their knowledge to make transformative change a viable and lasting process. Sharing the Maori manifesto of Aotearoa (New Zealand) in "Protecting and Respecting Indigenous Knowledge," Graham Hingangaroa Smith addresses some of the central themes of decolonization and offers the Maori experience to illustrate some of the resistance and proactive strategies that have resulted in many of their successes. No longer content with mere social equality or good race relations that serve the status quo, the Maori have coalesced their struggle into a vision of self-determination. Drawing on their own schools and language to educate their children to their greater destiny, they have merged their Indigenous knowledge with their objectives and have developed the holistic vision and philosophy of Kaupapa Maori. Kaupapa Maori has defined and solidified their individual and collective roles, responsibilities, and processes to empower their vision and their future.

The need for a decolonized context inspires Indigenous peoples to break their silence and regain possession of their humanity and identity. Linda Tuhiwai Te Rina Smith, a leading Maori scholar, identifies the challenges for Maori people in making research a retrieved space from which to carry out the aims of Kaupapa Maori philosophy. Her essay, "Kaupapa Maori Research," maps out the developing field of an Indigenous epistemology that is as much emerging philosophy as it is adherence to a cultural worldview and process. It involves Maori peoples taking responsibility for what gets researched, as well as for how research is done, not just from some vague Western codes of ethics but also from within the parameters of Maori language, culture, and philosophy. Good Kaupapa Maori research takes into account the people, their history, their philosophy and principles, their legitimacy, and their struggle for autonomy over their own self-determination, their *tino rangatiratanga*.

The remaining obstacles to understanding Aboriginal consciousness and order are challenged in Sákéj Henderson's final essay, "*Ayukpachi:* Empowering Aboriginal Thought." Sákéj explores the application of the Aboriginal mind, spirit, and language to modern challenges and explores how that application remains interrelated with their traditional ecology and the knowledge base developed within their worldview and language. Mapping out some of the "langscape" of those Indigenous worldviews, he illustrates how an indeterminate yet empowered future can unfold from reliance on Indigenous thought, rather than from total reliance on Eurocentric thought.

References

Battiste, M. 1986. "Micmac Literacy and Cognitive Assimilation." In J. Barman, Y. Hébert, and D. McCaskill, eds., *Indian Education in Canada: The Legacy*, 23-44. Vancouver: UBC Press.

–. 1995. Introduction. In M. Battiste and J. Barman, eds., *First Nations Education in Canada: The Circle Unfolds*, vii-xx. Vancouver: UBC Press.

Calliou, S. 1995. "Peacekeeping Actions at Home: A Medicine Wheel Model for a Peacekeeping Pedagogy." In M. Battiste and J. Barman, eds., *First Nations Education in Canada: The Circle Unfolds*, 47-72. Vancouver: UBC Press.

Hampton, E. 1995. "Redefinition of Indian Education." In M. Battiste and J. Barman, eds., *First Nations Education in Canada: The Circle Unfolds*, 5-46. Vancouver: UBC Press.

Macedo, D. 1994. *Literacies of Power: What Americans Are Not Allowed to Know*. Boulder, CO: Westview Press.

Smith, G.H. 1997. "The Development of Kaupapa Maori: Theory and Praxis." Unpublished PhD diss., University of Auckland, New Zealand.

Reclaiming Indigenous
Voice and Vision

Prologue:
The Experience of Colonization
Around the World
Erica-Irene Daes

It is a particularly great honour, as well as a great challenge, for me to introduce the subject of this important and unprecedented effort to understand colonization and its remedies for Indigenous peoples. If my personal experience working within the United Nations system had not already given me such strong feelings about the terrible legacy of oppression of Indigenous peoples around the world, I would not have dared to attempt the awesome task with which I am entrusted.

I do not wish to intellectualize the experience of oppression. The significance of the theme of the 1996 International Summer Institute was that it focused on the personal and spiritual dimensions of experiencing, and liberating ourselves from, oppression. This was not a typical scholarly program, then, but an experiment in healing. I congratulate the organizers of the institute for their vision and express to the editor of this collection my gratitude for the invitation to open this book.

In keeping with the spirit and purpose of this collection of essays, I will begin on a personal note. I am Greek; my roots are in the island of Crete, the site of one of the first great civilizations of the world. In the eyes of most of the world, I represent Europe, the centre of global power and wealth, a continent to which most nations attribute a large share of their historical suffering. But my own people suffered for centuries under the yoke of the Ottoman Empire and fought a particularly bitter and bloody war for national liberation more than 150 years ago.

At one time my country was also a province of the Roman Empire. To be precise, the Greek cities were governed as protectorates of the Roman Empire, based on peace treaties that Roman lawyers conveniently interpreted, years after the fact, as surrendering absolute sovereignty to the emperor. Readers may recognize a parallel with their own history, here in Canada and elsewhere. As a result of widespread looting, particularly during successive wars, some of our greatest historical and cultural treasures are found today in foreign museums, including the marbles of the famous Parthenon.

Our struggles have continued into the modern world. As a young free-dom fighter, I personally took part in the struggle against Nazi domination in Europe. And, today, many thousands of people of Greek origin are still experiencing discrimination and oppression, particularly on the island of Cyprus, in Polish Turkey, and in Northern Epilus in South Albania.

Nearly every people has its legacy of oppression and injustice; some cruelties have been worse or more recent than others. I say this not to diminish the injustice of what occurred in North America but to make the point that the experience of oppression is universal. European peoples dominated one another long before they developed the power to domi-nate peoples in other regions of the world. For this reason, I do not think it is particularly useful to divide all modern humanity into the oppressed and the oppressors. I would like to argue that we differ more with respect to the extent that we recognize and grapple maturely with our common historical experiences of injustice.

There is an expression, "You cannot be the doctor if you are the disease." What I am saying is that Europeans themselves have had the disease of oppressed consciousness for centuries, and, as a result, they have grown so used to this experience that they do not always appreciate the fact that they are ill. Indigenous peoples, by comparison, are much closer in time to the experience of spiritual independence and therefore are generally far more aware of the extent to which the symptoms of the disease persist, even after the formal institutional machinery of alien domination has been dismantled and replaced by the appearance (at least) of renewed self-government and self-determination. This is why I consider this collection to be so important, to Indigenous peoples as well as to the rest of us. Indigenous peoples may feel particularly marginalized and threatened at this point in world history, but I submit that Indigenous peoples are the closest to an understanding of oppression and to the sources of their own healing and renewal. To continue the medical analogy, they may become the vaccine for a disease that is as old as humanity.

I would like to speak more concretely about the symptoms of this dis-ease, drawing on my own personal observations and perspective. I do not claim to be an expert psychiatrist or sociologist, but my work has involved me with the victims of colonization and oppression to an extraordinary degree, and I have been impressed by certain shared characteristics of their experiences.

Let me begin with the philosophical concept of "free will," which, we should all realize, is something of an illusion. None of us is ever completely free to do as we wish. We are guided, albeit often without our conscious knowledge, by the past – our memories, the values that we have been taught, the actions of our ancestors. We are also limited by the cir-cumstances of the present, including a great variety of physical elements and forces that exist beyond human control. Freedom is unavoidably experienced within boundaries or constraints – which is to say that it is relative.

Despite these constraints, it is fundamentally human to desire freedom. Moreover, it is our spiritual side that motivates us to pursue freedom, not our physical nature, our intellect, or our culture. A unique spirit within each of us strives to express itself, to be recognized, to have a name and a destiny. Each one of us is born with the innate spiritual optimism that our existence is not irrelevant but is an important part of the larger pattern of life. Through the pain and confusion of childhood, we are consoled by the growing awareness that every one of us will become a brush stroke in the evolving portrait of our families and nations – a single musical note, however small, in the symphony. In discovering and developing our individuality through our relationships with others, we find our joy and our solace.

All forms of oppression involve a denial of the individual spirit and its quest for self-expression. Colonialism, slavery, intolerance, discrimination, and war – all these cruel experiences share a common element: the utter denial of the victims' relevance. They do not exist except insofar as their lives – or their deaths – advance the desires of others. The victims provide the pigment, but somebody else holds the brush. The individual consciousness of the enslaved and the oppressed is superfluous; oppressed peoples are made to realize that they could serve their purpose equally well if they were mindless robots.

The experience of oppression is spiritual death. It is about the destruction of our inborn spiritual faith in the importance of individuality and, indeed, in the value of trying to stay alive. Victims of oppression not only lose interest in self-preservation but also find it difficult to maintain their relationships as parents, friends, and neighbours. If you have been made to feel irrelevant, you cannot understand why anyone could possibly love you, and you anticipate betrayal from anyone who tries. Oppression undermines love and trust among its victims.

Life is like a journey. We encounter mountains that must be climbed, rivers that must be crossed, and dark forests through which we must try to find our way. We gain wisdom and self-confidence from the choices that we make on this life journey. For the oppressed, however, a stranger is always by their side, blocking their chosen destination, saying to them, "Not that way." Eventually, the experience of oppression becomes internalized as an accumulation of implicit, subconscious limitations on freedom. External oppression becomes self-oppression. The victim of oppression travels the road of life thinking at every crossroads "Not that way," until the result is immobility, inaction, and self-isolation.

All peoples have been oppressed at one or more times in their histories. They differ mainly in their awareness of the effects of the experience on their beliefs and their behaviours. Consider, for example, the terrible conflicts that have been erupting recently in my part of the world, the Balkans. It seems impossible to reconcile the various parties. The only solution appears to be to separate them geographically. The second stage of the conflict is already becoming apparent, however, with the rise of mistrust and repression within the newly segregated states — particularly in Serbia. Many of the same processes can be detected in the Middle East.

External aggression and domination are inextricably bound to internal domination, repression, and violence. Although the oppressor seems to be in control of events, and thus immune from the spiritual erosion of domination, the oppressor and the oppressed are witnesses to the same cruel historical process – a process that denigrates the relevance and meaningfulness of individual human lives. Oppressive nations may win wars of conquest, but their external aggression returns to haunt them in a cycle of internal mistrust, domination, and violence. In the course of mobilizing their power to dominate others, they suffer their own spiritual deaths.

Let us consider the relatively recent history of the region where we met together for the 1996 International Summer Institute. Everyone is aware of the tragic nature of daily life in Aboriginal communities: unemployment, self-rejection, addiction, family violence. Many of the writers of this collection have been instrumental, as scholars and community leaders, in bringing these tragedies to public attention, as well as in tracing their causes to the waves of military, missionary, and bureaucratic intervention that gradually stripped the Indigenous nations of the Prairies of their chosen destinies. Without excusing themselves from responsibility for remedial action, Native people in Canada have correctly attributed the mistrust and unrest in their communities to the historical experience of colonization.

But now if we were to look across the road, so to speak, from the Indian reserves to the small towns and big cities of the North American Prairies, and if we were to look closely behind the facade of neat houses and shopping malls, here too we would find family violence, gang violence, abuse of children, and widespread alcohol and drug addiction. The pain and ugliness over on the non-Aboriginal side of the road is less visible, less publicized, less a topic of scholarly debate and official scrutiny. It is nonetheless there, a mirror image of the spiritual erosion on Indian reserves.

Are the two patterns unrelated? I think not. From a historical perspective, moreover, is it any wonder that the intensity of violence at the family and community levels is so much higher just a few hundred kilometres to the south, in the United States? I will leave you with this question. The tragic experience of colonization is a shared experience, and the oppressors as well as the oppressed need healing if the cycles of external aggression and self-destruction are to be discontinued.

Having made these points, I would like to turn briefly to a more hopeful discussion of what I see as positive developments in the decolonization of Indigenous peoples. I will not address decolonization in the legal or political sense, as that is addressed in some of the essays. My chief goal here is to understand colonialism at the subjective, social, and spiritual levels. What I wish to share with you are some personal insights into the impact of the work of the United Nations – in which I have been fortunate to be able to play some role – in the countercolonizing, or liberation, of Indigenous thought.

Let me begin by stating something that may seem obvious: isolation is an important tool, and a devastating result, of colonization. A fundamental weapon used by most colonizers against colonized peoples is to isolate the colonized from all outside sources of information and knowledge – and then to bombard them with propaganda carefully aimed at convincing them that they are backward, ignorant, weak, insignificant, and very, very fortunate to have been colonized!

This strategy of colonialism is designed to break down any resistance by persuading the colonized people that not only are they powerless to resist, but they would also be naive to attempt to do so. It aims to inculcate the colonized people with the idea that they are out of step with the rest of the world; that they have no friends; and that their feelings of resentment and resistance are foolish and, far from being justified, simply prove just how savage and ignorant they must be. By this means, the colonized society as a whole is made to think of itself as entirely alone in the universe – completely vulnerable and unprotected. At the individual level, colonized people learn to hide their real feelings and sincere beliefs because they have been taught that their feelings and beliefs are evidence of ignorance and barbarity.

I would like to submit, then, that one of the most destructive of the shared personal experiences of colonized peoples around the world is intellectual and spiritual loneliness. From this loneliness comes a lack of self-confidence, a fear of action, and a tendency to believe that the ravages and pain of colonization are somehow deserved. Thus, the victims of colonization begin, in certain cases, to blame themselves for all the pain that they have suffered.

What is the antidote? The answer to this question is clear to me, for I have seen the proof of it in my capacity as chairperson of the Working Group on Indigenous Populations for almost thirteen years. The antidote is travel, the rebuilding of old alliances and kinships across borders, and the discovery of like-minded peoples in other parts of the globe. In other words, the antidote is the discovery of other colonized peoples who share the same experiences and feelings. This discovery, I submit, demonstrates that the colonizers lied and that the feelings and beliefs of the colonized, far from being strange or backward, are the feelings and beliefs of most of humanity.

In psychological terms, travel, communication, and alliances tend to validate the feelings, beliefs, and aspirations of peoples who have suffered under colonialism. The experience is like stepping into the sunshine after many years of sitting in a darkened room, being told, confidently, that there is nothing but darkness. The sunshine wipes away the dark loneliness of colonization.

In my humble opinion, this is the real story – the real triumph – of the Working Group on Indigenous Populations. It is important because it has become the place of meeting for hundreds of Indigenous peoples, coming from every continent and nearly every country of the globe. It gives Indigenous peoples the opportunity to discover – with their own eyes and ears – the powerful truths that they number in the hundreds of millions and that they are not alone. This is why I do not despair at the political frictions and repeated delays in achieving our goal of the adoption of a United Nations declaration on the rights of Indigenous peoples. Each year that the struggle for the declaration continues, Indigenous peoples are growing morally, spiritually, and politically stronger as they rediscover one another.

The 1996 International Summer Institute on the Cultural Restoration of Oppressed Indigenous Peoples was a small part of that global process, yet it was one more step toward reaffirming the shared experiences of all the colonized peoples of the world and toward giving them strength in knowledge.

Western Door: Mapping Colonialism

Clay Pots and Bones

Dear successive fathers:
Explain to me please, when did the
change take place, from owners
to wards of the selfish state?
Write down the reasons why
the land under our feet became
foreign soil in perpetuity.
Say again how the signers of
1752 lost as much as they
gained while the ink from a
quill pen rested in its
blackened Royal well.
What justification exists that
allowed our mounds to be
desecrated, clay pots and bones.
Rock glyphs painted over by
cfc-propelled paint.
Our songs and stories protected
by copyright and law, not in the
bosom of our grandmothers or
grandfathers of yesterday.
The cost of keeping us does
not reflect the real cost.
How many ghostly sails with
reeking holds did English
ports comfort in early fog?
Have you much experience in
the destruction of people,
besides us?

– Chief Lindsay Marshall,
    in *Clay Pots and Bones Pka'woqq aq Waqntal*

1
The Context of the State of Nature
James (Sákéj) Youngblood Henderson

Terror and suffering have always been integral to European life and thought. Modern European political thought is constructed on the idea that terror is a legitimate source of sovereign power and law. What modern European political thought conceals, however, are the effects of such terror on those who suffer under the rule of this law.[1] Following the tradition of ideographic mapping on birch bark used by the Aboriginal peoples of the eastern forests of North America, I want to map the cognitive contours and choices that have led to the domination and oppression of Indigenous peoples and their terror and suffering. Specifically, I want to map the British seventeenth-century construct of the "state of nature," show how this idea created the competing frameworks of treaty federalism and colonialism, and critique the relevance of the construct in Indigenous struggles.

Modern European political thought has its roots in the "state of nature" theory propounded by the seventeenth-century English political philosopher Thomas Hobbes. Hobbes's vision of the state of nature remains the prime assumption of modernity, a cognitive vantage point from which European colonialists can carry out experiments in cognitive modelling and engineering that inform and justify modern Eurocentric scholarship and systemic colonization. Indigenous peoples have experienced this concept as slavery, colonization, and imperialism, as well as liberalism, socialism, and communism. These derivatives of Hobbes's vision are the source of our difference, our suffering, and our pain, and it is our experience of them that unites us against continued domination and oppression.

Since the Hobbesian vision of the state of nature and the ideas derived from it exist in our minds as part of the cognitive prison imposed on us by our Eurocentric educations, Indigenous peoples need to understand both the nature and the function of this ideology. To understand why and how we were taught in these ideas, which constrain both our present abilities and our children's future, we have first to understand the artificial context of European thought. The best way to understand this phenomenon is through the idea of contextuality.

The Idea of Contextuality or Artificial Paradigms

In attempting to understand our changing views of the natural order of the world, Thomas Kuhn, a historian and philosopher of science, in *The Structure of Scientific Revolutions* labelled the process of those changing views "paradigm shifts."[2] Kuhn argued that long periods of "normal science" have existed in history, periods in which the fundamental assumptions and concepts are accepted and not seriously questioned. The unreflective era gives way to a "scientific revolution" in which new assumptions, theories, and ideas change the existing conceptual foundations of science. Kuhn calls these competing conceptual foundation "paradigms." Paradigms include not only fundamental assumptions but also systems of theories, principles, and doctrines. A paradigm shift occurs when scientists cannot explain certain data or natural phenomena (often called "anomalies") by reference to established scientific theories. Periodically, certain scientists discover that these anomalies have a unity that requires a new theory, and a new scientific paradigm is created. The paradigm shifts in the history of science, from the Copernican to the Newtonian, and from the Newtonian to the Einsteinian, demonstrate how scientists change their views about how the world works.

In law and the social sciences, such explanatory paradigms are called "contexts." Contexts are related to the paradigm shifts in natural science. Just as a paradigm reflects current scientific thought about the natural world, so a context reflects current social, political, and legal thought about the human social order. Roberto Unger, a Brazilian legal scholar, has asserted that, if a context allows people to move within it to discover everything about the world that they can discover, then it is a "natural" context. If the context does not allow such natural movement, then it is an "artificial" context derived from selected assumptions.[3]

Unger asserts that three theses define artificial contexts. The first thesis is the principle of contextuality. Contextuality is the belief that assumptions or desires that humans take as given shape people's mental and social lives. These givens can be either institutional or imaginative. These assumptions form a picture of what the world is really like and even a set of premises about how thoughts and languages are or can be structured. They also provide a framework for explaining and verifying worldviews. These worldviews are artificial because they are dependent on assumptions made about human nature or society and not on what the world is really like independent of people's beliefs about it.[4]

Unger's second thesis is that these artificial worldviews are conditional and can be changed but that such changes are exceptional and transitory.

Any context can be supplemented or revised by other empowering ideas about features that make one explanatory or society-making practice better than another.[5] Thus, small-scale, routine adjustments in a context can turn into a more unconfined transformation. If the conditionality of any context is overcome, then people do not simply remain outside all context but also create new assumptions and contexts: "At any moment people may think or associate with one another in ways that overstep the boundaries of the conditional worlds in which they have moved till then. You can see or think in ways that conflict with the established context of thought even before you have deliberately and explicitly revised the context. A discovery of yours may be impossible to verify, validate, or even make sense of within the available forms of explanation and discourse; or it may conflict with the fundamental pictures of reality embodied in these forms."[6]

Like Kuhn's "normal science," Unger's third thesis is that the conditionality of any artificial context is rarely replaced. Changes to artificial context are exceptional and transitory because the context is viewed as "normal" or "natural" and is relatively immune to theories or activities. Disregarding the distinction between routine and transformation maintains the immunity of artificial context and prevents its conditionality from being questioned or opened up to revision and conflict.[7] As Unger explains, however, the more people become aware of the conditionality of a context, the more likely they are to be able to effect meaningful change to that context:

> But you can also imagine the setting, representation, and relationship progressively opening up to opportunities of vision and revision. The context is constantly held up to the light and treated for what it is: a context rather than a natural order. To each of its aspects there then corresponds an activity that robs it of its immunity. The more a structure of thought or relationship provides for the occasions and instruments of its own revision, the less you must choose between maintaining it and abandoning it for the sake of the thing it excludes. You just remake or reimagine it.[8]

Certain humans, for example, created modern society. Modern society is a human artefact. It has been derived from an artificial context, an assumption about the "state of nature" that has been unquestioningly accepted by modern thinkers. Indigenous people must remember that modern thought is conditional upon this assumption. If this assumption about the state of nature is wrong, then Indigenous peoples have the right to reject modern thought and assert a new assumption for the state of nature and an Indigenous theory of society.[9] This is precisely what the international human rights movement and current constitutional and legal reforms are attempting to accomplish by rejecting the idea of the Indigenous savage. We are seeking to challenge and transform the modernist vision of the state of nature and to replace it with an extraordinary context-breaking vision that relies on Indigenous teachings about our place in nature. For the present, it is sufficient to state that Indigenous peoples are attempting to effect a paradigm shift to replace the Eurocentric way of viewing the world with a new context that would be an ecological or natural context of Indigenous knowledge rather than a refined artificial one.

Unger asserts that no social theory or thinker has ever taken the idea of society as artefact to its ultimate conclusion. Most Eurocentric social theories have either ignored this idea or balanced it with an ambition to develop a lawlike explanation of history, such as Marxism. Most liberating Eurocentric political movements based on lawlike explanations have failed. Unger argues that the failures of these schemes have prepared the way for a more radical revision of the context. He argues that understanding artificial contexts allows people to explain themselves and their societies and enables them to broaden and refine their sense of the possible. If society is constructed with a disbelief in natural contexts and on artificial assumptions, then oppressed peoples can break loose from established views of themselves as helpless puppets of social worlds that others have imagined, built, and inhabited and from the lawlike forces that supposedly brought these worlds into being. Moreover, Unger argues that, by understanding how contexts stick together, come apart, and get remade, people can disrupt the "implicit, often involuntary alliance between the apologetics of established order, and the explanation of past or present society,"[10] and they can understand how the failures of artificial contexts prevent people from revising them. Faced with the immunity of artificial contexts and power of human-made legal orders of colonization, Indigenous peoples need a deeper understanding of the modernist theory of context and its immunity from transformations.

Unger's central thesis is that all major aspects of human empowerment or self-assertion depend on our success at diminishing the distance between context-preserving routines (law) and context-transforming conflict. Human empowerment relies on people's ability to invent institutions and practices that manifest context-revising freedoms.[11] From an understanding of artificial contexts, Indigenous peoples can understand how to inspire alternative contexts to end the domination and oppression that are the residue of colonialism. A constructive understanding of contexts also gives us greater mastery in reconstructing a more equitable society and more equitable human relationships. From this framework, let us turn to the artificial construct of the state of nature.

The Artificial Construct of the State of Nature

The construct of the state of nature emerged from the political thought of seventeenth- and eighteenth-century Europe, and it formed the basis for the artificial context of the modern state. The artificial context argued against established political context and discourse developed by Aristotle that held the state and village emerged from the hierarchical male-dominated family.[12] The seventeenth-century Dutch jurist Hugo Grotius developed the first comprehensive theory of international law by translating Aristotle's concepts into a belief that humans by nature are not only "reasonable" but also "social." For Grotius, "natural" was derived from reason alone (whether God exists or not), and he believed that it was because people were naturally reasonable that they were able to live in harmony with one another.

The British philosopher Thomas Hobbes argued that no such natural order exists. Hobbes considered philosophy to be a practical study of two kinds of bodies: natural and civil. He declared that "natural bodies" included everything for which there is rational knowledge of causal processes. He rejected the Platonic view that there was an objective reality that corresponded to ideas and words; he considered all reality to be subjective and all groupings to be created by artificial agreements.

After experiencing the ruinous English Civil War of 1642 to 1648, Hobbes was convinced that the ancient political and religious edifice was ending. While the Restoration court of Charles II sought his prosecution for heresy, during his exile in Paris Hobbes wrote his main work, *Leviathan; or the Matter, Forme, and Power of a Commonwealth, Ecclesiastical and Civil,* published in 1651.[13] The book was a philosophical study of the political absolutism that had replaced the supremacy of the Church. He created the context of the modern, artificial state out of the central concepts of fear, distrust, misery, and passion.

According to Hobbes, the state of nature was "the Naturall Condition of Mankind, as concerning their Felicity, and Misery."[14] The Hobbesian state of nature was a condition in which many European peoples existed under conditions of "high moral density" or morality but with no "common power to keep them all in awe."[15] He argued that the state of nature was a nonpolitical and antipolitical condition. The constitutive elements of the natural state were primarily and fundamentally individuals who were free and equal and who lived in natural associations such as families or households.

In the state of nature, a scarcity of desired things created competition for resources, distrust ("diffidence"), and glory (war and conquests). In Hobbes's view, the natural condition for each European man was to be in a state of fear of desiring others, resulting in personal and collective wars.

Self-preservation was the necessary condition for all of his satisfactions and pleasures, and each European man was equal with respect to his ability to preserve his life and realize his wants. Since each was equally able, each had an equal chance to fulfil his desires. Hobbes builds human equality not from cognitive facilities[16] but from an explosive concept that every human is at once vulnerable to being killed and capable of killing.[17]

Hobbes did not see European men as naturally social. He argued that the natural passions of European men were directed toward "good" – being their self-interests and desires – and that they had to be educated to see the long-term best interests of everyone.[18] To redeem them from their natural passions and aggressions and to educate them, the artificial man-state, the absolute sovereign, must be created by personal convenants.

Hobbes's state of nature was derived not from a scientific analysis of nature but from his understanding of European "human nature." Hobbes characterized the state of nature as a condition of desires and passions that creates distrust and universal enmity among people in a realm where nothing is unjust: "The notions of Rights and Wrong, Justice and Injustice have there no place. Where there is no common power, there is no Law: where no Law, no Injustice."[19] The natural state is a state of war that "consisteth not in actual fighting; but in the known disposition thereto."[20] Thus, "a state of war" is a condition in which each individual or group is ready to fight with the others and in which this fact is common knowledge. It is a condition in which human stagnation and misery is self-evident: "In such condition, there is no place for Industry; because the fruit thereof is uncertain; and consequently no Culture of the Earth; no Navigation, nor use of the commodities that may be imported by Seas; no commodious Building; no Instruments of moving, and removing such things as require much force; no Knowledge of the face of the Earth; no account of Time; no Arts; no Letters; no Society; and which is worst of all, continually feare, and danger of violent death; And the life of man, solitary, poore, nasty, brutish, and short."[21]

Hobbes is concerned with irrationality rooted in the passions, which he believes lead to conflict. Even if a person is rational, no one is assured of the rationality of others, and, lacking assurance about the rationality of others, rational individuals can land in a state of war.

Hobbes did not assert the universality of the state of nature. He did not believe that the state of nature "ever generally" existed "over all the world."[22] Instead, he asserted that there were "many places" where the state of nature did exist: "the savage people in many places of *America*, except the government of small Families, the concord whereof dependeth on naturall lust, have no government at all; and live at this day in that brutish manner, as I said before."[23] Hobbes used savages in America to illustrate the universal negative standards of primal chaos and the natural state of war.[24] The savage state envisioned by Hobbes provided more than the force creating and sustaining law and political society, however; it also created a spectacular repository of negative values attributed to Indigenous peoples.

Hobbes asserted that the state of nature and civil society are opposed to one another. The state of nature has a right of nature (*"Jus Naturale"*): "the liberty each man has to use his own power, as he will himself, for the preservation of his own nature, that is to say, his own life; and consequently, of doing any thing which in his own judgment and reason he shall conceive to be the aptest means thereto."[25] By the right of nature, "every man has a right to every thing, even to one another's body."[26] This reinforced the wretched and dangerous condition of the state of nature.

Hobbes emphasized the tendency toward the state of nature in European society by noting the existing civil wars. He thought that these wars testified to the fact that European sovereigns remained in a state of nature toward each other as well as toward their subjects. He also believed that, with the separation between political and ecclesiastical authority in European society, the whole of Europe was not far from falling into the state of nature or the image of civil war, much in the same way as the ancient republics had been transformed into "anarchies."[27]

After Hobbes made this distinction between the state of nature and civil society, the state of nature became the starting point in Eurocentric discussions of government and politics. The state of nature was the conditionality or the assumption or the given upon which the idea of the modern state or civil society was constructed. Those who attempted to construct a rational theory of the state began from Indigenous peoples in a state of nature being the antithesis of civilized society. These political philosophers ranged from Spinoza to Locke, from Pufendorf to Rousseau to Kant. These philosophers created the natural-law theory of the modern state. Hegel eliminated the state of nature as the original condition of humans but merged the theory in the relations among states.

By the early eighteenth century, the usual explanation of the origin of the state, or "civil society," began by postulating an original state of nature in which primitive humans lived on their own and were subject to neither government nor law.[28] As the first systematic theorist of the philosophy of Liberalism and Hobbes's greatest immediate English successor, John Locke took up where Hobbes left off.

In 1690, Locke published *Two Treatises of Government*.[29] Like Hobbes, he started with the state of nature. However, he opposed Hobbes's view that the state of nature was "solitary, poore, nasty, brutish, and short" and maintained instead that the state of nature was a happy and tolerant one. He argued that humans in the state of nature are free and equal yet insecure and dangerous in their freedom. Like Hobbes, Locke had no proof of his theory. Indeed, there is no proof that the state of nature was ever more than an intellectual idea, since no historical or social information about it has ever existed.[30] Of course, there was nothing to disprove the idea either, and Locke simply stated that "It is not at all to be wonder'd that *History* gives us but a very little account of Men, *that lived together in the State of Nature.*"[31] Following Hobbes, he argued that government and political power emerged out of the state of nature.

"In the beginning," Locke wrote, "all the World was America."[32] That America is "still a Pattern of the first Ages of Asia and Europe,"[33] and the relationship between the Indigenous peoples and the Europeans in America is "perfectly in a State of Nature."[34] Thus, Locke, despite his differences with Hobbes on the state of nature itself, used the idea to justify European settlement in America[35] and to give Europeans the right to wage war "against the Indians, to seek Reparation upon any injury received from them."[36]

The Artificial Man-State

From the idea of the state of nature, Hobbes and the political philosophers who followed him constructed the idea of the artificial man-state and the positive content of the law.[37] These philosophers believed that civil society arose to correct or eliminate the shortcomings of associations between people in the state of nature. The transformation from individual or family freedom and equality to civil society did not occur because of nature; rather, it took place through one or more conventions made by individuals who were interested in leaving the state of nature. Civil society "made by the wills and agreement of men" Hobbes called "the Commonwealth": "[Thus] is created that great LEVIATHAN called a COMMONWEALTH, or STATE (in latine, CIVITAS), which is but an *Artificall Man*, though of greater stature and strength than the Naturall ... The *Pacts* and *Covenants*, by which the parts of this Body Politic were at first made, set together, and united, resemble that *Fait,* or the *Let us make man,* pronounced by God in the Creation."[38]

According to Hobbes, the force that impelled the transfer of power to an artificial state was negative necessity. Given the state of nature, Hobbes argued, individuals needed a superordinate power to make and sustain a political covenant:[39] "I Authorise and give up my Right of Governing my selfe to this [artificial] Man, or to this Assembly of men, on this condition, that thou give up thy Right to him, and Authorise all his actions in like manner."[40] Consequently, the origin and foundation of government are voluntary and deliberate acts. The principle of legitimation of artificial civil society is consent, rather than a natural society of families or households.

For Hobbes, only the artificial man-state could end the savage state of nature and create civil society. He secured this pact and its artificial creations, the commonwealth and the sovereign, against any change or possibility of legitimate disturbance. The artificial man-state was total and eternal.[41] Hobbes concluded that rebellion against the man-state broke society's basic convenant and was punishable by whatever penalty the sovereign might exact to protect his subjects from a return to the original state of nature. The sovereign had to seek and maintain peace by putting the fear and terror of the state of nature to the law breakers. The sovereign subject who created the compact became comprehensively committed to all actions of the indivisible power of the sovereign "as if they were his own."[42] The great liberty of the subjects depended on the silence of the sovereign's law.

Locke rejected Hobbes's idea of the legitimacy of absolute monarchy or "absolute Arbitrary Power." He also rejected that for the sake of self-preservation individuals surrendered their rights to a supreme sovereign through a social contract and that this sovereign was the source of all morality and law. Locke argued instead that the social contract preserved the preexisting natural rights of the individual to life, liberty, and property and that the enjoyment of individual rights led, in civil society, to the common good: "Those who are united into one Body, and have a common establish'd Law and Judicature to appeal to, with Authority to decide controversies between them, and punish Offenders, *are in Civil Society* one with another; but those who have no such common Appeal, I mean on Earth, are still in the state of Nature, each being, where there is no other, Judge for himself, and Executioner; which is, as I have before shew'd it, the perfect *state of Nature.*"[43] In short, each individual who joined society retained fundamental rights drawn from natural law that related to the integrity of person and property. He accepted a right of rebellion or civil war against a despot or a tyrant.

In Locke's theory, a sovereign with limited powers was the source of governmental authority. "The Supreme Power," Locke wrote, "cannot take from any Man any part of his Property without his own consent ... it is a mistake to think, that the Supreme Legislative Power of any Commonwealth, can do what it will, and dispose of the Estate of the Subject arbitrarily, or take any part of them at pleasure."[44] The reason for this limitation on any government was that people bring property rights into political society, which was set up specifically to protect these rights: "For the preservation of Property being the end of Government, and that for which Men enter into society, it necessarily supposes and requires, that the People should have Property, without which they must be suppos'd to lose that by entring into Society, which was the end for which they entered into it, too gross an absurdity for any man to own."[45]

Locke saw property rights as a natural law that existed before society was formed. Other natural rights were the rights of subsistence, which included the right of each individual to the material necessities for support and comfort. Beyond subsistence rights, there were acquired natural rights. These rights included rights acquired as a result of actions and transactions that individuals had undertaken on their own initiative and rights acquired when individuals had laboured on a resource or put something of themselves into a resource that gave them an entitlement to that resource. These natural rights were independent of political society or any civil framework. They were established before the origin of political society and constrained the Crown and popular will. Therefore, it was not open for governments to abrogate, derogate, or reorder them based on what governments thought society ought to do.

Interestingly, although Locke allowed that individuals could acquire natural property rights through labour, he did not apply this theory of property to the Indigenous nations of America. He stated:

> There cannot be a clearer demonstration of any thing, than several Nations of the *Americans* are of this, who are rich in Land, and poor in all the Comforts of Life; who Nature having furnished as liberaly as any other people, with the materials of Plenty, i.e. a fruitful Soil, apt to produce in abundance, what might serve for food, rayment, and delight; yet for want of improving it by labour, have not one hundreth part of the Conveniencies we enjoy; And a king of a large and fruitful Territory there feeds, lodges, and is clad worse than a day Labourer in England.[46]

Locke tied entry into political society under a central, sovereign command with the need to secure property. "The great and *chief end* therefore, of Mens uniting into Commonwealths, and putting themselves under Government, is *the Preservation of their Property*."[47] He proceeded to delineate law as a response to "many things wanting ... in the state of Nature." The "Civiliz'd part of Mankind" was characterized by "positive laws"[48] that were absent in the natural state. These positive laws were a response to the natural chaos of individual assertions of passion and self-interest: "First, [in the state of nature] There wants an establish'd, settled, known *Law,* received and allowed by common consent to be the Standard of Right and Wrong, and the common measure to decide all Controversies between them ... *Secondly,* In the State of Nature there wants a *known and indifferent Judge,* with Authority to determine all differences according to the established Law ... *Thirdly,* In the state of Nature there often wants *Power* to back and support the Sentence when right, and to *give it* due *Execution*."[49]

The theory that Indigenous people lacked positive law had certain self-serving implications for Europeans. If they had nothing resembling European law, then they had no government until they allied themselves with a European Crown. The implication was that Indigenous nations needed a relationship with a European Crown. With some false pride, Englishmen looked upon their laws as the most rational, efficacious, and perfect in the whole world; hence, the Crown was initially uncritical of any proposals to impose English legal traditions on Indigenous societies. These attempts failed. The "lawless" Indigenous nations rejected the imposition of English (and French) law and the leadership imposed by Europeans.[50]

Positive Law as Command

Hobbes created the notion of positive law, and he is considered the father of legal positivism. His purpose was not to show what is law here and there but what is law in general.[51] In the man-state, laws were the "command" of the sovereign to the sovereign subjects,[52] and only the sovereign could make valid laws.[53] The "laws of nature" could not be "properly law" until they took form as a sovereign command.[54] However, once the absoluteness of the sovereign command was accepted, the sovereign's law, originally described as chains, turned into "hedges."[55] This command theory went on to become the predominant notion in English jurisprudence.[56]

Sir William Blackstone's version of the nature of law in the *Commentaries on the Laws of England* reflected the Hobbesian notion of positive law.[57] Blackstone acknowledged the command that humans should live honestly, hurt nobody, and render each his due, and he asserted that self-love was the constitution of humanity and universal principle of action, and divine law helped us to discover the original law of nature and the law of nations that depended on the rules of natural law.[58] Blackstone agreed with Hobbes and noted that municipal or civil law was created because natural law allowed man to pursue his own good. In contrast to convenants, compacts, or agreements of the law of nations, municipal law was a prescribed rule dependent "upon the maker's will," and those who were bound by it were notified of universal tradition and long practice. Municipal law was defined as "a rule of civil conduct prescribed by the supreme power in a state, commanding what is right and prohibiting what is wrong."[59]

In 1832, legal scholar John Austin reinterpreted Hobbes into English jurisprudence and colonialism.[60] A professor of jurisprudence at the University of London, Austin defined law as the command of a political superior to a political inferior.[61] In Austin's system, an exclusive and independent sovereign was accorded general and habitual obedience by its subjects. This subjection was a necessary precondition for "political society" and law to exist.[62] Thus, positive law depended on the existence of a sovereign.[63]

The exclusive foundation for Austin's positive law was savagery in nature. Austin distinguished a general state of savagery that he called "natural society" as opposed to "political society." He stated that "A natural society, a society in a state of nature, or a society independent but natural, is composed of persons who are connected by mutual intercourse, but are not members, sovereign or subject, of any society political. None of the persons who compose it lives in the positive state which is styled a state of subjection: or all the persons who compose it live in the negative state which is styled a state of independence."[64] Following in the tradition of Hobbes and Locke, Austin illustrated natural society by "the savage ... societies which live by hunting or fishing in the woods or on the coasts of New Holland" and by those "which range in the forests and plains of the North American continent."[65]

Austin characterized the state of nature as completely wild and lawless.[66] Moreover, even if natural society were not wild and lawless, he asserted that "Some ... of the positive laws obtaining in a political community, would probably be useless to a natural society which had not ascended from the savage state. And others which might be useful even to such a society, it probably would not observe; inasmuch as the ignorance and stupidity which had prevented its submission to political government, would probably prevent it from observing every rule of conduct that had not been forced upon it by the coarsest and most imperious necessity."[67] Thus, the irredeemable savage and natural society are the ultimate limiting case against which Austin's theory of law was constituted.

European philosophers have noted that the elaboration, transmission, and refinement of the theory of the state of nature and the rise of the artificial state accompanied the rise and development of bourgeois society in Europe. Few have noted that the rise of the artificial state also accompanied the rise and development of colonialism. The meaning of the artificial state spanning artificial colonies in various states of nature has been largely ignored.

The Law of Nature and the Treaty Commonwealth

According to these early political thinkers, colonialism and the artificial man-state's law as command were not the only options available to people in the state of nature, and the ideology of the state of nature did not condemn Indigenous peoples to lives of slavery and oppression. In *Leviathan*, Hobbes devoted most of the first two chapters on the law of nature to a discussion of contracts and covenants (mutual promises) between sovereigns and their subjects, and he asserted that justice demands that these covenants be kept. The importance and interrelations of justice and these covenants in moving to civil society have often been overlooked.

According to Hobbes, the prudent and rational rules of the laws of nature *("Lex Naturalis")* provided savages with a means of escaping the state of nature. The laws of nature are precepts or general rules, discovered by reason, that preserve life by prohibiting activities that destroy life.[68] To Hobbes, the first law of nature was that everyone ought to seek peace but could defend himself by war.[69] The second law asserted that in seeking peace people needed to lay down their natural rights to all things and transfer them to a sovereign who, in return, would look after the safety of the people.[70] The third law asserted that, in transferring their natural rights to a sovereign, people must be willing to keep their covenants with this sovereign, and the sovereign, in turn, needed to keep his convenants with his subjects. The idea of transferring natural rights to an artificial man-state is integral to Hobbes's idea of civil society, but it is also integral to creating peace between sovereigns in the law of nations: when rights are transferred, obligations are created.

Hobbes argued that only through binding convenants between a sovereign and his subjects is the state of nature transcended. Without convenants, a sovereign would only be a man of strength, who would remain an enemy. The artificial man-state and civil society arose to correct the shortcomings of natural associations in the state of nature. The transformation took place through one or more convenants made by individuals who were interested in leaving the state of nature. Without these convenants, men remained in the state of nature toward one another, where no act was unjust.

Hobbes placed a limitation on the convenants that could be made: no one could contract away self-preservation, for that right is inalienable; no one could contract to do anything impossible; and no one could contract away a right that had already been transferred. Hobbes thought that convenants were impossible between people who could not share speech, since language created the structure and validity of the convenants.[71]

These convenants had to establish a "common Power set over them both, with right and force sufficient to compell performance."[72] They created an absolute sovereign, and the absolute sovereign made the convenants secure.[73] Thus, civil society "made by the wills and agreement of men" Hobbes called "the Commonwealth." This process was the original foundation of the law of nations and international law.

The international treaty order began at the end of the Holy Roman Empire in the 1648 Treaties of Westphalia. It was a conventional community of sovereign and independent, secular, artificial man-states associated by treaties of alliance, commerce, or "protection," under a conception of natural law that recognized the equality of all peoples and states.

In America, Hobbes's concept of the law of nature created the additional idea of treaties of peace and friendship with Indigenous nations, a notion that Locke was later to call the treaty commonwealth. The idea of treaty commonwealth with the British sovereign was the alternative idea to colonialism. The order of the treaty commonwealth was built on a theory of a compact between sovereign nations. It was the original form of covenant made with Indigenous peoples in North America. The treaties of the treaty commonwealth were voluntary and conditional commitments between artificial sovereigns, political societies, or nations. They manifested a customary law of nations. They were at that time and remain to this day the cement that has held and still holds the global artificial states together. The object of the promissory regime was to produce an ordered and just system between nations, grounded in principles of universal humanity, peaceful relationships, and protection.

Initially, the treaty commonwealth was based on European aristocratic customs and values.[74] It was an intellectual product of diplomats and jurists who were searching for an alternative to the law of war. This practical process ran parallel to the theoretical efforts of Hobbes and Locke to end civil warfare. The idea of an international treaty order was guided by the principle that states may impose obligations on themselves where none existed before. The idea was that agreements between artificial man-states could create a shared order based on accepted values of trust and promises. In the absence of agreement, no binding rules existed between artificial man-states. Thus, rules of international law emanated from the free will of artificial man-states. This is a classic illustration of the Hobbesian order. It is composed of principles and rules that the sovereigns have agreed to observe. It is a unique kind of legal order that is not built on either force or coercion.[75] At one level, the treaty order represents universal rules of negotiation, consent, and remedies. At another level, specific agreements between communities vary from place to place, creating locally binding principles and rules. Rules can be expressed by written conventions or discovered in generally accepted usage. The collected treaties and practices are the closest things to sovereign will and legislation in international law.

The original treaty commonwealth is best understood from a historical survey of practice, but it is useful to settle some questions of terminology. It is based on a recognition that *others* outside Europe are part of the same human world and can share in a single international order.

For example, Locke was aware that Indigenous nations had governments. Indigenous nations did not govern themselves in an individual and independent manner as laid out in the description of the state of nature. Locke asserted that Indians were grouped in nations[76] ruled by elected kings.[77] He also said that their kings were "little more than Generals of their Armies" who "command absolutely in war." In times of peace and in internal affairs, the kings or council or people "exercise very little Dominion, and have a very moderate Sovereignty."[78] The resolution of peace and war resided ordinarily either in the people or in a council.[79]

Locke argued that Indigenous nations lacked European institutions and desires, which he took as the universal criteria of political society. For example, he wrote that their kings did not have the exclusive right to declare war and peace.[80] Also, they lacked an institutional legal judiciary, legislature, and executive.[81] However, Locke asserted that the reason for the absence of these institutions was that the Indigenous nations had no need for them. They have "few Trepasses, and few Offenders," "few controversies" over property, and therefore "no need of many laws to decide them."[82]

In his analysis, Locke neglected the customary system of government and law that maintained such an order in Indigenous nations. Instead, he argued that the absence of European institutions was due to the limited desires of Indigenous people. "Confining their desires within the narrow bounds of each mans small propertie made few controversies."[83] Indigenous people, he argued, had "no temptation to enlarge their possessions of Land, or contest for wide extent of Ground," because they lacked money and large populations, which activated the desire to possess more than one needed.[84]

Locke's theory also created a need for Europeans to have a consensual relationship with Indigenous nations. In the early eighteenth century, the British Crown and Indigenous nations developed the coherent theory of treaty commonwealth or federalism. Prerogative treaties established a constitutional relationship between First Nations and Great Britain. These prerogative treaties respected Indigenous autonomy and legal institutions under international and civil law. They united the First Nations directly with the British sovereign as protected partners, distinct from European settlements.[85] These compacts allowed Indigenous nations to enter "civil society" in one body without surrendering their customs.

Consistent with Hobbes's and Locke's versions of a necessary compact, His Majesty's notion of a treaty commonwealth was posited in positive commands to colonial servants. The prerogative instructions in New England, Nova Scotia, and other colonies respected Indigenous governments and their legal systems. These prerogative instructions accepted Indigenous land tenure and started the policy of fair and honest purchases from Indian tribes under British law.[86] Beginning with the prerogative treaties such as the Wabanaki Compact of 1725, and extending across both Canada and the United States, the British sovereign brought Indigenous nations under his protection through covenants or promises.

The scope of British authority or commonwealth in North America was dependent on consensual agreements with freely associated Indigenous nations. Creating an international treaty order with Indigenous nations was not a uniquely North American phenomenon. During the eighteenth and nineteenth centuries, treaties were made with many Indigenous nations in Latin America, Africa, India, the Pacific, and Asia. The French, Spanish, Dutch, and other empires made treaties with the same aims as those of the British.[87] These aims were to establish territorial claims and economic spheres of influence that would be respected by other European powers. In fact, the entire system of imperial relationships and colonization that dominated world affairs until 1914 relied on treaties with Indigenous nations. Thus, the treaty relations between the Indigenous nations and the United Kingdom can best be understood as a branch of international law.[88]

These treaties brought the Indigenous nations into "civil society." Under the prerogative law of the imperial Crown, these treaties formed the first and fundamental legal structure of the British Empire, often called the "hidden constitution of Canada."[89] They also formed part of the international treaty order that created relationships with European sovereign states. Locke argued that the relationships between independent states comprise the hypothetical original condition of humans without political superiors:[90] "Those who have the supreme power of making laws in England, France, or Holland are to the Indians but like the rest of the world – men without authority."[91] As independent states, the Indigenous nations could enter into treaties to create a more stable political environment and to secure their rights. Locke considered the resulting legal compact to be distinct from domestic government.[92] His treaty commonwealth was a limited contractual alliance in the law of nations, while the domestic social compact of the English realm was a more comprehensive subordination of individual wills. Both addressed the deficiencies of the imagined state of nature by guaranteeing possessions and by establishing laws for the peace, safety, and public good of the people concerned.

After the 1648 Treaty of Neutrality between Britain and France, the Atlantic colonies in North America saw the first application of Locke's treaty commonwealth principles. His Majesty's instructions directly incorporated Locke's suggestions by clearly requiring colonial governors to enter into treaties and political associations with the "several heads of the said Indian Nations or clans and promising them friendship and protection in his Majesty's part."[93] These prerogative treaties were to establish a formal alliance with the Indigenous nations and place them under the protection of the Crown. The treaties were also designed to terminate any competing Indigenous tenures among the settlers and to prevent the colonists from using tribal dominion to exempt them from His Majesty's authority and taxation. The issue of international treaty order and the relations between the European sovereign and Indigenous nations achieved its zenith in the 1880s, when the world system of treaty commonwealth linked the European states and about 1,000 Indigenous nations globally.

The Austinian definition of a determinate superior as sovereign was at the heart of the international treaty order: "If a *determinate human* superior, *not* in a habit of obedience to a like superior, receive *habitual* obedience from the bulk of a given society, that determinate superior is sovereign in that society, and the society (including the superior) is a society political and independent."[94] Under this definition, Indigenous leaders were no less superiors than British sovereigns were. In this international treaty order, the stronger state did not incorporate the weaker one into its municipal law: "There is neither a *habit* of command on the part of the former [stronger state], nor a *habit* of obedience on the part of the latter [feeble state]."[95] Each allied state retained its distinct force, its distinct centre of power. Each alliance created its own conditionality: "No indeterminate party can command expressly or tacitly, or can receive obedience or submission: ... no indeterminate body is capable of corporate conduct, or is capable, as a body, of positive or negative deportment."[96] This is compelling evidence of bridging the gap between the civilized and people in the state of nature, yet this compelling evidence was ignored as colonialism unfolded.

The Artificial Construction of Colonization

Colonialism was the choice of the immigrants; it was not inevitable or predetermined by their views of the state of nature. They could have adhered to the concept of the treaty commonwealth, but they chose to create an artificial context for their own benefit using the negative aspects of the state of nature. The actual practices of the treaty commonwealth in British history and law illustrate that the state of nature premise of colonization can be challenged, but few have done so. The idea of colonization has remained immune to the issues of the law of nature and the treaty commonwealth. This immunity resides in the belief that Indigenous people could not make treaties and flies in the face of evidence that the imperial Crown did make treaties with the Indigenous nations.

The colonizers argued that the existence of the prerogative treaties in the law of nature and nations had no bearing on the status of Indian nations in international or domestic law.[97] They took the view that Indigenous peoples were "savages" or "barbarians" rather than sovereign nations. They used the ideas of the artificial man-state and law as command to create colonial assemblies and to begin their quest for self-rule and responsible government.

Typically, the colonial ideology arose as resistance to the prerogative treaties entered into by the Crown. Relying on European fears of Indigenous savages living in the state of nature, the colonizers immunized the colonial order from reconstruction by the European homeland by threatening "nihilism." They stressed the Hobbesian savagery of Indigenous society in the state of nature rather than the existing compacts with the imperial Crown. They then used the ideology of the state of nature to justify using brute force and terror to maintain their artificial context, and they used colonial laws to justify the process.

Colonial thought ignored the political and legal meaning of the covenants of the treaty commonwealth. Some writers have argued that the historical agreements with Indigenous nations and tribes were mere agreements or contracts, not "treaties," and as such were respected only out of the honour and generosity of the European sovereign or state. This argument disregards the importance of history and custom in international law and adopts a post hoc colonial and racist theory that is completely inconsistent with the primacy of consensual obligations in international law. Colonial thought used the theory of the state of nature to incapacitate actual state practices in international law. The colonizers then constructed alternative theories and artificial histories to justify colonization.

The colonizers circumvented and undermined the principle of treaty commonwealth and reinscribed the state of nature on the Indigenous nations. They then created new forms of dominion and oppression. The colonizers created a legal order and consciousness around the sovereign or state, that great fictitious entity of Eurocentric thought by which everyone seeks to live at the expense of everyone else,[98] especially Indigenous peoples and their resources. Traditionally, Europeans have dominated and oppressed other peoples under a mandate from God or nature and a notion of sovereignty or rule from above. For example, Judeo-Christian biblical writings are a chronicle of the exploitation of the weak by the more powerful, of a minority ruling a majority because of the majority's alleged human frailties. Just as the Jewish peoples have endured their oppression, Indigenous peoples have survived the path of their holocaust and the subtle and innovative brutality of modern consciousness.[99] Afro-Caribbean psychiatrist Frantz Fanon has defined colonized people as "every people in whose soul an inferiority complex has been created by the death and burial of its local cultural originality ... [which] finds itself face to face with the language of the civilizing nation; that is, with the culture of the mother country. The colonized is elevated above his jungle status in proportion to his adoption of the mother country's cultural standards. He becomes white as he renounces his blackness, his jungle."[100] The tensions between cultures and languages, the inferiority complex, the assimilative choice are all elements of the subtle brutality of colonization.

The evidence used in justifying colonization was limited, and knowledge that would have undermined the strategy was ignored. Indeed, copious evidence existed that the Indigenous peoples of North America were not savage.[101] The colonizers manipulated descriptions of Indigenous peoples to show them as "without subordination, law, or form of government," and there were increasing efforts "to civilize this barbarism, to render it susceptible of laws."[102] Anthropologist Margaret Hodgen has rejected the concept of the savage and has challenged attempts to identify American savagery with classical antiquity or with older versions of savagery in European thought: "So much is certain: it was not because of the validity of the correspondences cited ... The number of plausible likenesses elicited ... were at best relatively few and usually trivial ... [and] they were offset, and the conclusions derived from them were neutralized, by an overwhelming body of divergences which were seldom mentioned, much less assembled for comparison of relative proportions."[103] The large kinship confederations to be found in North America were simply disregarded. Political and legal philosophers went so far as to change evidence to conform to their theories. For example, they identified Aboriginal cultures with a lack of progress despite powerful evidence to the contrary. When they did recognize the ability of these cultures to change, they attributed it to Aboriginal imitation of European culture.[104]

Four hundred years of colonialism around the Earth was a process of conscious choice supported by manipulated facts on the part of the colonizers. These 400 years have had tragic consequences for Indigenous peoples. The consequences are more than mere conquest or the exercise of tyrannical power, slavery, and genocide;[105] they go to forced cognitive extinction.[106] After the British treaties, the colonizers created a systemic colonialism and racism that estranged Indigenous peoples from their beliefs, languages, families, and identities; that deprived Indigenous peoples of their dignity, their confidence, their souls, and even their shadows. Their only choices were wretched assimilation to the colonizers' values and living a mistaken and disconnected life or existing in the colonizers' imposed misery of the state of nature.

The philosopher Iris Young provides definitions for this systemic colonization. She defines "domination" as the colonizers' established regimes that inhibit or prevent people from participating in political life and in legislative law making and decision making. "Oppression" she defines as the systemic processes in society that inhibit or prevent the oppressed from communicating in contexts in which others can listen or prevent them from developing their human skills to resolve material deprivations.[107]

According to historian Lise Noël, systemic colonization is grounded in intolerance.[108] Intolerance comes from unconscious assumptions that underlie "normal" institutional rules and collective reactions; it is a consequence of following these rules and accepting these reactions in everyday life.[109] The causes of this intolerance are embedded in the modernist concept of unquestioned norms, habits, symbols, and everyday practices of a well-intentioned liberal society. In systemic colonization, no single source of oppression or dominion can be assigned causal or moral primacy. Colonization theories are embedded in every consciousness and

work as routine or normal activities. Instances of intolerance are so pervasive in modern society that scholars cannot individualize them. If the
oppressed cannot point to single causes or forms of oppression, then the
oppressor and his consciousness become invisible:

> The oppressor has no apparent existence. Not only does he not identify
> himself as such, but also he is not even supposed to have his own real-
> ity. His presence is so immediate and dense, and his universe coincides
> so totally with the Universe, that he becomes invisible. Rarely seen, rarely
> named, he is unique, nonetheless, in having a full existence; as the keeper
> of the word, he is the supreme programmer who confers various degrees
> of existence on those who are different from himself ... As the embodi-
> ment of the universal, the dominator is also the only Subject, the
> Individual who, never being considered to belong to a particular group,
> can study those impersonal categories of the population who pose a
> "problem," represent a "question," constitute a "case," or simply have a
> "condition."[110]

Systemic colonization cannot be reduced to one essential definition or a
unified phenomenon; instances of oppression operate together as a collective consciousness and infect most modern theory. Young asserts that
there are at least five faces of oppression: exploitation, marginalization,
powerlessness, cultural imperialism, and violence.[111] Noël argues that we
must look at many levels of domination and oppression, since a person
and a group can be oppressed or dominated in many different ways. She
points out that a person can be defined by, and therefore oppressed
because of, general characteristics arising both from biological categories
(race, gender) and from sociological variables (age); membership in a
socioeconomic group (social class, poverty) or a sociocultural group with
or without specific physical traits (ethnicity or identity); or individual
characteristics, most often randomly transmitted, which relate to the individual's sexual orientation, mental or intellectual state, or physical condition – specifically his or her health, integrity, or appearance (shape, size,
beauty).[112] Only a multivoice or plural explanation of the consciousness of
the oppressed can comprehend the brutal magnitude of the systemic colonization that Indigenous peoples experience and have to transform.

Conclusion

The idea of difference arising from the theory of the state of nature created
the Eurocentric thought, consciousness, and reasoning that justify colonialism. The theory of the state of nature created an interpretive monopoly of human nature. From this interpretive monopoly, Eurocentric
thought has dreamed and created liberal societies using force. The social

and governmental theories of these liberal societies have remained flawed and have been experienced by Indigenous peoples as artifices of domination, oppression, and racism. Neither the Europeans' word-worlds nor their life-worlds have created human solidarity. Instead, they have created the global state of war itself. European artificial constructs remain unrealized realms contaminated with deep-seated economic, organizational, and psychological constraints.[113] Roberto Unger commented that Eurocentric thoughts and desires have never fit within the artificial structure that Europeans have imposed on their beliefs and actions:

> often we treat the plain, lusterless world in which we actually find ourselves, this world in which the limits of circumstance always remain preposterously disproportionate to the unlimited reach of striving, as if its structures of belief and action were here for keeps, as if it were the lost paradise where we could think about the thoughts and satisfy all the desires worth having. When we think and act in this way, we commit the sin the prophets called idolatry. As a basis for self-understanding, it is worse than sin. It is a mistake.[114]

Aboriginal thinkers have long noted this mistaken idolatry. As early as 1777, a Cherokee commented about Eurocentric thought: "Much has been said of the want of what you term 'Civilization' among the Indians. Many proposals have been made to us to adopt your law, your religion, your manners and your customs. We do not see the propriety of such a reformation. We should be better pleased with beholding the good effects of these doctrines in your own practices than with hearing you talk about them or of reading your newspapers on such subjects."[115] A century later, in 1880, a Lakota stated: "White men have education and books, and ought to know exactly what to do, but hardly any two of them agree."[116]

Indigenous peoples must transform the false assumptions behind the state of nature and its social theories to begin their transformation to a postcolonial order. It is the key to our cognitive confinement. We must clearly understand the disadvantages of creating artificial societies from wrong assumptions. We should avoid affirming or copying the distorted European views of the state of nature or accommodating their made and imagined "normal" social and political constructs. We must continue to see the organization of life in terms of the Indigenous knowledge about living in balance with an ecology. We must use our traditional knowledge and heritage to force a paradigm shift on the modernist view of society, self, and nature.

Contemporary colonialists violently resist remaking or reimagining or even changing their social or governmental constructs or institutions to accommodate Indigenous knowledge. They deny that their artificial construct can be reimagined and remade; they deny that its assumptions could be wrong, because if they were their privileges would be threatened. Such resistance is the immunity of modern contextual thought. Faced with the realization that the Indigenous view of ecological order might create a better context of sustainable development, Eurocentric thinkers and governments continually evoke the Hobbesian nightmare of the chaos that would ensue if the state of nature and its derivative theories were replaced. Yet they seem to be unaware that we have been living in the chaos caused by their artificial state and society for the past 400 years.

Eurocentric thinkers fear what would happen if their contrived superiority were challenged. As one Eurocentric scholar has suggested, "When we discover that there are several cultures instead of just one and consequently at the time when we acknowledge the end of a sort of cultural monopoly, be it illusory or real, we are threatened with the destruction of our own discovery. Suddenly it becomes possible that there are just others, that we ourselves are an 'other' among others."[117] Thus, Eurocentric consciousness and its imagined society live in endless fear of a cycle of routine and revolution that has haunted their colonization of the Earth's peoples. If limited strategies of reform and retrenchment do not affirm their imaginative contexts and structures, then the artificial man-state resorts to coercive authority or violence to maintain enslaving visions by means of either the legal system or the army. In our struggles with systemic colonization, it has not changed, but Indigenous peoples have.

Both Noël and Young stress that the brutal practices of colonization are united by a web of desire and intolerance that holds Indigenous peoples captive. Indigenous people must question whether they agree that without civil society and positive law humans become disoriented and lose all capacity for caring, loving, solidarity, and thought. As part of the restoration of Indigenous knowledge and heritage, Indigenous scholars must confront the assumption of the state of nature. The theories and the choices behind this assumption require analysis by those Indigenous peoples who have survived colonialism and are seeking to transform it. They require a critique from the vantage point of Indigenous thought.

We must question why Eurocentric thought has devoted so few resources to studying the violence inflicted on Aboriginal people after 400 years of colonization. Obviously, Europeans remain anxious about the possibility of impending chaos. Rather than leave these notions to oblique allusion and rapacious innuendo, Eurocentric thought needs to seek to understand Aboriginal knowledge, language, and legal order. Surely, these studies will be more important to everyone in the next century than the existing political rhetoric and legal myth of dead white men creating artificial societies.

Additionally, we must use treaty commonwealth to demonstrate how assumptions about the state of nature underlie modern theory. The treaty commonwealth united the best of Indigenous and European traditions. It should not be characterized as a series of small-scale, routine adjustments to the context of colonialism. It was an alternative context-breaking explanation of the law of nature and nations that respected our sovereignty, our humanity, and our choices to preserve peace. The historical and legal legacy of the treaty commonwealth brings into question the necessity of colonization. It can transform dominant assumptions about the artificial context of colonialism, it can illustrate an explanatory or society-making practice better than colonialism, and it can be used as a vantage point from which to evaluate the false necessity of colonialization.

Notes

1 See, e.g., W.E. Conklin, *The Phenomenology of Modern Legal Discourse: The Juridical Production and the Disclosure of Suffering* (Brookfield, VT: Ashgate Publishing, 1998).

2 Thomas Kuhn, *The Structure of Scientific Revolutions* (Chicago: University of Chicago Press, 1962); D. Bohm and F.D. Peat, *Science, Order, and Creativity* (New York: Bantam Books, 1987). A paradigm is a set of implicit assumptions, concepts, theories, and postulates held in common about the natural world by several members of a community, enabling them to explore jointly a well-defined and delimited area of inquiry and to communicate in a specialized language about the subject. These paradigms define the boundaries of acceptable inquiry and the limiting assumptions within a discipline.

3 R.M. Unger, *Passion: An Essay on Personality* (New York: Free Press, 1984) at 5–15; R.M. Unger, *Social Theory: Its Situation and Its Task: A Critical Introduction to Politics, a Work in Constructive Social Theory* (Cambridge: Cambridge University Press, 1987) at 18–25. In legal thought, a context is about a human-constructed view of society; it functions similarly to a natural paradigm. A legal context is the study of lawyers' fundamental assumptions, the explanatory or argumentative structures that ordinary legal inquiries take for granted. Jeremy Bentham spoke of it negatively as "the art of being methodically ignorant of what everybody knows." Every lawyer usually takes for granted the meanings of statements such as "that is a rule of law," "the decision is binding on the Court of Appeals," and "X has a legal right to be paid by Y." All these implicit assumptions create contexts. The relative strength of a context lies in its resistance to being shaken by the normal actions that it helps to shape. The purpose of jurisprudence and legal scholarship is to elucidate and evaluate rules of juridical contexts.

4 *Social Theory,* ibid. at 18-9. Unger explained the contextual or conditional quality of all human activity: "To say that extended conceptual activity is conditional is to say that its practice depends on taking for granted, at least provisionally, many beliefs that define its nature and limits. These assumptions include criteria of validity, verification, or sense; a view of explanation, persuasion, or communication, and even an underlying ontology – a picture of what the world is really like. It may even include a set of premises about whether and in what sense thought and language have a structure" (ibid.).

5 Ibid. at 9.

6 Ibid. at 20.

7 *Passion, supra* note 3 at 10.

8 Ibid. at 10.

9 Ibid.

10 Ibid. at 5.

11   Ibid. at 6–8.
12   Aristotle, *Politics*, trans. E. Barker (London: Oxford University Press, 1958) (1252b) at 4. See also Marsilius of Padua, *Densor Pacis* (Toronto: University of Toronto Press, 1967) I, III, 4–5 at 10–3; J. Bodin, *The Six Books of a Commonweale* [1606], reprint of Knolle's translation (Cambridge: Harvard University Press, 1962) I at 1; J. Althusiu *Politica Methodice Digesta of Johannes Althusius* (Cambridge: Harvard University Press, 1932) vol. 8 at 39.
13   Thomas Hobbes, *Leviathan; or the Matter, Forme, and Power of a Commonwealth Ecclesiastical and Civil*, ed. C.B. Macpherson (Baltimore: Penguin Books, 1968). See R. Tuck, *Hobbes* (Oxford: Oxford University Press, 1989). In his political treatise, Hobbes compares the state, with its innumerable competing members, to the largest of natural organisms – the whale or leviathan. By this analogy, Hobbes argued that the state, like the whale, requires a single controlling intelligence to direct its motion.
14   Ibid. Hobbes ch. 13 at 182. See parallel chapters in T. Hobbes, *De Cive* (Philosophical Rudiments Concerning Government and Society) in B. Gert., ed., *Man and Citizen* (Garden City, NY: Doubleday, 1972) ch. I; and T. Hobbes, *Elements of Law, Natural and Politic*, ed. F. Tönnies (Cambridge: Cambridge University Press, 1928) part I, ch. 14.
15   Ibid. ch. 17 at 223.
16   Ibid. ch. 13 at 183, and ch. 10 at 151. Hobbes notes that the equality of wits is evidenced by each man's deep-seated satisfaction with his own wisdom, which is the source of his ability to kill another and to secure himself from his enemies, ch. 15 at 203-5.
17   Ibid. ch. 13 at 187.
18   Ibid. ch. 14 at 192.
19   Ibid. ch. 13 at 187-8. This notion is contradicted in Hobbes's writing by his idea of the concept of natural law (*lex naturalis*) and rights (*ius naturalis*), ch. 14 at 189. Also see *De Cive, supra* note 14, ch. 14 at 274, and *Elements of Law, supra* note 14, part II, ch. 10 at 148. Hobbes resolved this dilemma by arguing that laws of nature were not the same as the civil law of the sovereign but personal "conclusions, or Theorems" concerning self-preservation. However, if the theorems were delivered by the word of God, then they were laws, see ch. 15 at 215.
20   Ibid. ch. 13 at 186.
21   Ibid.
22   Ibid. ch. 13 at 187.
23   Ibid.
24   Hobbes also invokes the similar antagonistic condition existing between "king and persons of sovereign authority" (ibid. ch. 17 at 223-8), but he does not develop the comparison.
25   *Leviathan, supra* note 13, ch. 14 at 189.
26   Ibid., ch. 14 at 189-90.
27   *De Cive, supra* note 14, ch. 12 at 246.
28   P. Stein, *Legal Evolution: The Story of an Idea* (Cambridge: Cambridge University Press, 1980) at 1.
29   J. Locke, *Two Treatises of Government* [1690], reprint 2 vols., ed. P. Laslet (Cambridge: Cambridge University Press, 1970) *Second Treatise* at para. 138.
30   In their historical political evolution, European states have gone from feudal states to the Standestaat, to absolute monarchy, to constitutional monarchy, and so forth. There has not been any reciprocal consent of free and equal individuals creating a state.
31   Locke, *supra* note 29, para. 101 (original emphasis).
32   Ibid. at para. 49.
33   Ibid. at para. 108.
34   Ibid. at paras. 14 and 109.
35   Ibid. at para. 36.
36   Locke, *supra* note 29, vol. I, *First Treatise*, at para. 130-1.
37   E. Cassirer, *The Philosophy of the Enlightenment*, trans. Fritz Koelin and James Pettegrove (Boston: Beacon Press, 1955) at 19.
38   Hobbes, *supra* note 13 at 81-2 (part of emphasis added). Ironically, this is the Roman legal idea of *status civilis* or "the civil condition"; at the greatest level of generality, the commonwealth does mean "condition" or "way of being" ("the state of one's health").

39 Ibid., part II of Commonwealth, chs. 17-31 at 223-408.
40 Ibid. ch. 17 at 227. This phrase is a negative act of renouncing right and agreeing to authorize his action, but it does not require a positive swearing of allegiance.
41 Ibid. chs. 18 and 19 at 228-51.
42 Ibid. The rise of state sovereignty had permanent effects on European political thought. It slowly limited the older contexts of ecclesiastical and private law and prerogative. This process was reflected in Immanuel Kant's 1797 declaration that the only natural political relation was that between single individuals and states. By this time, the medieval notion of a society made up of smaller societies had been generally discredited. G.W.F. Hegel argued that the modern state was the "mind on earth." The Hegelian state, however, was not a Hobbesian state. It was a monarchy moderated by the law-drafting functions of dis-interested civil servants and moderated above all by the Hegelian notion that individuals must be able to find subjective satisfaction in their being willing members of a rational, free institution that secures the pursuit of absolute values inherent in philosophy, art, and religion.
43 Locke, *supra* note 29, *Second Treatise* at para. 87 (original emphasis).
44 Ibid. at para. 138.
45 Ibid.
46 Ibid. at para. 41 (original emphasis).
47 Ibid. at para. 124 (original emphasis).
48 Ibid. at para. 30.
49 Ibid. at paras. 124–6 (original emphasis). Also see A. Smith, *An Inquiry into the Nature and Causes of the Wealth of Nations, 1776* (Oxford: Clarendon Press, 1976) ch. 1, part 2; W. Blackstone, *Commentaries on the Laws of England,* 14th ed. (Oxford: Clarendon Press, 1766–9) at 5.
50 Robert A. Williams, Jr., *The American Indian in Western Legal Thought* (Oxford: Oxford University Press, 1990) at 151–226.
51 *Leviathan, supra* note 13 at 130.
52 Ibid.
53 Ibid. at 131.
54 Ibid.
55 Ibid. Compare ch. 21 at 263 to ch. 30 at 388.
56 But it did involve an immediate problem in that people have to know of commands in order to obey them. Hence, the command of the commonwealth is law only to those who have the means to take notice of it. "Over natural fools, children or madman there is no law, no more than over brute beasts" (ibid. at 132). But if law were to be dependent on popular knowledge, this condition could undermine the whole edifice of authority. With uncharacteristic equivocation, Hobbes opts largely, and understandably, for the maxim that ignorance of the law is no excuse (ibid. at 139).
57 "On the Nature of Law in General" in *Commentaries on the Laws of England, supra* note 49.
58 Ibid., vol. I at 40-4.
59 Ibid. at 44-5.
60 J. Austin, *The Province of Jurisprudence Determined,* 2nd ed. (London: John Murray, 1832), and *Lectures of Jurisprudence,* 3 vols. (London: John Murray, 1861–3).
61 Ibid., *Lectures,* vol. I at 1, 5.
62 Ibid., vol. III at 170-3.
63 Ibid., vol. II at 313.
64 Ibid., vol. I at 176.
65 Ibid., vol. I at 184. Austin also draws on both a general and existent state of savagery and the "imaginary case" of a solitary savage child abandoned in the wilderness, which he takes "the liberty of borrowing from ... Dr. Paley" (*Lectures,* vol. I at 82). The borrowing could be W. Paley, *The Principles of Moral and Political Philosophy* (Dublin: [s.n.], 1785) at 5. This solitary savage was "a child abandoned in the wilderness immediately after its birth, and growing to the age of manhood in estrangement from human society" (*Lectures,* vol. I at 82). As such, it could not be a "social man," would not appreciate the neces-sity of property, would be in total conflict with "his" fellows, and hence "the ends of

government and law would be defeated" (*Lectures*, vol. I at 85). The savage "mind" is "unfurnished" with certain notions essential for society: they "involve the notions of political society; of supreme government; of positive law; of legal right; of legal duty; of legal injury" (*Lectures*, vol. I at 85).

66 Ibid., vol. II at 9.
67 Ibid., vol. II at 258. Additionally, Austin does take into account the domestic challenge of the "poor and ignorant" to British order (vol. I at 62). This affliction is attributed to their ignorance of "the imperative good of property and capital." Its cure lies in a full appreciation of the principles of utilitarian ethics, particularly of the Malthusian variety: "if they adjusted their numbers to the demand for their labour, they would share abundantly, with their employers, in the blessings of property" (ibid.). Distinguishing them from the "stupid" savage who can only respond to the imperatives of the inexorable (vol. II at 258), "the multitude ... can and will" come to "understand these principles" (vol. I at 60).
68 Hobbes, *supra* note 13, ch. 14 at 189.
69 Ibid. at 190-1.
70 Ibid.
71 Ibid. at chs. 14 and 21.
72 Ibid., ch. 14 at 196.
73 Ibid., ch. 29 at 364-8; ch. 30 at 376-85.
74 D. Kennedy, "A New Stream of International Law Scholarship" (1988) 7 *Wis. Int'l L. J.* 1, 3. Kennedy criticizes twentieth-century scholarly output in international law as bound in "European doctrinal formalism."
75 *Reservations of the Convention of Genocide Case*, Advisory Opinion I.C.J. Reports 1951: 15. (It is well established that in its treaty relations a state cannot be bound without its consent.)
76 Locke, *supra* note 29, *Second Treatise*, at para. 41.
77 Ibid. at para. 108.
78 Ibid. Cf. *First Treatise* at para. 131.
79 Ibid.
80 Ibid., *Second Treatise*, at paras. 144-8.
81 Ibid. at para. 87.
82 Ibid. at para. 107.
83 Ibid.
84 Ibid. at para. 108.
85 R.L. Barsh and J.Y. Henderson, "Aboriginal Rights, Treaty Rights, and Human Rights: Indian Tribes and Constitutional Renewal" (1982) 17 *Journal of Canadian Studies* at 55–81.
86 Royal Instruction of 1761, Royal Proclamation of 1763. See J. Borrows, "Constitutional Law from a First Nations Perspective: Self-Government and the Royal Proclamation" (1994) 1 *University of British Columbia Law Review* at 2, 6, 7, 41.
87 See, generally, R.L. Barsh and J.Y. Henderson, "International Context of Crown-Aboriginal Treaties in Canada" in CD-ROM, *For Seven Generations: An Information Legacy of the Royal Commission on Aboriginal Peoples* (Ottawa: Canada Communications Group, 1996); C. Alexandrowicz, *The European African Confrontation: A Study in Treaty-Making* (Leiden: Sijthoff, 1973); C. Alexandrowicz, *An Introduction to the History of the Law of Nations in the East Indies* (Oxford: Clarendon Press, 1967); Sir W. Lee-Warner, *The Native States of India* [1910] (New York: AMS Press, 1971); R. Strickland, ed., *Cohen's Handbook of Federal Indian Law* (Charlottesville, VA: Michie Company, 1982) at 62-126; M.F. Lindley, *The Acquisition of Backward Territory* (London: Longmans, Green, 1926); A. Morris, *The Treaties of Canada with the Indians of Manitoba and the North-West Territories* (Toronto: Belfords, Clarke, 1880, rpt. Saskatoon: Fifth House Publishers, 1991).
88 *Worcester v. Georgia* 31 US (6 Pet.) 515 (1832); F.S. Cohen, "The Spanish Origin of Indian Rights in the Law of the United States" (1942) 31 *Geo. L. Rev.* 1, 17; M. Savelle, *Empires to Nations: Expansion in America, 1713-1824* (Minneapolis: University of Minnesota Press, 1974), 138-43.
89 B. Slattery, "The Hidden Constitution: Aboriginal Rights in Canada" (1984) 32 *Am. J. of*

Comp. Law 361; and B. Slattery, "Aboriginal Sovereignty and Imperial Claims" (1991) 29 *Osgoode Hall L.J.* 1.

90 Locke, *supra* note 29, *Second Treatise,* at para. 4.

91 Ibid. at paras. 9, 105, and 108.

92 Ibid. at paras. 144-5. It was not every compact, Locke argued, "that put an end to the state of nature between men, but only this one of agreeing together mutually to enter into one community, and make one body politic; other promises and compacts men may make one with another, and yet still be in the state of nature. The promises for truck between a Swiss and an Indian, in the woods of America, are binding to them, though they are perfectly in a state of nature in reference to one another: for truth and keeping the faith belongs to men as men, and not as members of society," ibid., *Second Treatise,* at para. 14.

93 Cf. L.W. Labaree, *Royal Instructions to British Colonial Governors 1670-1776,* 2 vols. (New York: D. Appleton-Century, 1935), vol. II, 469, 478-80, 742, 806.

94 Austin, *supra* note 60, *Lectures,* vol. 1 at 170 (original emphasis).

95 Ibid. at 173 (original emphasis).

96 Ibid. at 175. Cf. E. Vattel, *Le Droit des gens, ou principes de la loi naturelle* (1758), *The Laws of Nations or the Principles of Natural Law* (Chitty tr. 1839, book I, ch. 18); and *Worcester* v. *Georgia* (1832) 31 US (6 Pet.) 515.

97 A.H. Snow, *The Question of Aborigines in the Law and Practice of Nation* (1918; rpt. Northbrook, IL: Metro Books, 1972) at 128.

98 F. Bastiat, *Selected Essays on Political Economy,* trans. S. Cain (Princeton: Van Nostrand, 1964).

99 See, generally, L. Noël, *Intolerance: A General Survey,* trans. A. Bennett (Montreal: McGill-Queen's University Press, 1994); I. Young, *Justice and the Politics of Difference* (Princeton: Princeton University Press, 1990); J.R. Ponting, *Arduous Journey: Canadian Indians and Decolonization* (Toronto: McClelland and Stewart, 1986); H.A. Bulhan, *Frantz Fanon and the Psychology of Oppression* (New York: Plenum Press, 1985); J. Axtell, *The Invasion Within: The Conquest of Cultures in Colonial North America* (New York: Oxford University Press, 1985); A. Nandy, *The Intimate Enemy: Loss and Recovery of Self Under Colonialism* (Delhi: Oxford University Press, 1983); A. Memmi, *Dominated Man: Notes Toward a Portrait* (Boston: Beacon Press, 1969); F. Fanon, *Black Skin, White Mask,* trans. C.L. Markman (London: MacGibbon and Kee, 1968); F. Fanon, *The Wretched of the Earth,* preface by Jean-Paul Sartre, trans. Constance Farrington (London: MacGibbon and Kee, 1965); A. Memmi, *The Colonizer and the Colonized,* trans. Howard Greenfield (New York: Orion Press, 1965).

100 Ibid., *Black Skin, White Mask,* at 18.

101 See, generally, J. Blaut, *The Colonizer's Model of the World: Geographical Diffusionism and Eurocentric History* (New York: Guilford Press, 1993); J. Weatherford, *Indian Givers: How the Indians of the Americas Transformed the World* (New York: Crown Publishers, 1988).

102 J. Axtell, *supra* note 99 at 50.

103 M.T. Hodgen, *Early Anthropology in the Sixteenth and Seventeenth Centuries* (Philadelphia: University of Pennsylvania Press, 1964) at 354–5. Also see H.S. Commager, *The Empire of Reason: How Europe Imagined and America Realized the Enlightenment* (Garden City, NY: Anchor Press-Doubleday, 1977); W. Brandon, *New Worlds for Old: Reports from the New World and Their Effect on the Development of Social Thought in Europe 1500-1800* (Athens, OH: Ohio University Press, 1986).

104 B.G. Trigger, *Native and Newcomers: Canada's "Heroic Age" Reconsidered* (Kingston: McGill-Queen's University Press, 1985) at 51, 65.

105 Noël, *supra* note 99 at 100.

106 M.A. Battiste, "Micmac Literacy and Cognitive Assimilation," in J. Barman, Y. Hébert, and D. McCaskill, eds., *Indian Education in Canada: The Legacy* (Vancouver: UBC Press, 1986); Assembly of First Nations, *Towards Linguistic Justice* (Ottawa: AFN, 1990); and Assembly of First Nations, *Rebirth of First Nations Languages* (Ottawa: AFN, 1992).

107 Young, *supra* note 99 at 33–8.

108 Noël, *supra* note 99 at 5. (Intolerance is the theory; domination and oppression are the practices.)

109 Young, *supra* note 99 at 41.
110 Noël, *supra* note 99 at 11.
111 Young, *supra* note 99 at 42-65.
112 Noël, *supra* note 99 at 5.
113 See, generally, R.M. Unger, *False Necessity: Anti-Necessitarian Social Theory in the Service of Radical Democracy,* part I of *Politics, a Work in Constructive Social Theory* (Cambridge: Cambridge University Press, 1987).
114 *Social Theory, supra* note 3 at 18.
115 Old Tasse, in N.S. Hill, Jr., ed., *Words of Power: Voices from Indian America* (Golden, CO: Fulcrum Publishing, 1994) at 36.
116 Spotted Tail, ibid. at 38.
117 P. Ricoeur, *History and Truth*, trans. C. Kelby (Evanston, IL: Northwestern University Press, 1965) at 278.

2
Indigenous Peoples and Postcolonial Colonialism
Robert Yazzie

Colonialism should have been dead after the end of World War II in 1945. While the world decolonization process is almost complete, it has not begun for Indigenous peoples. This chapter addresses the history of colonialism and Indigenous peoples in the past, the legacies of past colonialism, and the fact that Indigenous peoples are still being subjected to it. It will also suggest responses to the process.

When we talk about colonialism in the modern world, we are really talking about the conquest and control of nonwhite, non-European peoples. When we talk about "colonies" and colonialism, we are usually talking about the lands settled by Europeans following the arrival of Columbus in 1492. They include Canada and its Indigenous peoples, the United States and Indians, Indigenous Australia, Maori Aotearoa (New Zealand), the native Pacific Islands, Indian Latin America, and Indigenous Africa. Colonialism among Indigenous people in the Americas began with Columbus in 1492, but it did not reach its height until the close of the nineteenth century.

The "reservation period" of American history was at its zenith by 1880. The Indian wars of the United States were coming to a close, and the last free Indian nations were being herded onto reservations. One of the leading American military commanders was General William T. Sherman. On October 27, 1883, he made a report to the US Congress in which he said "I now regard the Indians as substantially eliminated from the problem of the Army. There may be spasmodic and temporary alarms, but such Indian wars as have hitherto disturbed the public peace and tranquility are not probable" (1975, 159). He went on to explain why the Indian wars were over: "Immigration and the occupation by industrious farmers and miners of land vacated by the aborigines have been largely instrumental to that end, but the *railroad* which used to follow in the rear now goes forward with the picket-line in the great battle of civilization with barbarism, and has become the *greater* cause" (ibid.).

The United States embraced technology in the early 1860s, and the US Civil War of 1861-5 was the first modern "industrial" war.[1] It introduced new kinds of warfare: air warfare (in the form of observation balloons); trench warfare, where soldiers went underground; and underwater warfare (limited experiments with submarines). It introduced new kinds of weapons: the Gatling gun, a hand-cranked machine gun; the revolver, a pistol that could quickly fire off six shots; and steel ships with torpedoes. The Civil War also produced the concentration camp, a place where you confine groups of people to control them. It is used to contain people whose race, religion, or political beliefs are "different." My people, the Navajos, were death-marched more than 400 miles from their homeland to a concentration camp at a place called Bosque Redondo, on the Pecos River of New Mexico Territory (Bailey 1970). Navajos are among the few Indigenous nations to have suffered the concentration camp experience, and it left lasting scars on Navajo society.

In 1882, a new secretary of the interior from Colorado wrote a furious letter to the commissioner of Indian Affairs, complaining about the "barbaric" customs of Indians (Prucha 1978, 295). He ordered the commissioner to develop a law to eradicate those customs and to suppress ancient Indian religious and cultural practices. The commissioner obliged by creating the Courts of Indian Offenses in April 1883 (ibid., 300; Hagan 1966, 104). The court was to be staffed by "civilized" Indian judges: men (and it was "men") who were willing to cut their hair, wear European-styled "citizens" dress, and have only one wife. The new code made it a crime to see a medicine man. It made it a crime to *be* a medicine man. Ceremonies were illegal.

The United States gradually imposed its law on Indians and their nations. When the US Supreme Court made its 1883 ruling that only traditional Indian law applied to crimes in Indian country, Congress responded in 1885 by passing the Major Crimes Act (Cohen 1982, 300-1). It punished certain major crimes committed by Indians in Indian country and subjected them to trial in a federal court far from home. Federal courts do business in English, not in Indian languages. They use Anglo-American law and do not consider the expectations Indians have under their own laws.

In 1887, Congress came up with a scheme to "civilize" Indians by dividing up reservations into small, individually owned parcels of land called allotments. Indian nations lost three-quarters of their land base as a result (Washburn 1971, 150). At about the same time, the US Supreme Court developed a new legal principle, called the "plenary powers doctrine" (Cohen 1982, 217-20). It states that Congress can override treaties if it wishes, and it can pass any law regarding Indians it wants, whether Indians agree or not.

What was happening in Canada at this time? The western part of Canada was once "owned" by the Hudson's Bay Company, which still has stores across Canada today. The company then "gave" the Canadian west to Canada. When settlers from the east began violating the land and water rights of Métis and Indians in what is today Saskatchewan, there was a revolt: the 1885 Northwest Rebellion. That was the war for the Canadian west, and the Indians and Métis lost. Railroads and settlers followed, with a race between the United States and Canada to occupy the western part of this continent.

There is a symbol for this period of time: the machine gun. The Battle of Batoche was the last conflict in the war for the Canadian west, and it took place just a few miles north of Saskatoon. The Canadian army used the Gatling gun at Batoche. Arthur L. Howard, a salesman for the Colt Firearms Company, brought his Gatling gun samples to the battlefield. He wore his Connecticut National Guard uniform and merrily cranked away, slaughtering Indians and Métis (Howard 1974, 450-4, 465, 468, 479).[2]

The Maxim gun, the first fully automatic machine gun, was invented in 1884 (Ellis 1975, 33). It was used only on Indigenous peoples up to World War I (ibid., 79-107).[3] The British loved their Maxim guns. In 1883, certain European nations met in Berlin to carve up Africa among themselves. The British marched off to Africa, singing "Whatever happens, we have got; The Maxim gun, and they do not" (Manchester 1983, 52). The European powers used the machine gun to occupy Africa, Asia, and other areas that became colonies, to secure new colonies, and to repress Indigenous peoples. In 1899, British poet Rudyard Kipling urged the United States to get into the game in the Pacific and urged Americans to "take up the white man's burden" to "civilize" Indigenous peoples (1899, 12).[4] Kipling described them as being "half demon and half child" in his poem "The White Man's Burden." Americans joined in the colonizing game and took the Philippines, Cuba, Puerto Rico, Hawaii, and other lands.

A total of 65,038,810 soldiers were mobilized in World War I, and there were 37,508,616 casualties. That was 57.6 percent of all soldiers who were mobilized; 76.3 percent of all Russian and French soldiers became casualties (Spartacus Educational, n.d.). Many casualties were caused by the machine gun. The League of Nations, the first modern international organization, was created in 1920 following the end of the war. The Covenant of the League of Nations said of Indigenous peoples that "The members of the League ... undertake to secure just treatment of the native inhabitants of its territories under their control" (Laquer and Rubin 1989, 151). This recognized the power of member nations to colonize Indigenous peoples and ratified control over them, saying only that they deserved "just treatment." There was no definition of what was "just" and no enforcement mechanism to ensure that the covenant, an international treaty, would be observed.

There was a dogma or theory for colonialism, called "Social Darwinism." After Charles Darwin developed the theory of evolution, Herbert Spencer came up with the concept of "survival of the fittest" (Burke 1985, 260, 268). He went on to argue that some people are "fitter" and thus "superior" to others.[5] His book *Synthetic Philosophy* was a bestseller in the United States when Spencer visited New York in 1882 (ibid. 271). Americans loved Spencer. At the time, there was a group of railroad owners and industrialists, the "robber barons," who needed a theory to justify their power and control of resources and people. The theory of Social Darwinism assumes that a certain group of people has the right to make decisions for others and to control the government and the economy. Who are these people? They are male, usually Protestant, and wealthy. Social Darwinism also assumes that there are "inferior people," and history and contemporary practice show that they are women, non-Christian, and people of colour. In North America, that includes Indians and other Indigenous peoples.

The notion that one class or group of people has the right to make decisions for others made its way into law. At about the same time as the developments discussed above, an English legal philosopher, John Austin, developed the doctrine of "parliamentary supremacy." According to Austin, the source of law was the British parliament (Morison 1982). In the British system, the parliament can pass any law it wants, and the courts do not have the authority to overrule it.[6] Canada used the doctrine of judicial supremacy until it received its own constitution in 1982. There appears to be a trend now in the United States for the US Supreme Court to adopt a version of Austin's parliamentary supremacy.

Austin's theories assume that national or regional legislative bodies truly represent all. In fact, minorities (particularly Indigenous peoples) are effectively disenfranchised. They do not have the numbers to assure effective representation. They do not have the money to finance campaigns and thus secure favour. Although many democratic societies look to civil rights and human rights law to protect those whose numbers may be insufficient to make them effective participants in democratic institutions, the implementation of civil rights law also depends upon non-Indigenous elites in the judicial systems.

Social Darwinism and its theory of superior people has had a strong impact on public policy. There is a direct link between Spencer's theories and the Nazi movement (Burke 1985, 265-7),[7] which claimed that Germans were a superior race. The Nazis killed millions of people they hated – Jews, gypsies, homosexuals, and people who believed in democracy. One need only look at the composition of national and local legislatures and of judicial systems and legal associations to see that Social Darwinism and the concept of "superior" peoples having control are alive today. Comparatively few of those who operate the institutions are women, Indigenous peoples, or poor people, because the entry pass to those institutions is wealth and class. Indigenous peoples are not wealthy, they do not have the educational opportunities to enter the halls of the elite, and they do not have an effective ability to influence public policy. Those who occupy positions of power and authority think they have the right to make decisions for Indigenous peoples, and they assume that their decisions are correct and acceptable. Frequently, they are not.

That is the way colonialism is structured. It is a triangle of power in which the people at the top claim they have the right to control the people at the bottom. After 1945, when the period of colonialism was to have ended, former British colonies such as Australia, New Zealand, and Canada achieved complete independence. However, the original inhabitants of those lands, Australian Aborigines, Maoris of New Zealand, and the First Nations of Canada, did not get their independence. The people who colonized those countries run them, effectively excluding the first inhabitants.

Indian thinking is a response to the ongoing pattern of the colonization of Indigenous peoples. One of the basic differences between Western law, the law in most colonial and postcolonial countries, and Indian law and government is the nature of democracy. The word *democracy* comes from the Greek, and it means "rule by the people." In the United States and Canada, we have "kakistocracy," which means "rule by the worst," and one need only consult *The Congressional Record* or *Hansard* for proof of that assertion.

Traditional Navajo law is based upon equality and consensus. When there is a problem, we do not ask an outsider to make a decision for us. We make our own decisions. We do have traditional leaders, but they were not the stereotypical and powerful "chiefs" who were recognized by the colonial powers. The name for a traditional Navajo leader is *naat'aanii*. Its word roots address concepts of planning and speaking well. The traditional Navajo civil leader is someone who has wisdom, spirituality, leadership ability, and the respect of the community. A *naat'aanii* is not a boss; that person does not make decisions for others. The reason for that is summed up in the Navajo maxim "It's up to him." When there is a problem, people look to someone who has wisdom, experience, and spirituality to teach and to give advice. The best decision is made by the agreement and consensus of everyone involved in a problem.

As a concrete example, consider the problem of domestic violence. In the usual domestic violence situation, a man thinks he has the right to control a woman, including the privilege to use physical violence for control. Unfortunately, that perception of "right" comes from general attitudes Western society introduced to Indigenous communities. We see a great deal of domestic violence in Indigenous areas because the non-Indigenous culture taught us that men are "superior" to women.

Western law addresses domestic violence through an arrest, following a report of crime. However, jailing and punishment do not effectively address an offender's attitudes or change the offender's mind. He (and it usually is a man) only thinks he was unlucky to have been caught, and he will have his chance to take it out on the woman later. Women have little effective say about the process. They want the hurt to stop, but unfortunately punishment or the likelihood of punishment does not effectively deter offenders. The relatives of people who are involved in domestic violence are also affected by it. We speak of children and the elderly as "tag-along" victims of domestic violence. Acts of domestic violence teach children how to behave when they grow up – as either those who inflict injury or those who receive it, thinking that is "the way things are." Parents and siblings must watch in horror as their relative is hurt or their relative hurts others. Those tag-along victims have no say in the process at all.

Most court proceedings are ineffective in dealing with domestic violence because the process does not reach inside the people involved or help them communicate their feelings. It does not involve others who should be involved or teach that there are other ways to deal with conflict. Navajo methods of justice address all these things: they help people to take a look at themselves and examine their own conduct; they foster communication of feelings; they involve everyone who is affected by the harm; and they teach proper behaviour. When there is a dispute, we most often make assumptions about others. In the usual domestic violence case, the woman feels trapped. She resents mistreatment but does not know what to do about it. She wants the hurt to stop, but she has difficulties dealing with her own emotions and cannot be an effective part of that process. Those who hurt also have assumptions about the correctness of and justification for their conduct. Violent behaviour is learned behaviour, just as thinking that you must live with violent behaviour is learned.

Navajo Nation law offers women remedies by way of Western restraining orders and traditional Navajo peacemaking. Sarah J. Foster, a Navajo Nation Judicial Branch staff attorney, reported that, when she did a survey of cases in the Window Rock Judicial District, she found that women prefer Navajo peacemaking over the restraining order procedure.[8] Peacemaking is a "walk-in" service in which a woman can request a traditional peacemaking session at a local court. The court then sends the case to a peacemaker, who invites everyone involved to attend, including the woman and her relatives, the man and his relatives, neighbours, and even social services workers. The session opens with a prayer said by the peacemaker or a respected family member. Prayer is important because peacemaking is actually a healing ceremony, and prayer gets people to commit to the peacemaking process. Next, the people who are gathered start "talking out" their problem. The woman gets to do something she cannot do in a courtroom:

she vents her emotions and tells the group how she feels about the event. She describes her fear and the impact of the violent act on her. The man then describes his feelings. Many men give the excuses "She deserved it" or "It was her fault. If she had had my dinner ready when I got home from work tired and hungry, I wouldn't have had to beat her." Another excuse is "It's traditional for an Indian man to beat his wife." It is not traditional; that is a stereotype that has made its way into Indian communities.

It is important for an offender to get a chance to give his or her excuses. Otherwise, we will not know what motivated that person to commit the offence. Once the excuses are on the table, they can be addressed. Domestic violence and alcohol are often related, although alcohol does not cause domestic violence. Getting drunk is used as an excuse. In one peacemaking case, the man claimed that he didn't have a drinking problem and that his conduct was not all that bad. The man's sister confronted and corrected him, and he responded positively out of his respect for her. She pointed out that he did indeed have a drinking problem and that he was abusive. The sister was able to reach beneath the excuses and act as a teacher to correct her brother's act. (In Navajo thinking, you do not correct the actor; you correct the *action*.)

Peacemakers also deal with false excuses. They are not "neutral," unlike in some mediation practices. Peacemakers are chosen by their communities because they are respected planners and teachers who have definite opinions when something goes wrong. Where there is domestic violence, peacemakers teach that domestic violence is against our Navajo traditions. There are prayers and teachings in the traditional Navajo wedding ceremony that teach how husband and wife must relate to each other. It is a relation of reciprocity, in which both husband and wife are equal, and they must do what they can to ensure the success of the union. Survival was hard in traditional times, and Navajos developed a strong ethic of survival within the family by fostering cooperation and solidarity.

The peacemaker prompts everyone in the group to talk about what should be done to address what happened – the act that brought them into peacemaking. This is a very practical planning process in which everyone has a say. The group takes steps to deal with the underlying problem, which may be alcohol abuse or dependence, drug addiction, or other behaviours associated with violence. The group may agree to a program of spirituality and ceremonies to correct false assumptions and attitudes. Peacemaking also uses Western treatment programs, such as Indian Health Service violence-control counselling. The peacemaking can conclude with a reconciliation between the man and woman or a family discussion and consensus about ending the marriage for the good of the parties and their families.

Ultimately, peacemaking is about healing. You cannot order someone to heal or force someone to heal. Fines and jail time are not tools for healing. Healing depends on a process that moves people from "head-thinking" to "heart-thinking" (Grohowski 1995). They need help to learn how to live in right relations with others. In Navajo thinking, a bad relationship is evil. Bad relationships are addressed through practical discussions about the cause of the problem and mutually acceptable ways of dealing with it.

Navajo peacemaking is an example of pure participatory democracy. Participatory democracy is a decision-making process in which everyone who is affected and interested is involved. It is group decision making by discussion and consensus and is distinct from representative or republican democracy. The latter assumes that we elect someone to make decisions for us and that the group of elected people will make wise decisions for the good of all. The problem with republican democracy in the United States and Canada is that people who are elected, as a group, care little about the concerns and feelings of Indigenous peoples.

There is a lot of talk about sovereignty, and the talk has become very stale. It is mostly about whether the United States or Canada will "allow" Indigenous peoples to control their own lands, lives, and destinies. "Sovereignty" is nothing more than the ability of a group of people to make their own decisions and control their own lives. Colonialism is a situation in which people in Washington, Ottawa, or other neocolonial capitals make decisions that affect the lives of Indigenous peoples without effectively involving them or reaching consensus *with* them. Postcolonialism will not arrive for Indigenous peoples until they are able to make their own decisions. Colonialism remains when national legislatures and policy makers make decisions for Indigenous peoples, tell them what they can and cannot do, refuse to support them, or effectively shut them out of the process.

Social Darwinism is colonialist thinking, and it is alive and well in the United States and Canada. Its assumption is that an elite has the moral and legal right to shape the destinies of Indigenous minorities. There is a micro-issue that demonstrates this. A non-Indigenous bureaucrat is sometimes puzzled by the hostility that he or she receives when talking with an Indigenous group. Traditional Indigenous communication is based on respect, using respectful language and respectful discourse. A great deal of non-Indigenous communication is designed to compel the listener to accept the position taken by the speaker. Another way of putting this is that Indigenous people are offended by bossy and pushy discourse. The discourse itself shows that the speaker is not willing to acknowledge the equality of the listener or talk out a decision.

Indigenous leaders go to seemingly endless series of meetings to discuss the latest policy that has been formulated in Washington or Ottawa. The catchphrase for a positive yet small and incremental initiative is "soon." "Soon" never seems to come. Otherwise, we gather to discuss the latest disaster in national policy, such as the latest decision of the US Supreme Court. The difficulty with this discourse is that it still smacks of Social Darwinism. Indigenous leaders go to meetings with the elite, knowing that its spokespeople will force the latest decision upon them. When domestic violence and rape are discussed, we hear of the imbalances of power between the victim and the perpetrator. Imbalances of power perpetrate and perpetuate violence, and they are the petri dish of violence.

The best response to violence is healing. It is a personal process and an internal process to be shared with others. While Indigenous peoples may not succeed with "macro" issues such as jurisdiction, land-use control, or dealing with outsiders and intruders, they can succeed with "micro" issues. Taking control of one's own life is a healing issue. Strengthening the family is healing. Communities must consider how they can effectively reassume control of their destinies. If Indigenous people give up responsibility for their lives to others, they lose control of them. If, however, Indigenous people take back responsibility for their lives, beginning with the individual, they can achieve internal sovereignty.

I will end this essay with a personal note. I have an undergraduate university degree earned in Ohio. I have a law degree from the University of New Mexico School of Law. When I returned home to assume a position of authority in my own community, I thought that I had superior knowledge. I thought that I could make positive changes, armed with the power that knowledge of Western law gave me. I was wrong. I had to relearn my language and traditions and go back to a spiritual power base before I could begin to change. I say that I have been to hell and back.

I use my position of authority to attempt to change things on national and international levels. I try to educate others about the forces that lie immediately beneath colonialism, but national and international officials refuse to acknowledge the existence of Social Darwinism in their institutions. They will not surrender their ability to dole out meagre "rights," and they will not listen.

Ultimately, the lesson is that we, as Indigenous peoples, must start within. We must exercise internal sovereignty, which is nothing more than taking control of our personal lives, our families, our clans, and our communities. To do that, we must return to our traditions, because they speak to right relationships, respect, solidarity, and survival. I cannot beg for political power, because I will not get it. However, I can pray for personal power and work with people around me to achieve internal sovereignty. That is our path to postcolonial existence, although at this point it is a unilateral declaration of postcolonial status. Given the structure of our colonies within, and our relationship with the colonizers, all we can do is to declare community and spiritual independence. No tank, no smart bomb, and no colonial cop can penetrate that.

Notes

1 Technology and industrialization are intimately linked to colonialism. Kurt Mendelssohn (1976) suggests, in *The Secret of Western Domination,* that the "secret" explaining the ability of Europeans to dominate the world is possession of the keys to technology. Now that non-European peoples possess them, things could change.

2 Joseph Howard explains that Arthur L. Howard was a "friend of the [Gatling] gun," and "when he learned that Canada was going to try it out against the rebellious Métis he hastened to offer his services" (1974, 450-2). When there was an outcry about the use of the gun, Colt Firearms, its manufacturer, the Connecticut National Guard, and the US government disavowed involvement. He was then "on his own." "He was not perturbed about any of this; he was blissfully happy; and he was not in the least 'brutal.' He was merely scientific." "He was also effective. The newspaper correspondents in the field, the troops in their letters home, and even the austere command sang the praises of 'Gatling Howard'" (ibid. 453).

3 John Ellis says that "the machine gun came to be regarded as a weapon suitable only for use against African natives and the like" (1975, 102). However, "Of all the chickens that came home to roost and cackle over the dead on the battlefields of the First World War, none was more raucous than the racialism that had somehow assumed that the white man would be invulnerable to those same weapons that had slaughtered natives in their thousands" (ibid. 102).

4 An excellent resource for Kipling's poem and the contemporary reactions to it is Jim Zwick, "'The White Man's Burden' and Its Critics," in *Anti-Imperialism in the United States, 1898-1935* (1999) www.boondocksnet.com/kipling/.

5 While it may not be good history to attribute motivations to characters in the past, and while Herbert Spencer, his followers, and those who still think that there are "better" people (most of them appear to occupy the opinion/editorial pages of newspapers), I have a right to express my opinion. Just as it is with the literature of those who believe their religion is "superior," I have the right to say "That's stupid and harmful!" They may have been sincere in their beliefs, but they did not consider their effects on my people.

6 This is a broad-brush statement that may have certain exceptions. Generally, however, there are countries that recognize judicial review and the ability of a court to strike down a statute enacted by a legislature if it is unconstitutional or violates human rights, while some countries retain the concept of nonreviewability.

7 James Burke's (1985) discussion of Social Darwinism and the rise of the modern authoritarian state is in the chapter "Fit to Rule" in his book *The Day the Universe Changed.* This is a book on modern technology, and it again shows the link between technology and authoritarianism, which is a hallmark of colonialism.

8 Sarah Foster, personal communication, 1996.

References

Bailey, L.R. 1970. *Bosque Redondo: An American Concentration Camp.* Pasadena: Socio-Technical Publishers.

Bennett, G. 1978. *Aboriginal Rights in International Law.* London: Royal Anthropological Institute of Great Britain and Ireland, Occasional Paper no. 37.

Burke, J. 1985. *The Day the Universe Changed.* New York: Little, Brown.

–. 1998. *Bosque Redondo: The Navajo Internment at Fort Sumner, New Mexico, 1863-1868.* Tucson: Westernlore Press.

Cohen, F.S. 1982. *Handbook of Federal Indian Law.* Charlotteville, VA: Michie Bobbs-Merrill.

Ellis, J. 1975. *The Social History of the Machine Gun.* Baltimore: Johns Hopkins University Press.

Grohowski, L. 1995. "Cognitive-Affective Model of Reconciliation: CAMR." MA thesis, Antioch University, OH.

Hagan, W.T. 1966. *Indian Police and Judges.* New Haven: Yale University Press.

Howard, J. 1974. *Strange Empire: Louis Riel and the Métis People.* 1952. Rpt. Toronto: James Lewis and Samuel.

Kipling, R. 1989. "The White Man's Burden." *Rudyard Kipling Complete Verse: Definitive Edition*. New York: Anchor Books.

Manchester, W. 1983. *Winston Spencer Churchill: The Last Lion: Visions of Glory, 1874-1932*. New York: Little, Brown.

Mendelssohn, K. 1976. *The Secret of Western Domination*. New York: Praeger Publishers.

Morison, W.L. 1982. *John Austin*. Stanford: Stanford University Press.

Prucha, F.P. 1978. *Americanizing the American Indian*. Lincoln: University of Nebraska Press.

Sherman, W.T. 1975. "General Sherman on the End of the Indian Problem." In Francis Paul Prucha, ed., *Documents of United States Indian Policy*, 295-305. Lincoln: University of Nebraska Press.

Spartacus Educational. N.d. "Armies Mobilized and Casualties: 1914-18." In *Spartacus Educational, First World War Encyclopedia*. www.spartacus.schoolnet.co.uk/FWWdeaths.htm

Washburn, W.E. 1971. *Red Man's Land/White Man's Law*. Norman: University of Oklahoma Press.

Zwick, J. 1999. "'The White Man's Burden' and Its Critics." In *Anti-Imperialism in the United States, 1898-1935*. www.boondocksnet.com/kipling/

3
Hawaiian Statehood Revisited
Poka Laenui (Hayden F. Burgess)

What a scene there was in Hawai'i on Statehood Day 1959! Celebration swept through these islands on news of our joining the union of states of the USA. Communities lit bonfires, neighbourhoods held impromptu dances, cars blared their horns, and people walked the streets with broad grins and greetings, seeing themselves as full-fledged Americans. Hawai'i Democrats and Republicans, the two political parties, were together in the quest for Hawaiian statehood. Hawaii's media were in full support as well. Opposition voices were silent.

One decade later, the modern Native Hawaiian Rights Movement emerged through a series of issues: opposition to the Kalama Valley evictions (where local farmers were pushed out to make way for housing developments); controversy regarding the inclusion of ethnic studies at the University of Hawai'i; and outrage over the bombing of the island of Kaho'olawe by the US military (Native people claimed the island as sacred, while the military claimed war preparedness was of greater importance to society). Another decade later, the Hawaiian Sovereignty Movement emerged through several court cases in which the defendants challenged the jurisdiction of American courts over Hawaiian citizens. These included the defences from prosecution of Nappy Pulawa (an alleged underworld leader) and me (a lawyer facing discipline for refusing to obey a court order) and defences arising from the Sand Island evictions (of largely Native Hawaiians, to make way for an industrial park) and the Makua evictions (of largely Native Hawaiians, to make way for a tourist park). The Native Rights and Sovereignty Movements often appear indistinguishable. As the political rhetoric grew, the Hawaiian language, hula dancing, canoe paddling, and music flourished anew, spreading across racial lines, giving an added dimension to both movements.

It is four decades since those celebratory days of statehood. Let us reexamine that statehood process through the view of the Hawaiian movement.

"A double fraud was committed when Hawai'i was declared a State of the USA" proclaims a paper from the Institute for the Advancement of Hawaiian Affairs, an early proponent of the Hawaiian movements. Black's law dictionary defines fraud as "an intentional perversion of truth for the purpose of inducing another in reliance upon it to part with some valuable thing belonging to him or to surrender a legal right." These are harsh words indeed to throw at a government generally considered a leader in human rights and fundamental freedoms. Yet such words are being thrown at the United States of America more and more often by the Hawaiian Sovereignty Movement.

This indictment of fraud is rooted in historical events. It is now uncontested by the US government that a unified monarchical government of the Hawaiian Islands was established in 1810 under Kamehameha I and that from 1826 until 1893 the United States recognized the independence of the Kingdom of Hawaii and extended to it full and complete diplomatic recognition, including entering into treaties and conventions with the Hawaiian monarchs. From 1889 to 1893, US Minister Plenipotentiar John L. Stevens, along with a small group of non-Hawaiian residents of Hawai'i, some of whom were US citizens, conspired to overthrow the Hawaiian government. In pursuance of this conspiracy, the US navy landed in an invasion of this country. A puppet government was formed that subsequently "ceded" Hawai'i to the United States in 1898. Two years later, Hawai'i was governed under the "Organic Act" as the "Territory of Hawai'i," its governor appointed directly by the president of the United States.

Two major wars swept through the world, and as the Second World War came to an end there emerged a new international organization, the United Nations. In San Francisco in 1945, leaders of nations gathered to sign a UN charter that called for self-governance of territories under colonial-style conditions. The charter did not specify to which UN members or which "non-self-governing" territories it would be applied. But the following year, the UN General Assembly adopted Resolution 66, in which specific UN members and the territories under their respective rule were named. The United States became obligated under a "sacred trust" to bring about self-governance in Alaska, Guam, American Samoa, the Virgin Islands, the Panama Canal zone, Puerto Rico, and Hawai'i.

Over the years, the United Nations clarified self-governance to mean giving the people of the territory choices on how they would relate to the UN member – by choosing integration, free association, or independence. This self-governance process was meant to break the chains of colonization that held territories within the grips of colonizing nations. As a result, many African countries began their emergence from colonization during these years. Countries in the Pacific and Asian regions also followed this process.

In Hawai'i, decolonization went awry. Rather than permitting the three choices called for by the United Nations, the United States limited the choice to "integration." In 1959, it placed before the people the question "Shall Hawaii immediately be admitted into the Union as a state?" A "yes" response resulted in Hawaii's integration into the United States as a state. A "no" vote would have resulted in continued territorial status in the US de facto integration. The choices of free association or independence were never presented to the Hawaiian people. No education was offered on these alternatives: no public debates on these matters were conducted, and nothing came from the campuses of schools or the University of Hawai'i. The US-appointed governor never raised these options, and the Democrats and the Republicans failed to point out the right to these choices. Thus, when the United States reported to the UN General Assembly in 1959 that Hawai'i had exercised its right to self-governance and, in doing so, had elected to become a state, it convinced the assembly to remove Hawai'i from the list of territories subject to self-governance. An intentional perversion of the truth was thus committed to induce the United Nations to deny Hawai'i the fundamental right to self-determination.

The "statehood process" for Hawai'i was a double fraud. It not only failed to provide the correct set of choices to be voted on, but also it altered the "self" that could exercise "self-determination." The qualified voters in this process were US citizens who had resided in Hawai'i for at least one year. Following the American invasion and annexation, and during its watch, thousands had migrated to Hawai'i from the United States, Europe, Asia, and other Pacific islands. Many were associated with the US military's presence in Hawai'i. Others came for employment, education, opportunities, or escape. Those who were US citizens or took up US citizenship were all permitted to vote, but those who dared to declare themselves Hawaiian citizens, refusing to accept the imposed American citizenship, could not vote.

The Americans controlled education, the economy, the media, and the judiciary, as well as the internal political processes, managing in these years to squeeze the Hawaiian identity from public life. This practice of altering the "self" by maintaining control over transmigration, public education, and economic dependence is familiar among colonizing countries not wanting to lose their colonial possessions. France's conduct in Tahiti and New Caledonia and Indonesia's in East Timor, West Papua, and the Moluccas Islands are mirrors of the US conduct in Hawai'i. Thus, forty years after the statehood vote in Hawai'i, the question of statehood is being revisited, pried open, in fact, by this better understanding in Hawai'i of the rights that should have been accorded the "real" people of Hawai'I, who were entitled to vote on such an important question.

Among sovereignty advocates, there has been a narrowing of the favourite models. Some are urging a "nation within a nation" model of integration, crafted along the lines of the treatment of American Indians by the federal government. A growing number are urging instead complete independence from the United States, as Hawai'i had been before the invasion and as we see more and more nations are becoming. Few are suggesting a free association relationship with the United States, and even those who are are suggesting it merely as a transitional stage to full independence.

Who should vote in such a decision? One group suggests that voters should be restricted by race, allowing only those of Native Hawaiian blood to participate. Such advocates generally support a position of integration, whereby Native Hawaiians are given a special position within the society. A second suggestion is that "Hawaiians at heart" should all be able to participate – that is, all those who practise the culture (hula, oli, plant taro) and who claim to be "Hawaiian." This approach, however, faces obvious difficulties of verification. A third and popular position is to follow the historical and cultural legacy of the Hawaiian Nation: that is, Hawaiian citizens under the nation were multiracial and multicultural, but their national allegiance was dedicated to Hawai'i. Under this approach, a wide range of people would be "eligible," but the real test would be to choose to undertake Hawaiian citizenship, thus disavowing any other citizenship. Hawaiian independence is the favoured position of advocates for this third position.

The Sovereignty and Native Rights Movements are providing fertile ground for reexamining Hawaiian statehood, the Hawaiian "self," and the multiple possibilities in Hawaii's future. This reexamination raises issues stretching far beyond these islands' shores and into international political arenas. (1) Are claims of self-determination ever "settled" by events later discovered to have been fraudulent? Are later discoveries by a colonized people of fraudulent acts committed by administrative powers grounds for reopening questions of self-determination for such people? (2) Which people are permitted to vote in the process of decolonization, citizens of the colonial government or the colonized people themselves?

The international community has struggled with these questions for a long time and continues to do so. As the years take us further away from the time of the 1959 vote on Hawaii's statehood, voices are growing louder, more insistent, and clearer for a reexamination of Hawaii's self-determination.

Northern Door:
Diagnosing Colonialism

Heritage

From my mother, the antique mirror
where I watched my face take on her lines.
She left me the smell of baking bread
to warm fine hairs in my nostrils,
she left the large white breasts that weigh down
my body.

From my father I take his brown eyes,
the plague of locusts that leveled our crops,
they flew in formation like buzzards.

From my uncle the whittled wood
that rattles like bones
and is white
and smells like all our old houses
that are no longer there. He was the man
who sang old chants to me, the words
my father was told not to remember.

From my grandfather who never spoke
I learned to fear silence.
I learned to kill a snake
When begging for rain.

And grandmother, blue-eyed woman
whose skin was brown,
she used snuff.
When her coffee can full of black saliva
spilled on me
it was like the brown cloud of grasshoppers
that leveled her fields.
It was the brown stain
that covered my white shirt.
That sweet black liquid like the food
she chewed up and spit into my father's mouth
when he was an infant.

It was the brown earth of Oklahoma
stained with oil.
She said tobacco would purge your body of poisons.
It has more medicine than stones and knives
against your enemies.
That tobacco is the dark night that covers me.

She said it is wise to eat the flesh of deer
so you can be swift and travel over many miles.
She told me how our tribe has always followed a stick
that pointed west
that pointed east.
From my family I have learned the secrets
of never having a home.

– Linda Hogan, in *Red Clay: Poems and Stories*

4

Postcolonial Ghost Dancing: Diagnosing European Colonialism

James (Sákéj) Youngblood Henderson

Many different strategies and techniques comprise colonialism. These strategies and techniques are a maladroit manifestation by colonialists of their inherited European culture and values. These colonialists saw themselves as continuing the work of the great seventeenth-century European thinkers who created the idea of an artificial society. In remote places, they constructed colonialism on their heritage of Eurocentrism, universality, and a strategy of difference. In the process, they either rejected or overlooked the Crown's vision of treaty commonwealth in international law.

An understanding of these competing components will allow Indigenous peoples to understand the nature of postcolonial self-determination, its movements, visions, and projects. The analysis that I present will be an exercise in postcolonial ghost dancing. Perhaps, for the benefit of an international audience, I should explain why I use this term.

Eurocentric writers have categorized the ghost dance as a type of messianic movement among North American Indians that expressed a desperate longing for the restoration of the past. The vision unfolded that, if followers would purify themselves, speak the truth, love one another, and participate in a special dance, then the dead would soon join the living and all would live happily together in the old way. One vision originated in the prophet dance in eastern British Columbia and Washington. The vision emphasized an imminent destruction of the world, return of the dead, and change to more righteous ways, and it may have been the ultimate source of the later movement.[1] Among the Plains Indians, my relatives, a related vision told that a tidal wave of new earth would cover the alien whites and Indian nonbelievers and renew the land.[2] The vision instructed Wovoka to teach people a sacred dance to be performed at regular intervals. This vision came to be known as the ghost dance.

Eurocentric writings about the ghost dance misunderstood the visions. The normative visions and the dances were not part of a messianic movement but a sustained vision of how to resist colonization. It was a vision of how to release all the spirits contained in the old ceremonies and rites. The dance released these contained spirits or forces back into the deep caves of mother Earth, where they would be immune from colonizers' strategies and techniques. Their efforts were a noble sacrifice for future generations. What is more important, the dance would allow the spiritual teachings to renew the ecology, and eventually the forces of the ecology would forge a traditional consciousness of the following generations. In time, through postcolonial ghost dancing, these forces would foster a new vision of Aboriginal renewal, thus restoring the traditional consciousness and order. Part of the renewal is understanding the colonizer's strategy of Eurocentrism, epistemological diffusionism, universality, and enforcement of differences.

Eurocentrism

Among colonized peoples, the cognitive legacy of colonization is labelled "Eurocentrism." Among some Indigenous peoples, Eurocentrism is known as the twin of the trickster or imitator,[3] or the "anti-trickster." Similar to the trickster who emphasizes Aboriginal thought and dramatizes human behaviour in a world of flux, the "anti-trickster" appears in many guises and is the essence of paradoxical transformation. The "anti-trickster" represents a cognitive force of artificial European thought, a differentiated consciousness, ever changing in its creativity to justify the oppression and domination of contemporary Indigenous peoples and their spiritual guardians.

In academic professorate, Eurocentrism is a dominant intellectual and educational movement that postulates the superiority of Europeans over non-Europeans. Modernists tend to think of Eurocentrism as a prejudice that can be eliminated in the same way that attempts have been made to eliminate racism, sexism, and religious bigotry. However, Eurocentrism is not a matter of attitudes in the sense of values and prejudices. It has been the dominant artificial context for the last five centuries and is an integral part of all scholarship, opinion, and law. As an institutional and imaginative context, it includes a set of assumptions and beliefs about empirical reality. Habitually educated and usually unprejudiced Europeans accept these assumptions and beliefs as true, as propositions supported by "the facts."

Historian Lise Noël has dramatically captured the consequences of this cognitive reality:

> Alienation is to the oppressed what self-righteousness is to the oppressor. Each really believes that their unequal relationship is part of the natural order of things or desires by some higher power. The dominator does not feel that he is exercising unjust power, and the dominated do not feel the need to withdraw from his tutelage. The dominator will even

believe, in all good faith, that he is looking out for the good of the dominated, while the latter will insist that they want an authority more
enlightened than their own to determine their fate.[4]

In Canadian universities and colleges, academic curricula support Eurocentric contexts. When most professors describe the "world," they
describe artificial Eurocentric contexts and ignore Aboriginal worldviews,
knowledge, and thought. For most Aboriginal students, the realization of
their invisibility is similar to looking into a still lake and not seeing their
images. They become alien in their own eyes, unable to recognize themselves in the reflections and shadows of the world. As their grandparents
and parents were stripped of their wealth and dignity, this realization
strips Aboriginal students of their heritage and identity. It gives them
an awareness of their annihilation.

At best, Canadian universities define Aboriginal heritage, identity, and
thought as inferior to Eurocentric heritage, identity, and thought. Typically, however, Eurocentric thought explicitly and implicitly confirms
Aboriginal inadequacy and asserts a negative image of Aboriginal heritage
and identity. Tragically, before long, Aboriginal students will succumb and
inwardly endorse Eurocentric thought and help to lay the foundations of
the relationship of domination that will entrench their thoughts.[5]

A strong critique of Eurocentrism is under way in all fields of social
thought.[6] This critique reveals that the assumptions and beliefs that constructed the context are not universal after all. Many are imaginative local
knowledge; some are false.[7] These critiques give rise to anguished discourses about knowledge and truths. Quickly the issue of respecting diversity slips into maintaining Eurocentric unity and canons. Roberto Mangabeira Unger has called this the burden of the past in social theory and law:

> It is commonplace that great men impose a burden upon those who come
> after them. When there has been remarkable achievement in politics, art,
> or thought, the generation that follows in its wake, and benefits from it
> may suffer the paralyzing sense that nothing really important remains to
> be done. It may feel that the most brilliant opportunities have already
> been explored and turned to advantage. As a result, the successors seem
> faced with a dilemma: either they become mere caretakers of the monu-
> ments the great have left them, or, desirous of independence, but despair-
> ing of excellence, they drastically narrow their ambitions and set out to
> till, with technical proficiency, a small field.[8]

Critical scholars today are aware, as most were not a few decades ago,
that the empirical beliefs of history, geography, and social science that
invented the context of Eurocentrism often gained acceptance because of

the way in which the evidence was presented. Scholarly beliefs are embedded in particular languages and cultures and are shaped by them. This helps to explain the paradox of Eurocentrism, which is resistant to change and continues to exercise a persuasive intellectual power. Its old myths continue to be believed long after the rationale for their acceptance has been forgotten or rejected (e.g., arguments grounded in the belief that the Old Testament is literal history). Newer beliefs gain acceptance without supporting evidence if they are properly Eurocentric.

James M. Blaut argues that modernists derive this resistance from their association with the most powerful social interests of the Eurocentric elites.[9] European colonialism initiated the development of the Eurocentric context, and its wealth formulated many academic elites. Consequently, the development of a body of Eurocentric beliefs has been, and still is, of great importance in justifying and assisting Europe's colonial activities. Eurocentrism is, quite simply, the colonizers' model of the world.[10]

Eurocentrism is the colonizers' model of the world in a very literal sense: it is not merely a bundle of beliefs. It has evolved, through time, into a finely sculpted model, a structured whole – in fact, an ultra-theory, a general framework for many smaller theories: historical, geographical, psychological, sociological, and philosophical. This ultra-theory is known as diffusionism.[11]

Epistemological Diffusionism

Eurocentric diffusionism has changed through time, but its basic nineteenth-century epistemological framework has remained essentially unchanged. Blaut argues that diffusionism is based on two axioms: (1) most human communities are uninventive; and (2) a few human communities (or places or cultures) are inventive and thus remain permanent centres of cultural change or progress. On a global scale, this gives us a model of a world with a single centre – roughly, Europe – and a surrounding periphery.[12]

The dualism of an inside and an outside is central to the ultra-theory.[13] The basic framework of diffusionism in its classical form depicts a world divided into two categories, one of which (greater Europe, "inside") is historical, inventive, and makes progress; the other (non-Europe, "outside") is ahistorical, stagnant, and unchanging and receives progressive innovations by diffusion from Europe. From this base, diffusionism asserts that the difference between the two sectors is that some intellectual or spiritual factor, something characteristic of the "European mind," the "European spirit," "Western man," and so forth leads to creativity, imagination, invention, innovation, rationality, and a sense of honour or ethics – in other words, "European values." The reason for non-Europe's nonprogress is a lack of this intellectual or spiritual factor. This proposition asserts that non-European people are empty, or partly so, of "rationality" – that is, of ideas and proper spiritual values.

Classic diffusionism asserts an emptiness of basic cultural institutions and people in much of the non-European world. This is known as the diffusionist myth of emptiness. This idea plays a role in the physical movement of Europeans into non-European regions, displacing or eliminating the native inhabitants. The proposition of emptiness makes a series of claims, each layered upon the others:

(1) A non-European region is empty or nearly empty of people (so settlement by Europeans does not displace any Native peoples).
(2) The region is empty of settled population: the inhabitants are mobile, nomadic, wanderers (European settlement violates no political sovereignty since wanderers make no claim to territory).
(3) The cultures of this region do not possess an understanding of private property, so the region is empty of property rights and claims (colonial occupiers can freely give land to settlers since no one owns it).
(4) The final layer, applied to all of the "outside," is an emptiness of intellectual creativity and spiritual values, sometimes described by Europeans as an absence of "rationality."[14]

Classic diffusionism also assumes that some non-European regions were "rational" in some ways and to some degree. Thus, for instance, the Middle East during biblical times was rational. China was somewhat rational for a certain period in its history. Other regions, always including Africa, are unqualifiedly lacking in rationality.

Diffusionism asserts that the normal and natural way that the non-European world progresses – or changes for the better, modernizes, and so on – is by the diffusion (or spread) of innovative, progressive ideas from Europe, which flow into it as air flows into a vacuum. This flow may take the form of ideas or new products through which European values are spread. Europeans themselves are the bearers of these new and innovative ideas.

The diffusion of civilizing ideas from Europe to non-Europe is compensation for the confiscation of material wealth by Europe from non-Europe – although nothing can fully compensate Europeans for their gift of civilization to the colonies since the possibility exists that ancient, atavistic traits will counterdiffuse back into the civilized core, in the form of evil things such as black magic.

Blaut outlined the characteristics of the dualism between the centre and the periphery in tabular form:[15]

Characteristic of Eurocentric centre	Characteristic of periphery
Inventiveness	Imitativeness
Rationality, intellect	Irrationality, emotion, instinct
Abstract thought	Concrete thought
Theoretical reasoning	Empirical, practical reasoning
Mind	Body, matter
Discipline	Spontaneity
Adulthood	Childhood
Sanity	Insanity
Science	Sorcery
Progress	Stagnation

This is a simplified version of the diffusionist world model. The debates between diffusionists and their opponents have been going on for more than a century in anthropology, geography, history, and all fields concerned with long-term, large-scale cultural evolution.[16] The antidiffusionists (often called "evolutionists" or "independent-inventionists") level two basic charges against the diffusionists: they hold much too sour a view of human ingenuity, and they believe in spatial elitism. Yet antidiffusionists have failed to grasp the full implication of their critique. None of them denies that the world has an "inside" and an "outside." While criticizing the diffusionists for rejecting the psychic unity of humankind, the antidiffusionists nonetheless believe that Europe is the centre of cultural evolution. Therefore, they accept the idea – explicitly or implicitly – that Europeans are more inventive and more innovative than anyone else is.[17] They make this assumption explicitly when they discuss the modernizing effect of European colonialism. The basic structure of their arguments is the same as that of the diffusionists.

All Eurocentric scholarship is diffusionist since it axiomatically accepts that the world has one permanent centre from which culture/changing ideas tend to originate and a vast periphery that changes as a result (mainly) of diffusion from that single centre. This ultra-theory of Eurocentric context is the intellectual tool of European colonialism. It asserts that colonialism brings civilization to non-Europe and is, in fact, the proper way in which the non-European world advances out of stagnation. Under colonialism, wealth is drawn out of the colonies and enriches the European colonizers. In Eurocentric diffusionism, Europeans see this as a normal relationship between European and Indigenous peoples. Although Eurocentric diffusionism is constructed on some unjustifiably restrictive assumptions, it nevertheless provides the context for colonial legal and political strategy.

Universalism

Eurocentric thought does not claim to be a privileged norm. This would be an argument about cultural relativism, which asserts that values are about specific cultural contexts.[18] Instead, Eurocentric thought claims to be universal and general.[19] Noël summarizes the function of universalism in colonialism: "To present himself as the ideal human type, the dominator often invoked irreducible laws sanctioned by Nature, God, or History. In his view, the power he exercised over the oppressed was not so much the result of undue reliance on force as the effect of uncontrollable imperatives, if not a Higher Will. In relation to the universal model that the oppressor seemed to represent, the dominated always appeared to be afflicted with some defect or intrinsic failing."[20]

European scholars have always held that their civilization had two sources of inspiration that forbade them to be content with developing their own society and part of the world. The first inspiration was the search for knowledge. This quest was an outgrowth of the "wonder" that Aristotle found at the beginning of all thought and of the talk in which Socrates sought to engage each person willing to listen. Every discovery was examined for its universality, and life was to be tested by questioning its universal good. This quest for truth, universal values, and virtue informs the idea of the universal civilization and begins to explain why Europeans left their lands and went to such efforts to discover, as they thought, the whole world and to see it as a "whole" world.

The other reason that Europeans could not rest content with perfecting their own part of the world is the messianic prophecy of monotheistic religions. Europeans had a belief in, and a commitment to, a messianic dream of a millennium: a new heaven, a new Earth, and a transformed people. The Judaic vision of linear time moved toward a predetermined end. Christianity supplemented this vision with divine commands to the disciples that they had something to do, and they were to be about it.[21]

What Socrates and the prophets of the Bible shared is the notion of a universal mission that invites the attention of all humans. It is ironic that national laws of the time attempted to end the idea of this new knowledge and the transformation to a universal civilization. The executions of Socrates and Christ were both legally sanctioned and, indeed, have served to make subsequent generations suspicious of legal institutions and aware of the inherent contradictions in preserving legal order and doing justice. With these deaths came questions about the limits and nature of politics and law, which led to the idea of a civil public. Central to the ideal of a civil public is a search for knowledge, truth, and a just legal order.

Universality is really just another aspect of diffusionism, and claiming universality often means aspiring to domination.[22] Universality creates cultural and cognitive imperialism, which establishes a dominant group's knowledge, experience, culture, and language as the universal norm. Dominators or colonizers reinforce their culture and values by bringing the oppressed and the colonized under their expectations and norms. Given the assumed normality of the dominators' values and identity, the dominators construct the differences of the dominated as inferior and negative.[23] Thus arises the consciousness of the immigrant-colonizer and the Aboriginal-colonized, which the colonized have to accept if they are to survive. This binary consciousness justifies the separation of Indigenous peoples from their ancient rights to the land and its resources and the transfer of wealth and productivity to the colonialists and the mother country.[24]

Often when the colonized others become aware of the colonizers' vision of them and reject it, they experience what W.E.B. Du Bois called "double consciousness": "This sense of always looking at one's self through the eyes of others, of measuring one's soul by the tape of a world that looks on in amused contempt and pity."[25] Double consciousness occurs when the colonized assert that they are human but the dominators reject this assertion and impose their standards as universal and normal. Noël writes:

> After long endorsing the logic of a discourse taught to them as the only one that was valid, the dominated began to feel doubts. At first vague and fleeting, these doubts were aroused by the oppressor's own failure to live up to his idealized model of humanity. As the oppressed became more actively aware of their own worth, their doubts grew more insistent. Gradually, the dominated ceased to see the oppressor's defense of his special interests as the inevitable tribute owed to a superior being. Divine, natural, or historical laws that espoused such narrow designs became suspect. It eventually came to mind that these laws were pure creations of a group wishing to legitimize its privileges.[26]

The colonialist or oppressor is immune from double consciousness because, as the embodiment of the universal, the dominator has the privilege of not being considered as a member of any specific group. "Unseen and often unnamed, the oppressor thus is the implicit incarnation of the supreme model, the ideal type, and the yardstick that measures the humanity of anyone who does not resemble him. Presented as the standard of perfection, his specificity appears to coincide with the main lines of the universal. The very fact that he exercises the right to examine others confirms his belief and, for a time, the beliefs of his victim in his intrinsic wholeness."[27]

Dominators are in a position to study others who pose a "problem," present a "question," or constitute a "case."[28] In searching for the answers for others, dominators believe that they not only maintain a universal discourse but also speak the language of objectivity or impartiality.

Typically, to succeed in creating this sense of objectivity, colonizers must obscure Aboriginal memory. To strip Indigenous peoples of their heritage and identity, the colonial education and legal systems induce collective amnesia that alienates Indigenous peoples from their elders, their linguistic consciousness, and their order of the world. Only the Eurocentric oppressor is the agent of progress, either by the will of God or by the law of nature. The sum of European learning is established as the universal model of civilization, to be imitated by all groups and individuals. The oppressors' imperatives monopolize history or progress. In the Eurocentric construct of three-dimensional time, whoever masters the present moulds the past.[29]

In Canadian thought, for example, Aboriginal nationhood, rights, and treaties are banished from mainstream history and law and replaced by the theory of two founding nations: the English and the French. These thoughts silence or circumscribe the dominated First Nations. Born out of colonialism, anthropology was marked initially by the desire to resolve the conflict raised for European colonialists. By rescuing Indigenous peoples as objects of specific academic observation, Eurocentric anthropology effectively isolated them from history.[30]

The anomalous ability of Eurocentric academics and lawyers to energize and legitimize the rhetoric of universalism in colonial society was vast and remains powerful. Such repression of Indigenous peoples by universal standards or general law was and is effective in immunizing Eurocentric assumptions and practices from examination. As Noël states, "The opinions of the theorists and functionaries of Religion, Law, and Science thus had the effect of legitimizing the relationship of domination by accrediting the thesis of the dominator as the ideal model for humanity. Taking their cue from the very inferiority that they have attributed to the oppressed, theologians and ministers of religion, legislators and magistrates, researchers and scholars believe they may claim the exclusive right to determine the fate of the oppressed."[31]

Differences
In contrast to universalism was the strategy of differences. Universal humanity was a key idea, but the dominants did not apply it universally. Because colonizers consider themselves to be the ideal model for humanity and carriers of superior culture and intelligence, they believe that they can judge other people and assess their competencies. In short, colonizers believe that they have the power to interpret differences, and this belief shaped the institutional and imaginative assumptions of colonization and modernism. Using the strategy of differences, colonialists believe that they have the privilege of defining human competencies and deviancies such as sin, offence, and mental illness. They also believe that they have the

authority to impose their tutelage on the colonized and to remove from them the right to speak for themselves.[32]

Michel Foucault locates at the outset of the colonizing period a shift in the fundamental mode whereby knowledge is acquired: "The activity of the mind ... will ... no longer consist in *drawing things together,* in setting out on a quest for everything that might reveal some sort of kinship, attraction or secretly shared nature within them, but, on the contrary, in *discriminating,* that is, in establishing their identities ... In this sense, discrimination imposes upon comparison the primary and fundamental investigation of difference."[33] The strategy of difference is not simply abstract or analytical. It directly affects secular Eurocentric identity and order.

The strategy of racism allows the colonialists to assert Eurocentric privileges while exploiting Indigenous peoples in an inhuman way.[34] As Albert Memmi explains, "Racism is the generalized and final assigning of values to real or imaginary differences, to the accuser's benefit and at his victim's expense, in order to justify the former's own privileges or aggression."[35] Memmi goes on to identify four related racist strategies used to maintain colonial power over Indigenous peoples: stressing real or imaginary differences between the racist and the victim; assigning values to these differences, to the advantage of the racist and the detriment of the victim; trying to make these values absolute by generalizing from them and claiming that they are final; and using these values to justify any present or possible aggression or privileges.[36]

Stressing Real or Imaginary Differences

The strategy of stressing differences between European "civilization" and New World savages recurs throughout seventeenth- and eighteenth-century texts, maintaining the separation of Indigenous peoples from colonialists. Memmi affirms that "The colonizer discriminates to demonstrate the impossibility of including the colonized into the community: because he would be too biologically and culturally different, technically and politically inept, etc."[37]

By 1800, European aristocracies controlled more than one-third of the Earth's surface. With its expansive claim to exclusive rationality and its arrogant assumption of a universal and uniform knowledge of the world, the colonialists had set a fateful dimension. Colonialists have a better claim to subjugate Indigenous peoples to Eurocentric thought if they define them as "other." These definitions are always simple and reductive.[38]

Difference is an extension of the noun-based linguistic structure of Eurocentric thought. With the rejection of the noun-God's commandments and the unitary, suprahistorical intelligible human essence of classical thought,[39] Eurocentric thought could only perceive categories and make inferences.[40] The two methods used to do this were logical analysis and causal explanation. Each provided an interpretation of what it means to account for something both in the sense of telling what it is like, which is description, and in the sense of establishing why it had to follow from something else, which is explanation in the strict sense.[41]

In the transforming Eurocentric thought, nature was distinguished from European culture.[42] Colonialists use culture to bring order to nature. The sovereign subject becomes the illimitable conduit for illimitable thought and reason. Yet the subject also retains a distinct identity from nature, asserting self-sufficiency.[43]

Not only did this process create a new European identity, but it also reduced the world to European terms. People who stood outside the universal European civilization could only be absolutely different from it. They could only be an aberration or something other than what they should be. Thus, Indigenous peoples were of nature rather than of civilization and were constantly compared to the devils of Christian belief. The identities of Europeans and their colonies were achieved by describing their foundational differences from Indigenous peoples.[44] European identity was different from a wild, disordered nature and, in particular, from "untamed ... natural man."[45] This identity is based in racism and became the strategy that underpinned Eurocentric systems of knowledge and law.

Len M. Findlay in "The Future of the Subject" reminds us that comparative grammar and linguistics comprise an imperial project of the late eighteenth and early nineteenth centuries. It created the Indo-European identity and languages to legitimize conquest and colonization: "The move away from cultural otherness toward a common linguistic ancestry would lead to the ruthless reconstitution of difference rather than its progressive elimination. If 'we' started at the same proto-linguistic place, then why have you progressed so little relative to us? If 'we' belong to the same Indo-European family, then who is to head the family household and direct its economy? If you end up as the subaltern or object and I as the sovereign subject of our erstwhile common discourse, then it is certainly no 'accident.'"[46]

Assigning Negative Values to Differences

Since the first encounter with different people in the medieval crusades, Europeans have sought to prove the inferiority of those who do not share their supposedly superior value system and civilization. They use the same process to describe those from whom they wish to take something. The assigning of values in a colonial context is always to the advantage of the colonialists and to the detriment of their Aboriginal victims. To Memmi, the fact that real differences might be the basis for assigning negative values is irrelevant: "The racist can base his argument on a real trait, whether biological, psychological, cultural or social – such as the color of the black man's skin or the solid tradition of the Jew."[47]

This comfortable strategy allows the colonizers to recognize the very differences that they themselves induce. Anthropologists saw what they wanted to see, and, because they came from the universal European culture, they assumed that their view was an objective one capable of discerning the patterns of another culture.[48]

Assigning negative values to Aboriginal differences has been a persistent strategy in slavery and colonization. It is a strategy grounded in ideology rather than in empirical knowledge, and even anthropologists' impartial accounts of Aboriginal culture complied with the ideology of colonialism: "The Lone Ethnographer depicted the colonized as members of a harmonious, internally homogeneous, unchanging culture. When so described, the culture appeared to 'need' progress, or economic and moral uplifting. In addition, the 'timeless traditional culture' served as a self-congratulatory reference point against which Western civilization could measure its own progressive historical evolution. The civilizing journey was conceived more as a rise than a fall, a process more of elevation than degradation (a long, arduous journey upward, culminating in 'us')."[49] Armchair Eurocentric theorists did not have to live among Indigenous peoples to present an authoritative opinion about them. Relentlessly, the strategy of differences reinforced the obviousness of the received idea of Indigenous peoples.[50] Noël points out this process of circular reasoning: "Repetition reinforces what seems obvious. Warned that the dominated have a particular character trait resulting from their 'difference,' the dominator will not be surprised to observe its frequent manifestation. Having taken note of all those who adopt the behaviour he expects of them, he will feel entitled to conclude, in all impartiality, that the entire group to which they belong do the same thing."[51] Thus, Eurocentric authorities developed the negative stereotype of Indigenous peoples into a comprehensive prejudice, a stigmatized identity, and negative attitudes. Racist discursive strategy, says Memmi, "always adds an interpretation of ... differences, a prejudiced attempt to place a value on them."[52]

The "discovery" of the Americas produced two negative and seemingly contradictory views of Indigenous peoples. The first vision was that Indigenous peoples were wild, promiscuous, propertyless, and lawless. The second vision was of the noble savage who lived with natural law but without government, husbandry, and much else.[53] Together these visions created the narrative tradition of Aboriginal deficiency and unassimilability. Racism resolved any inconvenient contradictions.

The secular European worldview affixes to the idea of race three correlates, which together underlie racism: (1) differences based on race are fundamental, intractable, and unerringly indicative of superiority and inferiority; (2) these differences exclude brown people from the domain of knowing, reason, equality, and freedom (this is more than simply excluding the enslaved or colonized from the realms of liberty and universal law, as Grotius and Locke did);[54] and (3) through taking identity against their construction of "Indians," Europeans and colonialists become bound in their own being by the terms by which they oppress others.[55]

The primary ordering of things by Europeans was visual observation.[56] Thus, Indigenous peoples were classified according to their physical appearance, usually skin colour. Outward features were massively generalized and became signs of inner characteristics and capacities. When equipped with such visual identifying marks, the classifying gaze could produce colonial order by hierarchical racial division. The second step was "to imagine ... that a mere negation of all our [European] virtues is a sufficient description of man in his original state."[57] European thinkers derive a "negative state which is styled a state of nature or a state of anarchy" from a "positive" image of European civilization. Lastly, there was the insight that Indigenous peoples in the state of nature needed European values, or the civilized "subjection," including the determining order of "positive" law.[58]

By logical or causal deduction, Europeans fabricated civilization and positive law. These methods prevented the imaginary subjects of the state of nature from contradicting the Eurocentric universal. In other words, universalism created and sustained the strategy of difference; European thinkers simply ignored empirical evidence that did not fit with the patterns that they were imposing on the world.

Making Values Absolute

Colonial thought asserts that all differences are final, thus confining Indigenous peoples to alienation in perpetuity. This return to universalism is a potent ideological weapon. Memmi explains: "So the discriminatory process enters the stage of universalism or 'totalization.' One thing leads to another until all the victim's personality is characterized by the difference, and all of the members of his social group are targets for the accusation."[59] Moreover, "The racist ascribes to his victim a series of surprising traits, calling him incomprehensible, impenetrable, mysterious, disturbing, etc. Slowly he makes of his victim a sort of animal, a thing or simply a symbol. As the outcome of this effort to expel him from any human community, the victim is chained once and for all to his destiny of misfortune, derision and guilt. And as a counterpart, the accuser is assured once and for all of keeping his role as rightful judge."[60] Racism, on whatever level it occurs, Memmi asserts, "always includes this collective element which is, of course, one of the best ways of totalizing the situation: there must be no loophole by which any Jew, any colonized or any black man could escape this social determination."[61] Noël affirms this insight: "There is no aspect of the oppressed's person over which the dominator does not claim some rights, at some time, or which the dominator does not feel authorized to dispose of in some way to his advantage. The method used by the dominator may be subtle or brutal, and the discourse justifying it may be open or implicit."[62]

The inviolability of that "other" against which European identity is formed was secured by elevating some kinds of knowledge and suppressing others. All Indigenous peoples are viewed as people in the state of nature, and collectively they suffer from defects. Because of these defects, they are doomed to extinction in the face of an imported civilization. According to the dominant society, only Euro-Christian values are a remedy for their defects, and often only words on pieces of paper – called laws – can protect their existence.

Totalization began with Locke's statement that "In the beginning all the World was *America*."[63] As a source of savage origins, the Americas remained the predominant source of the state of nature in British thought until expanding colonization displaced this state of nature. The totalization of the negative values associated with the state of nature ignored that European intervention was burdened with the deathly disordering of a situation that already had its own subtle order. The existence of an Aboriginal order different from the state of nature, however, was to the European and the colonialist "literally unthinkable."[64] Yet, by totalizing the colonial order, the colonial dominators created for themselves the curse of getting it right. Not only did the concept of colonial order work against the colonized peoples, but it also created standards that the dominators could not hope to achieve.

By basing their power on the supposed superiority of their culture and technology, the dominators denied themselves the right to fail. By creating the myth of the ideal, they condemned themselves to eternal perfection. The inability of the dominators to live up to these myths exposed them for what these myths really were: theoretical constructs sanctioned by the groups whose privilege they served. Leslie Silko magnificently captures this predicament of the dominators: "We invented white people: it was Indian witchery that made white people in the first place."[65]

Using Values to Justify Privileges

The final essential element of colonialism relies on the deficient, dehumanized victims and their cultures to explain and justify the racists' aggression and privileges.[66] Memmi notes that a racist "does not punish his victim because he deserves punishment, but declares him guilty because he is already punished."[67] The inferiority or crimes of the oppressed must justify the colonial Eurocentric order. This element establishes the intimate relationship between Eurocentric repression of devalued differences and colonialism and racism. Memmi explains: "Whatever is different or foreign can be felt as a disturbing factor, hence a source of scandal. The attempt to wipe it out follows naturally. This is a primitive, virtually animal reaction, but it certainly goes deeper than we care to admit ... However that may be, the mechanism remains the same. By an accurate or failed characterization of the victim, the accuser attempts to explain and to justify his attitude and his behavior toward him."[68] The cultural and biological inferiority of Indigenous peoples justifies their domination by the superior British colonizer, thus justifying his privilege: "The fact remains that we have discovered a fundamental mechanism, common to all racist reactions: the injustice of an oppressor toward the oppressed, the former's permanent aggression or the aggressive act he is getting ready to commit, must be justified. And isn't privilege one of the forms of permanent aggression, inflicted on a dominated man or group by a dominating man or group? How can any excuse be found for such disorder (source of so many advantages), if not by overwhelming the victim? Underneath its masks, racism is the racist's way of giving himself absolution."[69] Colonial dominators have an answer for everything because they constantly change their level of coherence to favour their domination.[70] In Aboriginal thought, this process creates the "anti-trickster" or the imitator of the Imitator, its twin.

In the strategy of difference, evidence was irrelevant as the Eurocentric critical mind reflected the clear and rational laws of the universe.[71] Developing difference relied on logic or causal thought and not on empirical evidence. This legacy created most elements of Canadian law and policy, particularly the false description of the lawless nature of the savage and the idea that society and law emerged with agriculture. In this process, artificial government was equated with law, and law was not deemed possible in the solitary state of the savage or the savage family.

Consequences

Colonialism as an ideology had profound consequences for human psychology, particularly for the relationship between people of European descent and Indigenous peoples. Each colonial power perfected its own style and system of exploitation, domination, and oppression. These elements and strategies have left a traumatic legacy in the world. As Frantz Fanon stated in *The Wretched of the Earth*, "The colonized will first manifest his aggressiveness which had been deposited in his bones against his own people" but will eventually turn on everything.[72] No ecology, no culture, no people, and no psyche remains untarnished. Oppression was everywhere, and so was the technology of social control and death.

The massive hemorrhage that colonialism inflicted on Indigenous peoples is well documented. The infamy of the Atlantic slave trade and the carnage of the Middle Passage represent the largest and most callous forced migration imposed upon any people in the world. Conservative estimates of Indigenous Africans forced to be a commodity of the Atlantic slave trade range from 15 to 20 million people; recent writers believe that a better estimate is 60 to 150 million. For example, in 1650, Africa's population was 21.2 percent of the known world population; by 1920, it was 7.7 percent. In contrast, between 1650 and 1750, Europe's population grew by only 3 percent, but at the height of colonialism (between 1750 and 1900) the population rose by 400 percent. By then, Europe's population was spilling over to the rest of the world, with a million emigrants a year going to other continents.[73]

In his classic book *Capitalism and Slavery*,[74] Eric Williams documents how the African slave trade to the Americas financed the British Industrial Revolution and made enormous profits for banking concerns as well as insurance companies, especially Barclays and Lloyds. He writes that it was the profits of the colonial slave trade that developed the English manufacturing centres. Others have commented that in the British Industrial Revolution the colonial slave trade was the mainspring of the machine that set every wheel in motion.

European society developed itself and simultaneously underdeveloped Indigenous nations. By 1914, Britain boasted of an empire 140 times its size; Belgium, 80 times; Holland, 60 times; France and Germany, 20 times.[75] These nations were on the verge of colonizing the entire peoples of the Earth militarily, economically, spiritually, and cognitively.

The colonists created new hierarchies and governments that believed in the absolute superiority of Europeans over the colonized, the masculine over the feminine, the adult over the child, the historical over the ahistorical, and the modern or "progressive" over the traditional or "savage." These artificial political orders reflected ways of thinking that were defined by polarities: the modern and the primitive, the secular and the nonsecular, the scientific and the unscientific, the expert and the layman, the normal and the abnormal, the developed and the underdeveloped, the vanguard and the led, the liberated and the saveable.[76] Force sometimes imposed these ideas, but just as often Indigenous peoples absorbed these ideas. These privileging norms released forces within the colonized societies that altered their cultural priorities. Colonization created new worldviews that were self-legitimizing. In this brave new world, through a curious transposition, the colonial dominators called upon the colonized to justify themselves.[77] A historical, primitive people would one day, the colonialists said, learn to see themselves as masters of nature and thus masters of their own fate and a brave new world.[78] The psychological consequence of this strategy is currently being unfolded as the "anti-trickster" struggling with *Nanabush*, the Anishinabe trickster.[79] Among the Aboriginal peoples of the northern Plains, the reconciliations of these knowledge systems are viewed as restorative processes; thus, these processes are organized under the term "postcolonial ghost dancing."

Notes

1 L. Spier, *The Prophet Dance of the Northwest and Its Derivatives: The Source of the Ghost Dance* (Menasha, WI: G. Banta, 1935), and *The Ghost Dance of 1870 among the Klamath of Oregon* (Seattle: University of Washington Press, 1927).

2 See, generally, in Eurocentric literature, J.W. Sayer, *Ghost Dancing the Law: The Wounded Knee Trials* (Cambridge: Harvard University Press, 1997); D. Lynch, *Wovoka and the Ghost Dance* (Lincoln: University of Nebraska Press, 1997); J. Vander, *Shoshone Ghost Dance Religion: Poetry Songs and Great Basin Context* (Urbana: University of Illinois Press, 1997); A.B. Kehoe, *The Ghost Dance: Ethnohistory and Revitalization* (New York: Holt, Rinehart and Winston, 1989); R. Thornton, *We Shall Live Again: The 1870 and 1890 Ghost Dance Movements as Demographic Revitalization* (Cambridge: Cambridge University Press, 1986); D.H. Gottesman, *The Politics of Annihilation: A Psychohistorical Study of the Repression of the Ghost Dance on the Sioux Indian Reservations as an Event in US Foreign Policy* (Ottawa: National Library of Canada, 1974, Canadian theses on microfiche, 18226 [MA thesis, McGill University, 1973]); W.L. Weston, *The Ghost Dance: Origins of Religion* (London: Allen and Unwin, 1972); J. Mooney, *The Ghost-Dance Religion and the Sioux Outbreak of 1890* (Chicago: University of Chicago Press, 1965); D.H. Miller, *Ghost Dance* (New York: Duell, Sloan and Pearce, 1959); P. Bailey, *Wovoka: The Indian Messiah* (Los Angeles: Westernlore Press, 1957).

3 Aboriginal traditions are taught through a paradoxical force in nature known as the "trickster." The Míkmaq refer to him as *Klooscap* or badger, the Anishinabe call the force *Nanabush,* among the Cree the force is known as *wisakedjak* or coyote or crow, the Blackfoot Confederacy call the force *nabi,* the Lakota refer to this force as spider, and the people of the western coast refer to this force as raven. In Aboriginal thought, these sounds present the forces of transformation or changing person. Lessons are learned from trickster actions and transformations that encourage new interpretations and awakening.

4 L. Noël, *Intolerance: A General Survey,* trans. A. Bennett (Montreal and Kingston: McGill-Queen's University Press, 1994) at 79.

5 Ibid. at 79–80.

6 J.M. Blaut, *The Colonizer's Model of the World: Geographical Diffusionism and Eurocentric History* (New York: Guilford Press, 1993) at 8. I have relied heavily on Blaut in my analysis of Eurocentric diffusionism below.

7 Ibid.

8 R.M. Unger, *Law in Modern Society: Toward a Criticism of Social Theory* (New York: Free Press, 1976) at 1.

9 Blaut, *supra* note 6 at 10.

10 Ibid.

11 Ibid. at 10–1.

12 Ibid. at 12.

13 Ibid. at 14. There are a number of variants of this framework. The classical division was one between "civilization" and "savagery." Sometimes this dualism is treated as sharply distinct, with a definite boundary between the two areas. (This form of the model is the familiar one; it is sometimes called the Centre-Periphery Model of the World.) Alternatively, this dualism is expressed as a clear and definite centre, but outside it there is a gradual change in the degree of civilization or progressiveness or innovativeness. Another variant depicts the world as divided into zones, each representing a level of modernity or civilization or development. The classical division was one with three great bands: "civilization," "barbarism," and "savagery."

14 Ibid. at 15. See also M. Weber, *The Protestant Ethic and the Spirit of Capitalism* (New York: Scribner's, 1958) at 30.

15 Ibid. at 17.

16 Ibid. at 11, citing M. Harris, *The Rise of Anthropological Theory* (New York: Crowell, 1968); J.H. Steward, *Theory of Culture Change: The Methodology of Multilinear Evolution* (Urbana: University of Illinois Press, 1955).

17 Ibid. at 13.

18 See R. Benedict, *Patterns of Culture* (Boston: Houghton Mifflin, 1934). Cultural relativists sought to demonstrate that standards of morality and normalcy are culture-bound and called into question the ethnocentric assumption of European superiority. See Alison Dudes Rentelin, *International Human Rights: Universalism versus Relativism* (Newbury Park: Sage Publications, 1990) at 66.

19 Relativists claim that such universality is a cloak for the projection of culturally specific beliefs onto other cultures that possess different worldviews or "inner logic." See Rentelin, ibid. at 67–72.

20 Noël, *supra* note 4 at 149.

21 There are many examples of the search for the millennium. For example, in the Hebrew Bible or Old Testament, when the Lord asked whom he should send on the spiritual journey, Isaiah replied, "Here I am: send me," Isaiah 6:8. In the New Testament, the disciples of Christ are told to go forth to baptize all nations and to teach the things that have been commanded to them, Matthew 28:19; Christ said to Peter "feed my sheep," John 21:17. Some time later, as the Acts of the Apostles narrated, those disciples who witnessed the Ascension were told immediately that they were wasting their time standing there "looking up into the sky," John 21:17.

22 Noël, *supra* note 4 at 12.

23 I. Young, *Justice and the Politics of Difference* (Princeton: Princeton University Press, 1990) at 58–61.

24 A. Memmi, *The Colonizer and the Colonized*, trans. Howard Greenfield (New York: Orion Press, 1965). (Originally *Portrait du colonisé précédé du portrait du colonisateur* [Chastel, Corrêa: Éditions Buchet, 1957.] "When all is said and done the colonizer must be recognized by the colonized. The bond between the colonizer and the colonized is thus both destructive and creative. It destroys and recreates the two partners in the colonization process as colonizer and colonized: the former is disfigured into an oppressor, an uncouth, fragmented human being, a cheat solely preoccupied with his privileges, the latter into a victim of oppression, broken in his development and accepting his own degradation" (at 126). Jean-Paul Sartre stated in his preface to Memmi (ibid. at 24–5) that, for the immigrant-colonizer, "privilege and humanity are one and the same thing; he makes himself into a man by freely exercising his rights. As for the other [Aboriginal-colonized], the absence of any rights sanctions his misery, his chronic hunger, his ignorance, in short, his subhuman status." See Sartre, "Colonialisme et néocolonialisme," in *Situation V* (Paris: Gallimard, 1964).

25 W.E.B. Du Bois, *The Souls of Black Folk* (New York: New American Library, 1969 [1903]) at 45.

26 Noël, *supra* note 4 at 149.

27 Ibid. at 12.

28 Ibid. at 11.

29 Ibid. at 12, 16.

30 R. Rosaldo, *Culture and Truth: The Remaking of Social Analysis* (Boston: Beacon Press, 1989) at 30–45.

31 Noël, *supra* note 4 at 48.

32 D. Kennedy, "A New Stream of International Law Scholarship" (1988) 7 *Wis. Int'l L. J.* 1. The differences created, however, are fallible, and contemporary thought has witnessed the demise of most of them.

33 M. Foucault, *The Order of Things: An Archeology of the Human Sciences* (London: Tavistock, 1970) at 55.

34 "Everyone has felt the contempt implicit in the term 'native,' used to designate the inhabitants of a colonized country. The banker, the manufacturer, even the professor in the home country, are not natives of any country: they are not natives at all. The oppressed person, on the other hand, feels himself to be a native; each single event in his

life repeats to him that he has not the right to exist." Jean-Paul Sartre, "Materialism and Revolution," in *Literary and Philosophical Essays*, trans. A. Michelson (London: Hutchinson, 1968) at 215.

35 "Attempt at a Definition," in A. Memmi, *Dominated Man: Notes Toward a Portrait* (Boston: Beacon Press, 1969) at 185. See Lumbee legal scholar Rob Williams's brilliant application of these principles to federal Indian law in R.A. Williams, "The Algebra of Federal Indian Law: The Hard Trail of Decolonizing and Americanizing the White Man's Indian Jurisprudence" (1986) *Wis. L. Rev.* 219.

36 Ibid. Memmi at 186.

37 Ibid. at 187.

38 Noël, *supra* note 4 at 109.

39 Ibid.

40 See, generally, R.M. Unger, *Knowledge and Politics* (New York: Free Press, 1975).

41 Unger, *Social Theory, supra* note 8 at 9.

42 L. Jordanova, in "Natural Facts: A Historical Perspective on Science and Sexuality," states that, "While it is important to realize that nature was endowed with a remarkable range of meanings during the period of the Enlightenment ... there was also one common theme. Nature was taken to be that realm on which mankind acts, not just to intervene in or manipulate directly, but also to understand and render it intelligible. This perception of nature includes people and the societies they construct. Such an interpretation of nature led to two distinct positions: nature could be taken to be that part of the world which human beings have understood, mastered and made their own. Here, through the unravelling of laws of motion for example, the inner recesses of nature were revealed to the human mind. But secondly, nature was also that which has not yet been penetrated (either literally or metaphorically), the wilderness and deserts, unmediated and dangerous nature." In C.P. MacCormack and M. Strathern, eds., *Nature, Culture, and Gender* (Cambridge: Cambridge University Press, 1980) at 66. Foucault stated a similar conclusion – the appropriated and the yet to be appropriated share in the same universal order of things, *supra* note 33 at 56–7.

43 See E. Cassirer, *The Philosophy of the Enlightenment*, trans. Fritz Koelin and James Pettegrove (Boston: Beacon Press, 1955) at 38.

44 This is a process similar to Edward Said's notion of "orientalism." Said underscored the links between power and knowledge, between imperialism and orientalism, but showed how seemingly neutral, or innocent, forms of social description both reinforced and produced ideologies that justified colonialism and the imperialist project. Under such descriptions, the Orient was a cultural entity that appeared to be both a benchmark against which to measure Western European progress and an inert terrain on which to impose colonial schemes of development. See E. Said, *Orientalism* (New York: Pantheon Books, 1978). See also E. Said, *Culture and Imperialism* (Cambridge: Harvard University Press, 1992).

45 See L. Poliakov, *The Aryan Myth: A History of Racist and Nationalist Ideas in Europe* (London: Chatto and Windus, and Heinemann, for Sussex University Press, 1974) at 241.

46 L.M. Findlay, "The Future of the Subject" (1992) *English Studies in Canada*, 18, 2, at 130-1.

47 Memmi, *supra* note 35 at 187–8.

48 The French sociologist Emile Durkheim was evoked as the model in British ethnology. Ibid. at 32.

49 Rosaldo, *supra* note 30 at 30-1.

50 Noël, *supra* note 4 at 109.

51 Ibid. at 116–7.

52 Ibid. at 188.

53 See J.Y. Henderson, "First Nations Legal Inheritance in Canada: The Míkmaq Model" (1995) *Manitoba Law Journal* 23, at 1-31.

54 See J.J. Rousseau, *The Social Contract and Discourses* (London: Dent, 1986) at 186; D.B. Davis, *The Problem of Slavery in Western Culture* (Ithaca: Cornell University Press, 1966) at 114–5; J. Locke, "The Second Treatise of Government," in *Two Treatises of Government* [1689], reprint, ed. P. Laslett (Cambridge: Cambridge University Press, 1970) at 325–6, 366, paras. 23–4, 85.

55 Cf. Hegel, *Phenomenology of Spirit* (Oxford: Clarendon Press, 1977) at 19 – B.IV A.
56 Foucault, *supra* note 33 at 138, 132.
57 A. Ferguson, *An Essay on the History of Civil Society, 1767* (Edinburgh: Edinburgh University Press, 1966) at 75.
58 J. Austin, *Lectures of Jurisprudence,* 3 vols. (London: John Murray, 1861–3) at 22.2–I.
59 Memmi, *supra* note 35 at 189.
60 Ibid. at 191.
61 Ibid. at 177.
62 Noël, *supra* note 4 at 96.
63 Locke, *supra* note 54 at 343 (original emphasis).
64 Memmi, *supra* note 24 at 137.
65 L.M. Silko, *Ceremony* (New York: Penguin, 1977) at 132.
66 Memmi, *supra* note 35 at 191–4.
67 Ibid. at 217.
68 Ibid. at 192.
69 Ibid. at 194.
70 Foucault invokes this process in his concept of "tactical flexibility of the discourse" in *The History of Sexuality,* trans. R. Hurley (New York: Pantheon Books, 1978) vol. I at 132–5.
71 See, generally, G. Mosse, *Toward the Final Solution: A History of European Racism* (London: Dent, 1978).
72 F. Fanon, *The Wretched of the Earth,* trans. C. Farrington (London: MacGibbon and Kee, 1965) at 40.
73 H.A. Bulhan, *Frantz Fanon and the Psychology of Oppression* (New York: Plenum Press, 1985) at 42–4.
74 E. Williams, *Capitalism and Slavery* (Chapel Hill: University of North Carolina Press, 1944).
75 Bulhan, *supra* note 73 at 43.
76 A. Nandy, *The Intimate Enemy: Loss and Recovery of Self under Colonization* (Delhi: Oxford University Press, 1983) at x.
77 Ibid. at ix, citing Albert Camus.
78 Ibid.
79 See the elegant works of John Burrows: "Constitutional Law from a First Nation Perspective: Self-Government and the Royal Proclamation" (1994) *U.B.C. L. Rev.* 1; "With or without You; First Nations Law (in Canada)" (1996) 41, 3 *McGill L. J.* 629; "Frozen Rights in Canada: Constitutional Interpretation of the Trickster" (1997) 22 *American Indian L. Rev.* 37.

5
Jagged Worldviews Colliding
Leroy Little Bear

No matter how dominant a worldview is, there are always other ways of interpreting the world. Different ways of interpreting the world are manifest through different cultures, which are often in opposition to one another. One of the problems with colonialism is that it tries to maintain a singular social order by means of force and law, suppressing the diversity of human worldviews. The underlying differences between Aboriginal and Eurocentric worldviews make this a tenuous proposition at best. Typically, this proposition creates oppression and discrimination.

Culture comprises a society's philosophy about the nature of reality, the values that flow from this philosophy, and the social customs that embody these values. Any individual within a culture is going to have his or her own personal interpretation of the collective cultural code; however, the individual's worldview has its roots in the culture – that is, in the society's shared philosophy, values, and customs. If we are to understand why Aboriginal and Eurocentric worldviews clash, we need to understand how the philosophy, values, and customs of Aboriginal cultures differ from those of Eurocentric cultures. Understanding the differences in worldviews, in turn, gives us a starting point for understanding the paradoxes that colonialism poses for social control.

Aboriginal Philosophy
In Aboriginal philosophy, existence consists of energy. All things are animate, imbued with spirit, and in constant motion. In this realm of energy and spirit, interrelationships between all entities are of paramount importance, and space is a more important referent than time. Although I am referring to the philosophy of the Plains Indians, there is enough similarity among North American Indian philosophies to apply the concepts generally, even though there may be individual differences or differing emphases.

The idea of all things being in constant motion or flux leads to a holistic and cyclical view of the world. If everything is constantly moving and changing, then one has to look at the whole to begin to see patterns. For instance, the cosmic cycles are in constant motion, but they have regular patterns that result in recurrences such as the seasons of the year, the migration of the animals, renewal ceremonies, songs, and stories. Constant motion, as manifested in cyclical or repetitive patterns, emphasizes process as opposed to product. It results in a concept of time that is dynamic but without motion. Time is part of the constant flux but goes nowhere. Time just is.

Language embodies the way a society thinks. Through learning and speaking a particular language, an individual absorbs the collective thought processes of a people. Aboriginal languages are, for the most part, verb-rich languages that are process- or action-oriented. They are generally aimed at describing "happenings" rather than objects. The languages of Aboriginal peoples allow for the transcendence of boundaries. For example, the categorizing process in many Aboriginal languages does not make use of the dichotomies either/or, black/white, saint/sinner. There is no animate/inanimate dichotomy. Everything is more or less animate. Consequently, Aboriginal languages allow for talking to trees and rocks, an allowance not accorded in English. If everything is animate, then everything has spirit and knowledge. If everything has spirit and knowledge, then all are like me. If all are like me, then all are my relations.

In Plains Indian philosophy, certain events, patterns, cycles, and happenings take place in certain places. From a human point of view, patterns, cycles, and happenings are readily observable on land: animal migrations, cycles of plant life, seasons, and so on. The cosmos is also observable, and patterns are detected from a particular spatial location within the territory of a particular tribe. Tribal territory is important because Earth is our Mother (and this is not a metaphor: it is real).[1] The Earth cannot be separated from the actual being of Indians. The Earth is where the continuous and/or repetitive process of creation occurs. It is on the Earth and from the Earth that cycles, phases, patterns – in other words, the constant motion or flux – can be observed. Creation is a continuity. If creation is to continue, then it must be renewed. Renewal ceremonies, the telling and retelling of creation stories, the singing and resinging of the songs, are all humans' part in the maintenance of creation. Hence the Sundance, societal ceremonies, the unbundling of medicine bundles at certain phases of the year – all of which are interrelated aspects of happenings that take place on and within Mother Earth.

All of the above leads one to articulate Aboriginal philosophy as being holistic and cyclical or repetitive, generalist, process-oriented, and firmly grounded in a particular place.

Aboriginal Values and Customs

Aboriginal values flow from an Aboriginal worldview or "philosophy." Values are those mechanisms put in place by the group that more or less tells the individual members of the society that, "If you pursue the following, you will be rewarded or given recognition by the group," or, alternatively, "If you pursue the following, you will be ostracized or punished by the group." Aboriginal traditions, laws, and customs are the practical application of the philosophy and values of the group.

Arising out of the Aboriginal philosophy of constant motion or flux is the value of wholeness or totality. The value of wholeness speaks to the totality of creation, the group as opposed to the individual, the forest as opposed to the individual trees. It focuses on the totality of the constant flux rather than on individual patterns. This value is reflected in the customs and organization of Plains Indian tribes, where the locus of social organization is the extended family, not the immediate, biological family. Several extended families combine to form a band. Several bands combine to form a tribe or nation; several tribes or nations combine to form confederacies. The circle of kinship can be made up of one circle or a number of concentric circles. These kinship circles can be interconnected by other circles such as religious and social communities. This approach to Aboriginal organization can be viewed as a "spider web" of relations.

Wholeness is like a flower with four petals. When it opens, one discovers strength, sharing, honesty, and kindness. Together these four petals create balance, harmony, and beauty. Wholeness works in the same interconnected way. The value strength speaks to the idea of sustaining balance. If a person is whole and balanced, then he or she is in a position to fulfil his or her individual responsibilities to the whole. If a person is not balanced, then he or she is sick and weak – physically, mentally, or both – and cannot fulfil his or her individual responsibilities. The value strength brings out other values such as independence and respect. Independence means being a generalist, which means knowing a little bit about everything. Independence manifests itself in many different ways. It may manifest itself in long absences from the group on the trapline, in not asking for assistance when in trouble, and in being a "jack of all trades." The quest for balance manifests itself in what Rupert Ross calls the ethic of "noninterference."[2] Noninterference is respect for others' wholeness, totality, and knowledge.

The Aboriginal value of sharing manifests itself in relationships. Relationships result from interactions with the group and with all of creation. Sharing speaks not just to interchanging material goods but also, more importantly, to the strength to create and sustain "good feelings." Maintaining good feelings is one reason why a sense of humour pervades Aboriginal societies. Sharing also brings about harmony, which sustains strength and balance.

Because the shared heritage is recorded in the minds of the members of a society, honesty is an important Aboriginal value. Honesty is closely related to strength and sharing and may be seen as a commitment to these values. It is based on being aware that every being is animate and has an awareness that seeks to understand the constant flux according to its own capabilities. Aboriginal people seek to use such understandings to maintain their balance and to sustain harmony and cooperation. Under the custom of noninterference, no being ought to impose on another's understanding of the flux. Each being ought to have the strength to be tolerant of the beauty of cognitive diversity. Honesty allows Aboriginal people to accept that no one can ever know for certain what someone else knows. The only thing one can go on is what the other human being shares or says to you or others. And, in all of this, there is an underlying presumption that a person is reporting an event the way he or she experienced it. For the purposes of social control, there is a strong expectation that everyone will share his or her truth (actually, "truthing" is a better concept) because people depend on each other's honesty to create a holistic understanding of the flux. Lies result in chaos and establish false understanding.

A reciprocal aspect to honesty exists. If people come to know another person as untruthful and a liar, they will eventually not use that person's actions and talk as a basis for their relationships and interactions. In other words, the liar's expectations will not be fulfilled. The message is, "If you want to be part of the spider web of relations, speak the truth."

Kindness is a value that revolves around notions of love, easy-goingness, praise, and gratefulness. If love and good feelings pervade the group, then balance, harmony, and beauty result. This is a positive rather than a negative approach to social control. If individuals are appropriately and immediately given recognition for upholding strength, honesty, and kindness, then a "good" order will be maintained, and the good of the group will continue to be the goal of all the members of the society.

Understanding the four interrelated petals of the flower demonstrates why collective decision making was and is such an important Aboriginal custom. It is important in all aspects of Aboriginal life, including decisions governing external relations, the utilization of resources, movements within the Aboriginal territory, and the education of the younger generation. Customs with regard to external relations include peace and friendship with other tribes and nations; trade with outsiders; treatment of visitors and adoption of outsiders; and warfare and defence of territory. Customs about the utilization of resources include collective hunting and harvesting of game and plants and the equal sharing of these resources. Traditionally, the families within a tribal territory did not move around the territory randomly. In fact, extended families had responsibility for certain parts of the territory and moved within that particular part even though there may have been no strong demarcation between families and even though extended families may have joined and moved around the territory together. The fact that many families moved around certain parts of the tribal territory is reflected in the Sundance camp, where certain bands occupy certain parts of the camp circle. This was also reflected in the original occupation of reserves: certain bands occupied certain parts of the reserve and, in many cases, reflected the occupation pattern of the traditional territory.

It is not the intent of this chapter to describe in detail every Aboriginal custom; anthropologists have done enough of that. They have done a fairly decent job of describing the customs themselves, but they have failed miserably in finding and interpreting the meanings behind the customs. The function of Aboriginal values and customs is to maintain the relationships that hold creation together. If creation manifests itself in terms of cyclical patterns and repetitions, then the maintenance and renewal of those patterns is all-important. Values and customs are the participatory part that Aboriginal people play in the maintenance of creation.

How do Aboriginal peoples educate and inculcate the philosophy, values, and customs of their cultures? For the most part, education and socialization are achieved through praise, reward, recognition, and renewal ceremonies and by example, actual experience, and storytelling. Children are greatly valued and are considered gifts from the Creator. From the moment of birth, children are the objects of love and kindness from a large circle of relatives and friends. They are strictly trained but in a "sea" of love and kindness. As they grow, children are given praise and recognition for their achievements both by the extended family and by the group as a whole. Group recognition manifests itself in public ceremonies performed for a child, giveaways in a child's honour, and songs created and sung in a child's honour. Children are seldom physically punished, but they are sternly lectured about the implications of wrongful and unacceptable behaviour.

Teaching through actual experience is done by relatives: for example, aunts teaching girls and uncles teaching boys. One relative usually takes a young child under his or her wing, assuming responsibility for teaching the child all she or he knows about the culture and survival. This person makes ongoing progress reports to the group, friends, relatives, and parents, resulting in praise and recognition for the child. There are many people involved in the education and socialization of a child. Anyone can participate in educating a child because education is a collective responsibility.

Storytelling is a very important part of the educational process. It is through stories that customs and values are taught and shared. In most Aboriginal societies, there are hundreds of stories of real-life experiences, spirits, creation, customs, and values. For instance, most Aboriginal cultures have a trickster figure. The trickster is about chaos, the unexpected, the "why" of creation, and the consequences of unacceptable behaviour. These stories are usually told by the loving grandmas and grandpas of the tribe.

The education a child receives and carries forward into adulthood transcends the boundary between the physical and the spiritual. For instance, the boundary between the state of being awake and the reality in dreamtime is almost nonexistent. Anthropomorphic form is not important; it is assumed that a being can readily go through metamorphosis. All of the knowledge is primarily transmitted from the older to the younger generation through language; consequently, language is of paramount importance.

Eurocentric Values

In contrast to Aboriginal value systems, one can summarize the value systems of Western Europeans as being linear and singular, static, and objective. The Western European concept of time is a good example of linearity. Time begins somewhere way back there and follows a linear progression from A to B to C to D. The linearity manifests itself in terms of a social organization that is hierarchical in terms of both structure and power. Socially, it manifests itself in terms of bigger, higher, newer, or faster being preferred over smaller, lower, older, or slower.

Singularity manifests itself in the thinking processes of Western Europeans in concepts such as one true god, one true answer, and one right way. This singularity results in a social structure consisting of specialists. Everyone in the society has to be some kind of specialist, whether it be doctor, lawyer, plumber, or mechanic. Specializations are ranked in terms of prestige. This, in turn, results in a social class structure. Some professions are higher up the ladder, and some are lower down it. In science, singularity manifests itself in terms of an expensive search for the ultimate truth, the ultimate particle out of which all matter is made. And so it goes.

The static way of thinking is probably best exemplified by the former CBS TV news anchor Walter Cronkite, who used to say at the end of his newscast "And that's the way it is on ... X day, X year." The static way of thinking is also exemplified by the experimental approach in science, in which an observation is attempted in isolation and in an artificial environment. What happens or is manifested during the experiment at a certain time and place brings about a conclusion that says "And that's the way it is."

Objectivity is a process that has its base in physical observation and measurement. Again, science is a good example. Even though observation and measurement are both necessary to science, measurement is stressed and emphasized. If something is not measurable, then it is not scientific. Observation by itself is not good enough. Of course, anything subjective is not measurable and, therefore, not scientific. This way of thinking leads one to conclude that only physical objects and processes are measurable. Of course, physical objects and processes are external to the person. Objectivity, in other words, is an externalization but also an appropriative process. Objectivity results in an emphasis on materialism. Objectivity concerns itself with quantity and not quality.

Every society has many deep-rooted and implicit assumptions about what life and reality are all about. These assumptions are the guidelines for interpreting laws, rules, customs, and actions. It is deep-rooted and implicit assumptions upon which attitudes are based and that make a person say "This is the way it is." It is these assumptions that make it hard for a person to appreciate an alternative way of thinking and behaving. This is why I have gone to considerable lengths to illustrate the worldview of Western Europeans, which is linear and singular, static, and objective.

Aboriginal and Eurocentric Values Contrasted

Given the opportunity, Aboriginal cultures attempt to mould their members into ideal personalities. The ideal personality is one that shows strength both physically and spiritually. S/he is a person who is generous and shows kindness to all. S/he is a person who puts the group's needs ahead of individual wants and desires. S/he is a person who, as a generalist, knows all the survival skills and has wisdom. S/he is a person steeped in spiritual and ritual knowledge. S/he is a person who, in view of all these expectations, goes about life and approaches "all his/her relations" in a sea of friendship, easy-goingness, humour, and good feelings. S/he is a person who attempts to suppress inner feelings, anger, and disagreement with the group. S/he is a person who is expected to display bravery, hardiness, and strength against enemies and outsiders. S/he is a person who is adaptable and takes the world as it comes, without complaint.

Every society, whether consciously or unconsciously, realizes that, given the nature of human beings, there will always be members of the society who will run afoul of the cultural values and customs. In Aboriginal societies, diversity is the norm, so deviation from acceptable behaviour is minimized. A number of different factors operate to create this value. One is that the philosophy, the values, and the customs in Aboriginal societies are also the law. Law is not something that is separate and unto itself. Law is the culture, and culture is the law.

Another factor that minimizes deviations and abrogation of the law is equality. Equality pervades Aboriginal societies because of values such as sharing and generosity, the importance of the group as opposed to the individual, and in general the concepts of wholeness and totality. These values and mechanisms neutralize disparity between individual members of the society and therefore reduce wants, desires, and aspirations that may result in the abrogation of the law. In other words, if no person has more than any other does, then no one has feelings of exclusion or being cheated or short-changed.

Internalization of knowledge is another major factor that minimizes deviation from socially acceptable behaviour. Internalization means everyone carries around the societal code, whereas in Western society everything is externalized. A police force is an externalization of social control. If there is a police force, then the only time I have to worry about legally incorrect behaviour is when I get caught. The only time I know something is wrong is when a police officer stops me. Police officers are the detectives of right and wrong behaviour – mainly wrong behaviour because you never get stopped by the police for proper behaviour.

For the most part, Aboriginal societies do not have complex societal organizations such as police forces. Such organizations usually were not needed because traditional tribal society collectively agreed on acceptable forms of behaviour. The "spider web" of relations ensures that the welfare of the group is the most important thing in Aboriginal societies. The value of wholeness tells the members that, if all do their parts, then social order will be the result. It is as though everybody is a "cop" and nobody is a "cop." If the "whole" is maintained, then beauty, harmony, and balance result.

It is because of this underlying philosophy that "collective agreements" or ideal personalities were internalized by each member of an Aboriginal society. In other words, if I were a member of that society, then I would carry the behavioural code around in my mind. Knowledge is internalized, and once internalized it is forever with me. This knowledge tells me what is proper and what is improper behaviour. So if all members of the society carry the code around within them, then it is as though everybody were a police officer, and only minor mechanisms are needed for the purpose of social control, mechanisms such as gossip. Although modern society attempts to use gossip in this way, it does not do so very effectively. Splashing a criminal's name around in the news media has little effect on controlling that person's behaviour. That person is a criminal because he or she has not internalized any social-control mechanisms in the first place.

Jagged Worldviews

Colonization created a fragmentary worldview among Aboriginal peoples. By force, terror, and educational policy, it attempted to destroy the Aboriginal worldview – but failed. Instead, colonization left a heritage of jagged worldviews among Indigenous peoples. They no longer had an Aboriginal worldview, nor did they adopt a Eurocentric worldview. Their consciousness became a random puzzle, a jigsaw puzzle that each person has to attempt to understand. Many collective views of the world competed for control of their behaviour, and since none was dominant modern Aboriginal people had to make guesses or choices about everything. Aboriginal consciousness became a site of overlapping, contentious, fragmented, competing desires and values.

Such jagged worldviews minimize legitimate cultural and social control; thus, external force and law, relatives of terrorism, become the instruments of social control. The externalization of social control through things such as a police force brings with it the notion of objectivity. Is there any such thing as objective knowledge? The short answer is "no," because anything you claim to know is your knowledge alone. In a context of jagged worldviews, I cannot take for granted that you see and know the same things that I see and know. If I were to point out to you my little dog over here, and if you didn't see it, you would have no way of knowing if I was or was not really seeing a dog. When jagged worldviews collide, objectivity is an illusion. The only things I know for sure are the things I experience, see, feel, and so on. The rest of it is presumption and persuasion. I presume that you know what I know, what I see, what I feel. Because of this subjectivity, people discuss and persuade. This is why people talk so much attempting to explain to each other what they know. That is why we engage in conversation, so I can share my experiences with you and make you understand what I am feeling. When you respond, you are doing the same thing with me.

Yet all colonial people, both the colonizer and the colonized, have shared or collective views of the world embedded in their languages, stories, or narratives. It is collective because it is shared among a family or group. However, this shared worldview is always contested, and this paradox is part of what it means to be colonized. Everyone attempts to understand these different ways of viewing the world and to make choices about how to live his or her life. No one has a pure worldview that is 100 percent Indigenous or Eurocentric; rather, everyone has an integrated mind, a fluxing and ambidextrous consciousness, a precolonized consciousness that flows into a colonized consciousness and back again. It is this clash of worldviews that is at the heart of many current difficulties with effective means of social control in postcolonial North America. It is also this clash that suppresses diversity in choices and denies Aboriginal people harmony in their daily lives.

Notes
1 Percy BullChild, *The Sun Came Down* (San Francisco: Harper and Row, 1985). This is a good collection of Blackfoot stories.
2 Rupert Ross, *Dancing with a Ghost: Exploring Indian Reality* (Markham, ON: Octopus Publishing Group, 1992), 12.

6

Applied Postcolonial Clinical and Research Strategies

Bonnie Duran and Eduardo Duran

The student, practitioner, and academic in the psychological arena may ask a very valid and practical question: Why another cross-cultural treatise dealing with Native American psychology? It seems that psychological literature dealing with some of the very complex issues of providing theoretical and practical guidance in this area already abounds. As we see it, the existing literature on the subject is sorely lacking in relevant theoretical constructions upon which to base a fundamental approach that actually has some efficacy in ameliorating some of the problems facing our community.

After a combined three decades of graduate training, clinical practice, and research, we have had some revelations regarding the use of psychology and the politically correctly phrased cross-cultural approaches. Early on, we began to realize that much of the study of cross-cultural issues and the resultant literature primarily comprised an exercise that had to be validated by the rules of the academy, thus making it a neocolonial experience. It did not take a great revelation to discover that the people who made up the rules of this academy were predominantly white men. It follows that knowledge from a cross-cultural perspective must become a caricature of the culture in order for it to be validated as science or knowledge. Borrowing from the imagery of Frantz Fanon, the study of colonized peoples must take on a "lactification" or whitening in order for the knowledge to be palatable to the academy. The consequences of such cross-cultural production of knowledge have been ongoing epistemic colonialism within the discipline of psychology. For example, intelligence testing and sciencing based on eugenics are the root metaphors upon which modern theory and practice are based. From here, we do not need to look far for a critique of psychology – particularly in its cross-cultural formation. Insofar as all the

[*Editor's note:* This chapter has been adapted from their book *Native American Post-Colonial Psychology*, reprinted with permission from the State University of New York Press.]

human sciences are founded on the Western philosophical tradition, that tradition itself contains the seeds of psychology's transformation. The "linguistic turn" uncovers our construction based on the binary opposites implicit in Western metaphysics, which in turn constructs all scientific discourse, including psychology. Rather than continuing the "will to power" of control over natural and human processes, new philosophical formulations herald a moral advancement while at the same time negating the teleological progress of history. Feminist studies, cultural studies, and literary criticism are prime examples of the way in which disciplines have been transformed via the incorporation of philosophical insight – much the same way as Freud reversed the value of the binary opposites of consciousness and unconsciousness. These transformations open the door for different/other models of healing, normalcy, and identity.

The study of cross-cultural thought is a difficult endeavour at best; the outcome of cross-cultural study may be the depreciation of culture rather than its legitimate analysis from another viewpoint. The reality of doing cross-cultural investigation is that most of this analysis is performed through the inoculated gaze of a psychology whose discourse is founded on the premise of the universal subject – the subject of a historical project of emancipation via reason. As long as the language implies that the discourse is cross-cultural, we are perpetuating the notion that other cultures do not have their own valid and legitimate epistemological forms. "Cross-cultural" implies that there is a relative platform from which all observations are to be made, and the platform that remains in place in our neocolonial discipline is that of Western subjectivity. When Western subjectivity is imposed on colonized peoples, not only will the phenomenon under scrutiny evade the lens of positivism, but further hegemony will also be imposed on the community.

In order for our discipline to lead the way toward a true integration, sincere work must be completed as we move toward a postcolonial paradigm. Put simply, a postcolonial paradigm would accept knowledge from differing cosmologies as valid in their own right, without them having to adhere to a separate cultural body for legitimacy. Frantz Fanon believed that the Third World should not define itself in terms of European values. Instead, Fanon thought, everything needed to be reformed and thought anew, and, if colonized peoples were not willing to do this, then they should leave the destiny of their communities to the Western European mind-set. The year 1992 marked an important anniversary of the onset of colonialism in the New World. In keeping with the spirit of our brother Fanon, thinkers from the Third and Fourth Worlds must create knowledge that is not only new but also liberating and healing.

The past 500 years have been devastating to our communities; the effects of this systematic genocide are currently being felt by our people. The effects of the genocide are quickly personalized and pathologized by our profession via the diagnosing and labelling tools designed for this purpose. If the labelling and diagnosing process is to have any historical truth, then it should incorporate a diagnostic category that reflects the effects of genocide. Such a diagnosis would be "acute and/or chronic reaction to colonialism." In this sense, diagnostic policy imposes a structure of normality based in part on belief in the moral legitimacy and universality of state institutions.

Generating healing knowledge from the lifeworld of the colonist – as has been the history of cross-cultural work – will no longer suffice. Our communities' Indigenous forms of knowledge were and continue to be relevant as we face the task of overcoming the colonial mind-set that so many of us have internalized. For this reason, as responsible postcolonial social scientists, we must address the colonial attitude of our discipline. We cannot continue to reward knowledge that reifies the thought processes of Western Europeans above all others.

We realize that colonization has had an influence on much of the current state of knowledge. In order to have a true integration of thought, we must make room for nonlinear thinking, which will yield a true hybrid postcolonial way of expressing subjectivity. As we move into the next millennium, we should not be tolerant of the neocolonialism that runs unchecked through our knowledge-generating systems. We must ensure that journals, media, and other avenues for the dissemination of thought have "gatekeepers" who understand the effects of colonialism and are committed to fighting any perceived act of hegemony over our communities. Postcolonial thinkers should be placed in positions to act as gatekeepers of knowledge in order to ensure that Western European thought be kept in its appropriate place.

If psychology continues on its present course, the judgment of history will continue to be unkind – as already described by Michel Foucault in *Madness and Civilization* (1967). It is no longer acceptable for psychology to continue to be the enforcement branch of the secularized Judeo-Christian myth. Through the worshipping of logical positivism, our discipline has been a co-conspirator in the devastation and control of those peoples who are not subsumed under a white, male, heterosexual, Christian subjectivity.

The Newtonian and Cartesian fundamentalists who continue to entrench themselves in kneeling at the altar of science must analyze and deconstruct their actions anew. A very simplistic analysis will illustrate that their so-called objectification of science is nothing but ongoing social control and hegemony. Our discipline prefers to think that psychological thought exists in a noncontextual form, emerging as the immaculate conception of the past century. In reality, psychological thought as an offshoot of medicine has been gestating since the Middle Ages and continues to be implicated in an ongoing system of social control, as it was during the heyday of the papacy. These notions are sure to disrupt the linear thinking of most of our objective scientific brothers and sisters in the profession. A postcolonial diagnosis for such objective scientists would perhaps be "chronic and/or acute Cartesian anxiety disorder." Fortunately, this is a disorder that has a good prognosis when treated with some of the new postcolonial therapeutic interventions. Postcolonial psychology will not operate on the basis of a logic of equivalence – A non-A – but on a logic of difference – A:B. Postcolonial psychology will celebrate all diverse ways of life rather than compare others to what they are not.

The current literature illustrates how contemporary service delivery is still failing not only Native Americans but also other ethnic groups who do not subscribe to only a Western method of thinking. Sue and Zane have found that, "regardless of utilization rates, all of the ethnic-minority groups had significantly higher dropout rates than whites" (1987, 37). One of the most important factors in the failure of the mental health delivery system is an inability of therapists to provide relevant forms of treatment to ethnic populations.

Most of the attempts to provide services to Native American people have ended in failure. For the most part, the blame for this failure has been placed on the patient instead of on a delivery system that is still brazen with overtones of the 1800s (assimilation or termination of Native American people). Most providers are trained only in delivering services to the majority/dominant population. Usually, therapists are completely unaware of the life experiences not defined by Western subjectivity. In earlier works – *Archetypal Consultation* (Duran 1984) and *Transforming the Soul Wound* (Duran 1990) – a theoretical construct was initiated (though never fully developed). This construct was the result of the integration of Jungian psychology and community consultation concepts. The resulting mental health model was implemented in a Native American community in central and northern California and, when measured by some standard evaluation methods, was assessed as having some success.

Since the initial success of this program, there have been further developments in the way that psychology has been delivered to the aforementioned group of people. The program has expanded into a prevention and treatment model that has yielded a successful history of Native American people seeking relevant treatment for some of the problems they encounter as part of living in a colonialist setting. The purpose here is not to suggest that these paradigms are the final answer to the mental health problems in Native American communities. Instead, we would like to point out some possible weaknesses that may be inherent in the models that were developed and offer some new solutions that have emerged after decades of clinical practice and research with Native American people.

In the past few years, literature has emerged dealing with the issue of cross-cultural approaches. As yet, few models have shown a significant level of success, and they have been implemented on a small scale and need to be replicated. Most of the literature having to do with Native Americans continues to focus on the lack of relevant approaches to psychological treatment as well as to paint a very grim picture of the extent of the problems afflicting the Native American community. Most approaches implemented with Native peoples are ongoing attempts at further hegemony of their Aboriginal lifeworld. Alcoholism, chemical dependency, and high rates of suicide continue to plague these communities. Programs responsible for addressing these problems appear impotent in the face of such a Herculean task, although there are some isolated instances of success in treatment.

There continues to be discussion about integrating Western and traditional approaches in order to offer a solution to the problem; for the most part, however, the effort has remained in the realm of academic discussion. The problem is not so much with traditional practitioners in the Native American community as with the Western practitioners. Western practitioners approach traditional healing methods with scepticism while expecting traditional healers to have absolute faith in orthodox Western-oriented therapeutic strategies. A bridge between these two camps must be built. The bridging task is more difficult than it might appear, since most Western practitioners are deeply entrenched in a worldview that will not allow for openness outside rational empirical thought processes. In spite of the problems of bridging the two worlds, many non-Native American people are embracing and appropriating traditional concepts and actually portraying themselves as traditional medicine people or shamans. When Westerners portray themselves in this manner, they only increase the existing gap, since the Native American community perceives these impostors as exploitative and disrespectful.

Toward Understanding the Native American Worldview

Attempting to describe enough of the Native American worldview (also called "cosmology") so that the rest of this discussion makes sense is a difficult task. The description that we offer in this section is useful for operationally defining some of the terms and ideas in this chapter, but it is not an actual definition of what the experience of the Native American worldview is. In order to present a discussion of the experience of being in the world as a Native American, we would have to devote an entire thesis to the topic – since there is so much cultural diversity among different tribes – which would exceed the scope of this discussion.

One of the first ideas to keep in mind when thinking about the Native American worldview from a Western perspective is that the Native temporal approach to the world is different from that of Western people. Western thought conceptualizes history in a linear temporal sequence, whereas most Native American thinking conceptualizes history in a spatial fashion. Temporal thinking means that time is thought of as having a beginning and an end. Spatial thinking views events as a function of space or where the event actually took place. Understanding the space-time difference in conceptualizing history is necessary in order for the therapist to realize that the two ways of thinking are different yet part of the same continuum. Although the therapist/social scientist may be interested in when something happened, the client/community may be more interested in where the event took place. The idea of being in space versus time does not have to be a rigid one, and the client may or may not want to relate events in a more space-time integrated approach, although time may not have the same linear quality that it does for the Western person.[1]

The Native American worldview is a systemic approach to being in the world that can best be categorized as process thinking, as opposed to the content thinking found in the Western worldview. Process thinking is best described as a more action and "eventing" approach to life versus a world of subject/object relationships. Some Indigenous languages, for instance, are languages in which phenomena are experienced as the process of events. Western Indo-European languages describe the world predominantly by means of nouns or as relationships between objects, not as events.

Another crucial worldview difference of which the Western therapist must be cognizant is that of noncompartmentalization of experience. In Western experience, it is common to separate the mind from the body and spirit and the spirit from the mind and body. Within the Native American worldview, compartmentalization ideology is an imposition that attempts to displace a more interconnected experience. Most Native American people experience their being in the world as a totality of personality and not as separate systems within the person. This becomes more complex for the Western therapist/social scientist when the idea of the personality being part of all creation is discussed. Thus, the Native American worldview is one in which the individual is a part of all creation, living life as one system and not in separate units that are objectively relating with each other. The idea of the world or creation existing for the purpose of human domination and exploitation – the core of most Western ideology – is absent in Native American thinking.

Any psychology of Native American people must have a direct impact on the way that any type of relationship is experienced. The experience of therapy or healing is no exception to the experience of being in the world. The need for healing can be explained by the fact that the client/community has lost the ability to be in harmony with the life process of which it is a part.

Life experiences are process, which makes "being" a different experience than that in which the world can be explained by discussion of content. Whereas the Western approach to the world is one in which everything is categorized and named, the Native American way of being in the world involves a relationship and moving in harmony with the seasons, the wind, and all of creation.

The practice of Western psychotherapy entails a linear passage of time in which the client/community can resolve or be cured from its present problems. In Native American thinking, the idea of time having to pass in order to receive healing or blessing makes no sense. In Native American healing, the factor that is of importance is intensity, not passage of time. For instance, if a person dances with great intensity, that person achieves as much as a person who dances for a long time (if time is the only variable). When the Western therapist treats a Native American person, time passing may not be as crucial as the intensity of the therapeutic process.[2]

The process of psychotherapy is an arena in which the integration of worldviews is very important because psychotherapy attempts to restore balance in human beings. The restoration of balance demands that a relationship between psyche and matter (world, creation) be one of harmony; this is one of the paradigms that Jung discussed in his attempt to bridge the gap of psyche and matter that existed in his world. For Carl Jung (1960), the bridge was crossed through the use of symbols, as he believed that symbols provided the transcendent function that balances psyche and matter.

When working with traditional peoples, the therapeutic method must take into account the way in which traditional healers think. The notion of a personal layer of psyche surrounded by a tribal or ethnic strata lends itself to useful explanations in the arena of psychological work. Jung theorized that a symbol functions as the entity that transforms energy in the psyche. Culture plays an important role in the transformation of energy by providing a symbolic system that steers and guides the transformation of psychic energy for that particular culture. The development of the psyche cannot be accomplished by intention alone, and according to Jung "it needs the attraction of the symbol, whose value quantum exceeds that of the cause ... If man lived altogether instinctively and automatically, the transformation could come about in accordance with purely biological laws" (1960, 25). Since people do not live instinctively, we cannot simply resort to biological laws and explanations and must continue to work with laws that apply to the psyche in a purely psychological fashion.

Specific Problems with Western Psychological Worldviews

Western psychology (most psychology studied and taught is Western) has undergone a natural evolutionary process that has roots so deeply entrenched in classic Western philosophy that many scholars agree it is simply a footnote to Plato. In psychology, it matters little if the model or theory is Freudian, Jungian, or any of the other classical or contemporary theories. The critical factor in postcolonial psychological theory and practice is a fundamentally different way of being in the world. In no way does Western thinking address any system of cognition except its own. Given that Judeo-Christian belief systems include notions of the Creator putting humans in charge of all creations, it is easy to understand why this group of people assumes that it also possesses the ultimate way of describing psychological phenomena for all of humanity. In reality, the thought that what is right comes from one worldview produces a narcissistic worldview that desecrates and destroys much of what is known as culture and cosmological perspective.

The problem of irrelevant research and clinical practice would not be so destructive to Native American people if institutional racism did not pervade most of the academic settings for research and theoretical construction. These institutions not only discredit thinking that is not Western but also engage in practices that imply that people who do not subscribe to their worldview are genetically inferior. Stephen Jay Gould refers to the practice of valuing cultural experiences that are Western and white over any other cultural experience as biological determinism (1981, 325).

A good example of how some of the ideology of biological determinism affects people is seen in the field of psychometric assessment. The relevant literature is filled with studies showing cultural bias and outright racist practices, yet researchers continue to use the same racist tools to evaluate the psyche of Native American people. The very essence of Western science as applied to psychology is permeated with biological determinism that has as its sole purpose the demonstration of white superiority. Many examples can be cited of Native American people losing their freedom, being sterilized, or losing their children simply because they were not able to pass the white standards of a psychometric test.

Even though there are many obstacles to the development of relevant and practical psychotherapeutic interventions for Native American people, the fact that there are difficulties does not mean that we should simply despair and give up hope. We must keep an open mind by following the advice of Sitting Bull: "Take what is good from the White Man and let's make a better life for our children." There are valuable ideas in the Western world; we believe that by integrating worldviews and psychological understanding we can develop a model that will benefit Native American people as well as others. By reinterpreting some of the theoretical constructs developed by Jung, and by taking this reinterpreted psychology and integrating it with traditional psychology and other Native epistemologies, we can arrive at ideas with some theoretical and clinical relevance.

Problems in Implementing Traditional Approaches

Traditional approaches or practices are based on the concepts of illness and healing held by the group and may provide some insights into orthodox strategies as they are implemented among the Native American community. Traditional approaches are still used, but they are not very common in certain groups because of a loss of skills due to the colonization of the Aboriginal lifeworld. These traditional interventions receive criticism from the orthodox camp, and orthodox Western (usually medical) approaches do not accept or are not aware of Indigenous practices.

A very general and useful analysis of traditional concepts of illness and healing was formulated by F.E. Clements in 1932. Those guidelines are still useful in understanding traditional concepts as seen from a Western platform. The most widely held belief about illness is the personal belief that a diseased object has intruded the body, thus causing sickness. The obvious therapy for this type of illness is to have the object removed by physical means such as cutting or bleeding and sucking out the diseased objects or body parts. The Westerner does not have to stretch his or her imagination any further than the surgical table upon which all of this removal and sucking of bad blood and diseased organs is performed daily in all hospitals across the United States. There is so much belief in object extraction in our society that surgery is used almost as a placebo, creating the belief that the physician is actually performing the needed cure. According to Clements, the second most popular belief about illness involves loss of the soul. The illness in this case may derive from two means. One cause of the illness is the departure of the soul from the body. The second possible cause of this illness is the theft or abduction of the soul by ghosts or sorcerers. The treatment for this illness comes through the restoration of the soul by the healer. Of the traditional concepts, loss of the soul may be the most difficult for the Western worldview to accept. However, there is common ground between the two different paradigms. Many therapists talk about loss of ego, alienation, and patients being beside themselves; the task, then, is to place the person back in touch with reality.

Another belief about illness involves spirit intrusion and/or possession, which occur when the person is made ill by an evil spirit invading the body and causing the illness. In this case, the therapy may be done by three different means: the spirit may be expelled mechanically by bleeding, by beating, or by presenting noises and smells; the spirit may be transferred to another being; or it may be exorcized.

A concept of illness that may have more cross-cultural applications is the notion of illness being caused by a transgression against social or religious mores. According to some anthropological accounts, serious sickness and even death may be possible due to the breach of taboo. The most common treatment for this condition is confession or catharsis to a healer or priest.

This notion is closely related to the practice of psychotherapy, in which many sessions are used by the patient to clear himself or herself of the guilt of actual or perceived violations of some societal taboo or norm.

Sorcery is a method whereby sickness is caused by an individual who has power and can will an illness on another individual. The most common treatment for this form of illness is an appeal to a person who has the power to counter the spell, thus alleviating the sickness. There are some parallels in psychotherapy in which a therapist either consciously or unconsciously inflicts pathology on the patient. In this case, the usual cure is to go to another therapist who can counter the illness, thus countering the evil therapist's actions.

Because of the tremendous influx of Native American people into urban areas, providing traditional therapy is further complicated. By leaving traditional lands and moving to where there are more economic opportunities, it becomes difficult for Native Americans to maintain traditional ways. Yet the bleak realities of staying in a place where there is little hope of finding work puts the modern Native American in a double bind. In the San Francisco Bay Area, there are currently 100,000 Native American people from at least 300 different tribal groups. Attempting to serve all of these people in a relevant manner is extremely difficult, so one must begin to find commonalities not only within different traditional groups but also within the orthodox Western camp.

The lack of traditional Aboriginal practitioners and researchers in the urban setting presents a major difficulty in the attempt to serve the Native American community. In order for a client to be treated by a traditional healer, she or he must undergo substantial expense due to the distances that must be travelled in order to be treated. As the reader may suspect, the practitioner dealing with severe problems in this setting must be creative and flexible if he or she is to be of any use to the individual or community. Researchers as well must use creative methodologies that do not reinforce scientific and epistemic colonialism.

The empirical methodological paradigm of most research contributes to the lack of its acceptability within Native American nations and communities. Even when academics pretend to study cultures different from their own, most dare not ask the most logical of all questions: What is the point of reference for the interpretation of data? D. Sinha eloquently captures this problem: "There are several reasons for this retardation. First, modern psychology has been a product of the West and has been imported almost wholesale to Third World countries. Too often, problems taken up for research have been mere replications of whatever had been done in Europe or the United States with little relations to the needs of the country. Such unimaginative replications of Western research have been decried and called caricatures of Western studies" (1984, 20). To assume that phenomena from another worldview can be adequately explained from a totally foreign worldview is the essence of psychological and philosophical imperialism. This lack of theoretical and clinical relevance is clearly demonstrated all over the Third and Fourth Worlds and is currently the topic of theoretical debate within the academy.

Postcolonial practitioners and intellectuals have convincingly discredited the Eurocentric historiographic narrative of people of colour (Murray 1991; Said 1978) and have delineated how this production of meaning not only fails to capture any "truth" of Native and tribal lives but also infiltrates Native lifeworlds in the form of "epistemic violence" (Spivak 1988, 126). Social scientists have been rewriting tribal canonical texts (i.e., ritual) via anthropology and other disciplines since first contact and therein have produced meaning that has changed and distorted tribal understandings or forced them underground. Clinical psychology as well as research-oriented psychology is extremely narrow-minded. The assumptions of these fields are based on a utilitarian worldview. According to Sinha, "its orientation is basically micro-social, concentrating itself almost entirely on personal characteristics of the individual actors in social processes rather than on sociostructural factors" (1984, 21). Western empirical research is based on the illusion of objectivity, with a transhistorical, transcultural orientation. It operates within an a priori essentialist Cartesian model of a unified, rational, autonomous subject, the construction of which is problematized in the work of French poststructuralism and German critical theory. Guha and Spivak, Derridean deconstructionists, posit a decentred self: "that which operates as a subject may be part of an immense discontinuous network of strands that may be termed politics, ideology, economics, history, sexuality, language and so on" (1988, 12).

Social scientific investigation into mental health deproblematizes the material history of science as well. Michel Foucault (1973) brilliantly dissected what he called "technologies of power" authorized by the science of medicine. He illustrated that, far from objective statements of truth, the science of medicine emerged fully implicated in practices of domination. The objectification of Native American psychological problems deprives them of their material history and hence of a crucial aspect of their truth. Context plays no part when the goal is transcendental truths about human nature. Sinha believes, however, that within this orientation "one is disappointed by [these truths'] artificiality, triviality, and lack of relevance to real-life psychological phenomena. The methodology of psychological research has to be broadened to make it more relevant for the study of complex social problems facing Third World countries in the process of development" (1984, 21). Some postmodern theorists have gone so far as to say "once we give up metaphysical attempts to find a 'true self' for man [sic], we can only appear as the contingent historical selves we find ourselves to be" (Rorty 1992, 62). The history of Native-white relations since colonization not only presents the context for the treatment of family violence but must also illuminate the knowledge/power construction of the Native subject that has infiltrated Native subjectivity and identity.

Successful clinical interventions are not possible in a Native American setting unless the provider or agency is cognizant of the sociohistorical factors that have had a devastating effect on the dynamics of the Native American family. One of the most traumatic sociohistorical factors was the boarding school policy. Beginning in the late 1800s, the American and Canadian governments implemented policies whose effect was the systematic destruction of the Native American family system. These policies were implemented under the guise of educating Native Americans in order to assimilate them into Western society, while at the same time inflicting a wound to the souls of Native American people that is felt in agonizing proportions to this day. This pain is obvious when the family system is examined in a clinical context that employs sociohistorical honesty as a fundamental premise of prevention/intervention.

Scepticism concerning the applicability of a purely psychological model to represent problems of family violence for Native American peoples does not mean denying the need for or the contribution of psychology in the prevention or treatment of behavioural problems. Rather, our purpose is to look deeper into the multidimensional nature of mental health for fresh perspectives and empowering interventions instead of privileging a universal scientific discourse over the voice of the subjects. A richer perspective is vital in the work of mental health professionals involved in reeducation and resocialization into appropriate family behaviours, the definitions of which are politically discursive.

The therapist must understand that until recently Native American people had a culture that abounded with the resources needed for a harmonious existence. The Native American person was a human being trying to understand and live in peace within his or her cosmological reality. Special care must be taken at this point not to confuse this idea with the image of the noble savage. The noble savage projection is when a Native American is seen as a mystical being who can do magic and other spiritual tasks but is not too adept at thinking things through in day-to-day existence. This fantasy material is portrayed in the media and carried into the therapeutic session by many Western therapists. Native Americans had a well-structured society in which everyone's role and place was well defined. Our family systems and self-governance supported these roles and functions, and everyone felt valued as a member of the collective.

Holistic worldviews such as the one expressed above allowed Native American people to experience the world as a totality of which they were an integral part. This experience does not necessarily imply that Native

Americans were completely immersed in "participation mystique" (the notion that there is little or no ego differentiation and that the individual cannot determine a sense of self and merely sees himself or herself as a part of the world), as some anthropologists have speculated. This holistic worldview allowed Native Americans to have a unified awareness or perception of the physical, psychological, and spiritual phenomena that make up the totality of human existence or consciousness. In the experience of such a unified awareness, there was also a close integration with cosmological realities as they were experienced or perceived.

Native American people were able to have a centred awareness that was fluid and nonstatic. This centred awareness allowed for a harmonious attitude toward the world, as exemplified by a tribal collective way of life versus an individualistic approach. The harmony idea is best illustrated by the acceptance and being part of the mystery of existence versus the ongoing struggle to understand the world through a logical positivistic approach, as exemplified by Western science.

The core of Native American awareness was the place where the soul wound occurred. The concept of soul wound can best be understood as the trauma suffered by the psyche over half a millennium of systematic attempts at genocide directed toward Indigenous peoples. This core essence is the fabric of the soul, and it is from this essence that mythology, dreams, and culture emerge. Once the core from which the soul emerges is wounded, much of the emerging mythology and dreams of a people reflect the wound. The manifestations of such a wound are then embodied by the tremendous suffering that the people have undergone since the collective soul wound was inflicted half a millennium ago and continues in different guises even to this day. Some of the diseases and problems that Native American people suffer are a direct result of the soul wound. These self-destructive behaviours may be a desperate attempt to bring back a harmonious soul.

Conclusions

Attempts have been made to discuss healing from perspectives that bridge the colonized personal experience by using analytical systems of both the colonized and the colonizer. The task seems to be doomed from the beginning, since by looking through the lens of the colonizer and his systems of critique we only continue the hegemonic process experienced by the colonized. As well, this situation is not helped by the use of the English language in presenting the discussion. We believe that there can be an integrated system of analysis that lends itself to a discourse that need not be hegemonic to either tradition and may actually be liberating for both.

Some of the notions discussed in this chapter may be seen as strange and outside the paradigm of Western psychology. For us to have maintained a

Western outlook would have merely contributed to the epistemic violence from which Native American communities have been suffering for many generations. Western thinkers must acknowledge that there are legitimate forms of generating knowledge in the Native community and that this knowledge is valid in its own right, standing alongside that of other cosmologies. Western psychology is in desperate need of explanations for many of the illnesses that plague society in general; critically, the Western system of disease conceptualization and treatment is inadequate for many of these problems.

If the Western categorization of illness is falling short of the mark in the white community, then these categories must obviously fall much shorter when applied to the Native client. In the future, it will be beneficial to Native American people if the diagnostic manual takes into account some of the issues presented in this chapter. Many Native American people are diagnosed based on erroneous criteria; the diagnostic process never takes a historical perspective in placing a diagnosis on the client. We fantasize that one day the DSM (Diagnostic Statistical Manual for Mental Disorders) will have diagnostic criteria such as "acute or chronic reaction to genocide and colonialism." Until that day comes, there will be little honesty from the Western healing traditions in their relationships with Native Americans. Under the guise of Western healing, which is in fact an ongoing attempt to control the lifeworld of Native people, the epistemic violence will continue. Unless Western systems are reformulated in a manner in which traditional sciences and treatment strategies can flourish in an A:B framework, there will continue to be a lack of efficacy from these Western systems of healing.

The legitimization of Native American thought in the Western world has not yet occurred, and it may not occur for some time. This does not mean that the situation is hopeless in the Native American community. This community can help itself by legitimizing its own knowledge and thus allowing for healing to emerge from within the community. If the perpetrators prefer to live in denial, then that is an issue with which they will have to deal currently and historically. Clinically, once the pathology is cured in one area of the system, another area of the system will begin to show symptoms. At present, there are many programs and approaches dealing with healing in the Native American community. It is interesting to see who is beginning to lurk around the periphery and who wants some of the healing insight from Native American communities. The perpetrators, tired of living with a mythology that is no longer applicable, appear thirsty for these Indigenous forms of healing and are willing to pay money for them. Although resources are valuable, there is an additional offering that must be made in order to complete the healing circle between the colonizer and the colonized – historical honesty and amends must be made.

Notes

1 For a deeper discussion of worldview, see Vine Deloria's book *God Is Red* (1992).
2 We want to impress upon the reader that this discussion is a generalization, since there are tribes who do not think in this manner. The intertribal glossing in which we are engaged is necessary in order to stay within the scope of the project at hand. In no way do we pretend to understand and speak for all Indians – this would be an act of colonization. In postcolonial paradigms, we believe that by discussing this limitation some honesty is incorporated. This honesty is a small step toward respect.

References

Clements, F.E. 1932. "Primitive Concepts in Disease." *University of California Publications in Archaeology and Ethnography* 32: 185-252.

Deloria, V. 1992. *God Is Red: A Native View of Religion.* Golden, CO: North America Press.

Duran, E. 1984. *Archetypal Consultation.* Berne: Peter Lang.

–. 1990. *Transforming the Soul Wound.* Berkeley: Folklore Press.

Foucault, M. 1967. *Madness and Civilization.* London: Tavistock.

–. 1973. *Birth of the Clinic.* London: Oxford University Press.

Gould, S.J. 1981. *The Mismeasure of Man.* New York: W.W. Norton.

Guha, R., and G.C. Spivak. 1988. *Selected Subaltern Studies.* New York: Oxford University Press.

Jung, C.G. 1960. *The Structures and Dynamics of the Psyche.* Princeton: Bollingen.

Murray, D. 1991. *Forked Tongues: Speech, Writing, and Representation in Native North American Texts.* Bloomington: Native American University Press.

Rorty, R. 1992. "Cosmopolitanism without Emancipation: A Response to Lyotard." In S. Lash and J. Friedman, eds., *Modernity and Identity,* 58-72. Cambridge: Blackwell.

Said, E. 1978. *Orientalism.* New York: Pantheon.

Sinha, D. 1984. "Psychology in the Context of Third World Development." *International Journal of Psychology* 17-29.

Spivak, G.C. 1988. "Can the Subaltern Speak?" In C. Grossberg and N.L. Grossberg, eds., *Marxism and the Interpretation of Culture,* 271-313. Urbana: University of Illinois Press.

Sue, S., and N. Zane. 1987. "The Role of Culture and Cultural Teachings in Psychotherapy: A Critique and Reformation." *American Psychologist* 42: 37-45.

7
Transforming the Realities of Colonialism: Voyage of Self-Discovery
Ian Hingley

> In order to have a true integration of thought we must make room for nonlinear thinking, which will yield a true hybrid postcolonial way of expressing subjectivity. As we move into the next millennium, we should not be tolerant of the neocolonialism that runs unchecked through our knowledge-generating systems.
>
> – Eduardo Duran and Bonnie Duran
> *Native American Postcolonial Psychology*

The term "postcolonialism" implies that colonialism is a phenomenon that has been relegated to the history books. To truly achieve postcolonial status for nations and a global community, as individuals we must embark on personal voyages of introspection. We must face the disturbing fact that factions of society have systematically internalized the colonial mind-set and have overtly or covertly benefited from the oppression and subjugation of other groups of people. With this knowledge comes the personal responsibility to make a conscious choice for change.

In their book *Native American Postcolonial Psychology*, Eduardo Duran and Bonnie Duran state that "we face the task of overcoming the colonial mindset that so many of us have internalized" (1995, 6). Our introspection should not be viewed as static and unchangeable. We can and must view our neocolonial oppressor mentalities as holding transformative powers whereby we can consciously change ourselves and the world in which we live. This change must start within each and every one of us. We must, as Paulo Freire (1970) suggests, reflect within ourselves and then take action on our individual realities. This ideological change involves a radical transformation. The ways in which we perceive the world, relate to the world and to one another, will be altered forever.

Many influential writers have helped to chart my course of personal introspection directed toward identifying the systematically ingrained world of the oppressor. They include mid-century writers such as Freire (1970), Fanon (1968), and Memmi (1991), as well as contemporary writers such as Duran and Duran (1995), Cajete (1994), and Battiste (1986). In exploring the worlds of the oppressor and the oppressed, I found the words of French Canadian Lise Noël (1994) in her book *Intolerance: A General Survey* inspirational. These individuals provide the theoretical foundation that guides my voyage of discovery, and this essay seeks to reflect their wisdom. My voyage has just begun, but it is my hope that some day the tireless efforts of individuals fighting oppressive systems will result in a postcolonial world.

The Voyage of Discovery

Liberal humanists believe that they understand the needs and desires of the oppressed. The liberal-minded individual seeks to fully recognize inequities while trying to make a fundamental difference in society. The humanist exemplifies love and compassion for all human life. While I consider myself a humanist, I have come to realize that I may not fully understand what it means to be oppressed. Until recently, I would have stated that I was an active participant in the quest for a better global society and a champion of equality for all. I have come to realize that I was seeing the world through rose-coloured glasses.

The voyage of discovery can be described as a journey in which each individual plots his or her own course while not knowing the true destination. In this chapter, I will explore my life experiences as a Euro-Canadian male and seek to understand my role within the realm of the oppressor and the oppressed. I will further this exploration by correlating my experiences in childhood, early adulthood, playing hockey, coaching in the Special Olympics, and teaching school, with the philosophies discussed in Noël's *Intolerance*. Finally, I will explore the benefits that I have received from covert, systematic levels of oppression.

As a middle-class Euro-Canadian child in southern Saskatchewan, I received the benefits that family, friends, and hobbies had to offer. While I was receiving these benefits, however, my parents constantly reminded me that they were not to be taken for granted. My mother is a teacher, and my father is a United Church minister. Both are actively involved in social justice issues. My parents instilled in me an awareness of social issues such as racism, poverty, and sexism, all of which are the results of oppression. I became a pow wow dancer at the White Bear Indian Reserve and made many acquaintances and friends there; however, I always had the luxury of returning to my house and friends in Carlyle.

A favourite pastime for us town children was to visit the drugstore uptown and buy candies and read the latest comic books. On the way, we would take a path between two buildings to save time. On occasion, an intoxicated person would be lying on the ground in a state of unconsciousness. My friends would comment, "There's another drunken Indian." As I reflect on my early childhood, I find it sad how children so young can inherit and develop racist attitudes. It would not be fair to say that all the town children shared these racist beliefs, but unfortunately those who did were in the majority.

In school, I would find myself alienated from the town children if I played with my friends from White Bear at recess. The Aboriginal children could not choose to play with the town children. That choice was not theirs to make. The Aboriginal children were deemed a subculture, and the other students entrapped them into a state of alienation. This resulted in negative judgments of their value and self-worth, as Noël argues. I vividly remember hearing the Aboriginal children saying how they longed to join in the frequent football or soccer games. They were not invited to play because they were viewed as inferior. The roles of dominator and dominated were formed at a young age.

The stigma attached to the oppressed by the oppressor is an example of the so-called primitive mind theory illustrated in L. Lévy-Bruhls's book *How Natives Think* (1966), which implies that Aboriginal people are driven primarily by their emotions and are incapable of higher theoretical and abstract ideas. The parents in Carlyle viewed the Aboriginal people from the White Bear Reserve as inferior. They planted seeds of hatred and prejudice in their children and nurtured their growth. The system of oppression was ingrained within the hierarchical levels of the small town. This thinking is reflected in Noël's comments: "Thus, it is through another's eyes that the dominated receive their identity and, therefore, their relative worth and place in society. The dominator looks right through the oppressed without seeing them, to mark their social insignificance and relegate them to anonymity, or else focuses on them, to emphasize their visibility and stigmatize them" (1994, 110).

These examples from my early childhood demonstrate how the oppressor's mentality can be introduced even at a young age. Although I may not have been an active participant in this process of alienation, I unwittingly benefited from it. While I chose to associate with the Aboriginal children, I also associated with the town children. Many were unable to make these choices. I benefited from the oppressor's Eurocentric model because I was given options based on my race, gender, and class.

My family moved to Nova Scotia in 1976. We returned to Saskatchewan in 1979 to the town of Davidson, where I spent my adolescent years. In my adolescent and early adulthood years, I witnessed a continuing trend into this dichotomous relationship between the oppressor and the oppressed. Davidson was not an easy place for a preacher's kid with an acquired Nova Scotia accent to live. We had moved from Nova Scotia in time for me to enter grade six. It took me a long time to adjust to my new peer group. I had to change my identity to fit stereotypes defined for me. The world of sports was my opportunity to gain the recognition that I desired. I was actively involved in many sports, but none played a more important role in my life in this respect than hockey. Although playing hockey made me popular among the "in crowd" at the time, I now find myself asking if the broken bones, facial lacerations, concussions, and pain were all worth it.

The intense competition in sport can be compared to the oppressor's desire to dominate others. As Noël states, "When exercised against the human body, the power of the oppressor is revealed as direct and immediate. It expresses the oppressor's supremacy in all its force, while reminding the dominated of their own powerlessness" (1994, 107).

Young hockey players are taught to pick out the weaknesses of the opposition, with the objective of creating a system of alienation and control. We were trained to think of the opposing players as something other than human. They needed to be dominated and forced into submission. This attitude was reflected in the relationships between team members. If a player made a play to win the game or was victorious in a fight, fellow teammates, management, and the fans held him in high esteem. This promoted violence, oppression, and negative attitudes in the young hockey players.

When I moved to northern Saskatchewan, I played hockey for teams in La Ronge and Ile-à-la-Crosse. Here I came to discover the impact of the oppressor in the sport. In provincial and league games, we would hear the voices of racism rise from the stands and the opposing players as they cursed the Aboriginal teams. Many comments directed at me reflected the oppressor's superiority complex, as players and fans yelled such things as "welfare boy" and "half-breed." These are the comments that I feel comfortable repeating; others were too degrading to mention. On one occasion, they egged our bus; on another, we were spat upon. The harassment and intimidation were relentless.

The first question that we were asked when we proposed to enter the southern league was "How many Indians are on your hockey team, and can they play hockey?" This left an awful feeling in our hearts. Our team, the La Ronge Islanders, was allowed into the league on probationary status. Our team had to travel south every second weekend, while the southern teams only had to make one trip north a year. Noël discusses this issue of the dominator developing rules and laws: "Not only is the dominator capable of legislating in various ways depending on whether or not a group is different from him, he is also allowed to establish contrary laws for comparable categories of the dominated" (1994, 54).

Knowing that it would be a long struggle, we welcomed the southern teams to our community, fed them fresh fish, and held banquets in their honour. After our inaugural season, the teams could not wait to return to the hospitality of La Ronge and northern Saskatchewan. The question of whether we could play hockey against the southern teams had been answered clearly. Despite controversial refereeing, we made it to the league finals. One linesman for the final game apologized for the officiating, stating that there was no reason for our team to receive twenty-four penalties while the other team received only five. While we felt cheated and wronged, we took the experience as a learning one, rebounding to become league champions the following year.

While I experienced alienation from the southern teams as a result of my association with Aboriginal people, I also experienced alienation from a segment of the Aboriginal population. Some Aboriginal people called me "moonias," which I inferred was a derogatory name referring to my Euro-Canadian status. Many people questioned my involvement in Aboriginal hockey tournaments. My response was that we are all equal, and we all deserve to play. Although I was subjected to some name-calling, I was blessed overall by the experience of knowing Aboriginal people. The friendships and warm hospitality that I experienced in communities such as La Ronge, Ile-à-la-Crosse, Beauval, Buffalo Narrows, Southend, LaLoche, Prince Albert, and Stanley Mission will last me a lifetime. These people opened their homes to me in a prime example of northern hospitality. I look back and wonder how I would have been received if I had been an Aboriginal person attending a white hockey tournament. Once again, I found myself with the option to choose.

The summer of 1996 changed the way in which I viewed the sporting world forever. The Zone Five sports council in Humboldt asked me to coach two athletes, Wayne and Nathan, for the Special Olympics at the Saskatchewan Summer Games in Moose Jaw. The experience brought home to me my ingrained dominator philosophies.

Wayne made it to the final of the men's 100-metre running event. While he was warming up for the race, he began talking to the other racers. I quickly told him to concentrate on the task at hand. Shortly after the race began, I realized how inappropriate my attitude had been. Wayne was in the lead with about forty metres left when the second-place runner stumbled and fell. Wayne stopped running, helped the individual up, and went on to finish in third-to-last place. This went against the dominator's attitude of winning at all costs. Wayne taught me that being a winner does not necessarily mean finishing in first place.

Nathan helped to nurture within me the concept that winning is an intrinsic sense of self-gratification. This was Nathan's first time away from home. He was a victim of low self-esteem because of negative stereotypes in his hometown community that people with Down syndrome are stupid and worthless. Nathan constantly repeated the words "I am stupid." In a section titled "A Stigmatized Identity," Noël attributes this to the dominator's attitude: "As soon as they are seen, they are seen not only as 'other' but also as beings of lesser value. The greater the difference, the more it will be discredited in the dominator's view: having become a stigma, a mark of shame, this difference will be perceived as revealing an identity that is stained and compromised. Thus, for some people, the simple act of leaving one's home is a constantly repeated test, a genuine ordeal ... Simply mingling with a crowd to run their errands will subject them to stares, and even to the cruellest remarks" (1994, 111). During the opening ceremonies, Nathan risked the negative comments and started dancing in front of the stage to the band's music. Several coaches expressed embarrassment and shock that several of us were standing by while Nathan was "running wild." This mirrors Noël's statement: "Yet mental illness itself, in general, was defined as 'abnormal behavior,' meaning that it was behaviour different from that of the majority" (1994, 29). For my part, I felt that, if Nathan was having fun, then I was too. Nathan, being away from home, needed this sense of belonging. Soon many of the 5,000 people present joined in. The headlines of the local Moose Jaw paper reported "Hubick Livens Crowd." The article continued:

> Nathan Hubick rose to his feet in front of a large – and seated – stream of humanity. He took a quick glance around. Then he boogied. Hubick was the 1996 Saskatchewan Summer Games ice-breaker; a dancing, pom-pom waving Special Olympian who single handedly turned Sunday's opening ceremonies into a party ... Before Hubick donned his dancing shoes, the eight zones sat quietly on the field grass ... then Streetnix, a Saskatoon-based a capella band, took the stage. Hubick was soon on his feet, dancing up a storm, by himself. A minute past [sic] then another, as thousands looked on, he continued to dance and wave his pom-pom. Finally, a group of girls from Zone Seven got up, ran to his stacked-out area in front of the stage, and joined the action. Then more athletes picked up the beat. And more. Soon, the grass was packed with jiggling, jumping jocks. (Mitchell 1996)

Nathan had not only excited the masses with his exhilaration but also displayed the principle of emancipation, which Noël defines as "marked by the aspiration for autonomy." She writes that the process of emancipation "is one of discovering the difference, a discovery that is reached through the process of proclaiming pride" (1994, 203).

The process of emancipation, however, would not be an easy one for Nathan. In the high jump event, he was one of only two individuals entered, so he was guaranteed a silver medal. We expected that this would be a major confidence booster for him. However, Nathan is very short, and he did not attempt a jump because the bar was placed too high for him. The judge declared that Nathan would not receive a medal because he had not made a qualifying jump. This seemed rather harsh. I asked the judge to explain her reasoning. She replied: "If they want to be treated like the other athletes, then they have to make a qualifying jump." True enough, they needed a qualifying jump, but what did she mean "like the other athletes"? They *were* the athletes, not some sideshow. Finding this decision most inappropriate, I made a formal complaint to the track officials and the Special Olympic committee at the event. Nathan was able to make a jump and received his silver medal. The award ceremony was a very special occasion. It was a small victory over our society's oppressive ranking of individuals according to ability.

The Canadian Broadcasting Corporation interviewed the Zone Five Special Olympians, asking about our experiences at the games. After the interviews, a camera crew filmed the final race, in which, statistically, we finished last. I had a problem with how the CBC broadcast was presented. Our interviews were not in the news clip, and I was very disappointed to hear the interviewer state that, "Even though the Zone Five athletes came in last place in the relay, they still enjoyed their experiences and newfound friendships." I had specifically told the reporter that the week was a great experience for all involved and that all the athletes were winners. The news agency seemed determined to illustrate the values of the dominators: the need to win while creating a loser.

After the newscast aired, I was approached by a number of people who had viewed it. Most told me, "It was a special thing you did for those people." I felt proud of being recognized for my humanistic deed. While I truly believe that these people were sincere, as I was, we must learn to recognize the stigmas and stereotypes we create in the most innocent circumstances; otherwise, we unknowingly sustain the dominator's world. The Special Olympians were not charity cases whom I volunteered to assist. Rather, they were people who could learn from me and I from them.

While I may have helped these athletes in Moose Jaw, it was they who helped me to realize the true nature of sport. They made me see the world of the dominator that I had blindly adopted. Nathan, Wayne, and all the other athletes proved that all could work together in the spirit of cooperation and sportsmanship. It did not take long for me to develop a personal relationship with most of the athletes. I found myself, as a coach, congratulating all the athletes involved in every event, because they were all winners. It was a pivotal point for me: these outstanding individuals coached me in life.

As a teacher of the social sciences, I believe in creating opportunities for critical thinking and involving students at all levels, and I have sought to teach in the spirit of interactive lectures. One thing I have learned is that history is written by men, for men, and about men. In history we are taught about the men who have changed the structure of the world. So often the important contributions of women are ignored. G. Stanley Hall states, "The male ... tends by nature to expertness and specialization" (as cited in Noël 1994, 46). Noël quotes Schopenhauer to discredit Hall's comment: "Women ... always remain subjective; while granting that they sometimes had talent, he did not allow that they had genius" (46). Perhaps the problem was not whether women had genius or not but whether or not they had the opportunity to express and develop their genius. Traditionally, in European culture, women did not have this opportunity. In Aboriginal societies, such as the Iroquois, the clan mother played a key role in all decision making. Thus, many Aboriginal women had the opportunity to express and develop their genius.

Initially, I did not recognize these important issues, and I taught the curriculum as it was structured. It became ever more obvious to me that minorities were not given equal status. Furthermore, the curriculum was defined through the subjective attitudes of the oppressor. The teaching of the Riel Rebellion is a case in point. Was it really a rebellion, or was it more of a resistance? Noël comments on this scenario, stating: "When the resistance of the colonized peoples was expressed openly, the colonizers immediately felt themselves persecuted. Thus, Europeans saw themselves as 'the forces of order' dealing with 'rebels,' forces of order whose acts of 'courage' against 'fanatical' adversaries were reported by western media and history books. The impression of victimization felt by the White peoples in taking over foreign continents was manifested all the more intensely when the security of their own territory was in question" (1994, 136-7). As I attempted to combat such injustices in the curriculum, I was credited with the intention of making the curriculum more diverse and appropriate. I soon realized that I was teaching cultural and women's issues out of context. Who was I to speak for these groups? I sought further information through workshops and guest speakers.

My search led to my involvement with the Indian and Métis staff development program for the Northern Lights School Division 113. As an active member, I found myself again playing the role of the liberal-minded humanist. Noël states: "The dominator will believe ... he has truly understood the specific nature of the oppressed, since he recognizes the very characteristics he himself has induced. Whence his very clear impression that he possesses an intimate knowledge of the dominated ('I know these people') ... The oppressor's vision of the oppressed depends less on experience than on a predetermined conception of social relations, a conception this vision attempts to justify by permitting the dominator to see what he wants to see" (1994, 109). I have a need and a responsibility to create necessary change; however, I must seek further knowledge and have those who have been oppressed inform me how these issues are to be defined and what needs to be done to create solutions.

I recognize that there are many areas in which I have limited knowledge and that I need to expand my narrow understanding. For example, a secondhand encounter with institutionalized "welfare" provided another learning experience for me. The situation of a dear friend, one of my partner's relatives, helped me to see how dominators control employment opportunities. I had never realized that the state could promote welfare as a trap from which one could not escape. In my ignorance, I had branded my partner's relative lazy and unmotivated. Noël explains: "Rarely are the dominated conceded to have definitively positive qualities ... Blacks, Natives, and even foreign workers who are deemed to be taking undue advantage of the welfare and unemployment insurance benefits extended to them by the generosity of western countries are often accused of 'laziness'" (1994, 121).

I believed that this person could find a job if she really wanted to. I did not realize that she was a victim who illustrated the low self-esteem and alienation that Noël discusses as "a pedagogy of guilt" (1994, 123). This woman was a victim of the system. The dominator had trapped her into a state of dependency on welfare. She has since found full-time employment, working long hours at irregular intervals. Even though she is earning less than if she were on welfare, the government has refused to continue paying support for her and her three children. In essence, it is as though she is being punished for obtaining employment. Yet I have seen an immense change in her disposition and overall attitude. She has a renewed sense of self-worth and self-esteem.

I had adopted the dominator's perception of laziness, and my attitude exemplified the mentality of blame. Noël (1994, 130) quotes C.I. Waxman to illustrate this point: "Public opinion also continues to believe that poverty generally is due to a 'lack of effort' or some other form of character flaw. In North America, where the myth of equal opportunity is particularly prevalent, this reaction was lent credence by social workers in the early twentieth century, who held to the traditional belief that the poor suffer from 'emotional immaturity' and 'deep seated conflicts within the personality.'" If this is the case, then I have come to realize that such attitudes are an act of prejudgment by the oppressor.

My voyage of discovery thus far has been filled with times of sadness and times of jubilation. I needed to challenge everything that I knew, to broaden my perspective and redefine my personal position within the destructive and diverse realms of colonialism. Embarking on an introspective and reflective journey is a personal choice that is difficult. I learned that examining oneself honestly can create feelings of uncertainty, as one's secure position in the world may have to be reevaluated and reconstructed to reflect a newly developed perspective. This may cause feelings of isolation, but comfort can be found in the knowledge that others are on a similar journey and are more than willing to offer their support.

Many caring and compassionate individuals are there to help nurture growth and broaden horizons in the hopes of collaboratively structuring a postcolonial world. These individuals have been defined as "gatekeepers who understand the effects of colonialism and are committed to fighting any perceived act of hegemony on our communities" (Duran and Duran 1995, 7). Two such individuals have been my personal gatekeepers and deserve credit for their love, guidance, and inspiration. My partner, Jennifer, is a strong-spirited Aboriginal woman who is always willing to support and help her brothers and sisters in the global community. The other person who has nurtured my critical thinking and personal growth is Marie Battiste, a professor at the University of Saskatchewan. Marie is a unique educator who challenges students to reflect within themselves and to define their positions within a neocolonialist world of the oppressor and the oppressed.

As I progress on my journey, I continue to encounter individuals who are committed to creating a postcolonial world. We can make a difference, but it must begin within each and every one of us. I believe that I am among those individuals who "have realized that their individualistic worldview is not working and are looking elsewhere for a more community-oriented way of life that is more existentially and spiritually meaningful" (Duran and Duran 1995, 155).

Conclusion

By correlating my life experiences in childhood, early adulthood, and as a teacher – including lessons learned from playing hockey and coaching for the Special Olympics – to issues addressed in Lise Noël's *Intolerance,* I have discovered a system founded on inequality – a system that serves to exploit and alienate. I have illustrated this with the choices that I could make in childhood because of my Euro-Canadian status (choices not available to my Aboriginal friends) and by drawing parallels with the sport of hockey. Hockey exemplifies the ideology of the oppressor, with its attempts to dominate the opposition, whereas my Special Olympian friends taught me that this oppressive mentality can be replaced with compassion and cooperation.

I have been an unknowing benefactor of a world created by the oppressor, and I had not fully realized the severe implications of acts of oppression. Nor had I realized how I had become encased within the oppressor's world, a world about which I had no critical knowledge. I had thought that I understood the plight of the oppressed, but I have come to realize that my narrow perceptions were defined by oppressive institutions that only give an adulterated version of suffering. Learning that I receive benefits based on my gender and the colour of my skin has been a powerful discovery. I have come to terms with the knowledge that I have benefited from, and owe my position in society to, the many backs that have been broken by oppression. While I have exposed several parts of the entrenched and elusive doctrines of the oppressor, I realize that my voyage of discovery has just commenced.

References

Battiste, M. 1986. "You Can't Be the Doctor if You Are the Disease: The Tenets of Systematic Colonialism in Canadian Language Education." Unpublished ms., INEP, University of Saskatchewan.

Cajete, G. 1994. *Look to the Mountain: An Ecology of Indigenous Education*. Durango, CO: Kivaki Press.

Duran, E., and B. Duran. 1995. *Native American Postcolonial Psychology*. Albany, NY: State University Press.

Fanon, F. 1968. *The Wretched of the Earth*. New York: Grove Press.

Freire, P. 1970. *Pedagogy of the Oppressed*. New York: Herder and Herder.

Lévy-Bruhl, L. 1966. *How Natives Think*. New York: Washington Square Press.

Memmi, A. 1991. *The Colonizer and the Colonized*. Boston: Beacon Press.

Mitchell, K. 1996. "Hubick Livens Crowd." *Times Herald: Sports Extra*. August 6: 2.

Noël, L. 1994. *Intolerance: A General Survey*. Montreal and Kingston: McGill-Queen's University Press.

Eastern Door:
Healing Colonized
Indigenous Peoples

The Rose of Hope

The Rose of Hope is what we need, for the
aroma of its fragrance is so dear.
We can feel the softness of its petals
as we tend to hold it near.
We must handle it with care, for the
thorns of life can cause us pain.
But the fragrance will help us forget
we'll soon forgive it once again.
The Rose of Hope is all we need, but for
it to grow, we must first sow its seed.

– Kelusultiek/Shirley Kiju Kawi, in
Kelusultiek: Original Women's Voices

8
A Different Yield

Linda Hogan

Hosanna! The corn reached total zenith in crested and entire August.
The space of summer arched earth to autumnal fruit. Out of cold and
ancient sod the split of protein, the primal thunder. In the Mayan face
of the tiny kernel look out the deeps of time, space, and genes. In
the golden pollen, more ancient and fixed than the pyramids, is the
scream of fleeing Indians, germinal mirror of endurance, reflections of
mothers of different yield.

– Meridel Le Sueur, *Harvest Song: Collected Essays and Stories*

A woman once described a friend of hers as being such a keen listener that
even the trees leaned toward her, as if they were speaking their innermost
secrets into her listening ears. Over the years, I've envisioned that
woman's silence, a hearing full and open enough that the world told her
its stories. The green leaves turned toward her, whispering tales of soft
breezes and the murmurs of leaf against leaf.

When I was a girl, I listened to the sounds of the corn plants. A breeze
would begin in a remote corner of the field and move slowly toward the
closest edge, whispering. After the corn harvest at my uncle's farm, the
pigs would be set loose in the cornfield to feed on what corn was left
behind, kernels too dry for picking, too small for sale, or cobs that were
simply missed by human hands. Without a moment's hesitation, the pigs
would make straight for any plant that still held an ear of corn, bypassing
the others. They would listen, it seemed, to the denser song of corn where
it still lived inside its dress of husk.

When I first heard of Barbara McClintock, it confirmed what I thought
to be true about the language of corn. McClintock is a biologist who
received a Nobel Prize for her work on gene transposition in corn plants.
Her method was to listen to what corn had to say, to translate what the
plants spoke into a human tongue.

In *A Feeling for the Organism,* Evelyn Fox Keller (1983) writes that
McClintock came to know each plant intimately. She watched the daily
green journeys of their growth from earth toward sky and sun. She knew
her plants in the way that a healer would know them, from inside, from
the inner voices of corn and woman. Her approach to her science was
alive, intuitive, and humane. It was a whole approach, one that bridged
the worlds of woman and plant and crossed over the boundary lines

between species. Her respect for life allowed for a vision expanded enough, and sharp enough, to see more deeply into the mysteries of matter than did other geneticists at work on the same problems. Revelation of her method astonished the scientific community. She saw an alive world, a fire of life inside plants, even plants other than corn: "In the summertime, when you walk down the road, you'll see that the tulip leaves, if it's a little warm, turn themselves around so their backs are towards the sun. Within the restricted areas in which they live, they move around a great deal. These organisms are fantastically beyond our wildest expectations."

In her book *Adam's Task,* Vickie Hearne writes about the same kind of approach, only with animals, that McClintock used. She says that there are things to be gained by respecting the intelligence of animals: "With horses, respect usually means respecting their nervousness, as in tales of retreating armies on horseback traversing minefields, in which the only riders who survive are the ones who gave their horses their heads, or tales of police horses who snort anxiously when a car in a traffic jam turns out to be carrying the thieves who escaped capture six months earlier."

These past years, it seems that much contemporary scientific exploration has been thrown full tilt into the centre of one of those minefields and is in search of a new vision and of renewed intuitive processes of discovery that go beyond our previous assumptions about knowledge. This new requirement of thought turns out to be one that can only be called a leap of faith. "Over and over again," Keller says of McClintock, "she tells us one must have the time to look, the patience to 'hear' what the material has to say to you. One must have a feeling for the organism."

A few years ago, I was fortunate to meet a Jamaican artist named Everald Brown. Brown lives in a rural mountain town where houses have settled in with the enduring red earth. He creates carvings, paintings, and musical instruments that are radiantly alive with a resonance reaching far beyond the material and far beyond the creations of most other artists who work with the same wood and pigment. Brown is what Jamaicans call an "intuitive artist," though he himself says only that the doves have taught him his craft. One of his intricately carved stringed instruments is painted with a blue sky. White, luminous doves are flying across it. And his wood carvings, made of lignum vitae, the tree of life, are rich with the lives of animals and birds emerging from the heavy centre of wood.

Many creative people have called the inspiration "the muse." Often they say that their ideas come from a spirit world, from a life other than their own human life. Even the Bible is a work so described by its authors; it is the voice of God.

Artist Paul Klee once said that we must return to the origins of things and their meanings, to the secret places where original law fosters all evolution, to the organic centre of all movement in time and space, which is the mind or heart of creation.

This organic centre, the centre of creation, comes down to us through long traditions of learning the world's own songs. In American Indian traditions, healers are often called interpreters because they are the ones who are able to hear the world and pass its wisdom along. They are the ones who return to the heart of creation.

When we go back in human history, we find that it is not only the people now recognized as continuing in a tribal tradition who have known the voices of earth, how corn both sings her own song and grows better with the songs and prayers of the people. Western traditions of consciousness also derive from this approach to original, or Aboriginal, ways of knowing. Orpheus, for instance, was able to communicate with the worlds of animals, plants, water, and minerals. Psyche, for whom psychology was named, fell weeping on the ground, and while she was there the ants offered her a solution to the impossible task that she was assigned, that of separating a mountain of grain before dawn. The river reeds also passed along their secrets to Psyche, instructing her in the way to gather wool from golden sheep.

From nearly all traditions, account after account tells of stones giving guidance, as with Crazy Horse, the Lakota prophet and politician who took his direction from a stone that he wore beneath his arm. There are tales of the trees singing, of the corn called by the Mayans "the grace" telling stories of inner earth.

In recent times, the term "myth" has come to signify falsehood, but when we examine myths we find that they are a high form of truth. They are the deepest, innermost cultural stories of our human journeys toward spiritual and psychological growth. An essential part of myth is that it allows for our return to the creation, to a mythical time. It allows us to hear the world new again. Octavio Paz has written that in older oral traditions an object and its name were not separated. One equalled the other. To speak of corn, for instance, was to place the corn before a person's very eyes and ears. It was in mythic time that there was no abyss between the word and the thing that it named, but Paz adds that, "as soon as man acquired consciousness of himself, he broke away from the natural world and made himself another world inside himself."

This broken connection appears not only in language and myth but also in our philosophies of life. There is a separation that has taken place between us and nature. Something has broken deep in our core. Yet there is another world created inside the person. In some way, the balance between inner and outer worlds struggles to maintain itself in other and more complex ways than in the past. Psychologist C.A. Meier (1989) notes that, as the wilderness has disappeared outside us, it has gone to live inside the human mind. Because we are losing vast tracts of the wilderness, not only are we losing a part of ourselves, he says, but also the threat to life that once existed in the world around us has now moved within. "The whole of western society," he says, "is approaching a physical and mental breaking point." The result is a spiritual fragmentation that has accompanied our ecological destruction.

In a time of such destruction, our lives depend on this listening. It may be that the earth speaks its symptoms to us. With the nuclear reactor accident in Chernobyl, Russia, it was not the authorities who told us that the accident had taken place. It was the wind. The wind told the story. It carried a tale of splitting, of atomic fission, to other countries and revealed the truth of the situation. The wind is a prophet, a scientist, a talker.

These voices of the world infuse our every act, as much as does our own ancestral DNA. They give us back ourselves, point out a direction for salvation. Sometimes they even shake us down to the bedrock of our own human lives. This is what I think happened in the 1970s language experiments in which chimpanzees were taught Ameslan, American Sign Language. In *Silent Partners*, Eugene Linden (1986) discusses the results of experiments with American Sign Language and chimpanzees. Probably the best-known chimp is Washoe, a wild-caught chimpanzee that learned to use 132 signs, was able to ask questions, and could use the negative. The book is extremely significant to our times, not so much because of what it tells us about apes and their ability to communicate in signs as because of what it reveals about human beings and our relationships with other creatures.

The heated debates about the experiments came to revolve around whether or not it was actual language that the chimps used. The arguments centred on definitions of language and intelligence, obscuring the real issue, that of how we treat other living beings. A reader comes to wonder how solid we are in the security of both ourselves and our knowledge when an issue of such significant scientific and spiritual importance sparks such a great division of minds. However, if we are forced to accept that animals have intelligence, language, and sensitivity to pain, including psychological trauma, then this acceptance has tremendous consequences for our own species and for our future actions.

While Linden says that "it is a little unsettling to be confronted with an animal who does not automatically acknowledge your paramountcy in the natural hierarchy," he also says that the experiments were disquieting not only because of the tragic consequences that they created for the animals involved but also because they revealed the very fragile underpinnings of science. At the least, the questions raised throughout this project were primarily questions about ourselves, our own morality, our way of being in the world, and our responsibility for the caretaking of the earth.

Vickie Hearne, on the same topic of language experiments, says that we are facing an intellectual emergency. I want to take the word *emergency* a step further than the meaning that it has come to hold for us, for this is not merely a crisis of the mind but also a potential act of emergence, of liberation for not only the animals of the earth but also for our own selves, a freedom that could very well release us of stifling perceptions that have bound us tightly and denied us the parts of ourselves that were not objective or otherwise scientifically respectable. When Linden notes that one of the chimp experimenters who came to care deeply for her subjects was outlawed from the world of science, I was reminded of how, during the 1970s when Harry Harlowe was conducting torturous research on chimps at the University of Wisconsin, one of the female students was found holding and comforting a chimp that was in pain. This act of compassion led Harlowe to conclude that there was a maternal instinct in women that kept them from objectivity and that therefore they were not suited to the work of science. But even aside from that, the experiments were carried out to tell researchers what humans could have told them directly about their lives and needs and not have been believed.

We have arrived despairingly at a time when compassion and care are qualities that do not lend themselves to the world of intellectual thought. Jimmie Durham, a Cherokee writer who was a prime mover in the development of an International Treaty Organization, wrote a poem called "The Teachings of My Grandmother," excerpted here:

> In a magazine too expensive to buy I read about
> How, with scientific devices of great complexity,
> U.S. scientists have discovered that if a rat
> Is placed in a cage in which it has previously
> Been given an electrical shock, it starts crying.
> I told my grandmother about that and she said,
> "We probably knew that would be true."

It might be that Linden comes close to the centre of the dilemma about whether or not apes have language and intelligence when he says that "Perhaps it would be better to stick to figuring out the nature of stars and matter, and not to concern ourselves with creatures who threaten to paralyze us by shedding light on the true nature and origins of our abilities. Dismaying as this may sound, it is quite possible that we cannot afford to know who we are."

Not only have our actions revealed us to ourselves, and sometimes had dire results, but among many peoples educated in many European philosophical traditions there is also an intense reaction to the bad news that cruelty is cruelty. There is a backlash effect that resists peacemaking. In 1986, I heard Betty Williams, a 1977 Nobel Peace Prize laureate from

Northern Ireland, lecture in South Dakota. One afternoon Williams had witnessed the bombing death of Irish children. A little girl died in her arms. The girl's legs had been severed in the explosion and had been thrown across the street from where the woman held the bleeding child. Williams went home in shock and despair. Later that night, when the shock wore off, the full impact of what she'd seen jolted her. She stepped outside her door, screaming out in the middle of the night. She knocked on doors that might easily have opened with weapons pointed at her face, and she cried out, "What kind of people have we become that we would allow children to be killed on our streets?" Within four hours the city was awake, and there were 16,000 names on petitions for peace.

Williams's talk was interrupted at this point by a man who called out, "You're sick." Undisturbed by the heckler, Williams went on to tell how, touring the world as a peacemaker, she had left the starving people in Ethiopia for an audience with the Pope. He told her, "I feel so worried about the hungry people," to which Williams responded, "Don't worry about them. Sell the Michelangelo and feed them."

Such a simple thing, to feed people. Such a common thing, to work for peace. Such very clear things, to know that, if we injure an animal, ravage the land, we have caused damage. Yet we have rampant hunger and do not know, can hardly even imagine, peace. And even when animals learn to speak a language, and to communicate their misery, we still deny them the right to an existence free from suffering and pain.

I want to make two points here. One is about language and its power. While we can't say what language is much beyond saying that it is a set of signs and symbols that communicates meaning, we know it is the most highly regarded human ability. Language usage, in fact, often determines social and class order in our societal systems. Without language, we humans have no way of knowing what lies beneath the surface of one another. Yet there are communications that take place on a level that goes deeper than our somewhat limited human spoken languages. We read one another via gesture, stance, facial expression, scent. And sometimes this communication is more honest, more comprehensible, than the words we utter.

These inner forms of communication are perhaps the strongest core of ourselves. We have feelings that can't be spoken. That very speechlessness results in poems that try to articulate what can't be said directly, in paintings that bypass the intellectual boundaries of our daily vision, and in music that goes straight to the body. And there is even more a deep-moving underground language in us. Its currents pass between us and the rest of nature. It is the inner language that Barbara McClintock tapped for her research.

Hearne cites instances in which animals have responded to these inner languages of people. The famous case of the horse Clever Hans is one of these. Hans could do mathematical calculations and otherwise answer questions by tapping his hoof on the ground. As it turned out, Hans did not do the actual equations. Instead, he read the body language of the persons testing him: "Hans could always find out what the questioner thought was the correct answer, no matter how hard the questioner worked at remaining still and impassive. Hans apparently read minute changes in breathing, angles of the eyebrows, etc. with an accuracy we have trouble imagining." Hans's owner was denounced as a fraud. But, as Hearne points out, wasn't it a remarkable thing that the horse knew so well how to read people, even those other than his owner? They could not conceal from him the correct answer.

Critics of the ape language experiments worked vigorously to discredit the careful work of the researchers, and one of the variables they mentioned was this unconscious leakage.

Another point that needs to be made is that, when issues become obscured by distorted values or abstract concepts, we lose a clarity that allows us to act even in our own best behalf, for survival not just of ourselves but also of the homeland that is our life and our sustenance. These responses stand in the way of freedom from pain. They obstruct the potentials we have for a better world. It is a different yield that we desire.

It must have been obvious at the inception of the language experiments that their very design was to determine whether or not a speaking ape might have a consciousness similar to that of a human. However, the results were distressing, and the fate of the signing chimpanzees has been disastrous, some of them having been sold to research labs for other kinds of experimentation, including AIDS research.

We might ask what is to be gained by bridging the species gap? If it is, indeed, to determine intelligence levels, then it seems that the tally on the side of the chimpanzees adds up to more points than ours, since the chimps are now bilingual. But, whatever the impetus, Linden says that the loser in the conflict concerning human and animal community is science. And while the chimps are the primary victims of this ongoing struggle, we are also "victims of a skewed view of our relationship with the rest of the natural order."

What we really are searching for is a language that heals this relationship, one that takes the side of the amazing and fragile life on our life-giving earth. A language that knows corn, and the one that corn knows, a language that takes hold of the mystery of what's around us and offers it back to us, full of awe and wonder. It is a language of creation, of divine fire, a language that goes beyond the strict borders of scientific inquiry and right into the heart of the mystery itself. Le Sueur writes: "Something enters the corn at the moment of fusion of the male and female that is unknown to scientists. From some star, a cosmic quickening, some light, movement-fast chemical that engenders illuminates quickens the conception, lights the fuse." Life itself, though we live it, is unknown to us. It is an alchemical process, a creative movement and exploration with the same magic in mind as the researchers had when they originated their search for meaning within the world.

We are looking for a tongue that speaks with reverence for life, searching for an ecology of mind. Without it, we have no home, have no place of our own within the creation. It is not only the vocabulary of science that we desire. We also want a language of that different yield. A yield rich as the harvests of the earth, a yield that returns us to our own sacredness, to a self-love and respect that will carry out to others.

In most southwestern Indian cultures, the pollen of corn is sacred. It is the life-giving seed of creation and fertility. Anthropologist Ruth Underhill (1972) wrote that Papago planters of corn would speak to the life-sustaining plants. "Night after night," she says, "the planter walks around his field, singing up the corn":

The corn comes up;
It comes up green,
Here upon our fields
White tassels unfold.
Blue evening falls;
Blue evening falls;
Near by, in every direction,
It sets the corn tassels trembling.

I know that corn. I know that blue evening. Those words open a door to a house in which we have always lived.

Once, I ground corn with a smooth, round stone on an ancient sloping metate. Leaning over, kneeling on the ground, grinding the blue corn, seeing how the broken dry kernels turned soft, to fine meal, I saw a history in that yield, a deep knowing of where our lives come from, all the way back to the starch and sugar of corn.

She, the corn, is called our grandmother. She's the woman who rubbed her palms against her body, and the seeds fell out of her skin. That is, they fell from her body until her sons discovered her secrets. Before she left the world, she told them how to plant. She said, plant the beans and corn together, plant their little sister, squash, between them. This, from an oral tradition, came to be rediscovered hundreds of years later, almost too late, by agriculturalists in their research on how to maintain the richness of farm soil.

Cherokee writer Carroll Arnett once gave me a bracelet of corn. There were forty-nine kernels, representing the number of clans, stitched round in a circle of life. I said, "If I wear it when I die and am buried, won't it be wonderful to know that my life will grow up, out from beneath the earth? My life inside the green blades of corn, the stalks and tassels and flying pollen? That red corn, that corn will be this woman."

Imagine a woman, a scientist, listening to those rustling stalks, knowing their growth so intimately that "She could write the autobiography of every plant she worked with." What a harvest. What a different yield. In it is the pull of earth and life. The fields are beautiful.

Cornmeal and pollen are offered to the sun at dawn. The ears of the corn are listening and waiting. They want peace. The stalks of the corn want clean water, sun that is in its full clean shining. The leaves of the corn want good earth. The earth wants peace. The birds who eat the corn do not want poison. Nothing wants to suffer. The wind does not want to carry the stories of death.

At night, in the cornfields, when there is no more mask of daylight, you hear the plants talking among themselves. The wind passes through. It's all there, the languages, the voices of wind, dove, corn, stones. The language of life won't be silenced.

In Chaco Canyon, in the centre, my sister Donna told me, there is a *kiva*, a ceremonial room in the earth. This place has been uninhabited for what seems like forever. It has been without water so long that there are theories that the ancient people disappeared as they journeyed after water. Donna said that there was a corn plant growing out of the centre of the *kiva*. It was alone, a single plant. It had been there since the ancient ones, the old ones who came before us all, those people who wove dog hair into belts, who witnessed the painting of flute players on the seeping canyon walls, who knew the stories of corn. There was one corn plant growing out of the holy place. It planted itself yearly. It was its own mother. With no water, no person to care for it, no turning over of the soil, this corn plant rises up. Earth yields. We probably knew that would be true.

Do you remember the friend whom the leaves talked to? We need to be that friend. Listen. The ears of the corn are singing. They are telling their stories and singing their songs. We knew that would be true.

References

Fox Keller, Evelyn. 1983. *A Feeling for the Organism: The Life and Work of Barbara McClintock*. San Francisco: W.H. Freeman.

Linden, Eugene. 1986. *Silent Partners: The Legacy of the Ape Language Experiments*. New York: Times Books.

Meier, C.A. 1989. *Consciousness*. Trans. David N. Roscoe. Boston: Sigo Press.

Underhill, Ruth. 1972. *Red Man's Religion*. Chicago: University of Chicago Press.

9

From Hand to Mouth: The Postcolonial Politics of Oral and Written Traditions

J. Edward Chamberlin

I'm going to start off with a riddle, which I was reminded of by an old friend, the East Coast writer and critic Robert Finley. He knows as much about riddles as anybody I've ever come across – which is to say, he knows a lot about language and about its original, some would say aboriginal, powers – the powers of riddles and charms, of metaphor and magic, of reading and listening.

This is an old riddle, first put by a bunch of young boys to Homer, the legendary poet and oral performer and by reputation the wisest old man in ancient Greece. But he was no match for the youngsters. It's kind of a hunter-gatherer riddle, and it goes like this: "What we've caught and killed we've left behind. What has escaped us we've brought with us. What have we been hunting?"

Homer couldn't solve the riddle, so the story goes, and he was deeply upset not so much because of his inability – he was much too wise to be bothered by that – but because of the dilemma he now faced. Homer knew that what the boys were telling him was true – that is the convention of riddling. But he couldn't make sense of it. He knew all about hunting, he knew all about the world in fact, and he knew that what they said was nonsense. And yet he also knew that it was *true*. The stakes were higher than they might at first have seemed. He either had to change his understanding of the world – an understanding that had served him pretty well up to then – or had to solve the riddle, which would involve changing his understanding of its language. Fish or cut bait ... when there's nothing else in the world to eat but fish.

Eventually, Homer did solve it, with a little help from the boys. They had been hunting lice, it turned out – body lice on themselves. The lice that they had caught and killed they had left behind. What had escaped them they had brought with them.

Language put Homer in the dilemma, and language – a word, in fact the word *lice* – got him out of it. But the dilemma *was* real. It involved a framework – in this case hunting – within which words were to be understood and a challenge to Homer's understanding of what happens within that framework – that is to say, what happens when you go hunting. In a certain way, this riddle is an image of colonialism. Colonialism establishes a frame of reference; it says something with an authority that is rather more malicious than the mischievousness of those boys; and then it challenges us to believe it or not. What this creates is exactly what Homer experienced – an urgent fascination and enormous anxiety. And what it requires is that we either shift the frame or find the right language, the right word. In either case, it forces us to examine the nature of our belief in what we see and hear.

My topic is postcolonial theory and what it can tell us about oral and written traditions and the circumstances of many Aboriginal communities, but like these traditions I am beginning with language rather than politics. Often we are preoccupied with what language *is,* what it means, what it conveys by way of thoughts and feelings, what it cannot convey. For a minute, let's turn to what language *does,* what it makes happen, what it creates (also in terms of thoughts and feelings), what it brings into being that nothing else does (which is crucially important when we think about the loss of language or of some of its functions). Language makes things happen and brings things into being by means of what are sometimes referred to as "speech acts." I should add right away that like figures of speech –- metaphors, personifications, and hyperbole – speech acts are very much a part of writing (from graffiti and constitutions to all literary forms). And they are central to every society. For example, speech acts – in which language *does* something as well as *means* something – are part of praying and preaching, cursing and praising, bearing witness and giving evidence, pronouncing sentence and professing sanctioned truths. They are part of saying "I will" or "no" or "I love you," of repeating parables and proverbs, riddles and charms, and a wide range of code words and passwords and word magic. Sometimes these words can only be said by certain people, in certain places, to certain people. At other times they need to be said in congregation, by everyone. Always they have a kind of power, sometimes an awesome power. And usually they are necessary for our survival.

Words of power and words of survival have one thing in common. We remember them. That's part of their power. It's also how they contribute to our individual and collective survival, for we need a set of remembered words and occasions in order to maintain the coherence and continuity of our societies and to satisfy our spiritual and material needs. These are the words and the phrases that last.

"The phrase that lasts" is a line from a poem that also gave me my title, "from hand to mouth." It's called "Forest of Europe" and was written by Derek Walcott for his friend the great Russian poet and exile Joseph Brodsky. The poem is set in the grim cold of an Oklahoma winter, and it brings together a whole lot of experiences of dislocation and dispossession:

> There is a Gulag Archipelago
> under this ice, where the salt, mineral spring
> of the long Trail of Tears runnels these plains
> as hard and open as a herdsman's face
> sun-cracked and stubbled with unshaven snow.
> Growing in whispers from the Writers' Congress
> the snow circles like cossacks round the corpse
> of a tired Choctaw till it is a blizzard
> of treaties and white papers as we lose
> sight of the single human through the cause.[1]

Then, unwilling to surrender to all this, or to the loss of language that has accompanied it, Walcott talks about how a phrase of poetry or song – remembered, repeated, revered – can be "the bread that lasts." "What's poetry," asks Walcott,

> if it is worth its salt,
> but a phrase men can pass from hand to mouth?
>
> From hand to mouth, across the centuries,
> the bread that lasts when systems have decayed,
> when, in his forest of barbed-wire branches,
> a prisoner circles, chewing the one phrase
> whose music will last longer than the leaves,
>
> whose condensation is the marble sweat
> of angels' foreheads.[2]

We all know such words and phrases, the ones that last, the ones that make things happen. (The word *lice*, which solved the riddle for Homer, is another such word.) Both the enduring power and the survival rations provided by them function in two ways or, more precisely, in two worlds. On the one hand, they do things in the real world – the world of threats and promises, of demands and refusals, of weddings and funerals, of treaties and constitutions. On the other hand, and equally – or I would say even more – importantly, they function in the world of our imaginations, the world of stories and songs and performances in which we live our truest lives. This world, the world of the imagination, is not a world in which we escape from reality but one by means of which we engage reality on terms that reflect our own meanings and values. If our words and our several modes of imaginative representation are replaced by others that are not the reflection of our hearts and minds and experiences and the heritage of our people, then so is our sense of reality. This is the central insight of postcolonial theory, and it is why the "peopling and placing" of that imaginative world by others are so dangerous, for they alienate us from ourselves and from our home ... especially when, as is so often the case, we still live there. And although few would doubt the importance of this world of the imagination – the world of drumming and dancing, of carved chests and beaded belts, of condolence canes and ceremonial masks, of stories and songs – let me repeat an anecdote told to me by the Canadian geographer Peter Usher. It's about a meeting between an Aboriginal Tsimshian community in the northwest and a group of government foresters. The meeting was about jurisdiction over the woodlands. The foresters claimed the land for the government. The Indians were astonished by the claim – they couldn't understand what these relative newcomers were talking about. Finally, one of them put what was bothering them in the form of a question. "If this is your land," he asked, "where are your stories?"

This, in fact, was a revelation not about ownership in any simpleminded sense, because these stories didn't establish possession of the place. On the contrary, they showed how the people were possessed *by* it – owned and occupied, as it were, and answerable to it by means of their stories and songs. All of a sudden, those two worlds I talked about become much less distinct. Postcolonial theory can help remind us of this and get us back to the ways in which both the world of reality and the world of the imagination are sites of struggle for authenticity and authority, even though each may be menaced differently by change and may therefore offer different strategies for survival and power. For example – and I'm not being facetious here – the way in which a people define themselves may occasionally accommodate a forgetting of some of the events in their past, but it will always require a remembering of the words that constitute their history.

Now, in my view of it, postcolonial history *is* ultimately about all this – which is to say, it's about how language is an instrument of both survival and power. But because these words – "survival" and "power" – are so easy to bandy about, I want to try out a couple of others – "subsistence" and "sovereignty" – and consider them in a different kind of way. These words are highly charged – and widely misrepresented – politically, and for that reason they may give us a sense of how postcolonial theory can open up new understandings of the situation faced by peoples who are involved in the challenge of decolonization.

In the late 1920s, wracked with something like guilt for the destitute condition of Indian people in the United States, the Department of the Interior commissioned a report from the Institute for Government Research (later known as the Brookings Institute). Titled *The Problem of Indian Administration* and directed by Lewis Meriam, it provided an exhaustive catalogue of the relentless dispossession of Indian lands, the systematic destruction of Indian tribes, and the brutal dislocation of Indian peoples.[3] It was filled with righteous (and well-researched) indignation about the breaches of trust that had characterized Indian administration. It was harsh in its criticism of the land allotment policy that had been in place for half a century, and it recommended the reestablishment of tribal governments with control over lands and resources. It was eloquent in its celebration of the values of community and of place, and it stressed the interdependence of spiritual and material values in both Native and non-Native societies.

It was also incorrigibly utilitarian in the remedies that it proposed. And so, when it came to describing the situation of the Navajo, one of the largest and most powerful of the tribes, it forgot about their horses. Actually, it didn't quite forget. It dismissed them in one paragraph in its nearly 900 pages. The paragraph was titled "Worthless Horses."

Worthless? These were the horses that worked the land, pulled the wagons, carried the men and women, and herded the stock. They were the horses that also grazed wild on the grasslands, defying the immediate demands of subsistence and signifying not just prestige but also a kind of sovereignty. Seen in this light, a horse was its own reason for being – not a convenience or a commodity but a covenant linking Navajo survival with Navajo power. A covenant between fresh air and freedom to breathe. And this completely confounded those who wrote the Meriam report. To pick up my analogy of Homer and the riddle, they just didn't get it.

Oscar Wilde once said that art has two kinds of enemies: those who dislike it, and those who like it rationally. The second set, he insisted, is the real menace. Something of this menace now faced Navajo horses – and therefore the Navajo. The reforms that followed the Meriam report were designed to reclaim tribal authority from the Bureau of Indian Affairs and tribal land from overgrazing. Sheep and goats are a staple of Navajo life, and so the well-intentioned officials in charge proposed that a livestock reduction program be instituted immediately and that it be based on what were called "sheep units." Everything was to be calculated in sheep units ... even horses, which on average eat as much grass as five sheep.

The Navajo knew the state of their grasslands and the need for restrictions. They had survived as a people for thousands of years, and for several hundred years in the drylands of the Southwest, where, according to one story, they had come from the tundra lands and northern prairies that the Athapaskan people, to whom they are related, still call home. But they refused to have their sense of who they were and where they belonged determined by a diminished, impoverished vision that saw everything reducible to sheep units. The Indian agent for the Navajo at the time, Reeseman Fryer, said later that he thought that single phrase – sheep units – inflicted a deeper wound on the Navajo than almost anything else in those times of suffering and sacrifice. The federal government directed the Navajo to round up their five-sheep-unit horses and sell or destroy them. The Navajo said no.[4]

Their refusal had to do with more than just horses – but they were at the heart of it, for they represented Navajo resistance to those who deemed horses nothing more than a worthless indulgence and nothing less than an offence against the virtues of social utility and economic morality that informed the restructuring programs of the American New Deal.

Another anecdote catches something of where all this fits into the negotiation between survival and power. It's set in the early 1930s, just when sheep units had hit the charts. It had been a terrible winter up in the Rockies north and west of Edmonton. An Indian agent, Mindy Christiansen, visited the Beaver Indians, the Dunne-za – Athapaskan-speaking cousins of the Navajo, living in the mountains in the Peace River country near Fort St. John, British Columbia. "There are 170 Indians in the band," he wrote,

and they are simply on their last legs. They have absolutely nothing. I have never seen a band of Indians that had less. During the two days I spent with those Indians ... , it rained continually, and I noticed that these people did not even have tents. There were only two good teepees in the whole outfit and the only shelter they had was a piece of canvas hung over willows, under which I saw the old people and children huddled. They were very poorly clad and some of the children had practically no clothing on ... They haven't even any cooking utensils ...

In February all Indians were took sick with bad colds ... They lived on moose meat ... Sometimes a little flour. Sometimes no tea or tobacco.

Horses died 200.[5]

Two hundred horses for 170 Indians. A blessing in its way, the loss of those worthless horses. Now they could get on with living like the rest of us.

And yet, just a year later, Director of Indian Affairs Harold McGill came from Ottawa on a tour of the Indian reserves. "It is one of the finest reserves I have seen," he reported on a visit to the same band:

[They are] hunting and fishing Indians who do not live on the reserve but use it only for a camping ground in the summer ... There were about a couple of dozen tents and teepees in the encampment. The horses and dogs [of] the Indians appeared to be well nourished. The Indians had an abundance of moose meat drying on racks and a large quantity of Saskatoon berries were spread on canvas to dry in the sun. The tents that we visited seemed to be well supplied with moose meat and other varieties of food such as sugar, flour and tea. On the whole these Indians appeared well fed and happy.[6]

In the midst of recovering from the devastation of the year before, the Indians had taken pains to rebuild their herd of horses. That previous spring, they must have travelled far east to Manitoba, and south to Montana, to buy new animals and bring in breeding stock. Survival meant nothing without horses. More horses than they needed for their hunting, many more. But the horses did well in the river valley where they made their summer camp, and they gave the band a reason to go on.

"The tongueless man gets his land took" says a Cornish proverb. In 1986, I appeared in the Federal Court of Canada on behalf of that band, whose land had been taken and whose traditions had been trashed by a government that had become adept at cutting out tongues and counting the value of people and places in sheep units. The case was lost at trial. It was appealed to a higher court, which did not reverse the judgment but provided some satisfaction in a dissenting opinion. Finally, the case was won in the Supreme Court of Canada in December 1996.

But let's not be too quick to blame all our troubles on the government or on specific circumstances or story lines that discredit Aboriginal horses or homelands or whatever. The issue is both much more complex and much simpler. Understanding it is where postcolonial theory comes into its own, for it shows us that, just as in some important sense we *are* the government, so we live our lives in the orderings of our arts and our sciences, in the things we value and the subtle ways we convey the significance of those things, in the languages we use to talk about all of this. And if we are Navajo, or many other peoples, in our horses. Which is to say, in all of the activities we engage in, as individuals and as communities, which give meaning and value to our lives. The stories we tell: stories of the origin and purpose of things, of causes and effects and sequences of events, of what holds us together and keeps us apart. The institutions we establish and the covenants we enter into, secular and sacred, large and small. The ways in which we organize our communities: how we lay out the land, our patterns of ownership (of stories as well as of land), the buildings and roads we construct, the spaces we make open or closed. The priorities we give to health care, education, law and order, commerce, clean air and water, the arts ... and, just as important, the ways in which we divide these up in our minds. We live according to them all, practising subsistence – trying to live within our means, with a sense of spiritual as well as material fullness – and exercising sovereignty – using our intelligence and imagination to create an understanding of ourselves, individually and collectively, as human beings.

Which brings us right back to those Dunne-za and Navajo horses. There's surely a familiar instinct there, a perennial feeling about the importance of some things above and beyond their utility, an abiding faith in the value of more than merely getting by. Behind all this is a belief that survival is about being raised up rather than ground down and that power – a condition of survival, if survival is to mean anything at all – is an agent of the imagination as much as it is a function of reality. We keep separating them – survival and power, reality and the imagination, what is necessary and what is sufficient. We need to bring them back together. Which brings *me* back to postcolonial theory.

I must admit that I find "postcolonial theory" a rather intimidating phrase, partly because the word *theory* has become a mantra of the high priests of my profession and partly because postcolonial seems to assume that we're in a state of political grace – or a state of mind – that it's not always easy to recognize looking around at the conditions in which many people live. Yet that is the key, that state of mind, for the hopeful fact is that, despite the conditions of dislocation, dispossession, and disease that colonialism creates and postcolonialism chronicles, Aboriginal peoples the world over are still in possession of *powers*. Leave power aside. It's spiritual and imaginative powers I'm talking about, powers that defy the instrumental brutalities, the sheep-unit busyness of colonialism ... and the purely instrumental understandings of postcolonialism too.

Some years ago, when I was in Australia, I heard an Aborigine named Charlie Tjungurray talking to some visitors about his desert homeland. "I tell'im, you don't belonga this country! You got no *tulku*! *Tjukurrpa*! Only I got'em *tulku*. We bin live along this country. We know this country. I don't know where you come from. You not boss for this place!"

The issues he raised are clear, but the essential authority of his statement comes from two Pintupi words, *tulku* and *tjukurrpa*, which translate as "song" and "dreaming." The words represent all that is most significant about the relationship between his people and their land, between their past and the present, and between one and another. It has always seemed to me that what was ultimately important about those words was the fact that their full meaning and significance could not be translated. But their *un*translatability could. They were, they are, impervious to the enticements of European ways – or indeed anybody else's ways – of seeing and saying. Yet they provided the possibility of understanding, just like words in a riddle.

This raises a troubling question about postcolonial theory and its some-times extravagant claims. What postcolonial theory offers us, quite sim-ply, is a way of looking at things. That's all *any* theory offers – a frame and (if we're in luck) a focus. Despite all sorts of claims to the contrary, no theory offers *the* way, only *one* way ... to be put together, if we are knowl-edgeable enough, with other ways. That's why Charlie Tjungurray used both English and Pintupi words. Postcolonial theory certainly provides a *useful* way of looking at the lands, the livelihoods, and the languages of Aboriginal peoples. But it is not the only way. Other ways may comple-ment it or even contradict it. That shouldn't bother us. Despite Homer's anxiety, it turns out that we are much more comfortable with contradic-tions than we think, from looking at light (or, more precisely, the behav-iour of photons) as consisting of both waves and particles, to our everyday view of the sun rising in the east and setting in the west ... which we all know to be true (unless we live in the Arctic, that is) but which directly contradicts another truth, that the sun doesn't move at all (at least in rela-tion to the Earth); rather, the Earth revolves around it. When we go to a play – Shakespeare's *Hamlet*, say – we know that the actor is not Hamlet ... but then again he's not *not* Hamlet either. And so forth. As storytellers from Majorca say when they begin a tale, "It was, and it was not."

I mention all this because I want to emphasize what I believe to be one of the fundamental insights of postcolonial theory (though not by any means of all its supposed practitioners): its acknowledgment of contradic-tions; its insistence on their seriousness (in other words, not simply shrug-ging them off in a specious relativism); and its rejection of simplistic choices. Postcolonial theory does other things too, of course. It provides a way of interpreting the structural conditions of societies that have experi-enced colonial domination and exploitation and of the strategies they have adopted or the dilemmas they have found themselves in. And yet, even at that, I would note that postcolonial theory is notoriously nervous about some of the extremes of colonial brutality – slavery, the Jewish Holocaust, and the long-running war against the Indians (and the termi-nation and extermination policies that accompanied it). Postcolonialism is often unsure of whether these are different in kind or merely in degree from, say, the colonial organization of Africa or India. Questions of race are a complicated and contentious part of its analysis too.

I believe that it would be much better to focus on the encounter between hunter-gatherer and agricultural societies, which has a grimly predictable history in both ancient and modern times and is not amenable to these racial and national categorizations. Since the earliest develop-ments of farming, the history of the world's cultures has taken shape on the frontier between these two cultural forms: the hunter-gatherer, with a complex reliance on many resources in large, unfenced, but clearly defined territories, and the agriculturalist, with its systematic creation of pastures and arable fields that are then transformed, protected, and fenced.

Some of our deepest misunderstandings can best be understood with reference to this encounter, and much of the world's history has been about the conflicts that have arisen over perceptions of land, livelihood, and language. The first two have had a lot of attention. There is good reason to shift the focus to language, for the opposition between the two ways of knowing about the world has a corollary in two different kinds of language. There are certainly hazards to relying on binary oppositions in this (or indeed any) kind of analysis, but this one seems to offer significant new ways of understanding a profoundly human dilemma, one that typically – or perhaps archetypally – emerges in the dynamics of cultural encounter.

The encounter between hunters and farmers, which is by now internalized in many societies, seems to have an analogue in the opposition between the language of myth, poetry, and religion, on the one hand, and the language of what might be broadly described as evidence and opinion, on the other. These are obviously very general categories, but perhaps the plea that poets rather than politicians be called upon to write our constitutions catches something of the difference. Poetry, by common consent, is intrinsic to culture and identity; politics is associated with the homogenization, and these days the globalization, of cultures. Determined attempts by peoples the world over to maintain their linguistic and cultural heritage flow from their realization of this distinction and from the recognition that certain forms of language cannot be replaced by the standardized forms of national or international languages without profound loss.

We are often told that language defines what it is to be human, individually and collectively. Different languages, the argument goes, therefore define us differently; thus, while language in the abstract may be what defines us as human, language in practice – different languages in different practices – determines these differences. No matter how much we gloss over this for the sake of social or economic or political expediency, the blunt fact is that the loss of these languages means the loss of these differences. There are clear patterns to the loss – or often the deliberate destruction – of languages, and more often than not this pattern of loss is determined by the encounter between those two fundamental ways of being in the world.

Postcolonialism is quick to lament the loss of language, but it often fudges the awkward questions. It is not at all interested, for example, in the ways in which immigrants to the Americas, many of them fleeing colonial regimes of one sort or another, discarded their mother tongue in favour of the language (English or French or Spanish or Portuguese) of the settler society. We can say this is part of the coercion of colonialism, of course, but that does not get us around certain difficult questions, some of which we now face across Canada. They have to do not only with the difficulty of reconciling the English and French languages but also with the dilemma facing all nonhomogeneous societies: how to reconcile attachments to land with allegiances to language, and how to accommodate different allegiances and attachments, different lands and languages, within a single community. This problem bears on the situation of settlers, whose relationships with land and language may be the one thing of value they bring with them when they leave their homeland and the most useless of commodities when they arrive. But the most compelling expression of this conflict, and it seems to be the most intractable, is to be found in Aboriginal claims to land and language. In what sense are they negotiable, first of all? If they are, should claims to land determine the status of language, or the other way around? The ethical problems, and the practical quality of life difficulties in dealing with them, come into clearest focus when the quantities, as it were, are either very large or very small. An Aboriginal community that had jurisdiction over a very large area of land might insist that its language prevail there. Why would this be so troublesome? It is a version, perhaps, of the troubles associated with claims to French language rights in Quebec. At the other extreme, if the land claimed is negligible or the language is spoken by only a few, then why take such pains to preserve it? Small pieces of land are often identified as sacred sites, places where the spirits dwell, the locus of past, present, and future power. Should the same be said of small pieces of language ... that they are sacred sites, as it were? Certainly there are texts – the condolence ceremony of the Cayuga, the Gitksan and Nisga'a *ada'ox*, certain Haida songs – that are known by only a few remaining Native speakers. What is lost if and when they are lost? This is a perennial question; it is a profoundly Canadian one too. And it is at the centre of a set of questions of daily significance in the lives of our communities, questions that both move out in concentric circles and return us to that archetypal and historical encounter between hunter-gatherer and agricultural peoples and the ensuing conflicts over use and occupancy of the land, the division of the world into savage and civilized, the classification of cultures as oral or written, the distinction between ways of knowing and being.

Postcolonialism is also extremely uncomfortable addressing what might be called the internal colonialisms of a tradition – the ways in which, for example, the old can render the young speechless or the form of a story or song can shape or skew its subject. I think of a story from a quite different tradition, that of the Rastafarian communities of Jamaica. There are a number of plays and novels that reflect Rasta life and language, one of the most memorable being *The Harder They Come* (1980) by Michael Thelwell. It was inspired by a film of that title written by Perry Henzell and Trevor Rhone (and directed and produced by Henzell), which told the story of a legendary reggae songwriter, ganja trader, and gunman named Rhygin. In an article about the "translation" of the film to the novel form, Thelwell recounts his experiences and his anxieties. He quotes a particularly revealing conversation that took place when he was about halfway through the writing.

It was by way of a phone call from Jamaica: quite literally the voice of the audience, and calling about the work!

"Breddah Michael, we hear say you writing a book, is true?" The caller was Brother Sam, a poet-historian and theologian-in-residence with the Mystic Revelation of Ras Tafari, the very influential cultural ensemble centred on the master drummer and Rasta patriarch Count Ossie, who had recently died. Naturally I was surprised and very pleased – vindicated really – by this unexpected expression of interest from this militant of grassroots culture. I started to babble on about how very touched I was that he had called all this way and to explain the project, only to be cut off. (The call was, after all, much too expensive for pleasantries.)

"Dass all right Breddah Mike. Soun good. De book is bout us, right? Den dat mean the Count mus in dere, seen?" The phrasing was a little ambiguous, a question but not a question. It was too early. I wasn't quite sure I understood. So he explained.

"I an I the brederin say hear you doing dis mighty work, seen? Well den, we the brederin checking to mek sure that Count Ossie will get his due and rightful place derein. So long as it about us, the Count supposed to be in dere. True?"

"Wait, is dat you calling me for?" The tone of hurt indignation was not just tactical on my part. "My brother, you really believe say I could write a book about yard, and leave out the Count?"

"Well, not to say you would leave 'im out, but ..."

"Well, you can tell the brederin that the Count will certainly be in there. Seen, Iyah?"

Then, realizing that I might be making too hasty and sweeping a commitment, I felt compelled to launch into a discussion of the constraints of literary form. I explained at some length, and into a silence that somehow seemed to deepen as I spoke, that were I indeed doing a social or cultural study Count Ossie would inevitably have to be a major figure. Which was quite true. But this was a *novel*. And while I would wish the Count to be in it, and would certainly put him in if it proved possible, it would have to fit the context, and I couldn't categorically guarantee that the opportunity would present itself, or that if it did the Count would be as prominent as the brederin would wish. So much depended on the dictates of form, considerations of narrative structure, historical chronology, and the like.

"Surely you understand, my brother," I implored into the by now unnerving silence, fully aware of how fatuous and arty-farty I sounded as my words echoed back to my own ears. But in Sam there was neither mercy nor absolution.

"Understan?" he mimicked contemptuously. "Understan what? Stan under you mean. Iman must stand under say de man want to give praises and thanks to the Count, but it depend pon *form*? Pon *narrative struck-chah*? Pon *fictional integrity*? Tell me something, mi Lion?"

"Yes?" I asked timidly.

"Tell me dis – is who writing who? *Is you writing de book, or de book writing you?*"

And he did not wait for an answer, a kindness probably not intentional. For a long time after that, I was haunted by a vision of Sam dramatically recounting our conversation to the assembled brederin and concluding with apocalyptic solemnity, "Our brederin gann. Him laas. For is truly written, 'Many a foolish and heedless Ithiopian shall go down with Babylon.'"[7]

Still, the account that postcolonialism gives of the dispossession of land, language, and livelihood; of the dislocation of peoples, centres of power, modes of production; of the discrediting of meanings and values as well as of traditional forms and functions; and of the dynamics of disease – of mental unease as well as of physical distress – has been crucial to our understanding not only of the past and the present but also of possibilities for the future. Here I want to return once again to Australia and a comment by a *gubba* – a white man – named Bill Stanner, talking about the limits of language in a series of lectures he gave in 1969 that were gathered together under the title *After the Dreaming*.[8]

No English words are good enough to give a sense of the links between an Aboriginal group and its homeland. Our word "home," warm and suggestive though it be, does not match the Aboriginal word that may mean "camp," "hearth," "country," "everlasting home," "totem place," "life source," "spirit centre," and much else all in one. Our word "land" is too spare and meagre. We can now scarcely use it except with economic overtones unless we happen to be poets ... To put our words "home" and "land" together into "homeland" is a little better but not much. A different tradition leaves us tongueless and earless towards this other world of meaning and significance. When we took what we call "land" we took what to them meant hearth, home, the source and locus of life, and everlastingness of spirit. At the same time it left each local band bereft of an essential constant that made their plan and code of living intelligible. Particular pieces of territory, each a homeland, formed part of a set of constants without which no affiliation of any person, no link in the whole network of relationships, no part of the complex structure of social groups any longer had all its coordinates.

Stanner described the consequences as "a kind of vertigo in living":

> There was no more terrible part of our ... story than the herding together of broken tribes, under authority, and yoked by new regulations, into set- tlements and institutions as substitute homes. The word "vertigo" is of course metaphor, but I do not think it misleading. In New Guinea some of the cargocultists used to speak of "head-he-go-round-men" and "belly- don't-know-men." They were referring to a kind of spinning nausea into which they were flung by a world which seemed to have gone off its bearings. I think that something like that may well have affected many of the homeless aborigines.[9]

There is no discounting the terrors of this condition, which others can speak of with much more authority than I. But I want to add to this another anecdote, also from Australia, which opens up to my concluding remarks and opens up hope. It's from a book called *Kulinma*, which means "keep listening," by a man named Nugget Coombs.[10] I met him when he was in his eighties, and he was still at the centre of the struggle for Abo- riginal sovereignty. He told of an encounter, some years earlier, with what he described as "a rather broken down and derelict group of old chaps" in western Australia who were complaining that nickel mining had destroyed their tribe's sacred sites.

> We set out in a rather broken down old truck, shot a few kangaroos for food and went to Wingelina. There they took me to the sites, sacred to them and to their ancestors and to see the damage that had been caused ... As the day progressed there was an obvious increase in stature, an increase in authority in these men. Increasingly I became conscious of being a learner, someone who was being instructed in a mystery of infi- nite complexity ... We went out that night and sat in a circle in the sand with two or three fires between us as they sang [one of the song cycles about their ancestors]. The songs were sung in a kind of Gregorian chant style melody while the rhythm of the song was beaten into the sand with a stick ... In that circle I realised that these people, whom I had presumed to pity, had dignity and authority backed by a tradition infinitely older than our own.[11]

For all its litany of devastation and deprivation, postcolonial theory ultimately comes to rest on this belief: that there are things that have survived, that they do have power, that the margins are in fact the centres, and that the tidy alternatives that colonialism has somehow persuaded us to accept – between the worthy and the worthless, for example – are extremely hazardous and in every sense ultimately unholy. *And* that, if we don't get about understanding this, then we'll be living not a riddle, where two truths co-exist, but a lie, where we give up on trying to reconcile them. And they *do* need reconciling or reframing, for there *are* distinctions. All societies, including all Aboriginal societies, make them, and some even try to impose them on others. But they are notoriously contingent on cultural assumptions, and postcolonial theory has drawn our attention to the ways in which the framing of categories on the one hand can create an illusion of absolute meanings and values where these are only relative, and on the other can mask universal attitudes and beliefs by generating an array of apparently unique particulars or "differences."

One of the most debilitating choices that colonialism seems to have imposed on us, and that the academy of which I am a part sustains, is the choice between oral and written traditions, or between oral and written cultures. I want to say bluntly that there is no such thing as an oral culture, or a written culture, at least in the way in which these terms have come down to us from colonialism. This doesn't mean that there are not cultures whose primary forms of poetic and political expression are oral or written. But the fact is that we should be deeply uncertain about where to draw the line between oral and written traditions and indeed about whether there should be any lines at all. Every culture has eyes and ears, as it were, and the woven and beaded belts and blankets, the carved and painted trays, the poles, doors, veranda posts, canes and sticks, masks, hats, and chests that are variously part of many oral performances among Aboriginal peoples, especially those central to sacred or secular traditions ... *these* forms of writing are often just as important as the stories and songs. Every culture not only sees things but also *reads* them, whether in the stars or in the sand, whether spelled out by alphabet or animal, whether communicated across natural or supernatural boundaries. No hunter-gatherer society would last the year without sophisticated traditions of interpreting and evaluating written signs, and most such societies have generated forms of nonalphabetic writing (often in ancient days sufficiently sophisticated that we still haven't figured them out), using knotted and coloured strings, beads, and various performative and pictographic designs.

At the same time, every culture not only hears but also *listens* to things – one of the problems being that we are not very good at doing so across times and places and across cultures. In my own culture, which ostensibly is a written culture dedicated to the privileges of written texts, I spend much of my professional life *talking* about writing, and the most important institutions of this culture – the churches, the courts, and the parliaments

– are places where speech has a considerable presence. Separating oral and written traditions into tidy oppositions is like separating the worthy and the worthless. It is a debilitating preoccupation, about a foolish choice, between false alternatives. Like the alternative between separation and assimilation, grimly familiar to Aboriginal peoples in Canada. It is like giving someone a choice between being isolated and being overwhelmed, between being marooned on an island and drowned in the sea. Nobody should have to make that choice. Those of us who profess postcolonial theory and who try to put it into practice should ensure that nobody has to make such choices. We have not been doing our job, and to pretend that a choice between oral and written traditions is a real choice is to play right into the hands of those who benefit from these kinds of false alternatives.

In saying all this, I am not discounting how many imperial cultures have discredited the oral traditions of colonized Indigenous peoples, often in ways that have deeply damaged their viability in *both* of these worlds – the real world and the world of the imagination – to which I referred earlier. One of the central challenges that postcolonial theory presents to us is to counteract this, and one of the ways of doing this is to delineate the ways in which oral traditions have been misrepresented. Briefly, this misrepresentation tends to take one of two forms. First of all, there are the theories based on cultural typologies or on categories of mental aptitude that are essentially determined by evolutionary or developmental paradigms. These have produced conceptions of "oral cultures" and of orality that more or less presume a natural or historical development toward writing and literacy – which is to say, toward sophisticated thought and civilized behaviour. In their extreme form, these theories are pretty well discredited now, but (through the enormous impact of scholars such as Marshall McLuhan and Walter Ong) they have shaped most popular and some professional accounts of oral and written traditions over the past fifty years. And they continue to lurk within the terminology we use to describe those who do not possess what we call writing or who cannot read written texts. Their unwritten past is "prehistory," and they are "preliterate" ... or, even more negatively, "nonliterate" or "illiterate." Along with poverty and disease, these have become the conditions of the deprived in the contemporary lexicon.

Thus, people are inclined to think of oral traditions as less evolved than written traditions and of communities in which oral traditions flourish as correspondingly less developed – socially, culturally, and perhaps emotionally and intellectually. Or, as McLuhan put it, such communities exhibit that "utter inhibition and suppression of mental and personal life which is unavoidable in a non-literate world." (McLuhan relied for much of his information about such traditions on the written words of one J.C. Carothers, who ran the Mathari Mental Hospital near Nairobi during the 1940s and wrote books with titles like *The African Mind in Health and Disease,* published in 1953.) It is one thing to diminish the status of oral texts by considering them primarily as documents. It is quite another to discredit the societies whose lives they shape by considering them as condemned to the darkness of orality – the heart of darkness, in fact, for in McLuhan's own ostensibly enlightened phrasing the printed word has a "crucial role in staying the return to the Africa within" us.[12] This is pretty dubious stuff. It has also been immensely influential. Scarcely a day goes by that I don't hear one or two traces of it in conversation.

The second set of theories, "noble savage" New Age versions of the primitive typological ones, exaggerates rather than underrates the authority of oral traditions. In these theories, societies that claim an oral tradition – which for this purpose seems to include all Aboriginal and (in European terms) many "other" (that is, African and Asian) peoples – are celebrated for the refreshing vitality and natural power of their expression and for their freedom from the imperial corruptions and degenerate artifices of written forms. This is just as silly and just as influential.

There is no doubt that this kind of nonsense has taken its toll and continues to plague many of our discussions. Nobody with any experience of either oral or written traditions would buy fully into either. But there is a continuing attachment to both. In a sense, this is understandable. Oral traditions, like all traditions of expression, are closely involved in the conditions of their language. In the case of many Aboriginal peoples, this includes the conditions of dispossession and dislocation that they have experienced. In this scenario, it is fairly easy to take their oral traditions as reflections not so much of their primitive condition as of either their previously pure or their lately degenerate state, depending on the theory ... to which we then respond with either colonial superiority or postcolonial indignation.

Oral texts have suffered in another way, from our tendency to look through or around or behind them, rather than to look *at* them in and for themselves. In this sense, McLuhan's insistence that "the medium is the message" was salutary, even though it was applied more to writing and other forms of graphic expression than to speaking. Nevertheless, it reinvigorated the idea that texts (of any kind) are never just transparent agents of abstract meanings. Their material presence also generates meanings of some (usually a very significant) sort. This is especially so in oral traditions, where composition and performance in some measure constitute the end rather than merely the means of the communication.

It's no accident that many of the most profound truths are approached by negatives or by nonsense. In the religious tradition in which I was raised, one of the great hymns describes the Creator as immortal, invisible, inaccessible, unresting, unhasting ... and then, in a final bit of inspired nonsense, as silent as light. This is where language, and its ultimate agency for survival and power, come to rest. On the unspeakable. On the ways in which language reveals, rather than expresses, meaning. And on the ways in which it comes down to matters of belief rather than of truth.

Whether someone else believes what you say and do is much less important than whether you believe it. That's postcolonial theory at its purest and surest. And what it reminds us of, too, getting back to language, is that we all need – and we all have – a grammar of assent, a way of saying *yes*. Now *that's* a word with power. Postcolonial theory, I hope, is ultimately less about finding ways of saying no and more about finding ways of saying yes.

Notes

1 Derek Walcott, "Forest of Europe," *The Star-Apple Kingdom* (New York: Farrar, Straus and Giroux, 1979), 38-9.
2 Ibid. 40.
3 Lewis Meriam, *The Problem of Indian Administration* (Baltimore: Johns Hopkins University Press, 1928).
4 Reeseman Fryer, "Erosion, Poverty, and Dependency: Memoir of My Time in Navajo Service, 1933-1942" (December 1986). Unpublished.
5 From correspondence between Mindy Christiansen and Harold McGill, Calgary, July 14, 1933 (Exhibit No. 428/Exam. Leask in *Apssasin et al.* v. *The Queen* [Federal Court, Vancouver, 1986]), and the Field Notebooks of Mindy Christiansen, Notebook #2 (Glenbow Museum Archives, Christiansen Notebooks, BLC555).
6 Memorandum from Harold McGill, Deputy Superintendent General, to Thomas Murphy, Superintendent General of Indian Affairs, Ottawa, September 6, 1934 (Glenbow Museum Archives, McGill Papers, M742, f. 59).
7 Michael Thelwell, "The Harder They Come: From Film to Novel. How Questions of Technique, Form, Language, Craft, and the Marketplace Conceal Issues of Politics, Audience, Culture, and Purpose," *Grand Street* 37 (1991): 150-1.
8 W.E.H. Stanner, *After the Dreaming* (Sydney: Australian Broadcasting Corporation, 1969).
9 Ibid. 44-5.
10 H.C. Coombs, *Kulinma: Listening to Aboriginal Australians* (Canberra: Australian National University Press, 1978).
11 Ibid. 32.
12 From Marshall McLuhan, *The Making of Typographic Man* (Toronto: University of Toronto Press, 1962), 18, 45. Cited in Leroy Vail and Landeg White, *Power and the Praise Poem: Southern African Voices in History* (London: James Currey, 1991), 19.

10

The "Repressive Tolerance" of Cultural Peripheries

Asha Varadharajan

I find myself in the unusual position of advocating multiculturalism to an audience focused on the preservation and restoration of Indigenous cultures. My status as the migrant who negotiates between cultures seems curiously privileged when contrasted with that of Indigenous peoples who must consort with one world that is dead and another that remains powerless to be born. As I write this, however, I am immediately confronted by the realization that even if the nightmare of history for the Indigenous peoples of the world has been one of dispossession and deracination, it has simultaneously been the story of survival and spiritual regeneration – indeed, of the power of memory and invention. I hope that the experiences I can offer, although different from those of Indigenous peoples, suggest fruitful avenues for further investigation.

The multicultural worldview, because it emerges from the experience of migration and displacement, might initially seem like anathema to Indigenous peoples, whose worldviews are firmly rooted in a particular place. I think, however, that policies of evacuation, reservation, and decimation have created for Aboriginal peoples predicaments similar to those that confront migrant populations. Neither group is content to settle for empty nostalgia or idealized recollections of a lost organic community. I would like to suggest that for both groups there is now a movement afoot from restoration to reinvention, from traumatic repetition to healing and renewal.

Even though I am offering my comments from a multicultural perspective, I hope that my account of cultural and political negotiation with and resistance to inescapably Eurocentric models of value, education, and institution will spark productive moments of contention and insight that will illuminate desires and interests of Indigenous peoples. I share, after all, a history of colonization with them, even if its particular trajectory has been different in my country of origin and in my personal history. My vision for Canada, despite continuing evidence to the contrary, is an affirmative one. Because colonization in all its complexity affects all our lives on many levels, from the trivial to the profound, the process of decolonization cannot but be equally intricate and multidimensional. There is hope when we have the courage to reject quick fixes motivated by self-interest and embrace instead systemic, radical, regenerative, and communal change.

I will attempt to correct some misconceptions about multiculturalism and outline some of the unpalatable consequences of the way Canada has institutionalized racial and cultural differences. The polarizations that have structured the recent debates in the United States might prove instructive in our own context even as they reveal the pervasive *invisibility* of systemic inequities in Canada. Although I do not deny the importance of the social and economic inequities that prevent many students from entering institutions of higher learning, this chapter focuses on what happens *within* academic institutions, and on the manner in which these institutions, not altogether unwittingly, replicate the world without. I will also address the complications that arise from having a relatively small proportion of faculty from minority cultures in many institutions.

Let me begin with Michael Berubé's (1992) parody of the hysterical reactions of opponents of political correctness: "Readers who've followed the tortuous course of political correctness (PC) in the national press now know that there is no American intellectual community so benighted and blinkered as that of young faculty members in the humanities ... We 'reduce' knowledge to power, we read 'narrowly' for the ideological ramifications of literary texts. Yes, we plot no less than the destruction of the West" (124-5).

Berubé's wit, however, is careful not to obscure the seriousness of the charges levelled at proponents of curricular and institutional reform. The attempt by postcolonial critics to demonstrate the exclusionary biases of the Western intellectual tradition is, I think, in keeping with the critical spirit of that tradition. Yet it seems that in this debate, intellectuals are once again forced to identify with Culture fighting a losing battle against Anarchy. Established intellectuals have accused the "Visigoths in Tweed" (Dinesh D'Souza, as cited in Berman 1992, 125) of unilaterally rejecting Western culture and values, of dismantling the bases of aesthetic taste and judgment, of demanding attention to other cultures solely on the grounds of their historical victimization, and of turning education into a form of therapy, a touchy-feely route to self-esteem. All these charges are merely effects of the perception that the classroom is not the site of political transformation. In Irving Howe's ironic perception, those who wish to take over the world are ridiculously engaged in taking over English departments instead (Berman 1992, 153-72).

The unsavoury history of Canada's treatment of its Indigenous peoples and of its immigration policies – as well as the unmistakable presence of those who are sometimes patronizingly referred to as "visible minorities" – have in part been responsible for Canada's interest in engaging cultural differences. This interest has led to the idea of a cultural mosaic as distinct from a cultural melting pot, such as is found south of the border. All parts of the mosaic, however, are not created equal. The mosaic occasionally implies satellite cultures revolving around the two founding cultures or invokes the concept of unity in diversity, neither of which negates the peripheral status of "other" cultures. Even if one envisaged the mosaic as a whole that exceeded the sum of its parts, the opposite would not be permissible: that is, the parts could not exceed the whole and are more or less contained by it.

The problem is that there is often little to distinguish the process of integration from the process of assimilation, with its concomitant erasure of cultural distinction. Since Canada's claims to identity rest on its attempts to distinguish itself from the United States, the "official" representation of Canada is itself one of non-identity – in its most abject form, even one of non-entity (my apologies to the Mounties, ice hockey, toques, and beer). The contradiction between the ironic self-deprecation with which Canada represents itself on the outside and the demonstrable power differentials in the materiality of its existence on the inside only serves to cloud the issue further. In short, the grinning pluralism that the notion of harmonious diversity conjures up precludes the possibility of genuine difference – indeed, of dissidence. Multiculturalism should not be viewed as a state of quiescence. It should be envisaged as a domain full of conflict in which dominant and minority cultures contest meanings, identities, values, and interests on a regular basis. This characterization is not to be confused with a desire to foment hostility; rather, my intention is to insist upon the fraught nature of struggles for self-definition and equity, upon the difficulty they present and the intricate attention they demand.

Scholars of colour have resisted the homogenization of the "Third World" in Western discourse by calling for an acknowledgment of the fundamental differences between and within Third World nations. They have argued, simultaneously, that Third World cultures must be granted an existence independent of their erstwhile colonizers. They believe that the identity of these cultures should be formed in the process of contending with their own imperatives rather than in the process of reacting to colonial ones. Postcolonial critics are challenging Western critical frameworks on the grounds that they alienate members of Third World cultures from their own realities, induce slavish conformity on the part of postcolonial intellectuals (who should know better than to collaborate with their masters), and remain deaf to "Native" responses to the Western critical reception of texts as well as to the texts themselves. These polemicists categorically reject any attempt to make postcolonial literatures universally accessible and relentlessly expose the problems that emerge when texts from one culture are interpreted by readers from another.

Postcolonial critics also argue that seeking shared points of reference in the experience of colonization is a mistake because focusing on shared experiences obscures the difference, for example, between settler and Indigenous cultures, between civilizations that were deemed decadent (for example, India and the so-called Orient) and those that were deemed primitive or savage (for example, Africa). It is to be hoped that the realization that cultures are not interchangeable might force critical discourse to refrain from glib comparisons or gestures towards the essential brotherhood of "man" and make a sensitivity to other ways of apprehending the world possible instead.

The provocative energy of postcolonial criticism, however, occasionally produces overstatements that stall the move towards cultural translation. Cultures often congeal into static contradictions or stark oppositions that solidly confront each other. If the conflict is to be between the West and the rest, both are in danger of becoming impenetrable monoliths simply inconceivable or incommunicable to each other. This situation produce a paradox: "the West" can safely introduce a policy of "benign neglect" (see Mukherjee 1988) of other cultures because to do otherwise would only produce monstrous distortions of truth. As for "the rest," they must deny an ineradicable history of cultural imperialism that has made of them "mimic men" (V.S. Naipaul 1967), and they are left with no means of challenging Western misconceptions because the West would not understand them anyway. Neither side of the equation is granted the possibility of transcending its own limits, of imagining a world other than its own.

Just as it is a mistake to see Third World cultures as undifferentiated from each other, so it is a mistake to see the West as homogenous. Such misconceptions serve to entrench perennial themes rather than allowing individual cultures to develop into dynamic registers of historical and social becoming. I dwell on this misrepresentation of the Western tradition not because I want to reassure my colonizers that their lessons were not lost on me, but because I think such misrepresentation reduces resistance to a simple conflict between us and them. Cultural analysis, then, is reduced to seeking confirmation for what it has already discerned or for notions that the intellectual tradition already possesses. Ironically, therefore, postcolonial critics occasionally confirm what they attack – the self cannot help but iron out the wrinkles in the cultural constitution of whatever it perceives to be other. In order to align oneself with a political constituency of any kind, one becomes subject to prescribed choices that preclude the possibility of a form of opposition that caricatures neither the West nor the rest.

The increasing presence of postcolonial intellectuals or native informants in academia has led to a conflation of postcolonial interests with multicultural ones. This conflation seems to me a historical and categorical mistake. Decolonization in the Third World cannot be confused with the struggle of the "empire within," to use Salman Rushdie's (1991) phrase, even if the pressures of the global economy and the exigencies of modernity apply to both. For the purposes of this discussion, however, I would like to comment on the differences between experiences of migration within the multicultural community.

As Ali Behdad (1993) argues in "Traveling to Teach: Postcolonial Critics in the American Academy," the contemporary world seems inseparable from spatial mobility. This has particular consequences within the multicultural community. While geographical displacement distinguishes both immigrant communities in metropolises and the cosmopolitan immigrant intellectuals who presumably represent the interests of these immigrant communities, the privileges of access to the culture of imperialism do not accrue to both. Whereas the mobility of the intellectuals gives them the privilege of access to another culture, mobility at the community level merely makes these communities displaced.

Although immigrant intellectuals function as oppositional consciousnesses in universities, their resemblance to their perceived constituencies is forced at best. S.S. Sisodia's (Rushdie's character in *The Satanic Verses*) wry comment "The trouble with the Engenglish is that their hiss hiss history happened overseas, so they dodo don't know what it means" (1988, 343) is echoed in the reverse traffic from the colonies to the metropolitan centres. Behdad alludes to a T-shirt slogan that reads "We are here because you were there" to underscore the opposition to "racist images of 'swarthy aliens' flooding Western metropolises" (1993, 41). The conditions of displacement and transplantation produce, for the privileged immigrant intellectual elite, a fluid situation in which they can play with cultural boundaries, attest to the superior insight that the position of exile accords them, and revel in the plurality of subject positions afforded them. What is often missing among the intellectual elite is a trenchant sense of the economic and cultural disenfranchisement to which diasporic communities are subject, as well as of the pain of cultural dislocation. The struggles of Indigenous peoples within nations cannot be confused with migrant forms of estrangement, even though both communities seem condemned to a form of "uneven development" in the circulation of global capital. This state of affairs may well give them reason to combine forces against the enforced anomie they suffer.

The "split narratives" of migration experienced by the elite and the rest of the immigrant community have been expressed eloquently by Sarat Maharaj: "The one recounts entry into the Western world, becoming part of its modernity, its thrills, speeds, sensations, drifting with its fashions of life and living ... The second tale speaks of those who arrived in the modern West only to find themselves left behind by it, marooned, cut off within it" (as cited in Behdad 1993, 45). This savage discrepancy is exacerbated by a concomitant situation – second- or third-generation immigrants often bear little or no vital relation to the languages or cultures their ancestors left behind. They are sometimes subject to a form of cultural sclerosis in which their alienation manifests itself as a desperate clinging to cultural icons or rituals divorced from their contexts. They then are forced to deem their inevitable assimilation or the necessary amorphousness of their identities reprehensible, or to deny their pleasure in "Canadian" culture. For these people, hybridity or the continual process of cultural negotiation might actually be liberating, and Canada's vaunted non-identity might be fertile ground for the production of new forms of identity. Besides, the uncertainty of boundaries can also create the possibility of unexpected community, of coalitions that traverse the divides of class, gender, and race. I am not donning my Pollyanna hat at the expense of my Chicken Little one; I am merely suggesting an alternative approach to multicultural identity, one that does not view contradictions as always and necessarily debilitating.

I have composed this deliberately informal narrative in order to offer possibilities for exploration rather than to draw conclusions. I would like to conclude by suggesting avenues for discussion that I hope are useful to a laudable attempt to implement multicultural education. I offer the ensuing comments from the perspective of a female intellectual who veers between despair and optimism in her attempts to negotiate institutional authority.

First, the confusion of multiculturalism with political correctness, with a mealy-mouthed sop to guilty consciences, has precluded genuine debate. The "thought police" – as multiculturalists have often been called – are anything but. In their best moments they endorse a critical and scrupulously historical scrutiny of intellectual traditions. They insist on the self-scrutiny to which traditions routinely subject themselves in order to avoid attributing a false coherence to canonical forms. They do not engage in an empty valorization of subjugated cultures; instead, they restore these cultures to history and accord them their rightful status as dynamic, flawed entities subject to change. Because the history of modern colonization shows that cultures defined themselves in relation to each other, multiculturalists insist that imperial cultures should not be privileged over their subjects and should not constitute the frame of reference for anthropological analysis. While they rarely apologize for their interest in the dialectic of power and resistance, they are alive to the mixture of force, fraud, and consent that characterizes most social relations. All this is by way of saying that the intention is not to substitute one culture for another or to declare Western culture guilty until proven innocent but to see their interactions as a dialogue. This dialogue, however, does not prevent scholars from determining the often destructive power of Western concepts or, for example, from exploring the alarming implications of transnational capital and the unequal distribution of resources. The attempt, in short, is to interrogate the functioning of the West as a normative category, and to question the colonialism that survives the demise of empires (Ashis Nandy's [1983] phrase).

Second, Gerald Graff (1992), in his characteristically liberal fashion, proposes that English departments organize themselves around the teaching of ideological conflicts so that students are not excluded from the debate and have a stake in its outcome and representation. This seems a plausible solution, particularly because students and professors are often unconscious repositories of the assumptions that shape canon formation even if they do not always know the contents of this framework or if they cannot recognize any of the items in E.D. Hirsch's (1987) catalogue of cultural literacy.

Third, as a native informant of sorts, I have to be wary of colluding in the attempt to turn Third World literatures into raw material for the consumption of a literary tradition sorely in need of rejuvenation. I also have to be wary of being turned into the quintessentially exotic representative of "all things colourful and spicy" (Janaki Bakhle's phrase). As many have pointed out, minority faculty members are automatically presumed to teach minority disciplines, and little attempt is made to hire them to teach canonical fields. A subtle denigration of the scholarship and training necessary to communicate cultural differences is afoot here – a woman requires no training to be a feminist scholar, and so on. Teachers of postcolonial literatures are expected to "cover" the globe in isolation while three or four scholars work on individual historical periods of the Western literary tradition. Team teaching often does not solve the problem because race and gender complicate the issue – against their best intentions, white male professors come off as hip individuals with social conscience while female professors of colour are relegated to the status of victims who cannot get over themselves and bring their personal problems into classroom situations.

Fourth, my experience of teaching and working in racially homogneous intellectual environments has also acquainted me with the quixotic nature of my predicament. I am still routinely complimented on the fluency of my English at academic conferences in the same instant as my students mark speech communication as especially in need of improvement in my teaching evaluations. My failure to conform to the typology of an immigrant who, in the words of one of my interlocutors, has just stepped off the boat reduces my credibility even further. I do not wish to turn this into a confessional narrative, but I hope some of these examples suggest what racial and sexual markers signify and that those meanings are often at odds with the ones we want students to discover. This contradiction between intellectual authority and personal identity only reinforces the nagging feeling that native informants embody a docile version of difference, one that institutions can readily accommodate. The encounter with diversity, as many have already discovered, cannot be confined to ghettoized courses in which students and faculty perform as tourists; instead, cultural difference must function (dare I say it?) as a universal principle. I hesitate to say cultural pluralism because it could produce a curriculum modelled on the principle of accretion — that is, a curriculum produced simply by adding cultures while leaving structural hierarchies essentially unchanged.

And fifth, I want to argue for a version of cultural difference that is not simply a matter of individual style or costume or of a formal hybridity without content, but becomes the informing principle of a mode of anti-colonial dissent and of a vision of an anti-racist future. In this regard, intellectuals and critics must continually highlight their cultural, social, economic, and sexual determinants. Not only would such institutional practice align intellectual production and dissemination with ethical and political accountability, but it would also subject claims of universality and objectivity to the tests of history and of otherness.

References

Behdad, Ali. 1993. "Traveling to Teach: Postcolonial Critics in the American Academy." In Warren Crochlow and Cameron McCarthy, eds., *Race, Identity, and Representation in Education*, 40-50. New York: Routledge.

Berman, Paul, ed. 1992. *Debating P.C.: The Controversy over Political Correctness on College Campuses*. New York: Bantam.

Berubé, Michael. 1992. "Public Image Limited: Political Correctness and the Media's Big Lie." In Paul Berman, ed., *Debating P.C.: The Controversy over Political Correctness on College Campuses*, 129-49. New York: Bantam.

Graff, Gerald. 1992. *Beyond the Culture Wars: How Teaching the Conflicts can Revitalize American Education*. New York: W.W. Norton.

Hirsch, E.D. 1987. *Cultural Literacy: What Every American Needs to Know*. Boston: Houghton Mifflin.

Howe, Irving. 1992. "The Value of the Canon." In Paul Berman, ed., *Debating P.C.: The Controversy over Political Correctness on College Campuses*. New York: Bantam.

Mukherjee, Arun. 1988. *Towards an Aesthetics of Opposition: Essays on Literary Criticism and Cultural Imperialism*. Stratford, ON: Williams Wallace.

Naipaul, V.S. 1967. *The Mimic Men*. London: Deutsch.

Nandy, Ashis. 1983. *The Intimate Enemy: Loss and Recovery of Self under Colonialism*. Delhi: Oxford University Press.

Rushdie, Salman. 1988. *The Satanic Verses*. London: Viking.

–. 1991. *Imaginary Homelands: Essays and Criticism, 1981-1991*. New York: Viking.

11

Processes of Decolonization

Poka Laenui (Hayden F. Burgess)

Colonization and decolonization are social processes even more than they are political processes. Governance over a people changes only after the people themselves have sufficiently changed. This chapter presents observations on the process of colonization by the late Virgilio Enriques,[1] a Native son of the Philippines, an advocate for the integrity of Native wisdoms, and a professor emeritus of psychology at the University of the Philippines. The contribution from Professor Enriques is taken from my discussions with him in Wai'anae, Hawai'i, in the mid-1990s. Only portions of these discussions were recorded, and I confess to having expanded and expounded on this conversation over the years.

The process of decolonization described here follows that of colonization. My comments are based on my individual Hawai'i experience, my observation of others' experiences as they move from one phase of decolonization to the next, and my understanding of the broader societal experience in Hawai'i and of significant events that have taken place in the Pacific region and the rest of the world.

The Process of Colonization

Virgilio Enriques has suggested the following steps in the process of colonization.

(1) Denial and Withdrawal

When a colonial people first come upon an Indigenous people, the colonial strangers will immediately look upon the Indigenous people as lacking culture or moral values and having nothing of any social value to merit kind comment. Thus, the colonial people deny the very existence of a culture of any merit among the Indigenous people.

Indigenous people themselves, especially those who develop a closer relationship with the newcomers, gradually withdraw from their own cultural practices. Some may even join in the ridicule and the denial of the existence of culture among the Native people. They may become quickly converted and later lead in the criticism of Indigenous societies.

(2) Destruction/Eradication
The colonists take bolder action in step 2, physically destroying and attempting to eradicate all physical representations of the symbols of Indigenous cultures. This may include burning their art, their tablets, their god images, destroying their sacred sites, and so on. At times, the Indigenous people themselves may participate in this destruction – some may even lead in it.

(3) Denigration/Belittlement/Insult
As colonization takes a stronger hold, the new systems created within Indigenous societies, such as churches, colonial-style health delivery systems, and new legal institutions, will all join to denigrate, belittle, and insult any continuing practice of the Indigenous culture. Churches will style Indigenous religious practices as "devil" worship and condemn practitioners to physical torture or their souls to hell. Colonially trained medical practitioners will refer to Indigenous doctors as witches if their medicine is successful and as ignorant, superstitious fools if their medicine fails. The new legal institutions will criminalize the traditional practices and fine the practitioners, and they may declare illegal the possession of traditionally sacred or healing materials.

In this stage, symbols of evil must be imported by the colonizer in order for evil to gain legitimacy within the society. Thus, in many colonized societies, we find the importation of Dracula, Hallowe'en, or other representations of evil through the colonial societies' literature or legends, while the colonizers allude to the Indigenous peoples' representations of evil as ignorant superstitions.

(4) Surface Accommodation/Tokenism
In this stage of colonization, whatever remnants of culture that have survived the onslaught of the earlier steps are given surface accommodation. They are tolerated as an exhibition of the colonial regime's sense of leniency to the continuing ignorance of the Natives. These practices are called folkloric: "showing respect to the old folks and to tradition." They are given token regard.

(5) Transformation/Exploitation
The traditional culture that simply refuses to die or go away is now transformed into the culture of the dominating colonial society. A Christian church may now use an Indigenous person as a priest, permitting the priest to use the Indigenous language and to incorporate some Indigenous

terms and practices within the church's framework of worship. Indigenous art that has survived may gain in popularity and form the basis for economic exploitation. Indigenous symbols in print may decorate modern dress. Indigenous musical instruments may be incorporated into modern music. Supporting Indigenous causes within the general colonial structure may become the popular political thing to do, exploiting the culture further. This exploitation may be committed by Indigenous as well as non-Indigenous people.

Processes of Decolonization

I suggest five distinct phases of a people's decolonization. They are (1) *rediscovery and recovery,* (2) *mourning,* (3) *dreaming,* (4) *commitment,* and (5) *action.* Each phase can be experienced at the same time or in various combinations. Like the steps of colonization, these phases of decolonization do not have clear demarcations from one to the next.

Rediscovery and Recovery

This phase sets the foundation for the eventual decolonization of the society. People who have undergone colonization are inevitably suffering from concepts of inferiority in relation to their historical cultural/social background. They live in a colonial society that is a constant and overwhelming reminder of the superiority of that society over the underlying Indigenous one.

A person or a society may enter the stage of rediscovery and recovery for many different reasons. It may be out of curiosity or desperation, by accident or coincidence, to escape, or because of fate.

As a volunteer member of the US military, I came across a book at a military base library in Hawai'i, written by Queen Lili'uokalani, which started my entry into this phase of decolonization. Whether by accident or fate, I was curious enough to take it from the shelf and examine the words left by Hawaii's queen about fifty-five years earlier, telling of the conspiracy and overthrow of the Hawaiian nation. Having come upon these words, I could not let the matter alone. I had to take up my own study of my history, which I had never known before. I read and interviewed every source of information that I could find on Hawaii's history and Hawaiian cultural foundations.

Hawaiian society has been in this phase since the late 1960s, when greater sensitivity to racial identity and pride as well as growing distrust of the US government developed. The black struggle for equality in civil rights, the American Indian struggle for fundamental freedoms and recognition as the first people of the land, as well as the growing challenge to the righteousness of the US war in Vietnam played a major part in bringing Hawai'i to the recovery and rediscovery stage. Those challenges to the US government and its society showed us in Hawai'i that the great American society was not so great after all!

Around this time, information began to appear in Hawai'i about the overthrow of the Hawaiian nation in the latter 1800s by the US government: information about US government agents conspiring with residents in Hawai'i, many of whom were American citizens; American military spying while the government pretended to have no interest in grabbing Hawai'i; and US troops landing and acting as the military support for a puppet government. The disbelief and yet the complete inability to disregard the information stunned the general society. This was reflected in an interruption of the first criminal case in modern time that challenged the US court's jurisdiction over a Hawaiian citizen.[2] When defence counsel read President Cleveland's message to the US Congress[3] confessing to a litany of aggressive acts, circuit court judge John Lanham said that it was the most fantastic story he had ever heard, yet he could not deny the events having happened, since the words were taken from the US Congressional Record. Lanham was no neophyte to Hawai'i, having married a Native Hawaiian woman and served in the state legislature for many years and sitting, at the time, as a judge in the state circuit court.

As the rediscovery phase continued, new vigour in Hawaiian music and literature, both traditional and modern, added substantially to the recovery of pride. Social and political activities took on new momentum. Hawaiians were now willing to stand up against members of Hawaii's Supreme Court in their appointment of trustees to the Bishop Estate Trust, a nonprofit entity designed to educate Native Hawaiian students, with extensive assets of land throughout Hawai'i. There were new challenges to evictions of Native Hawaiians from beaches and valleys and challenges to the abuse of the island of Kaho'olawe as a US military bombing range. As this platform of discontent and awareness began to build, a plethora of new organizations emerged, pushing to the forefront the illegality of the overthrow of Hawai'i.

The phase of rediscovery and recovery has not ended. Many people are still "getting up to speed," not knowing many of the details but generally acquiescing to the overall theme of a grand illegality having occurred in Hawai'i 100 years ago – the theft of the Hawaiian nation.[4]

This phase of rediscovering one's history and recovering one's culture, language, identity, and so on is fundamental to the movement for decolonization. It forms the basis for the steps to follow.

One of the dangers in this phase is the elevation of form over substance, of dealing with a traditional culture from the perspective of a foreign culture. Indigenous people themselves can abuse their own culture, especially when they have been so long and completely separated from the practice or appreciation of their traditional culture, which they now see and treat from the perspective of the foreign one. This danger is evident among those who have taken on the trappings of their "traditional" culture by wearing forests of leaves and flowers on their heads, speaking the Indigenous language (which they learned at colonial colleges), and otherwise playing to foreigners' concepts of the Indigenous person. Theatrics that make good media clips could eventually be mistaken for substance.

The difference, therefore, between the final stage of colonization – *exploitation* – and the initial stage of decolonization – *rediscovery and recovery* – must be carefully distinguished. Caution must be taken in letting media select for the colonized people the leadership or the identification of their cultural roots.

Mourning

A natural outgrowth of the first phase is mourning – a time when a people are able to lament their victimization. This is an essential phase of healing. Even in individual tragedies in which one is a victim of a crime, has experienced the death of a close loved one, or has suffered from a sexual assault, the victim must be permitted a time of mourning.[5]

As a young member of the US military, plodding through the mounds of history and recovering from a loss of Native identity, I experienced great anger, wanting to blow up the colonial system, take up arms to drive that very military out of my Native home. Others have expressed themselves in very similar ways, finding that they had been lied to for so many years while in the "educational" systems in Hawai'i. Their anger and frustration have ranged from throwing chairs across a room to roaming streets wanting to beat Americans to contemplating paramilitary action.

The symbolic mourning of the loss of the Hawaiian nation took place during the centennial observation of the overthrow, held at 'Iolani Palace, where there was a gathering of over 10,000 people. Over the weekend of January 16 and 17, 1993, people came from all parts of Hawai'i and returned from other parts of the world for this centennial observation. It served as a focal point for mourning by most of those touched in one or another way by the overthrow.[6] Many more people remained at home but were tied to their radios, televisions, or newspapers as reports came in of the events at the palace.

The mourning stage can also accelerate the earlier stage of rediscovery and recovery. People in mourning often immerse themselves totally in the rediscovery of their history, making for an interesting interplay between these two phases, each feeding on one another.

This phase may also be expressed in great anger and a lashing out at all symbols of the colonizer. A sense of justified violence, either in words or in actions, can lull some into remaining in this phase, milking every advantage of the innocence of one's victimization. This abuse of the mourning phase can turn into an attempt to entrench the colonization in order to continue the mourning, the anger, the hatred, and the division among people. Some people are happy to go no further than mourning, finding sufficient satisfaction in long-term grumbling. People can be "stuck in the awfulizing" of their status as victims. Some build careers on it.

Dreaming

This phase is the most crucial for decolonization. Here is where the full panorama of possibilities is expressed, considered through debate, consultation, and building dreams on further dreams, which eventually become the flooring for the creation of a new social order.

It is during this phase that colonized people are able to explore their own cultures, experience their own aspirations for their future, and consider their own structures of government and social order to encompass and express their hopes.

So crucial is this phase that it must be allowed to run its full course. If the dreaming is cut short by any action plan or program designed to create a remedy for the issue at a premature stage, then the result can prove disastrous.

I liken this phase to the formation of a fetus in a mother's womb. That fetus must be allowed its time to develop and grow to its full potential. To attempt to rush the process, bringing the baby out sooner than his or her natural time, could prove dangerous if not disastrous.

An examination of the Pacific as well as the world's decolonization pattern may be helpful. There are many instances in which people who underwent "decolonization" merely underwent a change in position of the colonizer. Consider, for example, the constitutions of the newly emerged Pacific island nations as well as African nations. Do they reflect more closely the social and legal culture of the immediate preceding colonizer or of the Indigenous culture? Are those documents truly reflective of the hopes and aspirations of the people previously colonized? Or do they represent the colonial mentality that pervades the society at the time of foreign departure? Were they written or advised by colonial experts coming from a mind-set of Western political structures, or were they drafted by the people themselves?

True decolonization is more than simply placing Indigenous or previously colonized people into the positions held by colonizers. Decolonization includes the reevaluation of the political, social, economic, and judicial structures themselves and the development, if appropriate, of new structures that can hold and house the values and aspirations of the colonized people.

In Hawai'i, the dreaming is now vibrant. One ongoing process is called the Native Hawaiian Convention, in which delegates elected only by

Native Hawaiians convene to review all aspects of self-determination and make recommendations to the Native Hawaiian population. This convention will explore the full range of choices, from remaining integrated within the United States to complete independence from the United States.

Other organizations are also attempting to address the question of self-determination. Some have gone so far as to declare themselves the government *pro tem* pending success in achieving international recognition as an independent nation. Others are gathering and forming coalitions to promote continuing discussion of Hawaii's future. Still others are dedicated to remaining part of the United States but having the Indigenous people given formal recognition and equivalent treatment as many American Indian tribes, a nation-within-a-nation approach.

As the debate over Hawaii's future gains greater momentum, there is a matching hunger for solid background information and new visions upon which the dreaming can be built. Some of the areas now being explored include

(1)   ramifications of Hawaiian sovereignty on
   • tourism
   • population control
   • military presence
   • international trade and business
   • diversified agriculture
   • control over ocean resources
   • taxation
   • land relationships;
(2)   international legal principles that apply to the Hawaiian case – in particular, principles of decolonization, Indigenous peoples' rights, and ocean governance seen from new economic, environmental, and political world perspectives;
(3)   review of other cases in which people have exercised self-determination, both as Indigenous peoples' movements and as broader movements of decolonization;
(4)   identification and description of various models of nationhood; and
(5)   methods and processes by which non-Indigenous concerns and contributions can be incorporated into the overall study of Hawaiian sovereignty.

Hawai'i, however, continues to face the threat of rushing the dreaming. Now that the topic of Hawaiian sovereignty has "caught on" as one of the foremost political issues of the day, many are demanding immediate action, believing that reflection and introspection are not worth the time and effort in the development of a new social order. Those expressing impatience and even ridicule over the dreaming process often call for very short-sighted goals, generally measured by material gains. Thus, there is an immediate call for lands, dollars, and a "sovereign" nation whose jurisdiction and powers are fully within the US Congress or Supreme Court. Long-term planning for the future of Hawai'i in relation to the Pacific and the world is not included in such calls for an immediate remedy.

Commitment

In the process of dreaming, the people will have the opportunity to weigh the voices rather than becoming caught up with counting votes or bullets. They will be able to wade through the cult of personalities and family histories and to release themselves from the shackles of colonial patriotism. They will now be ready for commitment to a single direction in which the society must move. This phase will culminate in people combining their voices in a clear statement of their desired direction. There is no single "way" or process for a people's expression of commitment. In fact, over time the commitment will become so clear that a formal process becomes merely a pro forma expression of the people's will.

It can be difficult to distinguish between an early termination of the dreaming phase and the start of the commitment phase. In Hawai'i, in several corners of the society, we are hearing the call for a Hawaiian convention to create a founding document of the Hawaiian nation. This call is being made by bodies that include the Hawaiian legislature, semi-autonomous organizations such as the Office of Hawaiian Affairs, and even the umbrella organization supporting Hawaiian sovereignty education, Hui Na'auao. All such calls for a process must be carefully scrutinized and questioned as to whether they are consistent with the desire to allow the full process of decolonization to take place or to cut the dreaming short and force a premature resolution of historical injustices, thus limiting the losses of those whose interests are threatened in the decolonization process.

In recent years, the Hawaiian legislature and the Office of Hawaiian Affairs put up funds to conduct a vote among Native Hawaiians on whether or not to elect delegates to a Native Hawaiian Convention to propose a form of Hawaiian governance.[7] Suspicion was raised over the fact that funding for this process came from the State of Hawai'i and that the process was therefore tainted and not truly a self-determining process contemplated in international law. International policies – well established by the United Nations – do, however, call for governments to provide necessary resources to assist the people in their exercise of self-determination.[8] A vote was taken in which any person over the age of eighteen was permitted to participate, regardless of their residency or whether they were incarcerated or under other civil disabilities, such as losing the right to vote in a state election because of criminal conviction. Among Native Hawaiians throughout the world, 22,294 voted yes, while 8,129 voted no – a 73 percent response in favour of electing delegates to a convention. A second step was taken in January 1999 when delegates were elected to a Native Hawaiian Convention. That convention is now proceeding.

Several organizations are claiming that they individually represent the Hawaiian nation. They have gone forward and formed their "national" organizational structures, put in place their national leaders, and now proceed to speak for the nation. They are trying to be "first" in the action phase. Such elitist solutions are quick substitutes for the decolonization process, and they deprive the people of a participatory role in the formation of their own social order.

Action

This phase can be properly taken only upon reaching a consensus of commitment in the fourth phase. Otherwise, the action taken cannot truly be said to be the choice of the colonized people.

But the reality of many situations does not allow for the methodical, patient, time-consuming process of the four earlier phases. When a people are under physical attack, when a people are finding their children torn from their homes for reeducation in colonial societies, when a people are being removed from their traditional lands in droves, action may be called for prior to the society's completion of the dreaming phase. But that kind of responsive action to colonization's onslaught is not the action spoken of here. The responsive action is one for survival. The action called for in the fifth phase of decolonization is not a reactive but a proactive step taken based on consensus of the people.

The fifth phase may incorporate the full spectrum from a call to reason on one end to a resort to arms on the other. Under appropriate times and in the appropriate manner, all such actions are sanctioned by international law.[9] But the decolonization environment has so drastically changed in the past thirty years that the action phase today must include considerations beyond what has been historically undertaken to achieve independence. While the first thought for independence would have been to grab the rifle and march against the colonizer, it seems that the new weapons are dictated by technological development. The fax machine, computer, television, radio, and newspaper are perhaps more effective in executing the long battle plan. These new weapons notwithstanding, the rifle, it's been argued, may still be necessary to defend those other media of expression.

Not only have the methods of executing commitments changed, but also the arenas in which they are carried out are now not as geographically defined as before. To speak before a national congress or an appropriate body of the United Nations may be far more effective than to storm a mountain top within one's homeland in an armed battle.

Conclusion

I have presented specific steps in the processes of colonization and decolonization, based on two Indigenous people's observations of their own colonial and decolonizing experiences. For the purpose of illustration, these steps or phases have been presented here as distinct from one another, in a clear sequence. Yet the reality of colonization and decolonization is not so clear. In practice, we often see combinations of these social changes. We see them occur in individuals at different times and likewise in general society – some individuals being far ahead or behind in the process. The process of decolonization, for example, has actually begun in Hawai'i, where the general society has now gone through several years of the phase of rediscovery and recovery. In 1978, during the first criminal trial in which a Native Hawaiian defendant refused to dignify the court by entering a plea of guilty or not guilty to the government's charges, thereby challenging the court's jurisdiction to sit in judgment over Hawaiian nationals, less than 1 percent of the general and Hawaiian public understood his claim or cause. Twenty years later, the subject of Hawaiian sovereignty is on the agenda of almost every politician because both the vast majority of Native Hawaiians and the general public support some form of Hawaiian sovereignty. Even in the face of all this, we can still find individuals who remain in denial, pretending that there was no illegality in the overthrow of the Hawaiian nation, and who refuse to accept the general society's rediscovery and recovery.

Nor are the phases of decolonization such that, once passed through, they are never revisited again. As one goes through the phases of rediscovery and recovery, then mourning, next dreaming, it is at times helpful or even necessary to return to rediscovery and recovery to aid in the dreaming. For example, as the society engages in the dreaming by discussing the future of the Hawaiian nation, the question of who should make up the Hawaiian nation arises. The answer to this question lies partially in the exploration of Hawaii's history and culture, discovering the makeup of the earlier Hawaiian nationals and the cultural principles upon which these earlier national questions were answered.

The process of colonization and decolonization deserves closer consideration in attempting to refashion societies. Otherwise, we may find that we are merely entrenching ourselves deeper in the systems, values, and controls put in place by the colonizer.

Notes

1 The critique provided by Professor Enriques was aired on the Hawai'i Public Radio program "A Second Glance" on April 17, 1993. Copies of the program are available for $12 US from the Hawaiian National Broadcast Corporation, 86-649 Pu'uhulu Road, Wai'anae, Hawai'i 96792.

2 *State of Hawai'i* v. *Wilford N. Pulawa*, the 1977 and 1978 trial of the reputed Hawaiian underworld leader on charges of double kidnapping and murder. The jury reached a not-guilty verdict.

3 "Cleveland's Address to Congress, 18 December 1893," in James Daniel Richardson, ed., *A Compilation of the Messages and Papers of the Presidents: 1789-1907*, vol. 9 (Bureau of National Literature and Art, 1908).

4 Both the Hawai'i State Legislature and the United States Congress have admitted to the illegality of the overthrow of the Hawaiian nation. House Concurrent Resolution 147 of the Hawai'i State Legislature 1991, Act 359 of the Hawai'i State Legislature 1993, "Joint Resolution of Apology," US Senate Concurrent Resolution 19, PL 103-150 107 Stat. 1510, signed by President Clinton on November 23, 1993.

5 The Oglala Lakota nation has the "Wiping of the Tears" ceremony to fulfil the same need for mourning. Interview with Birgil Killstraight, "A Second Glance," April 11, 1992 (see note 1).

6 This event has been preserved in a nine-hour audiocassette, *Three Days in January: The Overthrow of the Hawaiian Nation*, and is available for $49.95 US through the Hawaiian National Broadcast Corporation (see note 1).

7 The Hawaiian Sovereignty Advisory Council and subsequently the Hawaiian Sovereignty Elections Commission were funded by the State of Hawai'i and the Office of Hawaiian Affairs.

8 See Chapter XI, Article 73, United Nations Charter; International Covenant on Economic, Social, and Cultural Rights and on Civil and Political Rights, Annex to GA Res. 2200 (XXI), December 16, 1966; Declaration on Principles of International Law Concerning Friendly Relations and Cooperation among States in Accordance with the Charter of the United Nations, Annex to GA Res. 2625, October 24, 1970; and ILO Convention 169 Concerning Indigenous and Tribal Peoples in Independent Countries, 1989.

9 See, for example, the American Declaration of Independence, 1776; the French Declaration des Droits de l'Homme et du Citoyen, August 6, 1789; the Universal Declaration of Human Rights, third preambular paragraph, 1948; the Declaration on the Granting of Independence to Colonial Countries and Peoples, GA Reso. 1514, 1961; and the UN Charter, Article 51, Declaration on Principles of International Law Concerning Friendly Relations and Cooperation among States in Accordance with the Charter of the United Nations, UN GA Res. 2525 (XXV), 1970.

12
Postcolonial Ledger Drawing: Legal Reform
James (Sákéj) Youngblood Henderson

How do Indigenous peoples create a postcolonial society? How do the powerless create a fair and just society and an innovative postcolonial consciousness? How do we heal people who continue to suffer from the demons of four centuries of colonialism? What is adjudicative legacy in contemporary legal analysis by Indigenous peoples? These are the questions that I have been struggling with during my formal education and legal experience. These questions are integral to transforming modern thought and moving beyond its ideology and its imposed script for Indigenous peoples. I am asking how Indigenous peoples can change existing Eurocentric legal thought so that it may fulfil its primary avocation of creating, sustaining, and protecting an enlightened and democratic society that respects Indigenous peoples. This chapter offers a personal example of the effort to penetrate the colonial legal order of Canada and to create a new postcolonial constitutional order, as well as the effort to create interpretive standards for the existing human rights covenants in international law in order to create a broader postcolonial order. Our postcolonial visions are thus enfolded in legal codes, nonnarrative legal documents, rather than in philosophical manifestos or grand narratives.

The Spirit of Ledger Drawings
Guiding my approach to and experience of constitutional reform have been the daunting spirits of my Tsistsistas (Cheyenne) ancestors, especially their approach to their imprisonment. After they entered treaty, the military forces of the United States imprisoned them for struggling to maintain the treaty order against its transgressors. Behind the grey stone walls of their prison, they had to learn English and another view of reality in the hostile classrooms – a worldview forced upon them, not one that was chosen. The military personnel offered them empty ruled accountants' ledger books as a gift. To the European immigrants, the ruled ledger books represented the medium and tool of capitalism, with its market vision of the

world. These books symbolized the economic promise and potential of the new continent to the aliens, supporting their desire for and goal of economic opportunity. To the imprisoned Tsistsistas, the ledger books were the symbol of their forced education within an imposed routine of confinement – a written medium by which they were supposed to acquire a new human identity, disconnected from their heritage. They turned their minds to this experience in an interesting way.

They recorded their experiences and the meaning of their experiences in these ledger books, in what others have labelled "ledger drawing" or "ledger art."[1] They ignored the overt purpose and principles of the ledger books and used them for iconic images of their experiences, ceremonies, and visions. Slowly, they filled the columns not with English script and numerals recording progress and prosperity but with their memories and drawings. They reclaimed the drawings from a vast ancient memory of pictographic symbols on rocks, buffalo robes, parfleches or saddle bags, shields, and teepee drawings. The fervent prison drawings unfolded the loves and passions of their lives. The drawings captured the integrity of their Aboriginal thoughts, with designs similar to those that had pervaded their lives and winter counts. They captured the tragedy arising from the row of smoking guns. They invented new symbols to describe complex ideas, such as dotted lines emerging from the mouth to represent speech or song. In abstract symbolism and narrative representation, they told of a different worldview and destiny. The drawing of their cultural heritage in the ledger books captured their idea of an infinite Aboriginal consciousness imprisoned within the finite ledger books of European consciousness.

Through the hybrid medium of European texts, these ledger drawings continued their autothonic heritage. The drawings represent a powerful Indigenous response to the colonial encounter. Indigenous peoples can see these ledger drawings as a troubled particularity concerning injustice, an Indigenous response to oppression and dominion similar to Gramsci's *Prison Notebooks*,[2] Solzhenitsyn's *Gulag Archipelago, 1918-1956*,[3] and Mandela's *The Struggle Is My Life*.[4] All these responses share a transformation of displacement and oppression into covert resistance against colonial violence, practices, and developmental economics.[5]

By invoking constitutional reform as another form of ledger drawing, I am seeking not only to honour their efforts but also to affirm their visions of how to deal with modern cognitive imprisonment. I may not use their precise visual icons, but our nonnarrative constitutional codes in Canada and the various Indigenous human rights treaties, such as the Declaration on the Rights of Indigenous Peoples, reflect the same cognitive icons when faced with similar colonized artifice and texts.

In many ways, all Indigenous lawyers are involved in a similar project.

We are seeking to sustain Indigenous worldviews and to protect them using modern legal thought and analysis. In terms of Poka Laenui's account of processes of decolonization (see Chapter 11 of this volume), our drafting of constitutional and international legal reforms was our way of dreaming while still imprisoned. It was the cognitive style and "spirit" of ledger drawing.

Many examples of this cognitive style exist. Often in very important meetings, other Indigenous lawyers and I would find ourselves drawing such icons and visual images on agenda lists and memos. More importantly, we would find ourselves transforming Indigenous worldviews and thought on written English legal texts by interpretation and nuance revision. Typically, these legal texts are the medium of a central, coercive will of the colonizers that protects their prosperity, their system of private rights, and their contrived institutions of government. The wording and style of these complacent texts create a social and cognitive world that usually oppresses Indigenous visions. Our efforts to transform these texts into inclusive documents of empowerment in international, constitutional, and legislative regimes have often been categorized by power holders as unnecessary chaos. But I see our efforts from our Aboriginal perspective as yet another manifestation of the spirit of ledger drawing in law. Perhaps we should call our legal reform efforts "postcolonial ledger drawing" rather than postcolonial law.

Colonized Indigenous peoples and their Indigenous lawyers are still imprisoned by colonization. We have not yet created a postcolonial society. Nevertheless, that is our hope and goal. The modern boundaries of our imprisonment are both cognitive and physical. Eliminating these prisons is the task of Indigenous lawyers and law students who are the first and fragile generation of legal warriors and ledger drawers. In this chapter, I would like to talk about how my generation has attempted to recognize and to end the cognitive or ideological prisons to move toward empowerment of our people. However, the physical prisons or correctional institutions that form a menacing background and symbol haunt my thoughts about all our efforts.

Eurocentric Cognitive Scripts

Colonized Indigenous peoples are still not flourishing. Their humanity remains problematic, and their human rights are still questioned. We live in endless poverty and need. Typically, the existing legal order continues its search for remedies for our past humiliations and the denial of human dignity and work.

In Eurocentric thought, the legal systems have been the place at which an ideal of colonization takes detailed institutional form. Its typical form is manifested as the ideal of civilization. Eurocentric legal doctrine supplies a way of representing and discussing civilization and its institutions that makes it possible to sustain and develop the privileges of the colonialists. We must grasp the negative role assigned to Indigenous peoples to acknowledge its transformative possibilities.

The governments of the day, our legal guardians and fiduciaries, do not want to discuss the transforming of legal or political institutions to include Aboriginal peoples in the nation. They do not want to end their national fantasies, artificial constructs, or myths about their nation, nor do they want to expose the injustice that informed the construction of their national and state institutions and practices. They do not want to create a postcolonial state or sustain these efforts at institutional reform. They reject a hybridized state and any insurgent indigenization of the political or adjudicative realm. Often they want us to vanish into separate replicative or imitative institutions or organizations without equalized funds or capacity or shared rule. All these efforts are an attempt to conceal the constitutive contradictions or unwanted side-effects of the imaginative settler or "sodbuster" state and the law.

Universities and educational processes also struggle with similar attitudes. Their categories and disciplines deny our holistic knowledge and thought. Indigenous people are forced to exist as an exotic interdisciplinary alterity. Our diverse legal order and consciousness are ordinarily dismissed as imaginary and not coercive enough to qualify as law. Our humanity and our very essence as human beings are ignored for Eurocentric models.

The Eurocentric curriculum and methods must renounce their assumed higher authority. Such authority has never been earned or properly possessed. To imagine the impossible and to talk about it effectively, we must confront Eurocentric thought and its fragmented disciplines. We must reveal to the Eurocentric specialists their significant biases and prejudices against Indigenous knowledge. These biases must be abandoned for a new style of intellectual and cultural collaboration with Indigenous knowledge to create a new vision of postcolonial society.

Thus, Indigenous peoples are living in a world according to imposed Eurocentric scripts. We are not living our own worldviews or visions. We exist in the contrived institutional and conscious realms of a failed colonization, often wrongly confused with the idea of civilization or modernity. We resist imitation of these colonial scripts but are partially complicit in maintaining these scripts even as we seek to change them. Thus, we live in contradiction. We resist these manifestations of what we should be, only to be forced to live life with a mistaken, and imposed, identity that is better suited to the imaginations of other peoples. Our educational and professional experiences make us feel and be disconnected from our worldviews, languages, and teachings. Our enormous creative and spiritual potential is not being used sensibly by Canadian and global orders. The imposed identity unbalances our capabilities and needs.

Constitutional Reform in Canada

In Canada, our attempts at dreaming were successful. Aboriginal peoples of Canada have argued for and articulated change in our constitutional status through our Aboriginal and treaty rights. Through our self-determination, self-consciousness, and self-realization, we have formally emancipated ourselves from colonial domination and oppression. At least on paper. We have refused to allow the Eurocentric constitutional experts to grant us formal legal equality before the law as individuals.[6] Instead, we demanded, and received, political equality consistent with the Aboriginal way of life and the Crown's treaty promises to Aboriginal people. Thus, we peacefully concluded our colonial legal servitude in Canada by restoring our rights to our worldviews, languages, identities, and treaty order as an integral part of the supreme law of Canada.

Before the constitutional reforms, the colonialists asserted exclusive parliamentary jurisdiction over "Indians, and Lands reserved for the Indians," under delegated powers from the imperial Crown.[7] Provincial governments may only exercise authority over these peoples under a lawful delegation of the federal power.[8] The supremacy of Parliament, the elected voice of the immigrants, was restricted by the 1982 constitutional reform. Section 35(1) of the *Constitution Act, 1982*, declares that "The existing aboriginal and treaty rights of the Aboriginal peoples of Canada are hereby recognized and affirmed."[9] Section 35 refers to two distinct categories of rights: rights of "Aboriginal" or customary origin,[10] and rights derived from specific written treaties that are an integral part of the supreme law of Canada.[11]

Constitutional respect for these rights continues our Aboriginal identity on this continent. It links the original treaty federalism with the colonial order. Creating this balance was a condition of Canadian independence from the imperial parliamentary supremacy over Canadian legislation. It was a belated nation-building process to create a significant postcolonial Canada.[12] Seeking to determine the meaning of this condition in British and Canadian law, the treaty nations of eastern Canada and Alberta raised this question in the British courts. These treaty nations sought a declaration that the treaty obligations are still obligations of the imperial Crown. In *Indian Association of Alberta*, Lord Denning concluded that the United Kingdom's responsibilities to these rights have been delegated to Canada;[13] however, he found that section 35 "does all that can be done to protect the rights and freedoms of the Aboriginal peoples of Canada," by making them part of the Constitution" so that they cannot be diminished or reduced."[14] No parliament should do anything to lessen the worth of these guarantees. The Crown in respect of Canada "so long as the sun rises and the river flows" should honour them. That promise must never be broken.[15]

Similarly, section 25 of the *Charter* provides special protection for these rights. It states that the *Charter* does not affect Aboriginal rights and freedoms: "The guarantee in the *Charter* of certain rights and freedoms shall not be construed so as to abrogate or derogate from any Aboriginal, treaty or other rights or freedoms that pertain to the Aboriginal peoples of Canada."[16] Neither section 25 nor the rest of the *Charter* lists these uniquely protected rights of Aboriginal people. Instead, section 25 is an analytical place-holder and protector for the "existing Aboriginal and treaty rights of the Aboriginal peoples of Canada" found in section 35 of the *Constitution Act, 1982*. These Aboriginal and treaty rights are sequestered from the colonizer's control by reasonable limits prescribed by democratic law in the *Charter*.

These two constitutional sections are complementary, and they locate a constitutional home for Aboriginal rights. They affirm and protect Aboriginal rights as fundamental rights in the conscience of the nation. In locating a constitutional place for Aboriginal and treaty rights, these sections also locate a constitutional source for Aboriginal orders, visions, and dream lines.

On the one hand, section 25 defines Aboriginal rights as an integral and legitimate part of the new constitutional order in Canada and explicitly protects these rights from Eurocentric personal rights guarantees and freedoms and from religious rules of popular morality. On the other hand, section 35 protects these fundamental rights as distinct from the secular and religious powers of the immigrants at large, who create legislation either in a popular assembly or in Parliament and who appoint judges to the courts.

These constitutional sections read very coolly, very self-confidently. As a part of the supreme law of Canada, our Aboriginal and treaty rights have been affirmed and recognized at every level of Canadian society.[17] We have come a long way from the attempt to totally reject our Aboriginal rights and to cash out our treaty obligations for individual equality. These new words in the Constitution of Canada are supposed to protect our collective consciousness and world order from any derogation by the Eurocentric immigrant regimes.

At the centre of this constitutional reform is Aboriginal people's ability to create a normative vision that defines their own contexts or ideas of existence, of meaning, and of spirituality surrounding the mystery of human life and to control their own thoughts and identities. We were supposed to be protected from the secular and religious rights of Eurocentric law, from the freedoms of individuals, and from the laws of their elected governments. Under the rule of law, these sections should have settled the public policy debate around these issues and should have created a legal shield around Aboriginal rights of spiritual teaching and practices. Often this megaright is talked about as a right to cognitive integrity from Eurocentric thought. Yet these words on paper have not changed the colonialist mentality in Canadian society and in political and adjudicative realms. A bias still exists in many conscious and unconscious forms.

Canadian context shows that constitutional words and guarantees do not have the power of a ghost dance shirt or a Plains Indian shield. The constitutional text is passive, its command yielding to the new ledger books mentality, called fiscal restraint. Perhaps the constitutional transformation to an alternative destiny happened too fast. We may have ended the constitutional legacy of colonization and created a new vantage point for Canadian thought and society – yet few can stand on the new ground. Since our transformation was led by Aboriginal visions and was not controlled or directed by any delegated powers from London, our constitutional reforms have perplexed colonial legal scholars, who have had a difficult time understanding the contextual shifts introduced by the new words in the Constitution.[18]

While the legal system is beginning to change, the dominant response of Canadian politicians, judges, lawyers, and scholars has been to unreflectively assert colonial privileges or power. Integral to these colonial privileges is pretending not to understand the constitutional reforms or even the meaning of sections 25 and 35. They demand English definition of these rights, as if the words are beyond the defined world and traditions that they inhabit. They assert that they cannot understand the meaning of Aboriginal rights or treaty rights and imply that it is beyond their "superior" intellect to comprehend such *sui generis* rights. They talk about these rights through the metaphor of an empty or full box. They demand definitions, as if English usage of words can save them from Aboriginal and treaty rights. All this incomprehension is contrived.

The words that the immigrants know define the world that they inhabit. The constitutional reforms are written in their vocabulary, reflecting the world that they live in, naming things, actions, and relations that are familiar to Eurocentric thought. These words, however, may have been placed into sentences and constitutional commands that are unfamiliar to them, because they suggest a constitutional order that is incomprehensible to their consciousness. The constitutional commands witness a partnership in Canada between the immigrants and the Aboriginal people and a limitation of Eurocentric, colonial privileges. These reforms insist on the end of colonization in Canada and the development of a more equitable society and an extraordinary legal system. Such thoughts seem so fair to us and so unrealistic to those in power and their supporters.

The incomprehensible nature of constitutional reforms requires Canadians to undertake a quest of understanding. They need to dream alternative visions. Their contrived response to these constitutional commands seeks to avoid the apparent: there is a new order possible, unknown to colonial thought or not known well enough. Canadians have a responsibility to discover the new constitutional order of Canada. They have to discover how their colonial contexts have been transformed into postcolonial government. Colonial governments can read the new words in the Constitution, but they must do more. They cannot refuse to understand how these words empower Aboriginal thought and law or refuse to consider how to blend the best of Aboriginal and Eurocentric thought to create an equitable multicultural Canadian society.

Declaring Indigenous Rights in International Law

Indigenous lawyers in Canada moved from constitutional debates to the UN Working Group on Indigenous Populations[19] to assist Indigenous leaders and lawyers to create new standards for Indigenous peoples in both international and UN law. The most comprehensive task was negotiating the Indigenous and Tribal Peoples Convention in 1989 (the International Labor Organization Convention 169),[20] which defined Indigenous self-government and cultural rights in national and labour contexts. It recognizes Indigenous people's rights to self-development, cultural and institutional integrity, territory, and environmental and human security.

We learned to lobby the UN General Assembly and were successful in getting the assembly to proclaim the International Year of the World's Indigenous Peoples (1990)[21] and later the International Decade of the World's Indigenous Peoples.[22] These resolutions assert a new relationship between Aboriginal peoples and the member states of the United Nations, described as a "partnership" and stressing "cooperation." The Indigenous network could lobby for and create new standards and describe the new vision, but we could not get the UN agencies or member states to implement our visions.

Indigenous lawyers and their friends created the foundation of an ecological order. We lobbied for a special provision for Indigenous peoples' programs (chapters 15 and 26) in Agenda 21, adopted by the UN Conference on Environment (1992), which supports traditional Indigenous resource management through "capacity-building."[23] We also lobbied for the inclusion of traditional ecological knowledge of Indigenous peoples in the UN Convention on Biological Diversity (1992).[24] These documents recognize Indigenous peoples as distinct social partners in achieving sustainable development, and they recognize our unique values, knowledge, and traditional practices and our role in environmental management and development. These UN documents manifest an Indigenous vision of our humanity for all people to read, and they unleash the power of a vision of an ecological theory of good order and human rights.[25]

The final unfolding of the Indigenous vision and theory was the Declaration of the Rights of Indigenous Peoples,[26] which aims to address the dreadful gap between the life situations and human rights of Indigenous peoples and other peoples. The UN Charter[27] and the Human Rights Covenants[28] declared self-determination and certain human rights to be universal, but most governments have interpreted them as not applying to Indigenous peoples. We argued that Indian peoples are "peoples" under the charter and covenants. The declaration is an interpretive tool for applying the UN Human Rights Covenants to Indigenous peoples of the Earth and to begin a belated design for postcolonial nation-building.

After twelve years of debate and reconciliation, we reached a broad consensus among the UN human rights experts and the Indigenous partners on a proper interpretive declaration, which articulates forty-five articles that set minimum standards for Indigenous peoples' human rights. This remedial task witnessed a new style of collaboration between technical experts and oppressed people. It was an enterprise of translating hope into insight and experience into enactment. Our emerging compromises were fragile, spoke tenderly of honour, caring, and healing, yet were drafted in the context of the aloof and sterile statutory protocol of UN conventions on human rights. The drafting style disguised and contained the bitterness of our experience with colonization.

The assumption that underscores the intricate declaration was stated in the preamble, which affirms "that Indigenous peoples are equal in dignity and rights to all other peoples, while recognizing the right of all peoples to be different, to consider themselves different, and to be respected as such." Article 3 articulates the new vision and operative principles of the declaration: "Indigenous peoples have the right of self-determination. By virtue of that right they freely determine their political status and freely pursue their economic, social and cultural development."

The declaration is a statement of principles or aspirations of postcolonial self-determination and human rights, and it is a binding treaty among all those Indigenous peoples who ratified it. The declaration is not legally binding on member states until it is passed by the UN General Assembly. However, it will have a certain intellectual force among member states and will carry some political weight and create some troubling inconveniences. If enacted as a convention, it will become a legal treaty among states that ratify it.

The Sub-Commission passed the declaration, but the Human Rights Committee found its articles too threatening. The review committee found them consistent with existing UN human rights, but member states intensively lobbied the committee not to adopt the declaration. Yielding to this pressure, the Human Rights Committee in 1995 created a working group of fifty-three representatives from the nation-states to review the Indigenous declaration. It is called the UN Working Group on the Draft Declaration of Indigenous Rights (WGDD). Thus, Indigenous peoples continue to be exposed to degrading ceremonies manufactured by the resisting states and colonizers.

Indigenous peoples have taken the position in the nation-states working group that we will accept no changes to or censorship of the existing compact in the declaration. The states have no authority to appropriate our visions or our consensus for their purposes. Human rights are universal and not relative. We feel that it would be pointless and unavailing to accept human rights standards lower than those that apply to other peoples of the United Nations, because this would mean accepting our legal inferiority. Never before have victims of colonization been asked to celebrate their inferiority and to feel guilty about wanting equality with other peoples.

We are now working on practical issues such as protecting our Indigenous knowledge and heritage, creating a permanent forum for Indigenous peoples in the United Nations, and studying remedies for the taking of our lands and resources. And we continue to require that national governments implement the existing international standards into domestic laws.

Sustaining Commitment and Action
Indigenous peoples will continue our journey. We need to heed Poka Laenui's processes of commitment and action. Passive words on paper are not enough to create the transformation to a postcolonial order. These words only express our vision; they manifest our commitment and action to all peoples. These words talk especially to our children, who have been deprived of our presence in this struggle, and to the future generations. The documents create a framework to be analyzed and evaluated, but the documents themselves cannot enforce compliance.

Our spirits and minds must continue to search for the manifestations of these processes of commitment to and action for our vision of a more equitable legal order built on respect for biological and human diversity, rather than on Eurocentric singularity. Like our ancestors, we need to continue the spirit of ledger drawing on Eurocentric legal texts, explaining why these texts deny our knowledge and heritage and regulate our destiny. We need to dream and realize new visions in the old ways.

Notes
1 See, generally, Janet C. Berlo, *Plains Indian Drawing 1865-1935: Pages from a Visual History* (New York: Harry N. Adams, 1996); J.M. Szabo, *Howling Wolf and the History of Ledger Art* (Albuquerque: University of New Mexico Press, 1994); Valerie Robertson, "Reclaiming History," *Ledger Drawings by the Assiniboine Artists Hoñgeeÿeesa* (Calgary:

Glenbow-Alberta Institute, 1993); Peter J. Powell, "Artists and Fighting Men: A Brief Introduction to Northern Cheyenne Ledger Book Drawing," *American Indian Art Magazine* 1,1: 44-8.

2   New York: Columbia University Press, 1992. Originally titled *Quaderni Del Carcere.*

3   New York: Harper and Row, 1974-8.

4   New York: Pathfinder Press, 1986.

5   L.M. Findlay, "Interdisciplining Canada: 'Cause Breaking Up Is Hard to Do,'" *Essays on Canadian Writing* 65 (1998): 1-15.

6   Section 25 of the *Canadian Charter of Rights and Freedoms,* Part I of the *Constitution Act, 1982,* being Schedule B of the *Canada Act, 1982* (UK), 1982, c. 11.

7   Section 91(24) of the *Constitution Act, 1867.* This has long been interpreted as applying to Inuit as well as to "Indians."

8   For example, in accordance with section 88 of the *Indian Act* or under federal fisheries legislation.

9   Schedule B to the *Canada Act, 1982* (UK), 1982, c. 11.

10   Aboriginal rights are found in the ancient base of worldview, language, customary teachings, knowledge, and practices of Aboriginal people. These rights are not found in Eurocentric religions or artificial laws based on rules from above or popular legislation or majority intolerance.

11   Section 52 of the *Canada Act, 1982* (UK), 1982, c. 11.

12   J.Y. Henderson, "Empowering Treaty Federalism," *Saskatchewan Law Review* 58 (1994): 234-329.

13   *R. v. Secretary of State for Foreign and Commonwealth Affairs exparte Indian Association of Alberta,* (1982) 2 W.L.R. 641, [1981] 4 C.N.L.R. 86, (U.K.C.A.).

14   Ibid., 99.

15   Ibid.

16   Schedule A to the *Canada Act, 1982,* (UK) 1982, c. 11.

17   April 17, 1982, section 35 of the *Canada Act, 1982* (UK), 1982, c. 11, Schedule B.

18   R. Romanow, "Aboriginal Rights in the Constitutional Process," in Meno Boldt, J. Anthony Long, and Leroy Little Bear, eds., *The Quest for Justice: Aboriginal Peoples and Aboriginal Rights,* 73–82 (Toronto: University of Toronto Press, 1985).

19   Economic Social Council Resolution 34, UN ESCOR, 38th Sess., Supp. No. 1 at 26, UN Doc. E/1982/59 (1982).

20   I.L.O. Cov. 169, I.L.O., 76th Sess., reprinted in 28 I.L.M. 1382 (1989).

21   General Assembly Resolution 164, UN GAOR, 45th Sess., Supp. No. 49, at 277; UN Doc. A/Res/45/164 (1990).

22   G.A. Res. 163, UN GAOR, 48th Sess., Agenda Item 114(b) pmbl. Para. 8 at 2 UN Doc. A/C.3/48/163 (1993).

23   See also ch. 15, Agenda 21, UN Conference on Environment and Development, Annex 2, ch. 26, para. 26.1, at 385, UN Doc. A/ CONF.151/26/Rev. 1 (Vol. 1) (1993); Rio Declaration on Environment and Development, UN Conference on Environment and Development, Annex 1, UN Doc. A/ CONF.151/26/Rev. 1 (Vol. 1) (1993); and Non-Legally Binding Authoritative Statement on Principles for a Global Consensus on Management: Conservative and Sustainable Development of All Types of Forest, UN Conference on Environment and Development, Annex 3, UN Doc. A/CONF.151/26/Rev. 1 (Vol. 1) (1993).

24   UN Doc. UNEP/Bio.Div./N7-INC.5/2 (1992).

25   S. James Anaya, "Indigenous Rights Norms in Contemporary International Law," *Arizona Journal of International Law* 8 (1991): 1-39; R.L. Barsh, "Indigenous Peoples in the 1990s: From Object to Subject of International Law?" *Harvard Human Rights Journal* 7 (1994): 33-86.

26   Report of the Working Group on Indigenous Populations on Its Eleventh Session, UN ESCOR, Comm'n on Human Rights, Sub-Comm'n on Prevention of Discrimination and Protection of Minorities, 45th Sess., Agenda Item 14, UN Doc. E/CN.4/Sub.2/1993/29 (1993).

27   UN Charter, art. 1, para. 4 ("respect for the principle of equal rights and self-determination of peoples").

28   International Covenant on Civil and Political Rights, 999 U.N.T.S. 171, art. 1(1) ("All peoples have the right to self-determination").

13
Invoking International Law
Ted Moses

I would like to reflect today on the international recognition of the rights of the world's Indigenous peoples.

The interests of the international community are thought to transcend somehow the interests of individual states. We stand in some awe when we think of the United Nations and other international bodies, because what these organizations decide, and do, must reflect some basic and ultimate standard of right and wrong, not just the national interests of their member states.

How is it, we have to ask, that in all these years of guardianship of the ultimate standards of justice – of right and wrong – that the international community did not speak out on the issue of the rights of the world's Indigenous peoples? What took it so long? Why have we Indigenous peoples been invisible?

We all wish for the concept of an international community whose interests transcend the interests of its member states. That certainly was the concept when the United Nations was formed. The world had suffered two world wars. We had witnessed the establishment and normalization of genocide and torture within the municipal laws of states – the legalization of murder as policy protected by the international standard of state security and the principle of noninterference – the line that the international community never deems to cross. But the principle of noninterference in the internal affairs of states led to the massive human rights violations of the Nazi era, and the world still feels the effects today.

The United Nations was founded on the principle that the interests of the international community would not be bound up in the lowest

[*Editor's note*: Ted Moses is Grand Chief and Ambassador of the Grand Council of the Cree to the United Nations. This essay is his original speech delivered at the 1996 Special Convocation at the University of Saskatchewan at which Dr. Ted Moses, Dr. Erica-Irene Daes, and Dr. Rigoberta Menchu Tum were honoured with honorary doctorate degrees (Saskatoon, June 27, 1996).]

common denominator of the legal systems of its member states. There would be a higher standard. States would have to acquiesce to the principle that the rights of human beings inhere in themselves, not in the state.

Unfortunately, the international community has not been completely successful in leaving behind the special interests of its members. Diplomats regularly receive instructions to vote in the United Nations so as to preserve the legal status quo of the states they represent. Then they proceed to dress this crude obedience to their ministers in a fabric of fine words expounding rights and precedents in international law.

When I first went to the United Nations, it took me a while to realize that this was how things worked. We explained the situations in our communities, and we appeared to be having discussions based on mutual understanding. However, when resolutions were to be drafted by diplomats, somehow none of this mattered. We were dealing with officials, I discovered, who had little serious concern with human rights. The officials and ministers who were making the decisions and formulating policy were not even in the room.

The Grand Council of the Crees first went to the United Nations in 1981. Tommy Wapachee, a Cree infant from Nemaska, had died on August 11, 1980. An epidemic of measles, gastroenteritis, and tuberculosis took the lives of eight Cree children before the end of that year.

It was not the first time disease had killed our children, but circumstances had changed. The James Bay and Northern Quebec Agreement, our treaty with Canada and Quebec, had promised clean water, sanitation, medical services, and clinics, and none of these had been put in place. The sad fact was that the children need not have died if the governments had kept their promises and respected their own laws.

We went to the international community because after five years, using every means to enforce and implement the treaty, we had essentially exhausted our remedies in Canada. We went to the courts, we lobbied, we spoke to the media, we brought in engineers and doctors, but the governments waited us out. At the time there was no Working Group on Indigenous Populations and no Martinez-Cobo Report on discrimination against Indigenous peoples.

By 1981 we had nowhere to turn, except to the international community. In Geneva we described our situation in Canada. Others described terrible atrocities in their own lands. Some who went to that meeting were never seen again after they went home. They were punished for telling us about their world. Some of our Cree delegates were told that "You are lucky you live in Canada where it is not that bad." I took no comfort in that. That was before Oka and, I think, before Restigouche. I was not going to let Canada off the hook because it was worse somewhere else. What logic supports that kind of thinking?

I knew also that if the government of Canada could be persuaded to support the recognition of strong international standards to protect the rights of Indigenous peoples, then not only would our lives be improved in Canada, but we would also have a means to address the terrible situations in other countries.

The 1981 meeting was one of the events that led to the establishment of the Working Group on Indigenous Populations in 1983. This and the International Labor Office, Convention 107 on Indigenous and Tribal Populations, were the only visible evidence that the United Nations had finally recognized our existence.

That recognition was minimal. The working group was established in a far corner of the United Nations system. People would laugh when I described where Indigenous peoples were at the United Nations. I would explain the General Assembly, the Security Council, ECOSOC, the Commission on Human Rights, the Sub-Commission on Prevention of Discrimination and Protection of Minorities, and, finally, that the sub-commission has a working group and that is where Indigenous peoples can be discussed. I also explained that the words *Indigenous peoples* couldn't be used because certain states – Canada among them – are fearful of recognizing our rights. As a result, the working group is designated as the Working Group on Indigenous Populations.

Nevertheless, we viewed the opportunity to bring the concerns of the Indigenous peoples to the United Nations very seriously, for it offered the hope of a brand-new, and badly needed, means of redress for our people. The working group had two essential mandates: to review current developments concerning our peoples, and to draft international standards to protect the rights of Indigenous peoples.

Members of the working group were cautioned not to hear complaints from the hundreds of Indigenous representatives who attended its five-day yearly sessions. That, of course, is difficult. How does one review current developments in communities whose members are being systematically murdered without appearing to make complaints? How does one describe dispossession of lands without appearing to be grieved? How do you describe your rivers being dammed, communities being flooded, burial grounds disappearing beneath reservoirs, hunting territories being denuded of trees – how do you describe these things and not object? How do you tell this story without demanding that the international community act to protect Indigenous peoples?

But the states that were behind these situations were sensitive about complaints being made before the United Nations. The working group was carefully and intentionally mandated so that it could not properly hear complaints. That was the rule. The chairperson, Dr. Erica-Irene Daes, would be obliged to caution the Indigenous representatives who were telling their stories, "This is not a chamber of complaints." She would, nevertheless, hear the grievances, because it was impossible not to hear them in the context of current developments. The working group would continue for another year, having survived the threat of being shut down by states that did not want the world to know what they were doing.

The work of standard-setting commenced. First, there were only five paragraphs of a declaration. Our work was blocked for a few years at that stage during which time various states argued that no declaration was necessary because the Indigenous "populations" were already protected by international standards concerned with cultural, religious, and linguistic minorities.

It took several years to convince the members of the sub-commission that the Indigenous peoples were not necessarily minorities. Imagine the reaction when diplomats learned that in some states the Indigenous peoples actually constituted the majority of the population. Even in these places, the Indigenous peoples were dispossessed, their rights were abused, and, of course, they did not have a voice in government.

The working group's mandate to review developments served to contribute directly and substantively to the work of standard-setting. It is important that this be understood. We did not work from theory or hypothesis about international law and international rights. There was nothing abstract about our work.

Indigenous people brought their experiences, their grievances, the histories of their lives and peoples to the working group. These experiences formed the basis for the proposals that eventually became the draft text. Every paragraph of the Declaration on the Rights of Indigenous Peoples is based on an abuse of human rights that the Indigenous peoples have experienced. The declaration proposes remedies in the form of human rights standards. These standards are not theoretical. We knew from bitter experience what needed to be in the draft. This is the unfortunate truth. And yes, every paragraph is also a demonstration that existing human rights law is not well respected.

The Declaration on the Rights of Indigenous Peoples is essentially an instrument that attaches the Indigenous peoples to the basic human rights instruments that already existed. This should not have been necessary. It became necessary because certain states – Canada was one of the most insistent – proposed that the international recognition of the status and rights of the Indigenous peoples be contingent upon the effect this recognition would have on municipal law.

In other words, states such as Canada deny our status in international law in order to avoid the recognition of the rights that status would confer upon the Indigenous peoples. This is in itself the most blatant form of racial discrimination, yet it is put forward as government policy without the least embarrassment.

Thus, when the Indigenous peoples proclaim themselves to be "peoples" who are subjects of international law, there is a chorus of objections from various states – Canada, France, Brazil, India, to name a few – that believe their interests would be adversely affected by the recognition of our status.

The high-minded sentiments and objectives of the Universal Declaration and the Charter of the United Nations, which expound the rights of peoples and nations, simply vanish. Diplomats tell us that, "If we recognized your rights, you would declare independence, you would want your lands back, you would prevent development, you would ask for compensation, you would want to have your own laws. Where would it end?"

Some states do not acknowledge this reasoning and resort instead to other strategies. Some argue that the Indigenous peoples are attempting to obtain special rights in international law. We are accused of seeking privileged status. The government of Canada put this idea forward with considerable effect in 1994 before the Commission on Human Rights. Others, such as France, argue that it is against their constitution to grant separate status to a nation within a nation.

When the French ambassador stated this position in Geneva in 1995, I asked him how France could recognize the right of Quebec to leave Canada and yet not recognize that the Indigenous peoples in Quebec have the same right if it is their choice to remain in Canada. He dismissed the objection: "You must understand, Quebec is a special situation. France is a unitary and indivisible state, and it would be contrary to our constitution to recognize the self-determination of the Indigenous populations."

How should we respond to such reasoning when it negatively influences the setting of international standards, which are in themselves intended to eliminate racial discrimination and prejudice? It seems that certain states are imbued with such a pervasive belief in their own superiority and supremacy that they fail to recognize the racial basis for their international policies. They use their enormous power to shape the meaning of international law, based on what I believe is a mistaken view of their own interests above all else.

It took me several years, as I have explained, to understand the mechanisms that influence the elaboration of what we call international law. In part I saw that international law was often just a matter of what a state could do and get away with. But it is obviously more than this.

Some states favour the recognition of the rights of Indigenous peoples; others oppose recognition entirely. Most states are indifferent on this issue and take positions on the basis of trade-offs and alliances with other states.

But some, thankfully, have a fundamental belief in the importance of human rights, international morality, and fair play.

It is in this context that we have worked to protect the rights of Indigenous peoples over the past fifteen years. I have often been told that the whole effort is useless. I cannot agree. I think we have little choice but to continue to defend our rights at the international level.

We have also had the opportunity now to see how critical it is that we demand our rights without reservation. The rights of the Indigenous peoples in Quebec have become a test case for the whole question of the rights of the world's Indigenous peoples. Is it possible for a mixed population of European origin to demand and exercise a right of self-determination but for the same population to deny that the Indigenous peoples have at least the same rights? The Quebec example clearly demonstrates a double standard based on race. In the separatists' view, Québécois, whoever they are, have the right; Indians do not.

If it had not been for our international work, this issue would likely already have been lost. We raised the question of Cree rights in the context of Quebec secession from Canada in Geneva in 1991. I was summoned by the Canadian ambassador in Geneva and reprimanded, as he said, "for bringing a domestic issue to international attention. Separation will never happen. Why discuss it here and make it a reality?"

We persisted, filing a large brief with the United Nations Commission on Human Rights in February 1992. That brief became the essence of the argument concerning our rights. It helped people to understand that Indigenous peoples must have the same status and level of recognition as all other peoples. It was no longer acceptable to propose that our right of self-determination be limited to internal self-determination. Sometimes, and the Quebec situation demonstrates this conclusively, Indigenous peoples may need to be able to exercise an external right of self-determination in order to protect their most fundamental rights.

The Draft Declaration on the Rights of Indigenous Peoples reflects this need. The international community can never predict when, and under what circumstances, a right will need to be exercised. That is why no conditions may be imposed upon the exercise of the rights of Indigenous peoples that do not apply equally to all of the world's peoples, Indigenous or otherwise. The principle is nondiscrimination.

I said above that we must continue. I say this only because some people have given us hope, and some people have been responsible for the considerable progress that has already been made. I am extremely pleased to be recognized today and to be honoured in the company of two other individuals: Dr. Erica-Irene Daes and Dr. Augusto Williemson-Díaz.

Let me tell you about our first meeting with Dr. Williemson-Díaz. In

1981 we requested the help of the World Health Organization (WHO) to stem the epidemic in the Cree communities. We wrote to the WHO and went to Geneva hoping to obtain that organization's assistance. We telephoned the WHO and asked for a meeting with primary health care officials. Everybody was polite and receptive, but the request for a meeting went unanswered. When we called again, our calls were not returned.

Someone suggested that an official at the United Nations Centre for Human Rights might be able to help. We met Augusto Williemson-Díaz in the hallway at the UN. We had no idea of his involvement in the protection of the rights of Indigenous peoples or of the important role he was to have drafting the Martinez-Cobo Report. He was a little larger then than he is now, and he was imposing. He offered, "Let me find out what is the problem." A day later we met him again. He was angry. He told us, "You have been going to the WHO, entering meetings without permission, barging into offices." We said, "We have never been to the WHO in our lives. We don't even know where it is." "Ahh," he said, "now I know what the problem is."

Canada, it turns out, was blocking our meeting at the WHO. The Canadian government had started rumours about us. Mr. Williemson-Díaz said, "Ask the Canadian mission to arrange the meeting. Bring a journalist to observe. You will have your meeting." That evening there was a report on CBC Radio and the BBC about our attempt to meet with the WHO. The next day the Canadian mission told us there was a meeting scheduled at the WHO. Augusto Williemson-Díaz is the father of Indigenous rights at the UN. He continues that struggle now in Guatemala. He has dedicated his life to that fight, and what a life it is.

Having said that he is the father of Indigenous rights, you can all easily imagine who is the mother of our rights at the UN. Erica-Irene Daes has said to me many times, "I love the United Nations." She even bought a blue car and explained to me that it was blue because that was the colour of the United Nations – "and Greece," she added.

Dr. Daes is an internationalist, and she truly does love the United Nations. Her vision of the United Nations brings us back to its original purpose – to place respect for human rights above the sovereignty of all states. Dr. Daes says that I am a member of her family. She is really the intelligence, the strategist, the force behind the gradual but significant steps the international community has taken to recognize the rights of the world's Indigenous peoples.

I can truly say this: the recognition of our rights at the international level is the dream of Erica Daes. Because she is there, she will have her dream, and we will have our freedom. I am patient. I will continue working, knowing that I am in good company.

Southern Door:
Visioning the Indigenous
Renaissance

Our Nation World

My eyes are wet
with the tears
of our loss.
As I stand alone
on the shore, on
top of these blue
rocks, I think back
to a time when all
voices heard were
in our language.
The very same that
Kluskap used to
teach the Mi'kmaq
about the ways of
our Nation World.
Now as I stand here,
the salt spray
washes away any
trace of my sadness.
I know now that
I will hear those
voices again as
I hear now the voices
of the Spirits who
speak to me through
Mother Earth.

– Chief Lindsay Marshall, in *Clay Pots
and Bones Pka'woqq aq Waqntal*

14
Indigenous Knowledge: The Pueblo Metaphor of Indigenous Education
Gregory Cajete

This essay reflects the efforts of Indigenous people to explore our own understanding of colonization relative to Indigenous education and the possibilities that Indigenous education may provide for creating the context we need to evolve a contemporized guiding philosophy for educating Indigenous people in the twenty-first century. In exploring our own expression of Indigenous education, an expression of education that is truly ours, truly coming from our sensibility, our understanding of the world and who we are, we are empowering not only ourselves but also the vision of a brighter future through education.

The Pueblo metaphors of Indigenous education I present here are a way to bring together some of the thoughts and ideas of various scholars about how to heal and transcend the effects of colonization. These metaphors – represented in words, images, and symbols – provide food for thought and a way to reflect on how we can use the tools of education in this process of reinventing a contemporary philosophy of Indigenous education.

When I was growing up, at Santa Clara Pueblo, I would hear many metaphors – from the old people, my parents, my grandparents, my relatives. A Pueblo community is a high-context learning environment in which we are constantly being taught. Every event and every situation we encounter in the community are usually learning experiences. The metaphor *pin peye obe*, which translated into English means "to look to the mountain," refers to striving to gain the highest perspective of a situation.

As Indigenous people recovering from centuries of colonization, we need a perspective from a higher place to understand where we have come from, where we are, and where we wish to go. As you imagine climbing this metaphoric mountain, this mountain within your heart and your soul, reflect on the place that you have come from, on the people who have taught you, who have shared with you their sense of place and their understanding of life. As we climb to the mountain and reflect on our past, we begin to understand that life and education are journeys. Indeed, life and knowledge are both ways of knowing ourselves in the context of the rich relationships that make up our communities, our environments, our world. I invite you to use the "Native eye" to look deeply into the nature of these relationships.

The "eye of the beholder" is both a visual and a linguistic metaphor for the tapestry of life, the interconnections, the relationships as seen from the Indigenous viewpoint. The "eye of the beholder" reflects the perspective and worldview that I believe we have to begin to teach in environmental education. We have to begin to advocate actively for this context of understanding not only for the education that our children receive but also in the renewal and revival of our own Indigenous sensibility and way of looking at the world.

Among Pueblo peoples there is a figure called Kokopelli. He is an archetypal figure who symbolically represents the procreative processes and energy in nature. He is said to go from village to village carrying a bag of seeds. In each place that he stops, he plants seeds. He then gathers seeds from that place to plant in the next place he visits. Those seeds are metaphors for thoughts and ideas; they are ways of looking at things. Kokopelli is a metaphor for the kind of understanding each of us must have as we set out on our journey. It is my belief that each and every one of us is Kokopelli. Each of us has a special bag of "seeds," of special gifts, that we bring and that we plant, and each of us collects seeds to take on the next step of our journey.

New Mexico has thousands of places where the stories of the people are depicted in petroglyphs. Wherever you see Kokopelli – and he is in many places – you can be sure that the story represented has some educational meaning. As we move through our inner and outer landscapes, we also move toward a greater understanding of ourselves. The Pueblo elders say that we emerged from a world before this world and that our journey is on a rainbow path on which we continue to walk. It is time to reflect on the meaning of that journey. The way Indigenous people do this is what we call Indigenous education. The Pueblo peoples say that there were three worlds before this one. Each world provided us with an environment in which we could become more human, more "ripened." In each world, we had a new opportunity to understand what it is to be human and to be fully alive.

The Pueblo elders say there was a time when Pueblo people began to congregate in larger and larger groups and create large communities. This process began 10,000 to 15,000 years ago as the first groups of Paleo-Indian people congregated in the caves and mesa lands of southern Colorado, Utah, and New Mexico. These people evolved primarily as simple hunter-gatherers who lived in extended families and who, through their connection with the land, became intimately intertwined with the cycles of nature.

There is evidence of these settlements throughout New Mexico, Colorado, and Utah in the form of communal pit houses. Pit houses – the archetypal Pueblo structures – began to appear throughout the land, and extended families began to form the nucleus of what we now call clan groups. Pit houses still exist today in the form of kivas and are traditional places of education for Pueblo peoples. In each place that we settled, we came to know ourselves more fully through our relationships with the places where we lived. We came to know the nature of water and of land. We came to know the nature of the desert and how to live there. In each place we stopped, we left evidence of our stay, but we also took something with us to our next stop. Some of these stops were by sacred waters that are so important in a desert environment like New Mexico. We came to know the importance of water for our life and our well-being. We began to reflect that understanding in a variety of ways, and we began to evolve technologies based on our growing understanding of the elements within our environment. We created baskets and pottery and distinctive patterns of architecture, all of which reflected our environment.

In time, extended families turned into clans, and those clans joined together to form villages. The villages evolved, and we learned what was required to live in a community and to establish a sense and understanding of the process of the social ecology. What we learned then extends into Pueblo life today.

There is a shared body of understanding among many Indigenous peoples that education is really about helping an individual find his or her face, which means finding out who you are, where you come from, and your unique character. That education should also help you to find your heart, which is that passionate sense of self that motivates you and moves you along in life. In addition, education should help you to find a foundation on which you may most completely develop and express both your heart and your face. That foundation is your vocation, the work that you do, whether it be as an artist, lawyer, or teacher. This, then, is the intent of Indigenous education. It is finding that special kind of work that most fully allows you to express your true self – "Your heart and your face."

Indigenous education is, in its truest form, about learning relationships in context. This context begins with family. It extends to the clan, to the community and tribe, and to all of the world. The purpose of Indigenous education is to help the individual become a complete man or woman. The goal is completeness. This is similar to the idea that we move through different worlds, evolving through these contexts to become more fully human. Our idea of education is a reflection of that social ecology. For instance, old people among Pueblos are loved not only as the carriers of the oral tradition, the history, and the customs of the community but also as people who are coming close to that ideal of completeness.

There are five major foundations that underlie Indigenous education. The first one, of course, is community. The next foundation has to do with technical environmental knowledge or making a living in a place by understanding and interacting with it. For instance, Pueblo people have a style of adobe architecture that reflects a particular way of living in the land. The third foundation is the visionary or dream tradition based on an understanding that one learns through visions and dreams. The fourth foundation could best be termed the mythic foundation. It reflects how we view the world through our mythic traditions. And finally there is a foundation that we can call spiritual ecology. It underlies the variety of expressions of Indigenous religion that we find around the world. It is the intimate relationship that people establish with place and with the environment and with all of the things that make them or give them life.

For the Pueblo people, the foundations of learning take many forms. They take the form of the hundreds of dances we perform during a year. They take the form of our teachings to our children about their relationships within their communities. Ultimately, the goal of Indigenous education is to perpetuate a way of life through the generations and through time. The purpose of all education is to instruct the next generation about what is valued and important to a society. Given this orientation, children are the most important focus of Indigenous education.

Pueblo children are taught the process of and participation in the ceremonial rituals that renew the relationships in their ecology. An example is the yellow corn dance, danced on August 12, our feast day in Santa Clara. In the final dance, mothers join their children to commemorate the connection between generations so the children know that they are part of a larger whole and that they have an important role to play within the context of that whole.

Every tribe evolves and develops a system and a way of living that focus on particular elements in its environment. For Pueblo peoples, agricultural traditions are well developed through time, through hundreds of generations of farmers. The symbol that reflects our farming way of life is corn. Corn is our metaphor for life, for being, and for community. There is a saying among my people that each of us is like the individual multicoloured kernels on a cob of corn: "We are kernels on the same corn cob." Each corn kernel has a particular shape, form, colour, and hue. No two are exactly alike, but each kernel leans up against another kernel to form a community, and that community is the corn cob.

The corn metaphor invites reflection in many forms. Beginning in July and continuing through the month of August, Pueblo corn dancers draw together in different communities to celebrate their sense of community and to honour corn as a symbol of their life and their well-being. Food is essential for life, and understanding the food you rely on and how that food gets to your table becomes in itself a lesson about life and living.

Visual art is another way Pueblo express their worldview. In art forms such as Pueblo pottery, we are reminded of our connection with those things that give life to ourselves and our community. The creation of pottery, or any traditional art form among Indigenous people, is filled with this understanding of relationship.

For Pueblo people, pottery is a prayer realized in a physical form. Every step in the traditional making of pottery is a reflection of who Pueblo people are and their respect for life. Pottery holds life because pottery is the vessel created from the sacred earth to contain our food. So Pueblo potters make their pottery beautiful, thereby making a prayer of thanksgiving and an offering in recognition of the sacredness of food and life.

The Pueblo wedding vase with one body and two spouts provides another artistic metaphor in the symbolic bringing together of male and female energy to make one family or one community. The vase is presented to a couple as they are joined in marriage to help them remember that their two individual lives are coming together to form a greater life. So it is that you see reflected in Pueblo pottery the foundations of Indigenous education: the sense of community, the way of knowing how to use your environment, the artistic and visionary foundation, and the foundations of tradition and spiritual ecology. All of these understandings are embodied in the creation of traditional art forms such as pottery.

Pueblo peoples also believe that we are the offspring of two sacred and primordial ears of corn. The great corn mother is the grandmother of all life. Several artistic representations by Pueblo artists reflect this understanding that we come from this greater whole. The hunter and the reflection of the heart line in the traditional earthen Pueblo hunter's canteen represents the relationship the hunter establishes with that which he hunts. Hunting is a spiritual journey and a way of understanding one's relationship with animals and with the world. The "hunter of good heart" becomes a metaphor for the variety of ways in which we understand ourselves as human beings. A typical scene in Pueblo communities is where the hunter brings his extended family together and, in the presence of the honoured guests and the deer he has taken, tells the story of the deer and the hunt and why it is important to respect all of those things that give people life. Then he shares the life he has brought with his family and with the community as a whole.

These relationships are expressed in many ways in the context of Pueblo life. The buffalo and deer dances we perform are two of the ways in which we honour these relationships. These dances are metaphors for the things that have meaning for us as Indigenous people. Our corn dances reflect our relationship to mother corn and the life she gives to us through our families, through our grandmas and our grandpas. The corn dances also celebrate the life of children, because ultimately they are the reason for the continuity of any culture through time and through place.

The two worlds of Pueblo life – the corn dancer and the buffalo dancer represented in murals – have evolved over thousands of years. Through our art forms and the ways that we create ourselves into a community, we come to recognize the important things that embody us as a people.

We are, in a sense, sharing with one another food for thought and relationship. That food can take a physical form, or it can take many other forms in the gifts that we give each other. Life is really about sharing with each other and with every generation the "food" or the seeds we bring with us in our seed bags, as Kokopelli would do. An understanding of this basic relationship is the foundation of what we are today calling spiritual ecology. In a sense, this is the relationship that Western ecology is so desperately looking for and trying to understand. It is in relationships with the land, with the places where we have lived for generations, that we come to understand the meaning of spiritual ecology. We understand it through our celebrations, the celebrations of our "old" people, the celebrations in which we share food and ourselves with each other. After the harvest, we feast and share with one another those things that are important and that give us life and generate love in our communities and our families.

These reflective metaphoric understandings are also images of our lives and families and tribal backgrounds. We are all like a harvest of many-coloured vegetables and fruit. Each of us has a role to play in the greater picture. The multicoloured ears of corn – the communities that have given us life and that we support – allow us to share with one another that life and become, in a sense, the bounty that we give to each other.

These Pueblo understandings reflect metaphorical perspectives, images of Pueblo life that are parallel images of Indigenous life and education. We, as Pueblo people, express our spirituality in a variety of ways. In the bread that we offer and in the smiles on the faces of our children, you see the reflection of peoples who have come through many trials and tribulations but who continue to exist today because we have not consented to allowing our traditions and our way of life to be negated. The purpose of any society or educational process is to engender happy children. The extent to which we are able to do that is the extent to which we are successful as a group or as a culture.

Among my people, the Tewa, we have a concept known as *pin geh heh*. When you are growing up, sometimes your grandma will call you *pin geh heh*, which means "split mind." It is our way of saying that you're not thinking, that you're not doing something with a whole mind. You're acting in a foolish or silly manner. As a result of colonization, Indigenous people are in many ways acting like the *pin geh heh*. We lead lives of paradoxical conflict and contrast. A pottery figure done by the daughter of one of my cousins from Santa Clara Pueblo at the Institute of American Indian Art illustrated this split-head concept. I asked her why she was making one of her pottery figures with a split head. She told me this is the way she feels as a Native woman in a society that does not honour who she is or where she comes from. She called the figure the *pin geh heh*.

I've seen the *pin geh heh* not only in myself but also in many of the students whom I have taught over the past twenty-five years. Today I do not consider myself successful in the teaching process unless I can at least begin a process of healing this split. The split head, of course, leads to things that we've talked about before: suicide; self-hate; the disintegration of our cultures; the lack of knowing where we are, where we are going, and where we are coming from. As educators, we see all these things in our students. When I am frustrated, I pull this image out and look at it closely because it is a reflection not only of many of my students but also of how I deal with two worlds and two ways of knowing.

Indigenous education is also about a true sense of being multicultural, because to begin to heal this split we have to honour the human being in each of us. It is like the Iroquois myth of the great turtle. We all ride the great turtle's back. It is time to take action, to heal that split in ways we're able to, through the work and professions that we have chosen.

The "Sun Dagger" is an Anasazi petroglyph and one of the only sites in the world that, through light and shadow, simultaneously marks the solstices, the equinoxes, and the nineteen-year cycle of the moon. This petroglyph is found in Chaco Canyon, New Mexico. At about eleven in the morning, as the sun is rising to its highest point in the sky, the sunlight begins to form an image of a dagger of light through three positioned sandstone slabs on a carved spiral petroglyph. For me this image is a metaphor for this point in history when we must take action to develop ways that will allow us to create a more sustainable society and to survive in future generations. We must preserve the reflections of our elders, our spiritual ecology, and our spiritual symbols such as the pipe. These are all part of Indigenous knowledge and can help us in our process of revitalization as we move into the twenty-first century.

Teaching is a way of healing and a way of life. As a teacher, I have to know something about almost everything. After twenty-five years of teaching, I just now feel that I am beginning to become a wise teacher. It takes that long.

There is a "Tao" of teaching. By this I mean that there is a complementary working of relationships. When you get into the Tao of teaching, you begin to get a feel for the spirit of teaching. Questions about what teaching means, what it is really about, flood your mind. There is the technique, of course, but the technique is nothing – literally nothing – without the ability to apply the essence of teaching. Indigenous people understand the Tao of teaching. They understand that teaching is really about finding face, finding heart, finding foundation, and doing that in the context of family, of community, of relationships with a whole environment.

I remember a quotation from Vine Deloria. He had asked an elder what it was that allowed him to know his environment and how he knew things without being in a place or even ever having been there. The elder told him, "I have a map in my head." Indigenous curricula are maps.

In Western education, curriculum is a contract a teacher makes to organize the content and to teach in a certain way. In Western education, curricula are very political. That's why certain courses have to be fought through the Western education system, because the system itself has a constructed sense of what it is about that it needs to defend. The map is the educational/political/social contract. The curricula, the maps, we as contemporary Indigenous people have been using have in many ways suppressed us. The maps we are operating with now support the very system that colonized us. Indigenous people are working with maps that are not of our own making. We are working with the colonizer's maps. It's only when we can become our own "cartographers" that we will be able to find our way through the territory and move once again into the Tao of teaching, into Indigenous education.

When I wrote *Look to the Mountain: An Ecology of Indigenous Education,* I came to realize deeply how Western education has colonized Indigenous peoples. I now know something about the Tao of teaching, and in writing *Look to the Mountain* I sought to challenge myself and others to look at education in a different way, to create new Indigenous maps.

As a teacher, I take action on this mapmaking "vision" on a daily basis. I have never left the nitty-gritty of everyday classroom life. We need to be teaching if we are going to have practical insights and truly understand what has to happen in education for Indigenous students. There are other prerequisites. We need to know the ecology of Indigenous science and education, our stories, and our songs. We need to understand and acknowledge the colonial shadow of history and of Western science.

In my teaching, I use a cultural historical foundation. My purpose is first of all to help young Native people truly understand their history. Students must begin with understanding where they have come from, and they need to understand it thoroughly. Indigenous educators have to be willing to turn history inside out and upside down. Indigenous educators have to look at things in a way that allows you to begin to understand how the compact works – how it oppresses. You have to understand the compact in order to make the kinds of changes necessary; otherwise, the changes are simply superficial. They don't change the basic contract.

We must examine our habitual thought processes. We all are creatures of habit. Institutions and organizations get into habits of behaviour because the people who run them get into habits of thinking. We have to examine those habits because we have been through the Western educational system and have been conditioned to think in a certain way about education, life, ourselves, the environment, and Indigenous cultures. We have to reexamine that way of thinking. We have to do it honestly even if it hurts. This includes thinking about things such as racism, sexism, and ageism. It includes learning things such as the battle that some Indigenous people have between being both the colonized and the colonizer, which causes the split head that my cousin's daughter represented. Her father, a non-Native, represented one worldview, one way of looking at life; her mother, a Native, represented the other. Being torn between those two ways of living and looking at life is a place of great confusion, but it can also be a place of great compassion and creativity, as it has been for my cousin's daughter.

We have to reflect on Indigenous thought, Indigenous science, and Indigenous education based on their own merits and on their own terms. That is a key. We have tried to validate these ways of knowing through the Western system, but there is a point at which you see that they are completely different systems, different ways of knowing the world, and that you have to look at them based on what they are. Indigenous knowledge is an internally consistent system. It validates itself. It does not need external validation. But you have to understand it and its principles through the maps that it has created. Finding a balance and attending to one's self and to where one stands are the first steps in our collective journey of rediscovery. We have then to be responsible to ourselves, our communities, our ancestry, and our personal gifts. That's difficult. You have to work at it every day. But we have to carry forward the best that we have and give that to the next generation.

It's hard to be a teacher. It's even harder to be an Indigenous teacher because you constantly have to work between two worlds. Many times you don't know if you are coming or going. But as an Indigenous teacher, you have a responsibility. We have, similar to the medical profession, an oath that we take, and that oath is to be responsible to the children who are given to our care and to the information and the knowledge that we convey. Thinking that they know the Native person's mind and being is a mistake that has been made many times by many non-Native people. That's the reason Native people have to begin to reflect and to write in their voices about their own experience. That is the only way to begin to correct that process of misunderstanding.

We as tribal people have maps in our heads. For some of us, much of that map has been stepped on, and it seems that it has been erased or totally eradicated, but it is still there. Knowledge is like a cloud. Clouds come into being, they form, and then they go out of being, and then they come into being again somewhere else. The maps that we have in our heads as Indigenous people are inherited and enfolded within our genes. Many Indian people and elders have said that we don't lose knowledge. Knowledge, like a cloud, comes in and out of being. Knowledge comes to us when we need it. It evolves and develops. When things are needed, they come. That's true. So the map in our heads is really what we have to begin to deal with.

My final words are about what we can do as designers of the educational experience for other educators. For me the curriculum is a creative process. As an artist, I look at every learning experience as an exciting creative event. I bring all I am, all I know, and all the technical knowledge I have to bear on creating an experience for the learner, for students, that helps them along the pathway of self-understanding and self-knowledge. I am a facilitator of learning processes and a creator of contexts for learning.

For example, when you deal with Indigenous science, you begin to realize that everything is alive. The Lakota talk about "the abiding stone." Everything, including the stone, can talk to you. Everything can teach you something. Everything is alive, related, and connected in the dynamic, interactive, and reciprocal relationships of nature. All events and energy unfold and enfold in themselves. That means that things come into being and that things go out of being when they are needed. This principle, this idea, is a part of Indigenous ways of knowing.

Indigenous people are interested in finding the proper moral and ethical relationship to the world in order for them to become "complete" human beings. Indigenous knowledge is derived from communal experience, from environmental observation, from information received, and from the visions attained through ceremonies and communion with spirits of nature. Indigenous people believe that the universe is a moral universe; we look at it and deal with it in terms of a moral framework. That's why Indigenous science would never come to a point where it would try to make a decision to alter a gene in order to create something better. I think the moral and ethical problems coming up in science today need the Indigenous sensibility so that moral development – a sense of ethics and way of compassionate knowing – becomes a part of the expression of science.

Indigenous relationships have a history. That is why it is important for me to create a context that allows young people to truly know their history. I am an artist and have used my paintings, in my curricula, teachings, and writings, to illustrate my own artistic vision. On the cover of my book *Look to the Mountain*, I use an illustration inspired by the tradition of Huichol Indian yarn painting that represents the first act in the journey toward understanding, that of "asking," and conveys a history and a process called the cycle of visioning. Looking to the "inner form" of an archetypal mountain, the human form asks for and receives understanding, with the trickster, in the form of a spider monkey, and four Kokopelli looking on. As the "flower and song" of the human touch the face of the great mystery, the human connects to a "great rainbow of thought and relationship" that brings illumination and true understanding of the "ecology of relationship" and of the inherent truth that "We are all related!" It's a generic view based on my own artistic vision. It's not meant to reflect any particular tribal point of view, but it does reflect Indigenous thoughts and ideas.

I spent some time with some Huichol Indians of Mexico when I sponsored them at the Institute of American Indian Arts a few years back. We shared such beautiful gifts with each other. In a way, the painting is honouring them. The painting represents the first stage of a creative vision process. In the book, I present seven stages in all. They include asking, seeking, making, finding or having, sharing, celebrating, and then centring or going back to the source or centre. The painting on the cover of my book is my asking, but I think it also represents the asking that each of us is in the process of evoking. We are asking for the direction. In the painting, the vision is connected with the rainbow running through the figure in the picture. He is a part of the rainbow, and so are we.

In Huichol art, when you represent a prayer or a song, you represent it as a flower going into the sky. For me, as a teacher, this image represents the first stage that we need to go through, indeed that we are going through right now. We are asking the kinds of questions that must be asked. What is our history? What are our tools? What action can we take for this process to manifest itself in ourselves and in our communities and in the ways in which we teach each other? For each of us is indeed a Kokopelli.

15
Maintaining Aboriginal Identity, Language, and Culture in Modern Society
Marie Battiste

Aboriginal people in Canada pose a serious question to the Canadian educational system: How should schools be structured and content developed and delivered to offer equitable outcomes for Aboriginal peoples in Canada? Aboriginal peoples articulated their goals for education in 1972, when the National Indian Brotherhood sought to take control of Indian education. These goals have not changed in the intervening years. Aboriginal parents still wish for their children to participate fully in Canadian society but also to develop their personal and community potential through a fully actualized linguistic and cultural identity and from within their own Aboriginal context.

There have been innovations in Aboriginal education in the past twenty-five years, both at the First Nations and at the provincial levels, but these reforms have not gone far enough. The existing curriculum has given Aboriginal people new knowledge to help them participate in Canadian society, but it has not empowered Aboriginal identity by promoting an understanding of Aboriginal worldviews, languages, and knowledge. The lack of a clear, comprehensive, and consistent policy about Aboriginal consciousness has resulted in modern educational acts that suppress these integral cultures and identities. Most public schools in Canada today do not have coherent plans about how teachers and students can know Aboriginal thought and apply it in current educational processes.

Educators have suggested that problems arise because the "style of learning" through which Aboriginal students are enculturated at home differs markedly from the teaching style of the classroom. Linguists have pointed out that these differences may lead to sociolinguistic interference when teachers and students do not recognize them. These theories, however, do not get to the root of the problem. Non-Aboriginal scholars have avoided the major evaluative issue, which I have previously called cognitive imperialism or cognitive assimilation.[1] Scholars within the United Nations have called it cultural racism.[2] Cognitive imperialism, also known as cultural racism, is the imposition of one worldview on a people who have an alternative worldview, with the implication that the imposed worldview is superior to the alternative worldview.

The 1996 report of the Royal Commission on Aboriginal Peoples reaffirms both the goals of Aboriginal parents for the education of their children and the gaps in the current educational system.[3] It explains how current educational policy is based on the false assumption of the cultural superiority of European worldviews, and it recommends ways to eradicate the many obstacles that stand in the way of the advancement of Aboriginal peoples in Canada today. The report attests to the need for the transformation of knowledge, curriculum, and schools. It recognizes that the current curriculum in Canada projects European knowledge as universal, normative, and ideal. It marginalizes or excludes Aboriginal cultures, voices, and ways of knowing. In this chapter, I will explore how Aboriginal identity, languages, and cultures can be maintained in the current educational system of Canada and what innovations are required to do this. I will also explore the challenges that lie ahead for educators in effecting an education that respects and nourishes Aboriginal languages, cultures, and identity.

It should be stressed that Aboriginal consciousness cannot be maintained without first challenging the assumptions of modern society. Confronting the difficulties in maintaining Aboriginal consciousness in modern thought may be too much for the current educational system, but language revival, maintenance, and development remain as a challenging task for Aboriginal peoples to undertake in their quest for decolonization and self-determination.

Public School Education: Benign Fragmentation

Most Canadians trust their educational system. Education is not only the arena in which academic and vocational skills are developed but also the arena in which culture, mores, and social values are transmitted to the student. The educational system, fostered by government and society, is the basis of Canadian cultural transmission. However, for children whose languages and cultures are different from mainstream immigrant expectations, this educational system is a form of cognitive imperialism.

The military, political, and economic subjugation of Aboriginal peoples has been well documented, as have social, cultural, and linguistic pressures and the ensuing detrimental consequences to First Nations communities, but no force has been more effective at oppressing First Nations cultures than the educational system. Under the subtle influence of cognitive imperialism, modern educational theory and practice have, in large part, destroyed or distorted the ways of life, histories, identities, cultures, and languages of Aboriginal peoples.

Most Canadians, both Aboriginal and non-Aboriginal, have long accepted some of the fundamental assumptions underlying modern public school education. We have assumed that education is a kind and necessary form of mind liberation that opens to the individual options and possibilities that ultimately have value for society as a whole. On the face of it, education appears beneficial to all people and intrinsic to the progress and development of modern technological society.

But public schooling has not been benign.[4] It has been used as a means to perpetuate damaging myths about Aboriginal cultures, languages, beliefs, and ways of life. It has also established Western science as a dominant mode of thought that distrusts diversity and jeopardizes us all as we move into the next century. After nearly a century of public schooling for tribal peoples in Canada, the most serious problem with the current system of education lies not in its failure to liberate the human potential among Aboriginal peoples but in its quest to limit thought to cognitive imperialistic policies and practices. This quest denies Aboriginal people access to and participation in the formulation of government policy, constrains the use and development of Aboriginal cultures in schools, and confines education to a narrow scientific view of the world that threatens the global future.

There are two different points at issue here. The first is the right of Aboriginal peoples to exercise their own culture; the second is the benefit that the Western world can derive from this culture. Western scholars are gradually realizing how important Aboriginal knowledge may be to the future survival of our world. Not only is it important that Aboriginal cultures are preserved and encouraged, but it is also important that they are recognized as the domain of Aboriginal peoples and not subverted by the dominant culture.

Two international conferences since the mid-1970s have drawn attention to the right of Aboriginal peoples to the preservation of their cultures in the face of cognitive imperialism. The World Conference on Indigenous People in 1978 "endorse[d] the right of Indigenous Peoples to maintain their traditional structure of economy and culture, including their own language."[5] In 1989, a United Nations seminar on the effects of racism and racial discrimination on the social and economic relations between Indigenous peoples and states concluded that global racism was taking on the new form of state theories of cultural, rather than biological, superiority, resulting in rejection of the legitimacy or viability of the values and institutions of Indigenous peoples.[6]

Ironically, although the value of Indigenous culture is devalued by cognitive imperialism, the dominant society has a tendency to take elements of traditional Aboriginal knowledge out of context and claim them for itself. In 1993, the chairperson of the Working Group on Indigenous Populations, Dr. Erica-Irene Daes, prepared a report condemning the widespread and continued exploitation of traditional knowledge and culture by Euro-centric institutions and scholars.[7] She described this as the final stage of colonialism, following the exhaustion of Indigenous peoples' tangible assets. Daes argues for the urgency of taking international action to pro-tect the dignity, privacy, and identity of Indigenous peoples without wait-ing for the adoption of the declaration. The principles laid out by the working group acknowledge that the heritage of an Indigenous people is a complete knowledge system with its own concepts of epistemology, philosophy, language, and scientific and logical validity that needs pro-tection from Eurocentric exploitation. In the 1990s, designated by the United Nations as the International Decade of the World's Indigenous Peoples, the Working Group on Indigenous Populations and related activ-ities are developing an understanding of and a cure for cultural racism and are furthering the immediate, practical processes of cultural restoration in decolonized states.[8]

Confronting cultural racism in Canada is a difficult task because cultural racism cannot be contained to any one portion of the state. It is a systemic form of racism that cannot be dealt with in schools through classroom supplements or add-on courses. Confronting the problem requires a holis-tic understanding of modern thought and the purpose of education.

Curriculum, Colonialism, and Incoherence

Although the notion of "one best educational system" has been largely discredited, the notion that there is "one best remedy" for our educational ills has not. Modern society is still looking for and frequently is offered simple cures for these ills, one-ingredient prescriptions that claim to be panaceas. But there is no cure-all, no educational antibiotic to be admin-istered externally by injection into the state to cure the modern ills.

To understand how education in Canada continues to suppress or exter-minate Aboriginal consciousness, one has to understand modern thought. The existing body of research, which normally provides reference points for new research, must be examined and reassessed. This is no small task. Few Canadians understand the relationship of modern thought to the educational system. Most educators assume that modern thought is an accurate description of reality, and this assumption is at the centre of the modern curriculum. Yet modern thought establishes an artificial and imaginary realm. The immigrants left their own societies and entered tribal Canada. In our Aboriginal homeland, they began to develop a soci-ety that they imagined into being through laws and regulations. The affir-mation and continuation of this imaginary realm are supplied through the provincial educational system. This imagined immigrant society is dis-tinctive from Aboriginal societies, whose customary rules are grounded in the laws of nature.

The purpose of education is to transmit culture to new generations. But culture remains elusive; it is implicitly summed up by skills and shared traditions. Since there is no agreement about transmitting culture, the real purpose of education is to affirm the political and social status quo. The task of education in Canada is to explain the immigrant's broad privileges and wealth in another's homeland. The curriculum has to justify immigrant privileges in Aboriginal America. In the past, the immigrants relied on the racism built into their political system to justify their privileges. Since the United Nations human rights declarations and covenants in the 1990s, these foundational standards have been universally rejected, and the necessary justification to sustain privilege has moved into the educational and cultural arenas.

In every educational circumstance, much of what is learned depends on the context in which it is learned. Within the context of public school education, one can identify a few basic preconceptions about reality that exercise an overwhelming influence over education in this country. The modern Canadian educational structure has its theoretical ambitions pinned to the development of a supposed science of history and society. This supposed science is based on false concepts of race and evolutionary thought; however, in the modern curriculum, these frameworks are taught as if Canadians were mere puppets of them and of the forces that generate and sustain them.

The supposed science of history and society presents humans as the product of an evolutionary or cultural logic on the one hand and of deep-seated, unalterable economic, organizational, or psychological constraints on the other. Educational institutions insist that abandoning this way of viewing the world would lead humans to theoretical nihilism and destroy the established social order. Educational theory does not argue that society can be remade or reimagined; instead, it postulates that, without recognizing this evolutionary logic and these practical constraints, humans and society will lose intellectual guidance. As a result, education must affirm the existing social order and its theory of control. Other forms of culture or social life are recognized in the curriculum as expressions of a different way of being human within the evolutionary logic or practical constraints.

The modern political theory of democracy, on the other hand, argues that humans can completely override these institutional arrangements. Modern experience in constitutional debates and in legislation with these arrangements shows that often these frameworks are put aside. Canadians think and act, incongruously and surprisingly, as if institutional arrangements or frameworks are not for real, as if they merely pretend to obey them while awaiting an opportunity to defy them. They can disrupt these established arrangements; they can replace them, if not all at once, then piece by piece.

Following the recent work done under the auspices of the United Nations, theorists of modern society in Canada have been forced to acknowledge that current social arrangements do not reflect a higher rational or practical necessity. Instead, modern political theory establishes immigrant society as a form of society that can be reinvented and reformulated at will. Modern educational theory is thus in a predicament. It is based on justifying and perpetuating the status quo, yet it has to acknowledge the recent shift in thinking that immigrant society is an invented society that can be recast. In defending immigrant society, it can no longer rely on discarded theories of racial or cultural superiority, but it cannot refer to an overarching set of objective values for justification either. Aboriginal societies reflect the patterns of nature; they are grounded in the world around them. In contrast to this grounding of Aboriginal society in an order outside itself, there exists no theory of Canadian immigrant society that reflects social order as an eternal pattern of human nature or social harmony. The contrast between the political theory of modern society and educational theory shows how fragile these arrangements and ideas are in daily life.

Schools affirm the status quo by talking of "training men and women the age needs." Who determines what the age needs? If there are some sorts of people every age needs, then there should be permanence in education. This training helps to preserve class structures and selects the elite rather than sorting everyone out according to their innate capacities. This sorting also passes family or parental responsibility on to the state, leading to a disintegration of the family for the abstraction of the society.

What is apparent to Aboriginal peoples is the need for a serious and far-reaching examination of the assumptions inherent in modern educational theory. How these assumptions create the moral and intellectual foundations of modern society and culture has to be studied and written about by Aboriginal people to allow space for Aboriginal consciousness, language, and identity to flourish without ethnocentric or racist interpretation. The current educational shortcomings may or may not be in the curriculum, or in finance, or in testing, or in community involvement, but no one will ever know this – nor the changes necessary for improvement – without a deeper philosophical analysis of modern thought and educational practices.

Decolonizing Education and Cultural Restoration

When most non-Aboriginal people think of why they would support the maintenance of Aboriginal consciousness and language in modern education, they view it as enabling Aboriginal students to compete successfully with non-Aboriginal students in the imagined immigrant society. Educators argue that school systems can maintain Aboriginal identity, culture, and languages by making a conscious effort to teach the children how to act in the modern classroom. They do not know or understand the cognitive shock they would be forced to endure if Aboriginal consciousness and language were to be respected, affirmed, and encouraged to flourish in the modern classroom.

Cognitive imperialism is a form of cognitive manipulation used to disclaim other knowledge bases and values. Validated through one's knowledge base and empowered through public education, it has been the means by which whole groups of people have been denied existence and have had their wealth confiscated. Cognitive imperialism denies people their language and cultural integrity by maintaining the legitimacy of only one language, one culture, and one frame of reference.

As a result of cognitive imperialism, cultural minorities have been led to believe that their poverty and impotence are a result of their race. The modern solution to their despair has been to describe this causal connection in numerous reports. The gift of modern knowledge has been the ideology of oppression, which negates the process of knowledge as a process of inquiry to explore new solutions. This ideology seeks to change the consciousness of the oppressed, not change the situation that oppressed them.

Whether Aboriginal or black or other visible minority in Canada, a similarity in treatment and themes of denial and oppression have resounded in society and through educational practices. In her book *Invisibility in Academe*, Adrienne Rich describes the result: "When someone with the authority of a teacher, say, describes the world and you are not in it, there is a moment of psychic disequilibrium as if you looked into a mirror and saw nothing."[9]

In the Canadian educational system today, Aboriginal people continue to be invisible.[10] Occasional pictures in books are the only images of our participation in the educational world. The content of these books, however, does not represent our worldview. Aboriginal people have had to endure a "planting out" of our systems when students were boarded in white homes to learn proper behaviour and acceptable skills for working in lower-class occupations. They have had to submit to child sexual and psychological abuse and boarding schools from age five to sixteen. The cultural imperialistic curriculum in these schools has degraded and demoralized cultural minority students, assigned them to transitional classes, failed them, and then accused them of lacking motivation, attention, or spirit.

As we approach the twenty-first century, we need to take a look at where we have been and where we are going. First we must become painfully aware of what has happened to children and to Aboriginal people across Canada, and then we must seek to find ways to resolve those problems. We must find resources to enable all children to have the rights outlined in the *Canadian Charter of Rights and Freedoms* and the United Nations *Convention on the Rights of the Child.*

Aboriginal languages are the basic media for the transmission and survival of Aboriginal consciousness, cultures, literatures, histories, religions, political institutions, and values. They provide distinctive perspectives on and understandings of the world, which educational research has ignored. The suppression or extermination of this consciousness in education through the destruction of Aboriginal languages is inconsistent with the modern constitutional rights of Aboriginal peoples.

Aboriginal languages are the means of communication for the full range of human experiences, and they are critical to the survival of the culture and political integrity of any people.[11] These languages are a direct and powerful means of understanding the legacy of tribal knowledge. They provide the deep and lasting cognitive bonds that affect all aspects of Aboriginal life. Through sharing a language, Aboriginal people create a shared belief in how the world works and what constitutes proper action. The sharing of these common ideals creates a collective cognitive experience for tribal societies that is understood as tribal epistemology.

Where Aboriginal knowledge survives, it is transmitted through Aboriginal language. There is clear and convincing evidence that student achievement and performance in school and pride in Aboriginal communities and heritages are directly tied to respect for and support of the students' Aboriginal languages.[12] Although it is clearly in the interests of the educational system to encourage the full academic and personal achievements of Aboriginal students, absolutely nothing has been done by the federal or provincial governments in Canada to remedy this educational problem. Nothing has been done to preserve, protect, and promote the rights and freedoms of Aboriginal people to use, practise, and develop Aboriginal languages in Canada. Canadian lawmakers and educators have overlooked the right of Aboriginal languages to exist as a medium of instruction in the schools, failed to recognize the official status of Aboriginal languages for conducting Aboriginal business, and failed to encourage educational institutions to allow the same academic credit for proficiency in Aboriginal languages as for proficiency in foreign languages. In contrast, the United States[13] and the United Nations[14] have passed legislation recognizing the right of Aboriginal peoples to use their traditional languages.

Many Aboriginal students still speak their Aboriginal languages, but there are no courses and extremely limited materials for helping them to make the transition to the working languages of Canada. These students, labelled "at risk," are relegated to the lower levels of academic achievement, where most remain. Limited ability in English (or French) impedes the progress of many minority children throughout Canada.[15] Teaching English (or French) as a second language must be unilaterally implemented in all schools where the students' language is different from the school's language.

Instead of requiring Aboriginal students to submit to a third language (French in English-speaking Canada and English in French-speaking Canada), they should have the opportunity to explore their first language in a provincially accredited course in elementary and secondary school, as well as to find appropriate ways to explore their understandings and expand their knowledge and usage of their second language of English or French. Being required to learn French or English as a third language, without a good handle on their first or second language, imposes yet another major hurdle that impedes Aboriginal students from achieving educational equity.

Books and materials in provincial public schools do not accurately depict the history and cultural diversity of Canada. Although some provinces have made great strides in correcting the blatant racism found in texts, the truth is still obscured in favour of a more rational and polished early existence in Canada. Beautiful images of Aboriginal peoples in Native regalia cannot be allowed to subvert the historical truths that publishers wish not to discuss. Polished texts obscure Aboriginal history, cultures, and languages while perpetuating the myth of an empty land in the New World that was ripe for discovery by European explorers. Kits and thematic units prepared by public education in some areas of Canada depict a prehistoric life of Aboriginal peoples, complete with teepees, skins, animal bones, rock tools, and arrowheads. Aboriginal peoples are depicted as primitives, gone after the arrival of the early settlers or working their way toward assimilation in urban areas.

Provincial public education has denied our people the right to speak to the issues of the past, to explain and understand the courses of action that we have had to take in these periods of adversity, and to be honoured for those choices. It is our heritage that we were given the right and the responsibility to pass on to our children. As yet, we have not been allowed the dignity to choose what is important to pass on through the public schools.

All First Nations and provincial schools require new teaching materials that depict, accurately and adequately, the culture, history, heritage, worldviews, and philosophies of Aboriginal peoples. Currently, only a few schools are producing materials in Aboriginal languages: most Aboriginal language programs publish their own. Book companies are reluctant to publish language materials that reach only a small group of people; however, the need has been established in Canada for the reevaluation of curriculum content in the schools and for a concerted effort to integrate Aboriginal knowledge into it. We need to encourage book companies to enlist other language groups into their book productions. Encouraging various Aboriginal communities to offer English texts so that they can decide if the content can be appropriately translated at a lower cost is an additional incentive to have materials in the Aboriginal languages.

Elders are the critical link to Aboriginal epistemology through the Aboriginal languages. The last vestiges of Aboriginal languages exist in pockets of the Aboriginal population. There they are secured by certain families in a collective community consciousness. By introducing language and cultural education in First Nations-operated schools, Aboriginal people are attempting to retain and sustain their languages, cultures, and tribal knowledge through the assistance of elders and a bare-bones curriculum development program.

Some First Nations schools have provided flexibility and openness to new ideas and have used Aboriginal pedagogy to bridge epistemologies. Taking schooling out into the bush and bringing elders into the classroom are two ways in which First Nations schools have enriched the knowledge not only of students but also of teachers.[16] This flexible approach helps to spread tribal knowledge, but it has sometimes been at a cost to some part of the compulsory public school curriculum. As one area is enriched, some other area of the regular school curriculum is affected. The result is that Aboriginal students sometimes do not have the same cumulative knowledge as their non-Aboriginal counterparts, just as the non-Aboriginal students do not have the cumulative knowledge of their Aboriginal counterparts.

To maintain its flexibility, community-controlled Aboriginal education must remain outside the arena of provincial administrative regulations. Another reason for this distance is to ensure that a central administration does not profit from the progressive ideas developed in such educational milieus. For instance, the acceptance of tribal knowledge by some scientists and scholars, including David Bohm, David Peat, David Suzuki, Rupert Ross, and others, and the elevation of tribal epistemologies in research and roundtables and think tanks will have the profound effect of pushing modern knowledge to new questions and ways of thinking about problems and solutions.[17] The ownership of these ideas must remain with Aboriginal people. We must nurture this growth, guide it with our elders and tribal scholars, and find ways to share tribal epistemology beyond history and culture.

The real justification for including Aboriginal knowledge in the modern curriculum is not so that Aboriginal students can compete with non-Aboriginal students in an imagined world. It is, rather, that immigrant society is sorely in need of what Aboriginal knowledge has to offer. We are witnessing throughout the world the weaknesses in knowledge based on science and technology. It is costing us our air, our water, our earth; our very lives are at stake. No longer are we able to turn to science to rid us of the mistakes of the past or to clean up our planet for the future of our children. Our children's future planet is not secure, and we have contributed to its insecurity by using the knowledge and skills that we received in public schools. Not only have we found that we need to make new decisions about our lifestyles to maintain the planet, but we are also becoming increasingly aware that the limitations of modern knowledge have placed our collective survival in jeopardy.

The public school curriculum is limiting the knowledge base of our children. They are being denied access to knowledge bases that they need to sustain themselves and the planet in the future. To deny that tribal epistemology exists and serves a lasting purpose is to deprive Aboriginal children of their inheritance, as well as to perpetuate the belief that different cultures have nothing to offer but exotic food and dance or a shallow first chapter in the story of what is to come. To allow tribal epistemology to die through the loss of the Aboriginal languages is to allow another world of knowledge to die, one that could help to sustain us. As Aboriginal peoples of this land, we have the knowledge to enable us to survive and flourish in our own homeland. Our stories of ancient times tell us how. Our languages provide those instructions.

With the recent development of First Nations schooling, we have once again resolved to involve the elders and our life ways in our development as human beings. We have begun by utilizing Aboriginal languages to teach the sacred knowledge of our ancestors. Our curriculum is based on the language, thematically taught, and aligned to the cycles, relationships, and rhythms of our existence. In this way, we are beginning to provide the balanced spectrum of education that we were denied under earlier federal policies of assimilation.

Western education has much to gain by viewing the world through the eyes and languages of Aboriginal peoples. The earth and its resources must be viewed through the lens of tribal knowledge if we are to understand how to protect the universe. Rituals and ceremonies that cleanse and heal, maintaining the balances, must be respected and honoured. Western science has promoted the development of modern society, which has initiated the best and worst of development from environmental and economic perspectives. Today we are faced with how we are to survive the global disasters created by our scientific ingenuity, as well as how we can bridge knowledge gaps created by the diversity of people and thought. Aboriginal languages and education can be the means to opening the paradigmatic doors of contemporary public education. Creating a balance between two worldviews is the great challenge facing modern educators.

Developing Legislation to Protect Constitutional Rights

Because modern society has no idea about the worldview within Aboriginal consciousness, the best way to encourage inclusion of this worldview in the modern curriculum is through a comprehensive federal act. Under the existing constitutional rights of Aboriginal people, the federal government must enact legislation to provide an adequate quantity and quality of educational services based on Aboriginal consciousness, as well as equal access for Aboriginal people to an education distinct from the needs of other groups or peoples in Canada.

While legislation appears to be an obvious solution to the problem, this course of action has not been proposed in the recommendations put forward by the Assembly of First Nations in *Toward Rebirth of First Nations Languages* or in the *House of Commons Standing Committee on Aboriginal Affairs Report* on Aboriginal literacy and empowerment. Both of these groups suggest consultation, task forces, and institutional arrangements, which I endorse. I also endorse the spirit and intent of their recommendations. Still, these consultations, task forces, and institutional arrangements must lead to a federal act implementing our existing rights in modern society. Such a federal act is a more permanent framework for understanding the problem and carrying out solutions.

Such an act should declare community-based education as an existing Aboriginal and treaty right that must be fully complied with and supported. A delivery system must be developed to facilitate the flow of service and program funds in the most direct and immediate manner to the local program level with a minimum of delay and administration. Such an act must recognize the viability of funding community-based educational institutions as conduits of all aspects of Aboriginal education.

Aboriginal languages are irreplaceable resources that require protection and support. In particular, Aboriginal languages require official status in Canada, constitutional recognition, and accompanying legislative protection. In addition, provincial and federal schools should provide credit within the school system for Aboriginal language study.

Experience has shown, however, that it is not enough to formulate policy that recognizes the viability of community-based educational institutions for Aboriginal people in an act. Funding and administrative policies must ensure that weighing criteria exist for preserving and developing Aboriginal consciousness and languages in those educational institutions. There are more than enough modern thought–based schools and classrooms in Canada; the problem is to create an Aboriginal language–based curriculum. No politician, administrator, or educator should be able to destroy Aboriginal consciousness or language because of other priorities. Thus, explicit funding and policies must ensure that First Nations politicians or administrators cannot confiscate funding designated for the preservation of Aboriginal consciousness or languages for other temporal schemes. This is the lesson of our history with education.

Aboriginal communities should be encouraged to assume full control of their education with adequate resources and funding to create an educational system that will develop Aboriginal consciousness through the development of Aboriginal language, culture, and identity. Where Aboriginal communities have instituted language policies in educational systems, these policies should be recognized and acknowledged by the federal government, and financial resources should be available to develop these policies and link these systems to other agencies and services that permit the development of languages.

Such an act must establish guidelines and funding incentives that will ensure that preserving and developing Aboriginal consciousness and languages is not viewed as a lesser part of the curriculum. Literacy is a Canadian resource that Aboriginal students must develop in their own languages before they are required to learn English. Funds must be provided to make Aboriginal literacy viable for schools to incorporate into their early childhood educational programs, in particular in the development of books and materials in the Aboriginal languages.

The act should encourage and require grantees to set aside a certain percentage of grant funds for in-service training and staff development programs on Aboriginal consciousness and languages to understand the scope and implication of the differences from modern thought. The existing network of provincial programs must be revamped to target program monies into enhancing Aboriginal consciousness and languages in all levels of the curriculum. The federal government should provide adequate resources to First Nations to ensure the development of language structures, curriculum materials, First Nations language teachers, resource centres, and immersion programs.

A network of regional curriculum centres for Aboriginal languages is justifiable. The regional centres would offer support for curriculum development with the assistance of local language informants and elders. Curriculum centres should be developed on a regional base suited to Aboriginal people so that they do not have to leave their communities for extended periods of time. Centres should be able to evaluate the established curriculum and work out solutions. The centres would offer curriculum developers and educational resources for the development of books by Aboriginal thinkers, as well as offer printing services at a reasonable rate. Some books may be accepted by other language groups in the region or nationally and, where appropriate, could be translated and printed, offering advantages such as lower rates due to the large number of books printed.

These centres should fund writing workshops and support writers who embrace Aboriginal thought and knowledge and apply it to methods of teaching. They should support and fund the research and writing of Aboriginal pedagogy and language curriculum and teaching. They should raise the consciousness of the Canadian public about the positive value to all society of inclusive education as opposed to the current exclusionary model. They should provide information to communities about the stages of language loss and the restorative process that they may use to guide the growth of a healthy language base. These centres should develop and/or encourage curriculum advisory boards or committees composed of elders in the community who will guide the development of curriculum and the development of language research for educational purposes.

Such an act must waive the requirement for teaching credentials and overcome other barriers to the employment of Aboriginal elders who speak their Aboriginal languages in federal or provincial schools. Elders in Aboriginal communities are the custodians of endangered Aboriginal languages, and they must have dignity and an acknowledgment of the value of their services. Elders require the support of other elders and flexibility in timing and scheduling. They should be provided with these necessary amenities.

It seems obvious that elders and others who can pass on Aboriginal identity, languages, and culture should be directly involved in the modern educational system. Yet seldom has any government confronted the educational biases in modern thought or educational practice that exclude them from this role. A modern legislative solution to this problem is found in the *Native American Language Act*.[18] Section 104(s) declares that it is the policy of the United States to "allow exceptions to teacher certification requirements for Federal programs, and programs funded in whole or in part by the Federal Government, for instruction in Native American languages when such teacher certification requirements hinder the employment of qualified teachers who teach in Native American languages, and to encourage State and territorial governments to make similar exceptions."

Aboriginal languages cannot be isolated in the way that politics or economics can be isolated in modern thought. Advocates of cultural studies argue that no person from another worldview can learn about other cultures except by being there and listening. (This is called "fieldwork.") Languages are said to be learned, not genetically encoded. Learning any language requires time and patience – one cannot simply use one's imagination to invent other cultural worlds, methods, and perceptions. Human imagination is as culturally formed as are distinctive ways of weaving, performing a ritual, raising children, grieving, or healing. All these activities are specific to certain forms of life.

In this era, discussion of limited funding is merely another way to avoid implementing constitutional rights and human rights. Yet without funding, the future costs for developing a curriculum that includes Aboriginal knowledge and languages are horrific. A base formula must be established to offer stable funding for Aboriginal education – funding at a level equal to provincial standards. The finances should be derived by implementing a procedure that identifies tax revenue already collected at the municipal, provincial, and federal levels, including money that normally flows into the existing tax revenue from treaty entitlements to the Crown, Aboriginal resources, and Aboriginal economic development activities.

This tax revenue has never been considered as having emanated from Aboriginal or treaty rights or from Indian reserves and communities, which in fact contribute a major portion of tax revenue to governments. After the federal government has identified and isolated dollars from a tax study and estimates have been made of these dollars, the monies may be supplemented by federal appropriations.

The act should encourage Aboriginal youth to obtain technical and professional levels of education once they have had the chance to learn the history of their own nations. When they perceive that education can have a positive impact on their own lives and those of their people; when there are Aboriginal role models who reflect the best values of their nations and who nurture culture and language development in their communities; and when good economic opportunities are created so that they can remain in their communities – all this can reflect on the existing body of Aboriginal knowledge. Still, each one of these solutions requires major changes.

Little classroom research has been done on the effects of teaching students about their culture, history, and languages, as well as about oppression, racism, and differences in worldviews, but consciousness-raising classes and courses at the elementary and junior high school levels, and at the college and university levels, have brought to the surface new hopes and dreams and have raised the aspirations and educational successes of Aboriginal students. Our people are slowly coming to understand that poverty and oppression are not their fault and are not the result of their faulty language, consciousness, or culture. They have begun to understand that poverty and oppression are tools created by modern society to maintain the status quo and to foster and legitimize racism and class divisions. As band schools offer courses in Aboriginal language and thought, and as economic opportunities are made available to Aboriginal peoples on reserves through education, racism and its residual effects in the non-Native community and family are being exposed.

First Nations government is a critical element in this development. First Nations must institute policies of hiring Aboriginal people whose first language is an Indigenous language and who will encourage its function and use in the workplace. If a language has little function in the daily lives of people, it will die. Leaders of the First Nations must inspire the youth to acquire an education so that they can benefit from increased responsibilities. The leaders must also inspire the youth to develop their skills for the nation and their valued language and culture. The First Nations must allow their own educated Aboriginal people to assume responsible positions in their community development, positions that nurture respect and honour, instead of passing these jobs to non-Aboriginal people or to family members with lesser qualifications. The strength of tribalism lies in our collective values, which must be fostered toward a collective consciousness as opposed to individual gain. Schools and community leaders must seek to nurture among the youth these traditional attitudes of collective community as they seek to develop their nation's growth. As the collective gains, so also do its parts. Collective healing in our community of the pains of the past and present will shape the attitudes of the youth. They must understand their past and the context of their present to embark on a new vision of the future.

Notes

1 Marie Battiste, "Micmac Literacy and Cognitive Assimilation," in J. Barman, Y. Hébert, and D. McCaskill, eds., *Indian Education in Canada: The Legacy* (Vancouver: UBC Press, 1986).
2 Report of the United Nations Seminar on the Effects of Racism and Racial Discrimination on the Social and Economic Relations between Indigenous Peoples and States. Commission on Human Rights, 45th Sess., UN Doc. E/CN.4/1989/22 (1989).
3 *Gathering Strength*, report of the Royal Commission on Aboriginal Peoples, vol. 3 (Ottawa: Canada Communications Group, 1996).
4 See, for example, Albert Memmi, *The Colonizer and the Colonized* (Boston: Beacon Press, 1963), and Paulo Freire, *Pedagogy of the Oppressed* (New York: Seabury Press, 1973).
5 See R. Barsh, "United Nations Seminar on Indigenous Peoples and States" (1989) 83(3) *Am. J. Internat'l L.* 599.
6 Battiste, "Micmac Literacy and Cognitive Assimilation."
7 Study of the Protection of the Cultural and Intellectual Property of Indigenous Peoples, UN Doc. E/CN.4/Sub.2/1993/28.
8 G.A. Res. 48/163, UN GAOR, 48th Sess., Agenda item 114(b), UN Doc. A/RES/48/163 (1994). See also Commission on Human Rights Resolution 1994/26 (March 4, 1994).
9 Adrienne Rich, "Invisibility in Academe," cited in Renate Rosaldo, *Culture and Truth* (Boston: Beacon Press, 1989), ix.
10 House of Commons Standing Committee on Aboriginal Affairs, *You Took My Talk: Aboriginal Literacy and Empowerment* (Ottawa: Queen's Printer, 1990), 29-35.
11 This is one of the findings of the United States Congress in *Native American Language Act*, P.L. 101–477, section 102(9) (1990).
12 Assembly of First Nations, *Towards Rebirth of First Nations Languages* (Ottawa: AFN, 1992); *You Took My Talk* (see note 10); Assembly of First Nations, *Towards Linguistic Justice for First Nations* (Ottawa: AFN, 1990); and Assembly of First Nations, *Tradition and Education: Towards a Vision of Our Future* (Ottawa: AFN, 1988).
13 *Native American Language Act*, P.L. 101–477, section 102(9) (1990).
14 Since Canada ratified the UN Human Rights Convention in 1976, Aboriginal people as linguistic minorities within Canada were supposed to enjoy freedom from discrimination and have the right to enjoy their own culture and to use their own language (GA Res. 2200a, 21 UN GAOR Supp. [No. 16] 49, UN Doc. A/6546 at 56). This right has never been translated into federal law or policy. The most recent UN statement is in International Labor Organization Convention 169, the *Indigenous and Tribal People Convention* 1989, articles 26, 27, 28. This convention has not been ratified by Canada.

15 See Mary Heit and Heather Blair, "Language Needs and Characteristics of Saskatchewan Students: Implications for Educators," and Catherine Littlejohn and Shirley Fredeen, "Indian Language Programs in Saskatchewan: A Survey," in Sonia Morris, Keith MacLeod, and Marcel Danesi, eds., *Aboriginal Languages and Education: The Canadian Experience* (Oakville, ON: Mosaic Press, 1995).

16 See Agnes Grant, "The Challenge for Universities," in Marie Battiste and Jean Barman, eds., *First Nations Education in Canada: The Circle Unfolds* (Vancouver: UBC Press, 1995).

17 See David Bohm, *Wholeness and the Implicate Order* (London: Routledge and Kegan Paul, 1980); David Peat, *Lighting the Seventh Fire: The Spiritual Ways, Healing, and Science of the Native American* (New York: Birch Lane Press, 1994); and David Suzuki, *The Sacred Balance: Rediscovering Our Place in Nature* (Vancouver: Greystone Books, 1997).

18 This federal act by the United States is part of the *Tribally Controlled Community College Assistance Act,* Public Law 101–477.

16
Protecting and Respecting Indigenous Knowledge
Graham Hingangaroa Smith

During the 1996 International Summer Institute at the University of Saskatchewan, I listened intently to the speakers and discussions and then organized my thoughts in order to respond interactively with issues previously raised. While the topic addressed at the institute generally kept faith with the theme of respecting and protecting Indigenous knowledge, I deliberately broadened my presentation to reflect upon some of the critical issues that had been raised by different speakers in the institute. This chapter closely reflects the original contribution made at the institute, which was presented in the traditional Maori form of oral presentation, *whaikoreo*. The appropriate *mihi* ritual introduction was performed, the words were spoken from the heart, the "truth" spoken by the speaker was laid out before the people for validation, the speech was delivered orally, and it was concluded with a traditional *waiata* or song. The presentation has been altered minimally to conform to printed conventions.

In this chapter, I will attempt to do three things. First, I want to deal with the protection of Indigenous knowledge within the context of the institute: that is, I want to respond to some specific challenges that came from voices gathered at the institute. Second, I want to explore what I call the "new formations of colonization" and look at one example in particular: the way in which Indigenous knowledge has become "commodified" as a result of the development of an emphasis on free-market economic forces. Third, I want to relate some of the specific strategies of resistance that are being developed within our context in New Zealand. In particular, I would like to describe the Maori case study as a possible example for other Indigenous communities to consider. I offer this example not to assert the definitive answer to the problems raised by colonization but to offer insights into what is and what is not working for us. You, of course, must decide for yourselves what is relevant and useful for your own situations. The key thing that I hope will interest people is the transformative processes we chose to adopt. This particular discussion is not so much about the structure of our interventions as it is about the processes we used to put those interventions in place. This, I think, is one of the ironies of Indigenous struggle: it is the actual process of struggle that makes us strong and committed and that helps us to consolidate why we are struggling. That is, struggle constantly forces us to identify and review what we stand for and what we stand against.

Seven Challenges Raised by the Summer Institute

The first challenge I want to respond to is what I call the challenge to Indigenous people to engage in positive, proactive initiatives rather than resorting to reactive modes of action. This proactive type of action can be illustrated in the tensions within the following dichotomies: the difference between having a fence at the top of the cliff and an ambulance at the bottom; the difference between prevention and cure; the difference between seeing oneself as responsible for Indigenous problems as opposed to understanding the wider societal structures; the difference between biological explanations and sociological explanations with respect to social and cultural differences. I am not suggesting that these positions are always absolute opposites; however, my view is that we Indigenous peoples should be concerned with accentuating preemptive and proactive actions rather than being sidetracked into being overly concerned with reactive responses. In Freire's terminology, we must "name the world for ourselves." While we should acknowledge that there are multiple sites where the struggle against oppression and exploitation might be taken up, Indigenous peoples must set the agenda for change themselves, not simply react to an agenda that has been laid out for us by others. With respect, I have felt a little uncomfortable with some of the discussion that has taken place at this institute when it has clearly come from a reactive mode of thinking. I would encourage the members of this institute to reflect carefully on the difference between being proactive and being reactive.

I would like to revisit some of the points made by Poka Laenui, who argued for the development and adoption of five steps of decolonization. My concern with this focus is that we might again be spending too much time in a reactive mode. The point here is the extent to which we are drawn into engaging with and justifying ourselves to the dominant society. I believe that such a process puts the colonizer at the centre, and thereby we become co-opted into reproducing (albeit unintentionally) our own oppression. While there is an important place for critical deconstruction of colonization (and I do not wish to diminish the powerful and valuable words offered by Poka Laenui), my concern is to concentrate our limited energies and resources on what it is that we want.

This latter point can be illustrated from the context out of which I've come. In recent years, Maori have penetrated the "politics of distraction" promulgated by dominant white non-Indigenous interests and have stopped feeling guilty about serving our own interests first.[1] We have challenged the hegemonies that maintain the status quo of *Pakeha* dominance and Maori subordination; for example, the beliefs surrounding the need to preserve "good race relations," "democracy," and "social equality" have been exposed as ideologies that thwart Maori interests and, conversely, serve to entrench existing *Pakeha* privilege. Maori have recently become less inclined to ask permission from or to seek support of non-Maori people with respect to meeting our needs and aspirations. We have increasingly moved to take action ourselves, implementing our own dreams with or without the consent of the dominant *Pakeha* society.

In short, Maori are sick of justifying and explaining our needs and aspirations to *Pakeha*. Maori themselves are now taking the initiative for transforming their own lives. In education, for example, Maori decided to initiate a range of educational and schooling initiatives to intervene in the twin crises of language loss and educational underachievement. Many Maori parents have opted out of existing state school structures and developed their own schooling responses – Maori parents have acted themselves. What Maori parents are saying to *Pakeha* society is that we know what we want. This is what we are going to do – you can help us (that is, get on the canoe and join us), or you can be left behind, because we're going to do this with or without you. My message to the institute members is that we have the option to set our own courses with respect to realizing our dreams and aspirations, and therefore we ought to be considering developing resistance initiatives around that kind of philosophy, initiatives that are positive and proactive. We must reclaim our own lives in order to put our destinies in our own hands.

The second challenge that members of the institute have talked about in various ways and that I would like to respond to is the whole notion of what counts as science. In particular, I have been concerned that the notion of "science" is talked about unproblematically. It worries me, as an Indigenous person, if we do not also see the dangers associated with the way in which science is constructed to promote the reification of Western thought. A particularly critical element for me here is the way in which technological rationality is embedded within science. Such positivistic framing of the world and social relations is at odds with Indigenous ways of thinking. I think that this is a dangerous form of knowledge for Indigenous peoples because it begins to switch our thinking from the circle to square boxes. It initiates a positivistic worldview that is fundamental to the New Right economic thinking that puts emphasis on competition rather than on cooperation, on the individual rather than on the collective, on regulations rather than on responsibility.

My reaction to an uncritical focus on Western science is very much one of resistance. I think that we should be cautious about inserting Western ways of thinking into the way we perceive knowledge. This is not an argument against science per se; it is an argument for developing a critical perspective on science in order to expose its colonizing potential. Science is not neutral. There are definitely implications for Indigenous peoples in engaging too seriously, in uncritical ways, with science. This is not to say that such an engagement may not be worthwhile. But I think, and Indigenous experience generally would support this stance, that we have to approach the issue with caution.

The third challenge that I want to respond to can be summarized as the issue of "naming ourselves." We need to be careful about how we label ourselves. The critical point here is the way in which labels can become self-fulfilling prophecies – labels can contribute to perpetuating our subordination and may both produce and reproduce our cultural oppression and economic exploitation. Thus, labels such as "minority," "oppressed," "exploited," and "subordinate" are useful when used sparingly and with critical understanding. There is something here related to the previous point about attempting to be positive and proactive. I think that this point was touched on in a previous session with respect to the word *democracy*. For example, if we spend time naming ourselves as a subordinate group, we're in danger of entrenching, producing, and reproducing our subordination because we also, in a relativist way, are naming the "others" as the dominant group.

There is a second critical element to this naming concern that has to do with democracy. One of the things that came out early in the institute was that we shouldn't name ourselves as a minority group. My opinion is that from time to time we do need to stand up and say that we are a numerical minority, because the notion of numerical minority critically engages with the taken-for-granted aspects relating to the democratic process. If we are trapped within the Westminster democratic model of "one person, one vote, and majority rule," then it needs to be understood that in such a system minority groups do not always have their rights recognized or supported by "democratic" processes. The Westminster model of democracy tends to reproduce the interests of dominant groups. So from time to time we need to remember that we are a numerical minority and therefore remind people that for Indigenous minorities the political "playing field" is not always level.

The fourth challenge that I want to respond to is a point argued by various speakers about the postmodern theoretical position. I want to support the way in which various speakers have outlined and deconstructed how "our stories" can be overly generalized. There is a need to sort out what is romanticized and what is real and to engage in a genuine critique of where we really are. Having said that, I think the point also needs to be made that it is all very well being engaged in deconstruction and going through an exercise of self-flagellation, but at the end of the day there must be room for change. The challenge for advocates of postmodern analyses is to find pathways that are positive and offer genuine opportunities for the transformation of our crisis circumstances. I think that an important point that has been missed in the postmodern critique is the level of accountability in regard to developing transformative outcomes for the Indigenous communities they purport to be serving. If a person is genuinely working on behalf of the community, then the community will also be part of the whole process, not simply be passive recipients of a grand "plan" developed outside themselves. Within the postmodern analysis, there is often an emphasis on the critique – that is, on what has gone wrong – at the expense of providing transformative strategies and outcomes. Many academics have their research shaped by the institution in which they work – for example, in order to fulfil the institution's academic expectations that research be positivistic and so on. A lot less emphasis is put on the critique that's developed out of the organic community context (it's not seen as real academic work). To put this another way, many Maori academics complain that we have to perform to two levels of accountability. Our academic credibility does not just depend on the institution we work for and the number of papers or books we produce. Our academic credibility is also set in very powerful ways by the communities in which we are located. I assume this is something that can be generalized in that many Indigenous academics are caught within similar multiple layers of accountability. If Indigenous academics, despite the burden, are not accountable to both community and academy, then they ought to be!

The fifth challenge that I want to take up is addressed to both the community and Indigenous academics. I have a concern with the often strident anti-intellectual and anti-academic stance of Indigenous communities. The distrust of academics, research, and institutions by Indigenous peoples is well founded and relates to a history of hurt, humiliation, and exploitation that has been perpetrated by some institutions and academics, with disastrous outcomes for some people. The problem is that this distrust is also directed at Indigenous academics. There is also good reason to be concerned that some Indigenous academics become "ivory tower intellectuals," disconnected from Indigenous communities and concerns, mere functionaries for the colonization of our peoples. While I accept that this does occur, I do not think that it serves the interests of Indigenous peoples to build a divide between our Native academics and our communities. Rather than dismissing all intellectual contributions as being unworthy and problematic, we should be seeking out those whose work is supportive and useful and ensuring that they are able to contribute to the struggle with appropriate support and guidance from the community. We all need to work hard to ensure that Indigenous academics are able to work positively and proactively for Indigenous communities. If and where necessary, academics should be brought into line. The main point here is that we need Indigenous academics working for the people; we cannot afford to have a divide between the interests of Indigenous scholars and academics on the one hand and Indigenous communities on the other. Indigenous struggle and transformation depend on these two groups working together. Later, I want to expand on this point by illustrating that the alliance between Maori academics and Maori communities has led to major gains in transforming Maori education and schooling crises. In this sense, the academy itself has been a site of struggle wherein Maori have attempted to reclaim research, teaching, and theory within the realm of Maori knowledge frameworks.

The sixth challenge is related to the previous point, and it is a challenge to reclaim the interventionary potential of theory. Again, I think that it is too easy for Indigenous people to dismiss theory – to be anti-theory. This is usually justified on the ground that theory is considered part of the Western colonizing agenda that serves to keep us oppressed. I would like to suggest that theory and academic research are important sites of struggle for Indigenous people, although I don't mean that we should take for granted that existing Western-oriented theories are at the centre. What I am talking about is the need to develop theoretical understandings and practices that arise out of our own Indigenous knowledge. Nor should we turn away from theory that may be developed elsewhere. We ought to be open to using any theory and practice with emancipatory relevance to our Indigenous struggle. Theory will enable us to move forward in the work that we are doing in our communities, in developing sound critiques and effective interventions. Theory is important in organizing struggle and transformative action. Theoretical understandings can provide appropriate frameworks for measuring the transformative actions that we are undertaking. On the other hand, I also think that there is an important place for critiquing Western theory, not in a reactive, negative way but in order to make space for our own theoretical frameworks. This has been an important part of the new Maori struggle. The academy has been critically engaged, not simply dismissed; theory and research have been critically reconstructed/reclaimed to work for our interests, rather than against them.

The seventh and final challenge is what I call the challenge of moving beyond the focus on the type of individualism that comes out of the new economic ideologies. The new focus on individual rights and freedoms and on individual choice is at once in conflict with one of the fundamental values associated with Indigenous peoples: the recognition of our collective solidarity. Such collectivity is embedded in our notions of family, tribe, cultural traits, values, and practices. It is often very easy to be seduced by the rhetoric of individual rights, but in reduction to such a focus our collective rights are undermined.

A further question to be explored around the notion of individualism is the extent to which we as individuals have the autonomy to make our own world versus the extent to which we are determined by wider structural forces that sit outside our individual control. In other words, how much agency sits with the individual? For example, we as Indigenous peoples have to consider the extent to which we can effectively change our conditions by simply changing people's behaviour and attitudes, in contrast to the need to engage in deeper societal change at the level of structures – such as those that may relate to economics, power, and ideology.

Anti-Colonization

All of the challenges that I have raised arise out of comments made at the institute, and these reflections provide a critical framework for the issues that I am going to address. I want to shift now the focus to what I term "new forms of colonization." I do not believe for an instant that we are in a postcolonial period. I do not think that we have seen the last of colonization; on the contrary, it is very much alive and well. What has happened in recent years is the creation of an illusion that colonization is no longer practised – that somehow the "white" world now understands this phenomenon and is able to desist from it. This, of course, is a myth; even in places where the colonizers have withdrawn politically, leaving the country to the original peoples (for example, India and Fiji), colonization persists. What has happened is that the processes of colonization have been reformed in different and more subtle ways. Many of these new formations are insidious, and many of them have yet to be fully exposed. Indigenous peoples generally have been slow to develop strategies to counter the influence of these new forms of colonization. I use the term "anti-colonial" to describe the proactive position of resistance that Indigenous peoples should adopt to these neocolonial formations.

In recent times, New Zealand has become a "laboratory" for an extensive experiment in free-market economics. We have moved away from the Keynesian economic model, in which the state had a central responsibility to nurture and care for all of its citizens. Since 1980, we have made some swift and far-reaching social changes derived from the free-market economic context. These changes have moved us away from the objective of a collective concern to provide "equal opportunity for all" to an individualistic notion of "the survival of the fittest." The economic reforms in New Zealand have headed us in the direction of the New Right policies promulgated by Ronald Reagan and Margaret Thatcher. A free-market economy has resulted in minimal state intervention or responsibility, and in effect our social and welfare services have been privatized. The shift to privatization has meant a shift to a primary concern for profit margins and a shift away from a concern for people first. The concept of "user pays" has replaced the ideologies of social justice, welfare rights, and equal opportunity. New Zealand citizens are now expected to purchase their education, health care, and other necessities that previously were provided free by the state. A major assumption made here is that all citizens in New Zealand are on a level economic playing field. This, of course, is a fallacy. In fact, Maori are the "worst off" group in New Zealand society – they occupy the worst-case scenario in statistics relating to social, economic, and cultural crises. In this sense, the majority of Maori do not start on an equal footing with *Pakeha*. The new free-market economy simply privileges the already privileged – the rich get richer. In this new economic structure, the rights of the individual consumer are paramount. This concentration on the development of the "competitive individual" who has "consumer sovereignty" has tremendous implications for a people whose culture is embedded in the collective.

Maori culture is centred on the values of sharing and cooperation that are embedded in tribal (*iwi*) and extended family (*whanau*) structures and responsibilities. The key point here is to understand the way in which cultural oppression converges with economic exploitation within these new formations of colonization. This to me is one of the fundamental ways in which colonialism is being reformed or repositioned by a small group of big business interests that has restructured the New Zealand economy. Multinational business interests probably have as much political influence now as our government. This situation is facilitated by the new free-market economy. We are governed to a large extent by multinational business interests that have infiltrated our own country. The new multilateral trade agreements such as GATT (General Agreement on Trade and Tariffs), NAFTA (North American Free Trade Agreement), EC (European Community), and APEC (Asia-Pacific Economic Consortium) are a reflection of these new multinational business interests. A major concern is the degree to which big business consortiums are so heavily into economic reductionism that Indigenous interests are merely to be tolerated insofar as they can be of assistance to the big business agenda. For the most part, these multinational corporate structures have little concern for Indigenous cultures or interests; certainly Indigenous claims to prior ownership of the land and sea resources are regarded as antagonistic to the position of the free-market economy.

An important point to emphasize about Maori experience is that in addition to the internal political and economic dangers are the external dangers associated with the politics of the global marketplace. For example,

New Zealand is part of GATT, which involves several different countries coming together to form baseline agreements in a single trading and labour-market economy. National boundaries as they relate to things such as labour conditions (wages and employment conditions) and intellectual and cultural property rights are broken down in the interests of the wider global market. Thus, Maori culture and other interests are no longer merely vulnerable within our own national boundaries; they have now been opened up to colonizing pressures from these other countries within the global alliance of the GATT. This is a new face of colonization. NAFTA, APEC, and the EC are all examples of this trend toward the formation of major global markets. I am asking Indigenous people to think carefully about the repercussions of this type of economic restructuring on our individual cultures within our own countries. Indigenous peoples must join together in a strategic global resistance to protect our interests. These resistance strategies must speak across national boundaries to the multinational interests that are at the seat of power in these new global alliances.

New Zealand is not and never has been a level economic playing field for Maori. There is a false assumption within New Right ideology that, when you have a free-market economy, everyone has an equal opportunity to access resources and to participate. Within the user-pays doctrine, everyone pays for the services and goods that he or she uses. This is considered a much fairer system in that those who use schools, hospitals, telephones, water, power, and medicines more should pay more. If we consider the case of Maori and schooling, then one of the major flaws in this ideology becomes apparent: it's assumed that all Maori have as equal access to education and schooling as non-Maori citizens. This, of course, overlooks the fact that our society is already unequal. While there may be many people in our New Zealand society who have two cars and who can therefore easily access the schooling of their choice, there are also many people, mostly brown, who have no car at all, and consequently their choice of schools is limited. Many people, mostly brown, live in single-parent families. Brown people form disproportionately high levels of crisis statistics across the board – incarceration rates, poorer health, under-achievement in schools, and so on. In our Maori experience, the opportunities under this kind of economic regime are not equal, and all indications are that Maori are becoming increasingly worse off. The detrimental implications for First Nations and Indigenous peoples across the world under this kind of system should be obvious.

Commodification of Indigenous Knowledge

I want to focus now in more definitive terms on how some of this marginalization of Maori actually occurs. I want to explain the process of "commodification" of Indigenous knowledge. Knowledge is commodified

to the extent that it is considered a "good" that can be traded or purchased. It's as though the world is to be considered a huge supermarket in
which knowledge can be packaged up to be bought and sold. This economic reduction of knowledge has had major implications for New
Zealand society in general and Maori in particular. The implications for
Maori knowledge have led to Maori concern for their intellectual and cultural property rights. The tensions between Maori and *Pakeha* cultural
interests and values can be generalized in the following diagram.

MAORI < – – – – – – – – – – – – – – – –> *PAKEHA*
Collective responsibility < – – – – – – –> Individual freedom
Cooperation < – – – – – – – – – – – – –> Competition
Aku (ours) < – – – – – – – – – – – – – > *Taku* (mine)

The diagram is fairly self-explanatory. It groups Maori around a set of
broad generalizations. The dotted line indicates that the positions represented as Maori and *Pakeha* are generalizations and that both Maori and
Pakeha individuals may be found anywhere along the continuum, but as a
generalization Maori tend to support one set of values and *Pakeha* the
other. For example, I draw your attention to the use of language – *taku*
refers to that which is mine individually, and *aku* refers to that which is
ours collectively. Maori cultural values and thinking tend to reinforce
the *aku* mode when we are talking about ownership of property. For
instance, in the cultural worldview, knowledge is perceived as belonging
to the whole group. Individuals do not hold knowledge for themselves;
they hold it for the benefit of the whole group. Individuals have a responsibility to share knowledge with the group. If one person in the group fails
to contribute, then the group as a whole loses, and the *mana* of the group
may be diminished. These traditional ways of thinking have been used
successfully in the organization of our university classes. They translate
into a positive, critical pedagogy that is success oriented rather than failure
oriented. Someone pointed out the other day that examinations should be
a test of what people know and not what they do not know – often a slight
change in orientation is all that it takes to achieve such an aim.

Let's now examine the ideas behind the notion of commodification.
Commodification is about compartmentalization. It is positivistic and
technological. If you can put the Maori into neat packages of tribal groups,
then you can split up the "money pie" and say this tribe has so much and
this tribe has so much. The state at the centre is then more easily able to
abdicate its treaty responsibilities. Note the key item here: treaty responsibilities. Maori have a treaty with the Crown. The Crown has embarked on
a series of initiatives that attempt to commodify the treaty rights and to

devolve responsibility back to Maori people themselves. Commodification is one way of doing that.

I want to give two specific examples of the way in which Maori knowledge has been commodified. In 1991, we had a census in New Zealand that asked Maori which tribe they were from. The form read, "State one *iwi* only." In Maori society, however, we can inherit our tribal affiliations equally through both mother and father. So if you have, as I do, a mother from one tribe and a father from another, then you have equal responsibilities to two tribes. What the census form was doing was forcing Maori to choose only one tribal affiliation. It seems that this would serve the *Pakeha* bureaucracy and technocrats better – they would then be able to allocate funding on a simplistic formula of "dollars to tribes" on a per capita basis.

A second example of the commodification of our traditional knowledge forms relates to the national Qualifications Authority (NZQA). In New Zealand, the Qualifications Authority is charged with developing the content of the curriculum. This bureaucracy hired a number of traditional Maori thinkers to come together to "package up" Maori knowledge into course units. These course units are not provided to schools in New Zealand; the schools have to purchase them. The knowledge is now owned by the Qualifications Authority and not by the *iwi* or Maori thinkers or their tribes. The course units can also be purchased by interested groups outside New Zealand. Intellectual and cultural ownership is legally vested through copyright with NZQA.

The consequences of NZQA setting itself up as the official authority over all knowledge in New Zealand, including Maori knowledge, is that people are categorized. You can no longer get inside the Te Kohanga Reo education system, a Maori preschool immersion program, to assist as a *kaumatua* (elder), to share your knowledge, unless you have a certificate. This certificate has on it the Qualifications Authority stamp and a stamp from the Kohanga Reo National Trust. What counts as a *kaumatua* is now also described outside our cultural context. It doesn't matter what the people say; the person who has the certificate is the one who qualifies. Translated into the context of the academy, the elders who come into the university setting to assist may in the future no longer come in unless they have a certificate from the national body to say that they are official elders. Such a system takes the power and control over our Indigenous knowledge out of our hands and puts them into the domain of officialdom.

Treaty rights have also been commodified. Rights embedded in the treaties are now all seen as property rights, even though notions of sovereignty and equality are personal rights. What is at stake is the protection of personal rights. By commodifying personal rights, the government has tried to pave the way for settling the treaties with a cash settlement. The essence of this is the abdication by the state of its original responsibilities in the treaty contract.

Anti-Colonial Resistance

I will now turn to some resistance initiatives that have been undertaken in New Zealand through the restructuring of schooling and education. Just to paint the picture, Maori people constitute about 15 percent of a total New Zealand population of about 4 million. We are about 20 percent of the school-aged population. We are very young, and our population is growing. We form, as I said, the bottom end of the social scale and contribute disproportionately to the crisis statistics in our society. Of the 66 million acres of land in New Zealand, 3 million acres remain in Maori hands today. The period that I want to address is the 1980s, when a number of things happened for the Maori. First of all, there was a mind switch away from being reactive, of fitting into the system, of trying to patch up the system of schooling in New Zealand. In 1982, Maori parents decided to take the cultural revitalization of language, knowledge, and culture into their own hands. They decided to start at the preschool level. The Maori language nests or Te Kohanga Reo quickly became a major institution. Structures were developed for creating an environment in which to learn the Maori language. The movement was embraced by the people, in particular by Maori women. Anywhere there was space, a preschool was established. In no time at all, we had something like 800 Kohanga Reo nationally, with an average of twenty children in each.

Maori language and culture are extremely vulnerable. Less than 10 percent of our population still speaks the language. The revitalization of our language and culture is of utmost importance. The preschool program was built around the revitalization of our language. The other key element in the program was building new family relationships. The 1950s and 1960s were a period of great dysfunction for Maori families in New Zealand. Some aspects of this dysfunction are seen in the somewhat romanticized film *Once Were Warriors*. Here we have domestic violence and drinking problems and families in complete disarray. One of the key things about Te Kohanga Reo has been the recentring of family units and the development of a new process of building the family. This was built into the system because it depended on family cooperation.

In 1982, when the first group of children who had been immersed in Te Kohanga Reo from birth turned five, a major dilemma was posed in terms of the future schooling options for a new generation of Maori children who were fluent Maori language speakers. They had to go to school somewhere, so a school movement was also developed. The school movement is about people, not individuals. So we began an alternative Maori elementary school system called Kura Kaupapa Maori, which offered total immersion in the Maori language. The parents opted to drop out of the regular school system, and it is interesting to look at the decisions that parents made, given this sense of autonomy, of being outside the system. What decisions did they make about what would count as the school curriculum? They decided, not surprisingly, that they wanted excellence in the Maori language, knowledge, and cultural frameworks for their children. They also wanted excellence in the New Zealand curriculum. It was not either/or. They picked both. To a certain extent, the two-pronged approach has been successful. It has depended on three things, which can be seen as the corners of a triangle. One corner is the attempt to alleviate the language and knowledge crisis in Maori communities. The second corner is the attempt to alleviate the learning crisis in Maori communities. The third and final corner is the development of the family, the extended *whanau* unit.

Any school curriculum is simply a selection of knowledge. Someone, somewhere, has decided what will count as the school curriculum. Moving outside the mainstream system, Maori parents put themselves in charge of these decisions. If you are involved in choosing the curriculum, you have a greater commitment to following through with it. Tests and examinations legitimize existing forms of knowledge. In our system, we are trying to reorganize the methods of evaluation. We are also trying to move away from conventional teaching methods, which used Maori perspectives in token ways simply to enable Maori children to feel good about themselves. It is not just that Maori knowledge is marginalized in the conventional school curriculum, but there are also structural problems with the way that learning is carried out. The key challenge being presented by Kura Kaupapa Maori is with respect to what learning is taking place: what is being learned. That question had not previously been asked with Maori interests in mind. Consequently, superficial aspects of Indigenous knowledge are used in conventional schools as a panacea, while the "real knowledge" is a narrowly selected curriculum based only on Western knowledge systems. By their very existence, Kura Kaupapa Maori offer a critical challenge to the selection of knowledge currently provided in conventional state schools in New Zealand. Kura Kaupapa Maori prioritize Indigenous Maori knowledge and select what other forms of knowledge will be taught and learned by students who attend these schools.

Maori people find themselves caught in social and economic problems that contribute to the social deficit model. The effect of these conditions is cumulative and contributes to Maori underachievement in society as a whole. Deficit explanations of the Maori condition usually highlight problems such as poor language skills, low incomes, poor health, and so forth. These conditions were all true in the 1960s and 1970s when these models were applied. The idea was that these social conditions explain Maori underachievement in the conventional school system. The problem with these explanations is that they focus on the Maori people as the problem. It deflects any criticism or critical inquiry of how the system is or is not working with respect to Maori. The questions about what is wrong with the system are being asked instead of the "victims" themselves. The existence of the alternative Maori schools critically engages the system as "problematic."

There are fifty-eight Kura Kaupapa Maori (1995) in New Zealand, including three that have moved into secondary education. We have changed the Education Act through protest, by negotiations, by threats, and through sit-ins. We were threatened by police and harassed, but eventually we got a hearing. Two years after we started our elementary schools, the government was in the throes of changing the Education Act, and the only other type of schooling inserted into the act is the Kaupapa Maori schools. The government has now come on stream and is funding the development of these schools at the rate of five new schools per year. The problem is that, when the government gives you money, there are strings attached. The liberating and transforming potential of these schools has been reined in as the state has started to fund these schools. I would argue that our view of the social transformation that has taken place is an incremental one. We understand that we have taken one of a number of steps that need to be taken. The big vision draws us along, but we must celebrate the small victories along the way. Anyone who thinks that he or she is going to get the whole social transformation and the utopian dream in one step would have to be lucky indeed. If you work out that formula, let me know. The existence of an alternative Maori school system is obviously a critique of the conventional state system. The state responds by reaching out and attempting to incorporate the Maori system back inside the mainstream.

Basically, the Maori school system is about incremental change. These schools have yet to realize their full potential, but they are growing to secondary and tertiary levels. There are several important elements that can be identified in Kura Kaupapa Maori and other Maori initiatives that address underlying structural issues. One of the key elements to social transformation is what Maori name *tino rangatiratanga*, translated to mean "absolute self-determination, full authority, and complete control." In the Maori school system, we have had to retrench a bit and settle for relative autonomy for the moment, but we do have a measure of self-determination. Many of the parents, because they have experienced language and cultural loss, are eager to get their children back to learning the language. The key in these schools has been to tap into that intense emotional energy for language and cultural revitalization so that it coincides with learning intervention. The essence is to bring these two things together. Of all the cultural elements required for excellence in education, the Maori stand by their traditional teachings. *Akonga* or Maori pedagogy is inserted into Maori schools, but not to the exclusion of other pedagogies. Teachers draw on a wide range of teaching methods.

It has also been important to train our own teachers. State schoolteachers cannot presume to teach in our schools. They have to go through a deconstruction process to get rid of some of the dominant cultural baggage that they already have on board. A lot of Maori pedagogy is intuitive to Maori teachers. Many teachers in the state system are good teachers, but many of them have lost confidence about using their cultural pedagogy. For example, in the Maori culture, the older siblings have a responsibility to the younger ones. There are important roles that the older children must play, such as making sure the younger children are fed first, making sure they are comfortable, and making sure there is no bullying – that kind of thing. It is a reciprocal relationship, because younger children also have a cultural responsibility in the way that they act toward the older ones. They are not to do certain things. When you invoke this and expand it to the educational setting, it's about more able kids helping less able kids. This leads to peer group teaching in the classroom. It can be expanded to cover discipline as well. A whole lot of things like that are embedded in the pedagogy of the teachers. All the children in the school are one family. All the parents are parents to all the children.

This next point is key and one that I find very exciting. Much research has been done in the Western theoretical world to describe how a student's social class and economic standing are related to the student's performance in school. This is a huge issue when you consider that most of our brown kids are also the kids who are marginalized socially and economically. The Maori school does not overthrow the social-economic impediment, but it provides cultural support networks that offset what might otherwise be the debilitating impact of social or economic standing. When you are treated as one family, everyone looks after everyone else. When a child comes to school with no lunch because his parents cannot afford lunch, others make sure he or she is fed. When a family is hit by unemployment, those who have jobs pay a bit more to cover the shortfall. The parents who are not working contribute in other ways – for instance, by coming in to the school to help out or by supervising on school trips. All the way through, we have our cultural support structures helping to intervene in the socioeconomic sector. Contrast this with the conventional school system in which children are individuals dropped off at the gate. They walk in by themselves. They sit in desks by themselves. They put their arms around their books and do their work by themselves. If their family is experiencing unemployment or discord, the burden is

carried by the individual child. In the Kaupapa Maori school, all of that
is shared collectively. Socioeconomic intervention is embedded in our cultural framework of nurturing. The trick is how we are able to stimulate
that nurturing even more by investing in and enhancing our cultural
support mechanisms.

The *whanau* or extended family is also an important element for Kura
Kaupapa Maori because it brings with it cultural obligations. Parents have
a responsibility to all of the children in the school. They have to come
to meetings. They have to get involved. Parents in extended Maori families have to fulfil certain cultural expectations to reinforce the Maori culture. It is not just a question of dropping your child off at the gate. The
parents are culturally contracted to support the school. This creates a very
powerful mechanism of support. The *Kaupapa* is the philosophy of Maori
education. It is written in Maori. These schools are total immersion environments. All the teaching is done in the Maori language. For those
parents who do not speak the language, there is a safe room where the
children come to talk to them in English.

The experiment of developing our own Maori schools has been reason-
ably successful. The number of schools has increased. Some parents have a
tremendous investment in these schools, and they have become intensely
Maori. While that is a good thing, it also creates difficulties in a situation
in which you are trying to make decisions collectively. We are experiencing some difficulties, but the important thing that we set out to do, which
is to revitalize the language and the culture, is being achieved. The educational process is going well, and our communities are united on a political
front. It is still a struggle to get resources in some areas.

In New Zealand, we have taken the initiative in reclaiming our educational system. We decided that we were no longer going to wait for others
to give their assent as to whether or not we could do things. In the early
stages, it meant a big commitment. It required a lot of will on the part of
the parents who formed the vanguard. The outcome has been a major
benefit to everyone, not just to the Maori communities, but to the country as a whole. The common perception at the United Nations is that the
New Zealand government has established Kohanga Reo and Kaupapa
Maori alternative systems of schooling for the "nice Natives." This is not
the case. Our gains have come out of intense struggle. The process of struggle has also educated us a lot.

Note

1 Our term for non-Maori is *Pakeha*, and I will use the term *Pakeha* rather than either white
or non-Indigenous.

17
Kaupapa Maori Research
Linda Tuhiwai Te Rina Smith

As mentioned in the previous chapter, the attitudes and feelings that Maori people have held toward research are shaped by how research has been conducted in their country. Research is implicated in the production of Western ways of knowing and in denying the validity of Maori knowledge, language, and culture. The previous chapter also mentioned the general legacy of *Pakeha* research on Maori attitudes toward theory and academic knowledge, attitudes that have led some Maori to be against *all* theory and *all* research.

One of the challenges for Maori researchers working in this context has been to retrieve some space. First, to convince Maori people of the value of research for Maori; second, to convince the various fragmented but powerful *Pakeha* research communities of the need for greater Maori involvement in research; third, to develop approaches to and ways of carrying out research that take into account, without being limited by, the legacies of previous research and the parameters of both previous and current approaches to research. What is now referred to as Kaupapa Maori research is an attempt to retrieve that space and to achieve these general aims. This chapter discusses Maori approaches to research and, in particular, the ways in which Kaupapa Maori has become a way of structuring assumptions, values, concepts, orientations, and priorities in research.

In February 1985, the general frustrations of Maori toward research were framed in a discussion paper written by Evelyn Stokes for the National Research Advisory Council. This paper was included in a more general discussion relating to the formation of new national science objectives. Stokes's paper argues for the acceptance of Maori knowledge and values, the desirability and social significance of more Maori research, and the need to train Maori researchers. The importance of Stokes's paper was its audience and its timing. It was directed at the top policy level, where decisions were being made that would dictate national priorities for research. Since then, those priorities and the ways in which they have been institutionalized have been radically restructured. The timing of the paper was, therefore, strategically well placed because it put Maori research interests on the national science policy agenda. Several writers had previously raised many of the same issues and had voiced similar concerns at conferences and seminars; however, these occasions tended to be disciplinary-based gatherings that did little to engage either the political realities of social science research or the attention of the few Maori who may have been in a position to carry out research.[1]

Later in the same year, I set out as a postgraduate student to interview a group of Maori women whose children were in Te Kohanga Reo. My daughter attended the same Te Kohanga Reo, and the women were well known to me. They had willingly agreed to be interviewed. I had found little help in the standard methodological guidebooks for the issues that I would confront as a Maori carrying out research on other Maori. Very little in the discussions of cross-cultural issues was useful because I was not working cross-culturally. I was, at three levels at least, an insider: as a Maori, as a woman, and as a mother. On other levels, I was an outsider: as a postgraduate student, as someone from a different tribe, as an older mother, and as someone who had a partner.[2] Much of the cross-cultural literature assumed that the researcher belonged to the dominant cultural group and was "doing" research to, for, and sometimes with a minority group. There were some studies that addressed issues faced by women researchers who were going to study in remote villages in Africa or South America. There were, of course, the romantic *National Geographic* accounts of women who spent years studying primates in various isolated spots, which frankly did not appeal to me. This literature reinforced the idea that one needed special skills, such as being culturally sensitive to ways of effectively gaining entrance into the community being studied and gaining the confidence of "informants."[3] There were few studies that critiqued methodological approaches, and those that I did find were authored by African American scholars rather than other Indigenous people.[4] There was nothing to help me think about and frame what I wanted to do within my own cultural context or how I might go about doing research in one of my own communities. Even previous research by other Maori academics appeared problematic to me, first because they wrote as if they were outsiders in their own world, and second because they were all men fluent in the Maori language and regarded as being deeply knowledgeable about Maori culture.[5]

I wrote a paper as a preamble to my research project, setting out the issues that I faced and attempting to articulate what it was that made those issues so problematic.[6] My concerns were also being voiced by other Maori in other contexts; however, our isolation from each other meant that we struggled through these issues alone. It has taken several years to bring what is still a small but active community of Maori researchers together.

Mapping Kaupapa Maori

At the outset, it needs stating that not all those who write or talk about Kaupapa Maori are involved in research. Kaupapa Maori has been applied across a wide range of projects and enterprises. Furthermore, not all Maori researchers would regard themselves or their research as fitting within a Kaupapa Maori framework. So not all Maori researchers claim to conduct Kaupapa Maori research. There are elements within the definitions of Kaupapa Maori that serve the purpose of selecting what counts and what does not count. One can ask, for example, if a *Pakeha* researcher can carry out Kaupapa Maori research. The answer based on current definitions is complex. It might be that a *Pakeha* can be involved in Kaupapa Maori research but not on his or her own, and, if involved in such research, he or she would have ways of self-positioning as *Pakeha*. A more radical interpretation might say that, by definition, Kaupapa Maori research is exclusively research by Maori. From these two answers it is possible to say something more about what Kaupapa Maori research is and what it is not. This section will map out the developing field of Kaupapa Maori research.

Kathy Irwin characterizes Kaupapa Maori as research that is culturally safe, that involves the mentorship of *kaumatua*, that is culturally relevant and appropriate while satisfying the rigours of research, and that is undertaken by a Maori researcher, not a researcher who happens to be Maori.[7] This statement implies that other forms of research – that is, culturally sensitive models – have not been satisfactory at the level of cultural safety. Irwin also grounds her work in a paradigm that stems from the Maori worldview and in *Te Reo Maori me ona tikanga*.[8] Bishop writes that Kaupapa Maori "addresses the prevailing ideologies of cultural superiority which pervade our social, economic, and political institutions."[9] Bishop's model is framed by the discourses related to the Treaty of Waitangi and by the development within education of Maori initiatives that are controlled by Maori. By framing Kaupapa Maori within the Treaty of Waitangi, Bishop leaves space for the involvement of *Pakeha* in support of Maori research (as treaty partners). Moreover, *Pakeha* who have a genuine desire to support the cause of Maori ought to be included because they can be useful allies and colleagues in research. The issue of control is linked, in Bishop's argument, with the goal of empowerment: "In the context of research, empowerment means that Maori people should regain control of investigations into Maori people's lives."[10] Bishop also argues that Kaupapa Maori research is located within an alternative conception of the world from which solutions and cultural aspirations can be generated. This alternative conception draws from an alternative code. Both Irwin and Bishop argue for the importance of the concept of *whanau* as a supervisory and organizational structure for handling research. Bishop refers to this as "a research *whanau* of interest." Irwin refers to a *whanau* of supervisors. For both Bishop and Irwin, the *whanau* provides the intersection where research meets Maori, or Maori meets research, on equal terms.

From these comments, it is clear that under the rubric of Kaupapa Maori research there are different sets of ideas and issues that are being claimed as important. Some of these intersect at different points with research as an activity. Some of these features are framed as assumptions and some as practices and methods, and some are related to Maori conceptions of knowledge. Smith summarizes these by saying that Kaupapa Maori research (1) is related to being Maori, (2) is connected to Maori philosophy and principles, (3) takes for granted the validity and legitimacy of Maori, the importance of Maori language and culture, and (4) is concerned with "the struggle for autonomy over our own cultural well-being."[11] He locates Kaupapa Maori research within the wider project of Kaupapa Maori, and he draws from the broader concept of Kaupapa Maori a set of elements that, he argues, can be found in all the different projects associated with Kaupapa Maori. Some of these principles will be discussed more fully later in the chapter. However, the general significance of these principles is that they have evolved from within many of the taken-for-granted practices of Maori and are tied to a clear and coherent *kaupapa*.[12] In terms of research –particularly in the attempt to develop empirical methods and, in a sense, operationalize the principles outlined by Smith – there is another set of steps to take beyond the working principles identified by Smith.

Kaupapa Maori as Localized Critical Theory

Most discussion about Kaupapa Maori is also discussion about critical theory, in particular the notions of critique, resistance, struggle, and emancipation. Previous sources, for example, situate Maori research within the antipositivist debate raised by critical theory. Pihama suggests that "intrinsic to Kaupapa Maori theory is an analysis of existing power structures and societal inequalities. Kaupapa Maori theory therefore aligns with critical theory in the act of exposing underlying assumptions that serve to conceal the power relations that exist within society and the ways in which dominant groups construct concepts of 'common sense' and 'facts' to provide ad hoc justification for the maintenance of inequalities and the continued oppression of Maori people."[13] Bishop goes further to suggest that critical approaches to research have in fact failed to address the issues of communities such as Maori, and the development of alternative approaches by Maori reflects a form of resistance to critical theory. Bishop makes these points in the context of the debate between Ellsworth and Giroux about the failure of critical pedagogy in relation to its emancipatory goals.[14]

Smith, however, argues that Kaupapa Maori is a local theoretical positioning that is the modality through which the emancipatory goal of critical theory, in a specific historical, political, and social context, is practised. The localizing of the aims of critical theory is partly an enactment of what critical theory actually offers to oppressed, marginalized, and silenced groups. The project of critical theory held out the possibility that, through emancipation, groups such as Maori would take greater control over their own lives and humanity. This necessarily implied that groups would take hold of the project of emancipation and attempt to make it a reality in their own terms while Western academics might quibble about the success or failure of the emancipatory project and question the idealism that lies behind it. There is a tendency to be overly precious about the project as a universal recipe that has to be followed to the letter if it is to be effective. Furthermore, this stance assumes that oppression has universal characteristics that are independent of history, context, and agency. At the level of abstraction, this is what has to be argued, in a sense, but it can never be so on the ground. There is also a naivety about what Stuart Hall has called the dirtiness of political projects, or what Frantz Fanon and other anticolonial writers would regard as the violence entailed in struggles for freedom. The end result cannot be predetermined. The means to the end involves human agency in ways that are complex and contradictory. The notion of strategic positioning as a deliberate practice is partially an attempt to contain the unevenness and unpredictability, under stress, of people engaged in emancipatory struggles. The broader *kaupapa* of Kaupapa Maori embraces that sense of strategic positioning, of being able to plan, predict, and contain across a number of sites the engagement in struggle.

Another dimension of Kaupapa Maori research is found clustered around issues of identity. Bishop, Irwin, Pihama, and G.H. Smith have all argued that being Maori, identifying as Maori and as a Maori researcher, is a critical element of Kaupapa Maori research. While this position is antipositivist, in that it is also saying that we look at the world through our grounding in Maori worldviews, most Maori researchers would also argue that being Maori does not preclude us from being systematic, ethical, and "scientific" in the way that we approach a research problem.[15] This positioning of the researcher and the views that he or she brings to research has been well argued in terms of feminist research. Feminist research maintains its focus on issues of gender (not just of women), but it has moved away from the view that only women can carry out feminist research to a view that is less essentialist.[16] Kaupapa Maori research, as currently framed, would argue that being Maori is an essential criterion for carrying out Kaupapa Maori research. At the same time, however, some writers suggest that we exercise restraint in becoming too involved in identity politics because of the potential that these politics have for paralyzing development.[17] This position is based on the specificities of our history and our politics. However, this does not preclude those who are not Maori from participating in research that has a Kaupapa Maori orientation.[18]

This latter point connects with the concept of *whanau,* as raised earlier, as a way of organizing research. Smith identified the *whanau* principle as an important aspect of Kaupapa Maori approaches. Both Te Kohanga Reo and Kura Kaupapa Maori have attempted to organize basic decision making and parent participation within each of these initiatives around the concept of *whanau.* It is argued that in precolonial times the *whanau* was the core social unit, rather than the individual. It is also argued that the *whanau* remains a persistent way of living in and organizing the social world. In terms of research, the *whanau* is one of several Maori concepts, or *tikanga,* that have become part of a methodology, a way of organizing a research group, a way of incorporating ethical procedures that report back to the community, a way of "giving voice" to the different sections of Maori communities, and a way of debating ideas and issues that have an impact on the research project. It also has a very pragmatic function, in that the *whanau* is a way of distributing tasks, of incorporating people with particular expertise, and of keeping Maori values central to the project. In Bishop's model, it would be at this level, for example, that *Pakeha* can be involved. The *whanau,* then, can be a very specific modality through which research is shaped and carried out, analyzed, and disseminated.

Whanau is one of several aspects of Maori philosophy, values, and practices brought to the centre in Kaupapa Maori research. Nepe argues that Kaupapa Maori is derived from very different epistemological and metaphysical foundations and that it is these foundations that give Kaupapa Maori its distinctiveness from Kaupapa Pakeha or Kaupapa science or any other *kaupapa.*[19] In other words, there is more to Kaupapa Maori than our history under colonialism or our desires to restore *rangatiratanga.* We have a different epistemological tradition that frames the way we see the world, the way we organize ourselves in it, the questions we ask, and the solutions we seek. It is larger than the individuals in it and the specific "moment" in which we are living. The significance of Kaupapa Maori to Maori language is tied to the connection between language, knowledge, and culture. According to Sir James Henare, one of the architects of Te Kohanga Reo, *"Ko te reo te kakahu of te whakaaro te huarahi i te ao turoa o te hinengaro."*[20] The revitalization of Maori language has brought with it the revitalization of Maori forms of knowledge and the debates that accompany those knowledge forms.[21] Kaupapa Maori, however, does not mean the same thing as *matauranga* Maori or Maori knowledge and epistemology. The concept of *kaupapa* implies a way of framing and structuring how we think about these ideas and practices. Nepe argues that Kaupapa Maori is a "conceptualisation of Maori knowledge."[22] It is a way of abstracting that knowledge, reflecting on it, engaging with it, taking it for granted sometimes, making assumptions based upon it, and at times critically engaging in the way that it has been and is being constructed.[23]

There is the possibility within Kaupapa Maori research to address the different constructions of Maori knowledge. A good example of this is in the development of Maori women's theories about Maori society. These theories question the accounts of Maori society provided by men, including Maori men, but still hold to a position arguing that the issues of gender for Maori do not make us the same as white women.[24] The critical theory of Kaupapa Maori also applies, therefore, to Maori ways of thinking, but it does not deny either the existence or the fundamental legitimacy to Maori people of Maori forms of knowledge. It seeks to understand these forms, however, on their own terms and within the wider framework of Maori values and attitudes, Maori language, and Maori ways of living in the world.

There is another feature of Kaupapa Maori research that is becoming increasingly important as research funding is restructured around government priorities and policies. The state is the largest funding institution for research in New Zealand. The restructuring that occurred after 1994 separated the policy-making functions of government from the allocation of resources for research. The largest amount of money is institutionalized through the Foundation for Research, Science and Technology. Other ministries and government departments still fund research, but in the form of purchasing specific reports that fulfil the needs of the ministry concerned. In many cases, these reports are written over (rewritten) and subjected to Crown copyright. In this sense, the research is not research so much as a purchased product that becomes owned by the state. It becomes debatable, then, whether the purchased product is worth taking seriously outside government. The restructuring of research connects with the wider restructuring of the state in line with New Right economic policies. They have emphasized the importance of government objectives, of competition and contestability, of the separation of policy from funding, of outputs that are purchased, and of outcomes.[25] This shift toward the New Right has profound implications for Maori cultural values and practices.[26] It also has major implications for Maori in terms of its reinscription of positivist approaches to scientific research.[27]

Kaupapa Maori Research: In Which Fields?

In terms of Kaupapa Maori, the most important question is related to issues of social justice. The debate about social justice occurs at several levels. Reconciling market-driven, competitive, and entrepreneurial re-search, which positions New Zealand internationally, with the need for Maori to carry out research that recovers histories, reclaims lands and resources, and restores justice hardly seems possible. This is precisely why the debates around *rangatiratanga* and the Treaty of Waitangi have been significant. The attempt by Maori to engage in the activities of the state through the mechanism of the Treaty of Waitangi has won some space in which Maori can argue for different sorts of research priorities. This space is severely limited, however, as it has had to be wrestled not only from the state but also from the community of positivistic scientists whose regard for Maori is not sympathetic. Furthermore, the competitive environment created by the restructuring makes Kaupapa Maori research a competitor for resources with positivistic research. The problem is not just that posi-tivist science is well established institutionally and theoretically but also that it has a connectedness at a common-sense level with the rest of soci-ety, which, generally speaking, takes for granted the hegemony of its methods and its leadership in the search for knowledge. As far as many people are concerned, research is positivist; it cannot be anything else. Kaupapa Maori is a fledgling approach occurring within the limited com-munity of Maori researchers. It exists within a minority culture that con-tinues to be represented within antagonistic colonial discourses. It is a counterhegemonic approach to Western forms of research and, as such, currently exists on the margins of Western research.

Kaupapa Maori research is imbued with a strong antipositivistic stance. However, its wider *kaupapa* is to include all those researchers who are attempting to work with Maori and on topics of importance to Maori. The outer edges of Kaupapa Maori are not necessarily sharply delineated, although, as argued in the introduction, there is, at the political level, something at stake. One of the strands of a burgeoning Maori research community is the development of Maori health research. This develop-ment provides one interface between the more positivistic medical science approaches to research, particularly epidemiology, and social science approaches such as sociology and policy analysis. The "failure" of medical research to address the needs of Maori parallels the failure of educational research. Recognition of this has shifted some areas of health research toward developing more culturally sensitive research and employing Kau-papa Maori approaches. The changes include involving Maori researchers in large studies and the establishment of Maori health research units that focus on issues of Maori health, are managed and organized by Maori, and employ multidisciplinary approaches within a Kaupapa Maori frame-work.[28] Hence, large-scale epidemiological survey work and ethnographic, qualitative studies sit alongside each other in the same centre. The con-nection between the two highlights yet another feature of Kaupapa Maori research. Getting the *kaupapa* "right" is the first and major issue; the second issue is employing the most appropriate methods and people. Hence, sometimes a positivistic piece of research has been carried out by Maori researchers, but the questions it sought to answer, the problems it sought to probe, and the data it sought to gather have generally been priorities debated by Maori working in a Kaupapa Maori framework. There are three different points to be drawn here. First, there are politics attached to research. Most researchers understand that. Quite simply, positivistic research attracts funding. Second, there are accountabilities and preresearch discussions that have already framed and, to an extent, transformed the approach to research. Third, most of the Maori health research units have developed strong ties with specific Maori communities.[29] These factors are reflected in the way in which the centres are constituted and the geographical areas in which they work.

There may be a question about whether Kaupapa Maori research is its own paradigm. Irwin suggests that it is.[30] Others involved in Kaupapa Maori would deliberately be reluctant to engage in such a debate because it sets up comparisons with Western science, which is exactly what Kaupapa Maori is resisting.[31] Kaupapa Maori research is both less and more than a paradigm.[32] It does set out a field of study that enables a process of selection to occur and defines what needs to be studied and what questions ought to be asked. It also has a set of assumptions and taken-forgranted values and knowledge upon which it builds. In this sense, it fits into some of the ways that a paradigm is defined. However, it is also more than the sum of those parts. Kaupapa Maori research is a social project. It weaves in and out of Maori cultural beliefs and values, Western forms of education, Maori aspirations and socioeconomic needs, and Western economies and global politics. Kaupapa Maori is concerned with sites and terrains. Each site is one of struggle. Each has also been claimed by others as "their" turf. They are selected or select themselves precisely because they are sites of struggle and because they have some strategic importance for Maori. We are not at present interested in nuclear physics, but we are becoming interested in genetic science.[33] There are sound reasons why we are interested in education, employment, health, and history. Each of these domains situates us in crisis. They are more real and more pressing.

The Working Principles of Kaupapa Maori Research

Having mapped out some of the key points relating to Kaupapa Maori research, I will now shift my focus to issues that are more methodological.[34] Drawing together a range of experiences in research and work by other Maori, I will define some working principles based on the importance of Maori ways of knowing, Maori values, Maori processes and practices. This section will also address critical questions that frame Kaupapa Maori research and discuss issues arising from practices held to be important specifically for Maori researchers.

Graham Smith, in a series of papers on Kura Kaupapa Maori as an educational intervention, has argued that within the intervention are essential elements that make it successful for Maori. These elements encapsulate Maori values and knowledge, but they also provide bridges over which other educational strategies can be put into practice.[35] Briefly, Smith outlines six principles:

(1) *(tino) rangatiratanga* (relative autonomy principle)
(2) *taonga tuku iho* (cultural aspirations principle)
(3) *ako Maori* (culturally preferred pedagogy)
(4) *kia piki ake i nga raruraru o te kainga* (mediation of socioeconomic and home difficulties principle)
(5) *whanau* (extended family structure principle)
(6) *kaupapa* (collective vision, philosophical principle)

This list does not claim to be definitive, but it does capture the salient features of Kura Kaupapa Maori, and the same principles can be said to operate in any Kaupapa Maori context. However, some of these principles get reframed in the context of research, or, rather, the details are different but the basic principle remains the same. The following working principles for research have been taken not just from Smith's framework but also from research projects in which I have been involved in a number of roles and from discussions with Maori researchers at *hui* and conferences.[36] They incorporate the views, to some extent, of those who work in health, education, Maori studies, policy analysis history, and *iwi*-based research. In each case, there is a set of recent politics around these ideas, and, rather than ignore them and insert other concepts, I have taken each one and mapped it out in terms of its implications for Kaupapa Maori research.

The Principle of *Whakapapa*

A number of Maori have identified *whakapapa* as the most fundamental aspect of the way in which we think about and come to know the world.[37] *Whakapapa* is a way of thinking, a way of learning, a way of storing knowledge, and a way of debating knowledge.[38] It is inscribed in virtually every aspect of our worldview. In terms of Kaupapa Maori research, *whakapapa* is embedded in our own knowledge and is integral to what becomes taken for granted. *Whakapapa* intersects with research in a number of different ways. Furthermore, the shape that it takes varies according to the context, the time, the people, and the actual project.

It is through *whakapapa* that Maori people trace ourselves and our access to land, to a *marae*, and to a *turangawaewae*. *Whakapapa* also positions us in historical relationships with other *iwi,* with our landscape, and within the universe. One ancient *whakatauki*[39] tells us that we are the seeds or direct descendants of the heavens and can trace our *whakapapa* back to the very beginning of time and the creation of the universe.

E kore koe e ngaro, he kakano i ruia mai i Rangiatea[40]

Whakapapa also relates us to all other things that exist in the world. We are linked through our *whakapapa* to insects, fishes, trees, stones, and other life forms.[41] The concept of *whakapapa* embraces much of how we see ourselves in relation to everything else. It is the principle of a different code and, as such, is realized and elaborated through a wide range of practices.

John Rangihau, for example, wrote about the difficulty that the term "Maori" presents for him as a person with specific *whakapapa* that locates him in *whanau, hapu,* and *iwi.*[42] The "pan-Maori" approach to all things Maori was an identity imposed externally on all Maori people. Other definitions of identity, such as race classifications, have been equally problematic. These definitions resulted in the working out of mathematical equations that determined how much Maori blood you had and that did not take into account any notion of culture. People were asked to nominate a primary *iwi,* to choose one *iwi.* Maori can claim bilineal descent, and having to nominate just one lineage counters the principle of *whakapapa.* However, these external measurements of identity and attempts to regulate identity are significant at an ideological level because they become normative for what it means to be Maori.

The importance to Kaupapa Maori research of the principle of *whakapapa* is based on a number of interrelated issues. First, it needs to be regarded as an important way of thinking about Maori people generally. It is not the only way – gender, age, and the ability to speak Maori are just as important – but it is a culturally important way. It is about having a deep and thorough understanding of Maori society. Second, it is important when Maori people are the subjects of research, even in urban settings when one may not expect to be working with kinship-based groups. Many of the contemporary institutions to which Maori people in urban areas belong, such as sports clubs, housie schools, networks, and Kohanga Reo, still operate in some situations on the basis of *whakapapa.* This applies, for example, if they visit or receive visits from other Maori. It sometimes determines social support networks or access to a church minister of a *marae.* It may even shape friendships. The point is that, when Maori people are involved, you cannot assume that *whakapapa* is not working.

A third issue is related to the role of Maori researchers. The recent trend toward having more Maori researchers involved in projects often assumes that simply employing any Maori will be enough to satisfy the need to be culturally sensitive. However, a Maori researcher also has a *whakapapa,* also belongs somewhere, also has an identity that goes deeper than simply being Maori. Maori researchers need to think critically about what that means for the way in which they may think about themselves as researchers and about the Maori issues or Maori people they are researching. Being a Maori researcher does not mean an absence of bias; it simply means that the potential for different kinds of biases needs to be considered reflexively. Neither can it be assumed that a Maori will be more sympathetic to Maori issues or other Maori. Sometimes, in positioning themselves or being positioned as experts, they construct and apply a normative view of Maori culture based on their own experiences. Some Maori are perceived by other Maori as being more hostile to Maori than a *Pakeha* researcher might be. Some Maori are viewed as applying their own *iwi* belief systems over other *iwi*. One of the ways in which these issues are dealt with culturally is through the practice of *kanohi ki te kanohi*,[43] in which the researchers "front up" to the people and in the usual welcoming rituals of Maori position themselves publicly on the *marae* in terms of their *whakapapa*.[44]

The Principle of *te reo*

Maori language has been a site of struggle since the beginnings of state education. Practices to "get rid of" Maori language in the home have been well documented. The struggle to revitalize the language was central to the politics of Maori in the 1960s and 1970s. A petition to have Maori language taught in primary schools was organized in the 1970s by Nga Tamatoa. The development of Te Kohanga Reo in 1982 has been the most innovative approach to saving the language. Maori language was the subject of a claim to the Waitangi Tribunal in 1985. Kura Kaupapa Maori, the primary schooling alternative based on Maori philosophies and taught through Maori language, first started in 1986. The Maori Language Act was passed in 1987. This act declared Maori an official language, established a Maori language commission, and gave limited rights to speak Maori in judicial proceedings. Protection of Maori language has also formed part of subsequent claims to the Waitangi Tribunal and cases taken to the High Court. The most recent case was taken to the Privy Council in 1995. That year was also named by the government as *Te Tau O Te Reo Maori* (Maori Language Year), as part of the United Nations Decade of Indigenous Peoples.

As already mentioned, Maori language/*Te Reo Maori* is significant as a principle in Kaupapa Maori research. The survival of Te Reo Maori is viewed as being absolutely crucial to the survival of Maori people. It is an issue that brings together the support of a wide spectrum of Maori people. There are several ways in which Maori language is regarded by Maori. The following *whakatauki* give an indication of its value.

(1) *Ko te reo te mauri o te mana Maori.*
(2) *Toku reo, toku ohooho*
Toku reo, toku mapihi maurea
Toku reo, toku whakakai marihi.[45]

In terms of research, Maori language is important in a number of different ways. Maori worldviews are embedded in the language. There are some social practices that are only conducted in Maori. There are rich forms of expression that make sense in Maori because they connect with histories, values, and other images. Many of the early researchers, such as Elsdon Best, did much of their interviewing in Maori and gained access to whole bodies of knowledge that have still not been translated. The language, in this sense, is a window onto ways of knowing the world.

However, the language is also a way of interacting in the world. In this sense, Maori researchers need to have a range of skills with Maori language. There are age, gender, and *iwi* prescriptions on the ways in which they may use the language formally, but in most situations there are basic requirements to be fulfilled when the researcher is Maori and is in conversation with a Maori-speaking research subject. Not all Maori speakers choose to speak only the Maori language, but sometimes, even when they use English, they are making connections and using expressions that in Maori make a lot more sense.

There is an issue of dissemination of research results and the extent to which they are available for Maori speakers and readers. This has not as yet been a priority. However, there are three areas in which research could be carried out and made available in Maori: (1) the claims and findings of the Waitangi Tribunal, (2) the recovered histories specific to *whanau, hapu,* and *iwi,* and (3) the dissemination of information related to health, education, and other social policy areas. This aspect is about sharing knowledge and the results of research so that people can become better informed and make better decisions. It has another consequence further down the track of promoting different forms of literature in Maori.

The Principle of *Tikanga Maori*

Tikanga is regarded as customary practices, obligations, and behaviours, or the principles that govern social practices. It is about being able to operate inside the cultural system and make decisions and judgments about how to interpret what occurs. The concept of *tikanga* can be used as a rigid set of rules by which actions are judged as *tika*, or correct, although there are other values that mitigate against that rigidity. One example is the concept of *mana*, which was sometimes gained by those who dared to take risks and exploit or change *tikanga*. *Tikanga* applies to a wide range of social practices – for example, in relation to land, to the carving and construction of meeting houses, to health practices, to the use of *marae*, to the carrying out of *tangi* and unveilings, to *whaikorero* and *waiata*, and to the hosting of *manuhiri*.[46]

The concept of *tikanga* may also be used to convey the sense that something feels and looks "right": for example, the incline of the roof of a *wharenui* is at the "right" angle; the aesthetics of a carved house have the right balance; the way in which a *manuhiri* enters on the *marae*; and the way in which people present themselves on formal occasions. The sense of correctness, of having things set right, is important, because the alternative – "getting it wrong" – is considered to have consequences. This has direct implications for research. How researchers enter the research community, how they negotiate their project aims and methods, how they conduct themselves as members of a research project and as individuals, and how they engage with the people require a wide range of cultural skills and sensitivities. Maori researchers tend to take for granted many of these skills, but in doing so they tend to underrate the importance of such skills. Others may be so much in awe of getting it right that they end up getting it wrong. And getting it wrong in a traditional sense is viewed as having real (sometimes dire) consequences. For example, someone may fall ill. Obviously, "rational" science would not consider this a rational belief, but it is not important what the researchers think; important are what the research subjects think and their perceptions of the researchers. This is one of the primary reasons even Maori researchers need a mentor or *kaumatua* when they are entering the more formal domains of Maori communities. One of the roles of the *kaumatua* is to look after or attend to the formal, ritual, and spiritual dimensions of *tikanga*.

Intersecting this principle, and indeed all others, is the concept of *tapu*. Some forms of knowledge are regarded as *tapu,* and therefore access to these forms of knowledge is restricted. Even when access is given, such knowledge needs to be treated with respect and care. *Tapu* knowledge generally relates to knowledge that is specific to *hapu* and *iwi* and is of a more esoteric nature.[47] It has a particular impact on those researchers who work in the area of tribal history. Some of these histories are actually written down, and often it is the book in which they are written that becomes *tapu* and restricted. One of the obvious problems, however, is that Maori people have become less knowledgeable. This can lead to mystification of knowledge, which is not about *tapu* but about power of a different sort – that is, the power of an individual to claim resources and land and assert "traditional" claims that cannot be challenged. In general, however, *tapu* is an important cultural way of regarding knowledge, and in this sense it needs to be incorporated as a principle of respect for the people who choose to share their knowledge with you. In the words of a *whakatauki,* "*Ahakoa he iti, he iti pounamu.*"[48]

The Principle of *Rangatiratanga*

The concept of *rangatiratanga* has been used throughout this chapter. In Smith's framework, *rangatiratanga* is connected to the "goal of control over one's own life and cultural well-being." This involves control over decision-making processes. The usage of *rangatiratanga* is framed within the discourses related to the Treaty of Waitangi. In the Maori version of the treaty, Te Tiriti of Waitangi, article 2 says in part, *"Ki nga tangata katoa o Nu Tirani te tino rangatiratanga o o ratou wenua o ratou kainga me a ratou taonga katoa."*[49]

Although there is considerable linguistic and legal debate about the concept of *rangatiratanga* in relation to the text of the treaty and the obligations of the Crown, its wider use by Maori encapsulates a wide range of beliefs and aspirations.[50] These discourses, alongside the increasingly "expert" definitions of the Waitangi Tribunal and the Crown itself, have a major influence on the way that research is "governed." At one level, it is about control over the agenda for research and control over the resources and how they are distributed.

There are several sets of principles used in relation to the way in which the Treaty of Waitangi is being interpreted by the Crown. These principles should not be confused with the general principle of *rangatiratanga* being proposed here. In this context, *rangatiratanga* owes as much to the discourses around the Treaty of Waitangi as it does to the shifts in social science research toward more sympathetic and emancipatory research aims and practices. Community control, ethical practices, and research reflexivity have marked some aspects of this kind of research.

At a more pragmatic level, the principles of *rangatiratanga* would govern the ways in which the following critical questions are answered.

(1) What research do we want to carry out?
(2) Whom is that research for?
(3) What difference will it make?
(4) Who will carry out this research?
(5) How do we want the research to be done?
(6) How will we know it is a worthwhile piece of research?
(7) Who will own the research?
(8) Who will benefit?

The principle of *rangatiratanga* would consistently affirm the importance of addressing these questions to Maori people and not, as has previously happened, to *Pakeha* experts, with Maori being consulted on the side. Where discussions by Maori on these issues have occurred, it has not meant that *Pakeha* researchers have been excluded or restricted. Many *Pakeha* researchers have found the process far more collaborative and exciting than if they had attempted to carry out their research apart from Maori groups.

The Principle of *Whanau*

A *whanau* is an extended family. Smith suggests that the principle of *whanau* is important because it provides a support structure that has in-built responsibilities and obligations. The significance of *whanau*, especially as a way of organizing and supervising research, has been raised earlier in this chapter. However, there are other dimensions to *whanau* that need to be mentioned. One relates to *Mana Wahine* and *Mana Tane,* issues of gender. This is important on a number of grounds. At one level, Maori women have been absent from the way that research about Maori has been conducted, for example in tribal histories. In other ways, Maori women have been present, but as a subtext to the major story.[51] In other circumstances, Maori women have been the targets of research and of subsequent interventions. This has particularly been the case in the areas of health and education. At the same time, however, it needs to be recognized that research into Maori boys' education and personal development has not been sympathetic either. In terms of recovering histories, there is a need to look again at the ways in which gender issues are discussed, privileged, and/or silenced when Maori researchers think about research. Gender issues have become important for Maori women because of the exclusionary practices within Maori society, based primarily on gender, which seem to disadvantage women more than men. Many women would argue that these practices are recent ones and are becoming more entrenched as new, younger, and less secure groups of men take over positions of leadership within their *iwi.* These issues are frequently buried under *iwi* politics.[52]

If gender issues in the context of *whanau* are important, then so are age issues. In attempts to operate within Maori contexts, the role of *kaumatua* has taken on a new significance. Kathy Irwin, for example, sees their role as a mentoring and supportive one. Others have "adopted" *kaumatua* as part of their research team, as official members who bring expertise. Part of this exercise has been about gaining entry into a community. *Kaumatua* are also held to be those people who are knowledgeable about Maori things. This is based not simply on the fact that they are old and therefore wise but also on the premise that they have systematically gathered wisdom as they have aged. Not all older Maori are *kaumatua* in this sense of the term. Some *kaumatua,* for example, have kept written records and histories; they are experts in *whaikorero* and *waiata;* they can operate beyond their own immediate *marae;* they have earned respect; they have *mana* and can defend it if necessary through their skills in *whaikorero,* their knowledge of *whakapapa,* and their *matauranga.* Their status as *kaumatua* is directly linked to their knowledge and their ability to use that knowledge for the collective good.

Maori views about knowledge have been discussed in the wider literature; however, there are some aspects of knowledge that are important to Maori research. Levels or phases of knowledge are helpful concepts for thinking about Kaupapa Maori research. The notions of *mohiotanga, wananga, maramatanga,* and *matauranga,*[53] for example, indicate levels and processes by which we gain insight and deep clarification of what we are seeking. *Matauranga* is said to be attained when it is held or comes to rest within us. Eruera Stirling defines *matauranga* as "blessing on your mind, it makes everything clear and guides you to do things the right way."[54] One of the roles of *kaumatua*, then, is to make the pathways to knowledge clearer. This is achieved through their use of *karakia*, their involvement in the welcoming rituals and *mihimihi,* as well as through their intellectual involvement in analyzing data.

Within the dynamic of *whanau* exist other sorts of social relations. In terms of research, the *whanau* principle is generally regarded as an organizational principle, a way of structuring supervision, of working collaboratively, of ensuring that a wide range of Maori concepts is discussed rigorously, and a way of connecting with specific communities and maintaining relationships with communities over many years. The *whanau* can sometimes replace advisory committees, project teams, and supervisory roles. It includes all those roles that are technical and those that are about mentoring and support.

Maori Cultural Ethics

Ethical issues have become increasingly significant as research communities across all disciplines have been held up for public scrutiny and found wanting. The idea of a self-monitoring community of professional scientists, which adheres to codes of good conduct and exerts standards on its members, fell apart with the National Women's Hospital Cervical Cancer Inquiry. This inquiry shocked women and "ordinary people" as an exercise in academic, scientific arrogance. However, for Maori, the inquiry simply reinforced the sense that we have been objectified by research since our first encounters with the West. The ethical issues for Maori, then, have come out of a long history of being researched by outsiders and then having that research flung back at us.

Research ethics for Maori communities extend far beyond issues of individual consent and confidentiality. In a discussion of what may constitute sound ethical principles for research in Maori communities, Ngahuia Te Awekotuku has identified a set of responsibilities that researchers have to Maori people.[55] Her framework is based on the code of conduct for the

New Zealand Association of Social Anthropologists, which in turn is based on the American Anthropological Association's guidelines.[56] Te Awekotuku sets out fairly basic guidelines aimed at respect for and protection of the "rights, interests, and sensitivities" of the people being studied. There are, however, some culturally specific ideas that are part of Kaupapa Maori practices. These are not prescribed in codes of conduct for researchers but tend to be prescribed for Maori researchers in cultural terms.

(1) *aroha ki te tangata* (a respect for people)
(2) *Kanohi kitea* (the seen face – that is, present yourself to people face to face)
(3) *titiro, whakarongo ... korero* (look, listen ... speak)
(4) *manaaki ki te tangata* (share and host people, be generous)
(5) *kia tupato* (be cautious)
(6) *Kaua e takahia te mana o te tangata* (do not trample over the *mana* of people)
(7) *Kaua e mahaki* (don't flaunt your knowledge)[57]

These "sayings" reflect just some of the values placed on the way in which we behave. They are very different from the "public" image of Maori society as a forum for ritual, oratory, and chiefly leaders, but they are the kinds of comments used to determine if someone has "good" qualities as a person. There are several other *whakatauki* that contain the ideals and aspirations worth seeking as well as the moral messages for those who decide not to conform to the rules of practice.

It has been suggested that research in Maori communities can be reduced to a set of simple steps or procedures because they assume that the single most important issue is access to Maori communities. These "procedures" include, for example, finding a *kaumatua* willing to help, going to the local *marae* with the *kaumatua*, and being introduced to and employing local people as research assistants.[58] There is a danger that such "procedures" become fixed criteria for determining ethical practices and good conduct. But the reduction of Maori attitudes, values, and experiences with research to simple procedures, while helpful to outsiders, masks the underlying issues and is a deeply cynical approach to a complex history of involvement as research objects. For Maori researchers, the above steps are far too simplistic in that our choices, culturally, are much more flexible, the community networks are more established, and there are more opportunities to discuss issues and to be seen. At the same time, the accountabilities and responses from the community are more immediate and last longer.

Questions of Method

The main focus here has been on underlying aspects of Kaupapa Maori research and how it is situated as a theory about research. These final comments, then, briefly address the actual practice of determining how to gather "data." People engaged in Kaupapa Maori research have been trained in different disciplines, each with its own methods for carrying out research. To date, many of these researchers have had to develop a critique of their own disciplinary approach to research and to Maori issues and then struggle to make space for their projects within the constraints of the methods imposed. How easy or difficult this is depends on the discipline (and the particular orientation within the discipline) and on the nature of the issues being researched.

Increasingly, Maori research projects have employed multidisciplinary approaches to a research "problem." Maori researchers have themselves developed methods and approaches that have enabled them to do what they want to do. They have gone into the field (that is, their own territory or *rohe*) to interview subjects (sometimes their own relations or *whanaunga*) whom they have identified through various means (including their own networks). They have now filled out their questionnaires or interview schedules and have gone back to the office to analyze and make sense of their data. During the course of their encounter, they are often fed and hosted as special guests, they are asked questions about their family backgrounds, and they are introduced to other members of the family, who sometimes sit in on the interview and participate. Sometimes, if the subject is fluent in Maori, they switch back and forth between the two languages, or, if they think that the researchers cannot understand Maori, they try even harder to speak "good" English. If the researchers are in their homes, they may see photos of family members in the lounge. Sometimes it is hard to tell that the "subject" is Maori. Sometimes they say things a researcher may feel uneasy about, sometimes they come right out and ask the researcher to do something for them, and sometimes they are cynical about and hostile to the questions being asked. When the researcher leaves, it is with the silent understanding that they will meet again. The researcher may return to work and feel good about the interview. Was it an "interview," a conversation, or perhaps a dialogue? Or was it something more than that?

So much of the "method" used in this kind of empirical research gets "written out" that the voices of the research subjects become increasingly silenced as the act of organizing, analyzing, and interpreting the data starts to take over. Time passes by, because these processes take a long time to work through. In Kaupapa Maori research, as a final point, there is the commitment to report back to the people concerned. It is partly a commitment to reciprocity and partly a process of accountability. Students who have written theses, for example, have taken a copy back to the families whom they interviewed; other researchers have invited people into their centre for a presentation; still others have made use of an occasion to publicly thank the participants concerned. The significance of these acts is that sometimes a written piece of work is passed around the *whanau*, other people phone and ask for their own copies, and others put it alongside the photos of family members that fill their sitting rooms. This final reporting closes off one part of an activity; it does not close off the relationships established.

Conclusion

This chapter has mapped out some of the parameters of Kaupapa Maori research, its concept, its context, and its application to research. I have also discussed the connection between Maori cultural values, principles, priorities, and the emancipatory aims seen by those who write in this area as a significant component of Kaupapa Maori research. They are very different from other forms of research – for example, models of cultural sensitivity. The connection between cultural systems and emancipatory goals gives what has been called a "local" context for what critical theoretical approaches mean for Maori. This makes it unique. Also significant about these developments is the involvement of Maori conceptually as well as in the field. This is different from other models of culturally sensitive research, in which the space to be involved at the beginning is often not up for negotiation. Some critical tensions exist, one of which is the involvement of non-Maori researchers. Although there are some examples in which non-Maori researchers have become involved through *whanau* organizations, this does not by any means open involvement. It is one issue that will continue to be contested and debated. "Researching back," like "writing back," is partly about talking back to the West or, in this case, to *Pakeha* and partly about talking to ourselves. Kaupapa Maori research is a way of organizing such processes.

Notes

1 Annual disciplinary conferences are often dominated by academic presentations, and the political nature of research is kept well away. In some cases, it is regarded as a contaminant, and people who raise or address political issues are considered polemicists! On the second point, there were and still are few Maori with postgraduate qualifications, which tend to be a prerequisite for most research positions. Even fewer of these attend conferences or belong to disciplinary societies.

2 Most of the parents in our Te Kohanga Reo were single mothers, very young, and living in the state housing units down the street from the Kohanga Reo. I had a job, as did my spouse, and we had a car, so there was also an issue of socioeconomic circumstances.

3 I had always seen myself as belonging to the "informant" community and thus felt well trained to inform on myself but insufficiently trained to get others to do it for me! And, of course, I "read" what I was being told in the interviews as if I were still a member of the "informant" community and was very conscious of the way in which the words given to me were being carefully selected and framed.

4 For example, J. Mitchell, "Reflections of a Black Social Scientist: Some Struggles, Some Doubts, Some Hopes," *Harvard Educational Review* 52,1 (1982): 27-34.

5 None of which is how I saw myself.

6 L.T. Smith, "Te Rapunga Ki Te Ao Marama" (Education Department, University of Auckland, 1985), the first of a series of papers.

7 K. Irwin, "Maori Research Methods and Practices," *Sites* 28 (1994): 25-43, at 27.

8 Ibid. 28. *Te reo Maori ona tikanga*, trans. "Maori language and its customs."

9 R. Bishop, "Initiating Empowering Research?" *New Zealand Journal of Educational Studies* 29,1 (1994): 175-88, at 175.

10 Ibid. 176.

11 G.H. Smith, "Research Issues Related to Maori Education," paper presented to NZARE Special Interest Conference, Massey University, 1990. Reprinted as "The Issue of Research and Maori" (Research Unit for Maori Education, University of Auckland, 1992).

12 In this sense, *kaupapa* means "project" or plan.

13 L. Pihama, "Tungia te Ururua, Kia Tupu Whakaritorito Te Tupu of te Harakeke: A Critical Analysis of Parents as First Teachers," MA thesis, University of Auckland, 1993, at 57.

14 This debate began formally with a paper by E. Ellsworth, "Why Doesn't This Feel Empowering? Working through the Repressive Myths of Critical Pedagogy," *Harvard Educational Review* 59,3 (1989): 297-324. Ellsworth questioned many of the basic assumptions of critical pedagogy. This provoked a response by Henri Giroux, and the broader issues of the debate are summarized more fully in P. Lather, *Getting Smart: Feminist Research and Pedagogy within the Postmodern* (New York: Routledge, 1991), 43-9.

15 L.T. Smith, "Re-Centring Kaupapa Maori Research," paper presented at Te Matawhanui Conference, Maori Studies Department, Massey University, 1995.

16 This is not without contention, in that some feminist groups would still argue that men, because they are men, cannot possibly articulate a feminist position or carry out feminist research. What I want to signal, however, is that feminist scholarship has moved from its early foundations, and, as a parallel, the same possibility exists for Kaupapa Maori research.

17 For example, Kathy Irwin writes that "There is still a destructive debate taking place in some quarters over who are 'real' and, heaven forbid, 'acceptable' Maori women ... Precious time is wasted debating amongst ourselves, who is and who isn't an 'acceptable' Maori." "Towards Theories of Maori Feminisms," in R. Du Plessis, ed., *Feminist Voices: Women's Studies Texts for Aotearoa/New Zealand* (Auckland: Oxford University Press, 1992), 1-21, at 3.

18 Nor does it preclude those who identify themselves as Maori but cannot speak Maori language, those who are Maori but do not know their *whakapapa,* or those who are Maori but have lived away from their *iwi* or *whanau* territories.

19 T. Nepe, "E Hao Nei e Tenei Reanga: Te Toi Huarewa Tipuna, Kaupapa Maori, an Educational Intervention System," MA thesis, University of Auckland, 1991.

20 Trans. "The language is like a cloak which clothes, envelopes, and adorns the myriad of one's thoughts," cited in ibid. 15.

21 See A. Salmond, "Maori Epistemologies," in J. Overing, ed., *Reason and Morality* (London: Tavistock, 1985), 240.

22 Nepe, "E Hao Nei," 15.

23 For example, those involved in Kaupapa Maori projects question attempts to mystify Maori knowledge or use either their identity and knowledge of *whakapapa* or Maori language as a way of excluding other Maori from participation in decision making or other forms of involvement.

24 See, for example, N. Te Awekotuku, "He Whiriwhiri Wahine: Framing Women's Studies for Aotearoa," in *Te Pua* 1 (Puawaitanga, University of Auckland, 1992): 46-58.

25 For a further discussion of these points, see J. Clark, "The New Right and Educational Research," *Input* (New Zealand Association for Research in Education) 16,1 (1995): 2-8.

26 For further discussion of this point, refer to G.H. Smith, "The Commodification of Knowledge and Culture," *Overview* 49 CORSO (November 1993): 149-53; and G.H. Smith, "Maori Culture for Sale," *Polemic* (University of Sydney Law Society) 4,3 (1994): 149-53.

27 See, for example, the guidelines and policies for the Foundation for Research, Science and Technology and their application forms.

28 Two such units, Te Pumanawa Hauora at Massey University and the Eru Pomare Research Centre at the Wellington Clinical School, are funded by the Health Research Council. Another unit exists at the University of Auckland Medical School, and other units operate inside existing centres – for example, the Alcohol and Public Health Research Centre at the University of Auckland.

29 These include rural and urban communities and several *iwi* groups.

30 Irwin, "Maori," 27.

31 See, for a further discussion, G.H. Smith, "Falling through the Cracks of the Constructivism Debate: The Neglect of the 'Maori Crisis' within Science Education," *Access* (Education Department, University of Auckland) (1995): n. pag.

32 I am using the definition of paradigm by T. Kuhn, *The Structure of Scientific Revolutions, International Encyclopaedia of Unified Science*, 2nd ed., vol. 2 (Chicago: University of Chicago Press, 1970).

33 It is not that nuclear physics is not thought to have an impact on our lives, but it is not yet as real as the advances currently being made in genetic engineering and the possibility that now exists under GATT for "our" genetic material to be copied and patented.

34 S. Harding, *Feminism and Methodology* (Bloomington: Indiana University Press, 1987), 2-3.

35 G.H. Smith, "Kaupapa Maori Schooling: Implications for Educational Policy Making," in *Proceedings of the Conference for the Royal Commission on Social Policy* (Wellington: New Zealand Council for Educational Research, 1988).

36 Rather, say, than in the context of Kura Kaupapa Maori or other types of *hui*. The "community" of Maori researchers is a specialist community that includes health, policy, educational researchers, and postgraduate students.

37 J. Rangihau, "Being Maori," in M. King, ed., *Te Ao Hurihuri: The World Moves On*, 3rd ed. (Auckland: Longman Paul, 1981), 165-75.

38 Graham Smith, for example, identifies *whakapapa* as a strategy for learning how to read print material. G.H. Smith, "Akonga Maori Teaching and Learning Methodologies," in G.H. Smith, ed., *Nga Kete Wananga Readers 2* (Auckland: Auckland College of Education, 1987).

39 *Whakatauki* are similar to proverbs or sayings.

40 Trans. "You will never be lost, you were a seed planted at Rangiatea."

41 See, for an example of such a *whakapapa*, S.M. Mead, "Ka Tupu Te Toi Whakairo ki Aotearoa Becoming Maori Art," in S.M. Mead, ed., *Te Maori: Maori Art from New Zealand Collections* (New York: Harry N. Abrams for the American Federation of Arts, 1984), 63-75, at 67.

42 Rangihau: "Being Maori."

43 Trans. "face to face."

44 For further applications of this concept to research practice, see R. Bishop and T. Glyn, "He Kanohi Kitea: Conducting and Evaluating Educational Research," *New Zealand Journal of Educational Studies* 27,2 (1992): 125-36.

45 Trans. (1) "The language is the life principle of Maori"; (2) "My language, my inspiration, My language, my special 'ornament,' My language, my precious 'treasures.'"

46 *Tangi* are our mourning rituals, which include the funeral; *waiata* are chants and songs often used to give "relish" to a speech; and *manuhiri* are guests or visitors.

47 This is sometimes referred to as *Te Kauwae Runga*, or the "upper jaw" form of knowledge, while more accessible forms of knowledge are referred to as *Te Kauwae Raro*, or the "lower jaw." This can be found in the account by Te Matorohanga, who was Percy Smith's key informant. See P. Smith, *The Lore of the Whare Wananga* (New Plymouth: Polynesian Society, Thomas Avery, 1913).

48 Trans. "Although small it is [like] a precious greenstone."

49 Trans. "[The queen agrees to give] to chiefs and *hapu* and all the people of New Zealand the full chieftainship of their lands, their villages, and all their possessions." (Trans. from Project Waitangi).

50 See, for example, I.H. Kawharu, *Waitangi Maori and Pakeha Perspectives of the Treaty of Waitangi* (Auckland: Oxford University Press, 1989).

51 A good example of this is the Maori story that, in oral accounts, is a story in which Maui engaged in different ways with his grandmothers – for example, to acquire fire and wisdom and to attempt to gain immortality. However, even in some recently written children's stories, the grandmothers have all been transformed into men. It has become a story about men. For a discussion, see K. Jenkins, "Reflections on the Status of Maori Women," in *Te Pua* 1 (Puawaitanga, University of Auckland, 1992): 37-45.

52 See, for example, A. Mead, "Maori Leadership," in *Te Pua* 3,1 (Puawaitanga, University of Auckland, 1994): 11-20.

53 Salmond, "Maori Epistemologies" (see note 21), discusses these concepts in more detail. They are all terms for different sorts of knowing.

54 Cited in A. Salmond, *Eruera: The Teachings of a Maori Elder* (Wellington: Oxford University Press, 1980), 205.

55 N. Te Awekotuku and Manatu Maori, *He Tikanga Whakaaro: Research Ethics in the Maori Community* (Wellington: Manatu Maori, 1991).

56 New Zealand Association of Social Anthropologists Principles of Professional Responsibility and Ethical Conduct (adopted in 1987 and amended in 1990).

57 I have selected these sayings, having heard them used on several occasions as evaluative comments on people. The saying *"titiro, whakarongo, korero"* comes from Te Atarangi, the Maori language program for adults. It seems to be a basic code of conduct for researchers in a number of situations. Actually, these sorts of sayings are often made by the *kuia,* or older women, on a *marae* as they watch, very keenly, what people are doing.

58 For example, *New Zealand Doctor* (June 9, 1995) has a fifteen-step guide for visiting a *marae.* The Race Relations Office also used to publish ways to gain easy access to Maori communities.

18

Ayukpachi: Empowering Aboriginal Thought

James (Sákéj) Youngblood Henderson

> Tribal territory is important because the Earth is our Mother (and
> this is not a metaphor: it is real). The Earth cannot be separated
> from the actual being of Indians. The Earth is where the continu-
> ous and/or repetitive process of creation occurs. It is on the Earth
> and from the Earth that cycles, phases, patterns, in other words,
> the constant flux and motion can be observed and experienced.
> In other words, creation is a continuity, and if creation is to
> continue, then it must be renewed, and consequently, the
> renewal ceremonies, the telling and re-telling of the creation
> stories, the singing and re-singing of songs, which are the
> humans' part in maintenance of creation. Hence, the annual
> Sundance, the societal ceremonies, the unbundling of medicine
> bundles at certain phases of the year. All of these interrelated
> aspects of happenings that take place on and with Mother Earth.
>
> – Leroy Little Bear, *Kainaiwa* (Blood Tribe)[1]

Aboriginal people are daily asked to acquiesce to Eurocentric theories of
legal context that are based firmly on fictitious state-of-nature theories
and cultural differences. In one way or another, they are being asked to
validate the colonialists' libel. They are being asked to affirm alien values
and to sacrifice Aboriginal values for them. Contemporary liberal society
argues that the best Aboriginal people can do is to avoid unnecessary
exclusion by fitting in with the Eurocentric version of society. In effect,
colonized people are being asked to give up their constitutional rights
(that is, their Aboriginal and treaty rights) and to recognize a Eurocentric
and individualistic legal tradition that perpetuates the colonial rule of law.[2]

On the various paths to decolonization, colonized Aboriginal people must
participate in Eurocentric society and knowledge. In the early stages of decolonization, survival depends on accepting Eurocentric worldviews. Jean-
Paul Sartre noted the existence of an "iron law which denied the oppressed
all weapons which he did not personally steal from the oppressor."[3]

Initially, the colonized are unaware that the Eurocentric standards do
not have an existence independent of their hierarchical relations. Only
gradually do they understand that they cannot win at a game with rigged
rules that are likely to change as soon as the colonized discover how
they work. The colonized are forced to look inward for a secure cognitive

foundation. Albert Memmi, a Tunisian writer, recounts from his experiences the process of how educated colonized people learn to know their own identity:[4]

> And [the colonized] who has the wonderful good luck to be accepted in a school will not be saved nationally. The memory which is assigned him is certainly not that of his people. The history which is taught him is not his own ... He and his land are nonentities ... or referenced to what he is not ... The colonized is saved from illiteracy only to fall into linguistic dualism ... In the colonial context, bilingualism is necessary ... But while the colonial bilinguist is saved from being walled in, he suffers a cultural catastrophe which is never completely overcome ... Suppose that he has learned to manage his language to the point of re-creating it in written works; for whom shall he write, for what public? If he persists in writing in his language, he forces himself to speak before an audience of deaf men ... It is a curious fate to write for a people other than one's own, and it is even stranger to write to the conquerors of one's people ... As soon as they dare speak, what will they tell just those people, other than of their malaise and revolt?[5]

Historian Lise Noël also captures the inherent dilemma:

> One of the not inconsiderable effects of oppression is that the dominator succeeds in imposing his logic even on the process adopted by the dominated to escape his control. This logic is double-edged, supplying the victim the weapons and the oppressor with pride in having produced them. For example, some westerners have boasted of having taught Africans and Asians the principles of a revolutionary and liberal heritage after these were invoked to launch decolonization ... The dominated must free themselves from the snares and pitfalls pervading the discourse that they did not initially recognize as alien because it presented itself as all-encompassing and impartial ... The first thing that will have to be called into question will be the principle of an ideal model of humanity or a complete objectivity. In seeking emancipation, the oppressed ... would do best to renew the prevailing discourse by emphasizing the relative nature of differences in identity and recognizing the inevitability of competing subjectivities in the development of knowledge.[6]

To acquire freedom in the decolonized and dealienated order, the colonized must break their silence and struggle to retake possession of their humanity and identity. To speak initially, they have to share Eurocentric thought and discourse with their oppressors; however, to exist with dignity and integrity, they must renounce Eurocentric models and live with the ambiguity of thinking against themselves. They must learn to create models to help them take their bearings in unexplored territory. Educated Aboriginal thinkers have to understand and reconsider Eurocentric discourse in order to reinvent an Aboriginal discourse based on heritage and language and to develop new postcolonial syntheses of knowledge and law to protect them from old and new dominators and oppressors.[7]

The crisis of our times has created postcolonial thinkers and societies that struggle to free themselves from the Eurocentric colonial context. While we still have to use the techniques of colonial thought, we must also have the courage to rise above them and follow traditional devices. It is this harmonization that haunts this chapter. We can learn from the efforts of colonized writers, such as Gandhi, who have shown British society that its self-legitimating and self-congratulatory colonial race-relations discourses were inconsistent with any concept of a rule of law. Additionally, we can seek dealienation and affirming identities from those colonized writers, such as Frantz Fanon and Albert Memmi, who have shown that the race-relations theories were grounded in and sustained by themes derived from European racism and imperialism. Some of the best Aboriginal enlightenment can be found in the work of Cree author Mary Ellen Turpel-LaFond (especially in her essay "First Nations Resistance: Postcolonial Law"), the writings of Anishinabe legal scholar John Borrows, Lumbee legal scholar Robert Williams, Jr., Chickasaw writer Linda Hogan, Seneca legal scholar Robert Porter, and Mohawk writer Patricia Monture (OKanee) Angus (especially in "Surviving the Contradictions: A Personal Note on Academia"[8] and her book *Thunder in My Soul*).[9]

The critical work of Brazilian legal scholar Roberto Unger is unique and empowering for Indigenous people. Although his writings are based on Eurocentric traditions, they provide inspiration for Aboriginal people seeking to understand the limits and patterns of Eurocentric thought. His works assist us in constructing postcolonial critical theory. His is a relentless attack on the contradictions of modern liberal thought. These ideas can be found in *Knowledge and Politics* (New York: Free Press, 1975); *Law in Modern Society: Toward a Criticism of Social Theory* (New York: Free Press, 1976); *Passion: An Essay on Personality* (New York: Free Press, 1984); and *The Critical Legal Studies Movement* (Cambridge, MA: Harvard University Press, 1986). His innovative explanatory theory of society and programs for social reconstruction can be found in *Politics* (Cambridge, UK: Cambridge University Press, 1987) in three books: *Social Theory: Its Situation and Its Task; False Necessity, Anti-Necessity: Social Theory in the Service of Radical Democracy;* and *Plasticity into Power: Comparative-Historical Studies on the Institutional Conditions of Economic and Military Success.*

Moreover, postcolonial writers can find strength in the common cycles and patterns of Eurocentric thought itself. The needed transformation in context is a common pattern in European legal thought. Indeed, it is a persistent cycle in all their cognitive reality. In the history of European ideas, these transformations have been introduced by scholars at a loss to solve particular problems in different fields of knowledge. Eventually, they discover that these problems are connected with one another. Then they find the sources of their bafflement in the premises that underlie the disciplines within whose boundaries they have been working. At last, they establish new systems of thought that sweep away the difficulties that they faced. Correspondingly, after mastery of a particular problem, there is a movement from ideological mastery to enslavement. As the eighteenth-century German philosopher G.W.F. Hegel showed with great brilliance, the history of European thought and culture is an ever-changing pattern of great liberating ideas that inevitably turn into suffocating straitjackets.[10]

In Eurocentric thought, it is essential to learn to think and act in a fragmentary manner, balancing the tensions of failing polarities. To have mutually exclusive, contradictory opposites, or dualism, requires a certain uniformity of thought about unpacking events in such a way that the opposites will come out the same regardless who does the unpacking. If there is no agreement on how to divide events or situations between the two poles or categories (or if one concludes that it no longer seems to make a difference), then the distinctions collapse into indeterminacy or contradictions. This collapse of dualism is fatal since modern legal thought is founded on a strategy of differences. Examples of this strategy are the distinctions between public/private, state/society, legislative/judicial, power/law, and law/policy. The collapse of difference illustrates the decline of a legal culture and a transformation (or paradigm shift) in contemporary thought.

The mechanics of failed polarities as explanatory contexts are intriguing in Eurocentric thought but unexplored. In modern thought and courts, the process begins when polarities such as savage and civilized peoples are denied by a judge and an intermediate category (called "quasi-civilized" or half-breed) is created. To prevent the collapse of the explanatory power of dualism, other judges reframe the contradictory opposites by affirming and extending the ambiguous intermediate category toward both polar concepts, thus creating a triad. Eventually, as the ambiguity over classification increases, the court has to balance the intermediate category against both conceptual ends of the polarity. As the opposing poles become closer to each other in balancing with the intermediate terms, the black and white concepts merge into grey law. What were originally linear opposites collapse into an expanded intermediate term, creating a new singularity (Indians), usually signified by the intersectionality of description, explanation, and justification of a failed polarity. The new singularity is contrasted against other singularities (Canadians), until a new polarity arises, and over time it begins to fail as an explanation.

These paradoxes operate in Canadian thought and law. Canada is a land of diversity, embracing vast differences within its borders and among its peoples. The Canadian legal profession needs to create an integral jurisprudence to meet the needs of all Canadians. Lawyers must accept multicultural law rather than colonial law and recognize cross-culturality as the potential termination point of Eurocentric thought. Canadian legal thinkers must understand that cross-cultural, syncretic thought and jurisprudence can create a legitimate place where postcolonial worlds can recover an effective identifying relation between self and place. This view provides a framework of "difference on equal terms" within which multicultural theories can continue to be fruitfully explored.

Eurocentric thinkers do not understand the elegance of Aboriginal thought and do not question the negative myths of colonial thought. They easily conclude that Aboriginal knowledge, consciousness, and language are irrelevant to contemporary Canadian thought. They see Aboriginal life as lifeworlds without systems (anarchy). Yet, when one aspires to decolonize Aboriginal people, these neglected lifeworlds contain the authority to heal Aboriginal identities and communities. Restoring Aboriginal worldviews and languages is essential to realizing Aboriginal solidarity and power.

Paulo Freire, a Brazilian social reformer and educator, has argued that only within the existing participatory relationship with natural, cultural, and historical reality can people be educated. He also argues that a critical consciousness of the cultural and historical roots of a people, as understood and expressed by them, is the foundation for their cultural emancipation. Moreover, he asserts that reformers must begin with the way in which a group communicates about its world.[11] Thus, it is fundamental to any Aboriginal emancipation that existing Aboriginal worldviews, languages, knowledge, customary orders, and laws must be validated by Canadian institutions and thought. Aboriginal people cannot know who they are through the structure of alien languages. They cannot read about themselves in books or reports written in alien languages. Since they do not know who they are, they remain trapped in another context and discourse that others have constructed on their presumed negative values.

Reliance on Aboriginal Thought

Aboriginal thought and identity are centred on the environment in which Aboriginal people live. As Aboriginal people experienced the forces of an ecosystem, Aboriginal worldviews, languages, consciousness, and order arose. With the elders' calls to return to Aboriginal worldviews, languages, knowledge, and order, we need to reexamine their ecological context. Such an inquiry requires us to learn from the ecosystem as our ancestors did, as well as to learn from our elders' experiences. Some Aboriginal thinkers have begun to deal with the gap between Eurocentric and Aboriginal worldviews and language structures. Aboriginal educators such as Marie Battiste, Murdena Marshall, and Eber Hampton have urged a return to Aboriginal worldviews, languages, and knowledge as a remedy for the failed experiment in assimilating Aboriginal people.[12]

This reexamination is difficult. Eurocentric thought was created on a negative vision of Aboriginal thought and life. It stressed the dissimilarities between Europeans and Aboriginal people, and it used this distinction to create barriers to Aboriginal rights and solidarity. At the heart of the conceptual oppression and confusion is the idea of the unimaginative savage with little culture or order who needs European civilization and thought to progress. A Laguna Pueblo writer, Leslie Silko, captures this quandary:

> But the fifth world had become entangled with European names ... All of creation suddenly had two names: an Indian name and a white name. Christianity separated the people from themselves; it tried to crush the single clan name, encouraging each person to stand alone, because Jesus Christ was not like the Mother who loved and cared for them as her children, as her family ... The old instinct had always been to gather the feelings and opinions that were scattered through the village, to gather them like willow twigs and tie them into a single prayer bundle that would bring peace to all of them. But now the feelings were twisted, tangled roots, and all the names for the source of this growth were buried under English words, out of reach. And there would be no peace and the people would have no rest until the entanglement had been unwound to the source.[13]

Like the fifth world described by Silko, eighteenth- and nineteenth-century Eurocentric thought created entangling names and concepts to describe Aboriginal peoples and their societies. We still struggle under those labels. Pioneering ethnographers had some insight into Indigenous consciousness, but more often they made interpretive mistakes.

Europeans assumed that it was a noun-God who created the world. Thus, they saw Aboriginal culture from an alien cultural perspective – as a set of solutions devised by a group of people to meet specific problems posed by a common situation. Based on this assumption, they believed that life was fixed and contained. They thus defined their task as discovering the coherent whole behind human behaviour by means of observation. Their European eyes created structural theories of Eurocentric thought that ignored Aboriginal thought and understanding.

"What does God look like?" asked Chickasaw poet and novelist Linda Hogan, and she answered, "These fish, this water, this land."[14] Aboriginal thought emphasizes coherent wholes or shared patterns at the expense of unique processes of change and internal inconsistencies, conflicts, and contradictions. Aboriginal thought honours the diversity of life and never developed any single theory or view of culture,[15] which knowing observers have attributed to it.[16]

In Eurocentric thought, the knowing observer's views became the "virtual" truth about Aboriginal cultures, and these views remain serious obstacles to understanding Aboriginal consciousness. European ethnographers spoke about Aboriginal life as webs of meaning and of Aboriginal people creating many different social worlds through symbols. Descriptive details reveal that Aboriginal culture is displayed through the identification and elaboration of matters such as language, child-rearing practices, totems, taboos, signifying codes, work and leisure interests, standards of behaviour and deviance, systems of social classification, and jural procedures shared by members of the studied people. From descriptive data, ethnographers infer patterns that knit society into an integrated whole as an all-embracing and largely taken-for-granted way of life. In addition, the analysts infer the pattern or patterns, differentiating them from others and urging analyses that mediate between deterministic and voluntaristic models of behaviour. In this sense, culture is seen as an abstract possession of Eurocentric writers, and the contents of Aboriginal knowledge are understood as merely symbolic and ideational.

Another flaw in understanding the Aboriginal worldview is derived from Eurocentric diffusionism. Eurocentric ethnographers represented Aboriginal people as objects of Europe's global enterprise, as if they were the ideal recipients of the white man's burden. Most often, Aboriginal people were depicted as members of a harmonious, internally homogeneous, unchanging culture. From such a perspective, Aboriginal culture appeared to "need" progress and economic and moral uplifting. This perspective, however, served as a self-congratulatory reference point against which Eurocentric society could measure its own progressive historical evolution. The civilizing journey is conceived of more as a rise than as a fall, a process more of perfection than of degradation – a long and arduous journey upward, culminating in being "them." Often this process is negatively characterized as assimilation. By assuming the answers to questions that should have been asked, Eurocentric disciplines confidently asserted that so-called traditional Aboriginal cultures do not change – only European society progresses.

Because the ethnographers were literate and the Natives were not, the ethnographers recorded the "utterances" of the Natives. Their written narratives became monuments to Eurocentric worldviews and diffusionism.

Because of their superior civilization, classic ethnographers assumed an illusion of objectivity, although few of them actually mastered Aboriginal worldviews, consciousness, or languages. Most re-created the Aboriginal realm in their own likeness and confidently taught it to Eurocentric society as the actual Aboriginal truth. Classic notions of Aboriginal stability, orderliness, and equilibrium still dominate contemporary thought. Part of this resilience is derived from the Eurocentric illusion of a timeless culture. The classic understanding of how Aboriginal people should look and act, and even of what lies ahead for them, is now seen as part of Eurocentric time and thought. So strong are the ethnographers' written views that often one can predict from them what modern society will demand of Aboriginal people; much too often these classic notions organize the lives of Aboriginal people for them and limit their future.

Aboriginal people's identities and aspirations suffer under the legacy of these entangling Eurocentric doctrines, names, and methodologies. Because the classic works do not present clear or fair interpretations of Aboriginal worldviews, Aboriginal people have had to suggest a total revision of anthropological and social analyses. Eurocentric thought has been resistant to such a revision. Around the globe, Aboriginal thinkers have had to prove that the received notion of "culture" as unchanging and homogeneous is not only mistaken but also irrelevant. We have had to prove to modern society that our worldview is distinct from the cultural ethnographies constructed for us by Eurocentric thought. We have had to prove that we are not brute, timeless events in the state of nature. We have had to use social analysis to attempt to reverse the process: to dismantle the ideological in order to reveal the cultural (a peculiar blend of objective arbitrariness and subjective taken-for-grantedness). The interplay between making the familiar strange and the strange familiar is part of the ongoing transformation of knowledge.

The timeless aspect of the Eurocentric view of Aboriginal culture has created the context for the total demise of our culture. Central to European cultural confusion is the myth of a "primitive culture" untouched or uncontaminated by Eurocentric influences. The ethnographic impulse to regard cultures as fixed images that have an integrity and coherence that enable them to be studied (ethnographic monumentalism) does have a solid, deep structure: all cultures are separate and equal; there is no cultural superiority. However, this thought equally encompasses the everyday and the esoteric, the mundane and the elevated, the ridiculous and the sublime. Understanding Aboriginal culture requires one to try to understand other forms of life on their own terms. Although some translation is necessary, one worldview should not impose its categories on other people's lives because they probably do not apply, at least not without serious revision to the assumptive realms.

What is more important about these Eurocentric constructs is that they are tools that terminate Aboriginality. The timeless aspect is a Eurocentric attempt to limit the future – another way of forcing Indigenous culture to accept the inevitability of imitating Eurocentric modes of thought and dress. Any changes in our lives are equated with the end of Aboriginality and the beginning of civilization.

Aboriginal thinkers can, however, avoid falling into the trap of applying the colonial strategy of difference between worldviews. Aboriginal thinkers such as Leroy Little Bear have attempted to broaden the linear quality of Eurocentric time or "history" into the spatial pluralities common to Algonquian worldviews and languages.[17] While it is tempting to create negative values in the alien worldview, to be a neocolonial Aboriginal thinker is no great achievement. It does not take much talent for an Aboriginal person to see that something is wrong, but it will take many visions to determine what may put it right again. I have a tentative and limited vision of how to make things right. It is a personal vision about Aboriginal thought. It has many gaps that need to be filled and lacks complete understanding. Many visions will be needed to create a complete vision. With this understanding, I want to look at the concepts of natural contexts, Aboriginal worldviews, languages, knowledge, and order to illustrate a framework for our emancipation from Eurocentric thought.

Natural Contexts

Unger asserts that a context of inquiry is natural if it allows those who move within it to discover everything about the world that they can discover. Such contexts make available to people all the forms of practical collaboration or passionate attachment that they might have well-founded reasons to desire.[18]

Ecological contexts as natural contexts are not discussed in modern social thought, but they are now emerging concepts in the natural sciences and sustainable development theory. These ecological contexts have always been indispensable parts of Aboriginal thought and life. Aboriginal natural contexts are not based on the instructions of a noun-God or on the reductionistic thoughts of great men. Aboriginal elders have insisted that Aboriginal people not fall into the trap of creating artificial contexts for the generations to come. To understand the meaning of life, they urge Aboriginal people to reestablish a relationship with their local ecological order. Ecological forces have always been the source of the most important lessons of Aboriginal thought and life. Aboriginal worldviews, languages, knowledge, order, and solidarity are derived from ecological sensibilities, so an understanding of these forces is essential to an understanding of Aboriginal contexts and thought.

Most Aboriginal peoples, for example the Mi'kmaq on the Atlantic coast, have no sound for nature.[19] The best translation of their natural context is "space" or "place of creation" (*kisu'lt melkiko'tin*). They call their understanding of the sea, rivers, and forests where they live the realm of the earth lodge (*maqmike'wi'kam*). The Cree or *nehiyawak*[20] have a similar concept, which they express as mother earth (*kikawinaw*). The Lakota languages[21] express this concept as *maka*.[22] The earth lodge is understood as an interrelated space where Aboriginal people have direct and extremely visceral relationships with the essential forces in nature. The Mi'kmaqs' understanding of their natural context establishes the vantage point from which they construct their worldview, language, knowledge, and order. They have no knowledge of the interrelated space outside the ecology of the Atlantic. They do not have an artificial notion of society or self independent of their place of creation.

Mi'kmáki became the concept that the allied people (Mi'kmaq) called their national territory. This translates as the "space or land of friendship."[23] The concept stresses the voluntary political confederation of various Algonquian families into the Holy Assembly or *Santé Mawiómi*, with a shared worldview. Wherever their language was spoken was *sitqamúk*, their ancient space, and every part of this territory is sacred to the allied people. *Mi'kmáki* is not a cosmological order; it is the result of millennia of field observations and direct experiences. The experiences of their ancestors are directly encoded within Mi'kmaq language and symbolic literacy. These understandings or sentiments furnish an important part of the implicit order in which they live, as well as their practical knowledge.

The sacred order in which the Mi'kmaq live is expressed as a mutually sustaining ecological relationship. Consistent with the people's action-oriented reality, a process of being with the universe was and is a widely shared, coherent worldview that connects all things. For example, the Mi'kmaq conceptualized every animal with a certain spirit and considered animals a "separate nation."[24] They adhere to an active principle of kinship with all life forms.[25] An important feature of their world order is the use of human kinship as a general analogy for ecological relationships.[26] The most obvious and widespread manifestation of this relationship is the totemic clan system. This system categorizes social obligations, such as sharing and deference, as well as proper moral and ethical considerations, with the reciprocal ecological relationship. Plants, animals, and humans are related, and each is both a producer and a consumer with respect to the other, in an endless cycle.[27]

The sacred order is also a place where the animate powers of the spirits (*mntu*) exist in harmony. The Mi'kmaq are conscious of and respect the animation of their environment. To them, every stone, tree, river, coastline, ocean, and animal is a discrete *mntu.*[28] They strive to respect and live in harmony with these intelligible essences. Within their space, a respectful and sacred relationship between all life forms is the highest form of existence. Such relationships are not always achieved, but they are the purpose of life.

Nestumou is the sound that describes the Míkmaq experiences on a part of the earth. The Cree call this realm *nistotamowin* or personal experiences. Both sounds validate the people's identity within an ecosystem and a langscape (a landscape of language) that creates an appropriate cultural literacy with the ecosystem. Literally, the Míkmaq sound means the "understood realms." *Nestumou* describes everything for which the Míkmaq have experiences, not everything that could exist. *Nestumou* includes both the visible and the invisible realms and is discussed in terms of lodges (*wikwóm*). *Nestumou* expresses the cumulative wisdom of the Míkmaq, with about eight levels of meaning or understanding (*nestunk*).[29] These levels are interconnected and transform from one to another. The *nestunk* are the deep earth lodge (*lamqamuk*),[30] the root lodge (*wjipisekek*),[31] the water lodge (*lampoqókóm*),[32] the earth lodge (*kinuwsitaqamino*),[33] the ghost lodge (*wskɨtékmujuiokóm*),[34] the sky lodge (*mooskoonwíkóm*),[35] the light lodge (*wásóqwíkóm*),[36] and the ancestors' lodge (*skɨtékmujuawti*).[37]

The centre of the sacred realm is viewed as the living lodge (*maqmikéwíkam*). The living lodge is composed of three realms: the underwater lodge, the earth lodge, and the ghost lodge. It comprises the spirals of the unfolding realms of daily Míkmaq life and the immanent enfolded realms of intuitive and transcendental experiences. Surrounding these realms are five other realms: the deep earth, root, sky, light, and ancestors' lodges. Interconnecting each of these lodges are the forces (*mntu*), and each lodge is associated with certain keepers of forces, regardless of form.

The earth and its forces are the living context that instructs Aboriginal teachings and order. Life and its forces are seen as a gift to be humbly accepted, not as something to be taken for granted or used to manipulate other life forms. Life is revered, acknowledged, and reaffirmed through prayer, ceremony, dance, and ritual. The earth and its forces create wholeness, which European thinkers often call objective reality. The earth, however, is an external reality that is in a continuous state of transformation. The Míkmaq see all the transformations as linked with each other. Some of these changes occur in cycles or patterns, and these cycles or patterns are understood as part of a whole. Usually, if the Míkmaq cannot see how a particular change is connected to the whole, they believe their perceptions are affected by their experience or perspective.

The realms of flux create a flowing, transforming existence. Aboriginal elders and thinkers relate each realm to the entire movement. They describe each realm only to understand the overall process of change.

Energies or forces of the realms change with transformations. These transformations do not always cause physical changes; they often cause changes in the manifestation or behaviour only of those who are aware of the subtle changes. If there is no change or renewal, then the energies or forces waste away. These realms are not outside each other but are interactive. The interaction among all these parts is what is felt to be important, rather than the different parts themselves. Thus, the sacred space is considered as a transforming flux that constitutes an indivisible web of meanings. The Míkmaq can perceive the web, and occasionally they can experience reflections of the realms. The total order, described as an indivisible world, can best be understood in English as the implicate order.[38] Traditionally, the Míkmaq have translated this order into the English words "the most" or the "great mystery" or the "great silence."

Aboriginal Worldviews

Most Aboriginal worldviews and languages are formulated by experiencing an ecosystem.[39] Linda Hogan has stressed our intimate relations to the ecological forces: "We come from the land, the sky, from love and the body. From matter and creation. We are, life is, an equation we cannot form or shape, a mystery we can't trace in spite of our attempts to follow it back to its origin, to find out when life began, even in all our stories of when the universe came into being, how the first people emerged."[40] Aboriginal worldviews are empirical relationships with local ecosystems, and Aboriginal languages are an expression of these relationships. By living in an ecological space for millennia, Aboriginal people have established a worldview that sees the order of life as a state of flux. However, this state of flux is not the product of human force and fraud or the manifestation of human will, which is typically one-sided and self-asserting. The Aboriginal worldview asserts that all life is sacred and that all life forms are connected. Humans are neither above nor below others in the circle of life. Everything that exists in the circle is one unity, of one heart.

The Aboriginal worldview teaches Aboriginal people to feel humble about their existence. They are but one strand in the web of life. In the circle of which all life forms a part, humans are dependent upon all the other forces for their survival. Aboriginal worldviews also teach that humans exist to share life according to their abilities. They exist to care for and renew the web of life, and therefore they must respect and value all the forces of life. Often this worldview is called the process of humility.

Most Aboriginal people see their environment as shaped and created by living forces. A Lakota thinker, Vine Deloria, Jr., observed that there are two great truths about Aboriginal people. First, there is a great unanimity among Aboriginal nations when they express their views on the natural world and on the behaviour of humans in that world. Second, because of the different places where they live and learn, Aboriginal nations are distinct from each other.[41] Their diverse ecologies or living lodges have created their diverse worldviews and languages.

Aboriginal understandings, languages, teachings, and practices developed through direct interaction with the forces of the natural order or ecology. This experience intimately connects their worldviews and knowledge with a certain space. This is more than mere ecological awareness; it is a living relationship with a specific environment that is not conceived of as either universal or conventional.

Most Aboriginal worldviews and languages are founded on the belief that all life forms were created to adapt to ecological change. As Chief Joseph, a Nez Percé, stated, "The earth and myself are of one mind. The measure of the land and the measure of our bodies are the same. Do not misunderstand me, but understand me fully with reference to my affection to the land."[42] Understanding life forms and how together they create and sustain a sacred, delicate balance is the foundation of Aboriginal worldviews and languages. We must learn to be patient with all the life forms in our surroundings and to give thanks for all things the life forms do for us. We must understand that it is our privilege to share with others the meaning of life. Understanding the delicate balance of the earth and its cyclic patterns provides an accurate impression of our natural, ecological context.

Most Aboriginal worldviews are founded on two understandings. First, they understand the ecosystem as an eternal system tolerant of flux and refined by endless renewals and realignments. Second, they understand that each ecosystem encapsulates and enfolds many forces or parts, none of which can enfold or encapsulate the whole. The forces express nature instead of creating it. These two understandings focus on the interdependence of the life forces. They also express the need for respectful behaviour to all parts of the sacred spaces. Thus, Aboriginal people perceive all the various forces of nature as connective fibres in a larger pattern that enfolds a fluctuating ecological system.

Together these understandings reinforce our belief that all life on earth is living and interrelated.[43] All forces of the physical environment have similar spirits and are subject to the forces of nature. Aboriginal people can understand anything if they are conscious of their relationships to other life forms and the relationship of these life forms to everything else. In translation, they call this interrelationship the law of circular interaction.[44]

The natural context and worldview of circular interaction is quite different from the formal but empty word-world created by the artificial contexts of Eurocentric thought. The universality of Eurocentric abstract thought assumes that all humans have a common heritage and a common destiny. Enfolded in this heritage and destiny are the ideas of a failed savage past and a better civilized future. Within this paradigm, Europeans self-righteously set out to convert all others with whom they came into contact to their understanding of an artificial future society.

I reject the concept of "culture" for worldview. To use "culture" is to fragment Aboriginal worldviews into artificial concepts. The worldview is a unified vision rather than an individual idea. Aboriginal worldviews assume that all life forms are interconnected, that the survival of each life form is dependent on the survival of all others. Aboriginal worldviews also note that the force of the life forms is derived from an unseen but knowable spiritual realm. Dr. Erica-Irene Daes, Special Rapporteur to the United Nations, has summarized a good way to view Aboriginal worldviews:

> In developing the principles and guidelines, the Special Rapporteur found it useful to bear in mind that the heritage of an indigenous people is not merely a collection of objects, stories and ceremonies, but a complete knowledge system with its own concepts of epistemology, philosophy, and scientific and logical validity. The diverse elements of an indigenous people's heritage can only be fully learned or understood by means of the pedagogy traditionally employed by these peoples themselves, including apprenticeship, ceremonies and practice. Simply recording words or images fails to capture the whole context and meaning of songs, rituals, arts or scientific and medical wisdom. This also underscores the central role of indigenous peoples' own languages, through which each people's heritage has traditionally been recorded and transmitted from generation to generation.[45]

Just as ecology defines Aboriginal consciousness, so it also informs Aboriginal teachings and knowledge. To generate stability in a transforming universe, Aboriginal elders say that individuals have to create consensual relationships with these forces. Thus, Aboriginal people are taught nourishing rituals and ceremonies for communication with these forces.

The discord between Aboriginal and Eurocentric worldviews is dramatic. It is a conflict between natural and artificial contexts. Aboriginal worldviews are not reductionistic. They have always stressed similarities rather than differences. The complexities of the forces of nature are always transforming, thus to begin studying one force of nature eventually entails understanding all its transformations.

The Aboriginal worldview may be understood from four complementary perspectives: as a manifestation of Aboriginal language; as a specialized knowledge system; as a unity with many diverse consciousnesses; and as a mode of social order, law, and solidarity. Each perspective of the worldview is learned, not genetically or racially encoded. Learning another worldview is a lifetime project that requires time and patience. One cannot simply use imagination to invent other cultural worlds. Even those so-called realms of pure freedom, our fantasies and "innermost thoughts," are produced and limited by consciousness and language. Human imagination is as culturally formed as are distinctive ways of weaving, performing a ritual, raising children, grieving, or healing.

Aboriginal Languages

Aboriginal languages express an awareness of a local ecology and are directed to understanding both external life forms and the invisible forces beneath them, which Algonquian languages describe by the sounds *mntu*,[46] *manidoo, manito, manitu,* or *manitou.*[47] These words can be equated with the forces or essences of life or spirit, knowledge, and thought. Aboriginal people explain their consciousness using these sounds: how they feel; what they see as beautiful, admirable, effective; what they perceive as odd or dangerous or dull. Perceiving these forces is a pathway to understanding multilevel sensations and instincts. These forces provide the link between the natural context and Aboriginal consciousness and order. They create continuity between one's inner life and one's capacity for action. These sounds create a dynamic consciousness between ease and unease with a changing ecosystem. The discussion here is not about introspection or inner life. It is about the affective forces or quality of the ecosystem, where relationships depend on the energy of natural forces. This can be viewed as similar to the ancient European quest to understand intelligible essences or Platonic forms.

The natural order is viewed as a complex cycle of renewing forces, energies, and relationships. Creating a relationship with the living energy in an ecosystem forges Aboriginal worldviews and languages. The Algonquian peoples are verb-oriented. Unlike most Europeans, they do not have a noun-oriented language that creates divisions or dualities. Their pursuit is to be with the flux, to experience its changing form, to develop a relationship with the forces, and thus to create harmony. Their language and thought are an attempt to learn from being part of the flux, to create a complementary and harmonious relation with nature, to experience the beauty of the moment, and to release such inspirations back to where they came from without fear of loss. Their language has not developed a method to explain the forces or change them, merely to contain them. This is the vital context of their worldview and life.

Because of the awareness of flux and its forces, the Algonquian language is an active relationship between the elements of a particular environment. Algonquian consciousness is one of common meaning (appositeness) or aptness. It is complementary to the flux and its forces. It recognizes that it is an integral accomplice to these ecological forces, not their master or witness. It is a unity of meaning, with each form of awareness representing a way of being with others and with self. In most Aboriginal languages, there are no fixed categories of objects, such as sun, wind, natural resources, minerals, plants, animals, or peoples. These categories are English translations of Aboriginal categories of being that describe the external patterns and interactions of life-giving forces.

In Aboriginal society, reason is the awareness of implicit forces in a changing reality, an understanding of solidarity, love, and caring. This linguistic awareness knows no distinction between is and ought or between theory and practice. The awareness is more an acrobatic patterning in which healthy, civil, unrestrained vitality and energetic movement are distinguished from heaviness, violence, tension, and passive movement. The process of maintaining the Míkmaq worldview is called *tliln-uo'lti'k*. It is distinguished from the process of maintaining their language or thought, which is signified by the sound *tlinuita'sim*. Additionally, they acknowledge a dynamic factor that is independent of consciousness: the unconscious, known among some tribes as the "other side," the *nagual*. Among the Míkmaq, the "other side" is known as *qame'k*.[48]

In comparing Aboriginal languages with the noun-based values of English, scholars have emphasized three distinct features of Aboriginal languages in America.[49] Aboriginal languages make a distinction between real and imaginary nouns; they do not fragment mass nouns, for example to specify measurement or individualize intangibles; and they treat time as being continuous with little difference in the tenses of verbs. In contrast, the English language uses the same linguistic, spatial, and metaphoric structure for both real and imaginary nouns; constantly tries to give form to intangibles and mass nouns, for example a glass of water; and has a fragmented and objectified (three-dimensional) concept of time.[50] Often these linguistic differences create an unbridgeable linguistic void between the two understandings.

Kiowi author N. Scott Momaday captures the modern irony of Aboriginal worldview and language: "One of the most perplexing ironies of American history is the fact that the Indian has been effectively silenced by the intricacies of his own speech, as it were. Linguistic diversity has been a formidable barrier to Indian-white diplomacy. And underlying this diversity is again the central dichotomy, the matter of a difference in ways of seeing and making sense of the world around us."[51]

Aboriginal consciousness and language are structured according to Aboriginal people's understanding of the forces of the particular ecosystem in which they live. They derive most of the linguistic notions by which they describe the forces of an ecology from experience and from reflection on the forces of nature. As the Cree elders say, "The Cree language is our identity (*kinêhiyâwiwininaw nêhiyawêwin*)."[52]

Like the functions of the periodic chart of elements in chemistry, the

Mìkmaq language is a "holafrastic" structure. Similar to most Algonquian languages, it affirms the implicate order of the world. Its speakers build up verb phrases from what we could call implicate roots, containing the action or motion of the flux, and have hundreds of prefixes and suffixes to choose from to express an entire panorama of energy and motion. The use of verbs rather than a plethora of noun subjects and objects is important: it means that very few fixed and rigid separate objects exist in the Mìkmaq worldview (or langscape). What they consider instead is great flux, eternal transformation, and interconnected space. With this fluidity of semantic-phonemes comprising the verb sounds, every speaker can create new vocabulary "on the fly," tailored to meet the experience of the moment and to express subtle nuances of meaning.

To take Aboriginal languages away from Aboriginal people in the name of a process toward a universal English language is the initial step in all legal annihilation.[53] To carry this badge of slavery in one's mind is to perpetuate colonization and alienation. As French philosopher Jacques Derrida noted, "The violence of an injustice has begun when all the members of a community do not share the same idiom throughout."[54] Similarly, he noted that a precondition to justice is the ability "to address oneself to the other in the language of the other."[55] Thus, language already has both knowledge and law enfolded in it. Without access to their Aboriginal language, Aboriginal people can neither create nor sustain a postcolonial order. They can have access to Aboriginal cultures through English, but they cannot grasp the inherent beauty of Aboriginal worldviews and language through English. They end up living a translated life.

Aboriginal Knowledge

Understanding and attempting to contain the energies that infuse everything is the goal of Aboriginal knowledge.[56] Aboriginal knowledge has developed a privileged place for space and all its energies instead of time as the most important ordering concept of reality. Most Aboriginal thought teaches that humans are the youngest life form on earth and the most dependent and the least knowledgeable. Our gift is our ability to learn and to think. Traditionally, Aboriginal people studied the behaviour of life forms and the seasons to develop an understanding of the dynamics of a space and the role of each life form in it. They also studied life forms and seasons to create a lifestyle that was harmonious with the local ecosystem. The ecosystem in which they lived was their classroom; the life forms that shared the land were their teachers. As a Lakota once stated about Aboriginal knowledge, "We may *misunderstand*, but we do not *misexperience*."[57]

Aboriginal knowledge rejects the claims of universal civilization and values. Instead, it reflects the complexity of a state of being within a certain ecology. Aboriginal elders and thinkers view universal knowledge as a cultural abstraction of Eurocentric worldviews, histories, neuroses, and value systems. These norms were tied to a belief in monoculturalism, to ancestry, gender, and purity of race or lineage.

Aboriginal people understand how limited their knowledge is about this realm of transforming flux. Experience is the way to determine personal gifts and patterns in ecology. Experiencing the realms is a personal necessity and forges an intimate relationship with the world. In the Aboriginal quest for knowledge, such experiences are focused on helping one understand the nature and structure of a particular realm, on how realms interchange yet remain related, and on how language may create an elegant way of explaining an implicate order composed of complex systems of relationship and interdependence. As a Lakota medical doctor stated, "I know that our people possessed remarkable powers of concentration and abstraction, and I sometimes fancy that such nearness to nature as I have described keeps the spirit sensitive to impressions not commonly felt, and in touch with the unseen powers."[58]

This search to respect the forces of an ecosystem taught the value of a tolerant and holistic approach to life. This process of experiencing and understanding nature was more than a matter of defining phonemes or phones or words and phrases. It made little sense to create any form of fixed language in this realm; the known truth is about unending change that requires flexibility, both cognitively and physically.

Aboriginal knowledge is not a description of reality but an understanding of the processes of ecological change and ever-changing insights about diverse patterns or styles of flux. Concepts about "what is" define human awareness of the changes but add little to the actual processes of change. To see things as permanent is to be confused about everything: an alternative to that understanding is the need to create temporary harmonies through alliances and relationships among all forms and forces. This web of interdependence is a never-ending source of wonder to the Aboriginal mind and to other forces that contribute to the harmony.

In most Aboriginal worldviews, people must struggle with the various keepers of the natural order to find and understand their gifts. No concept of equality in gifts exists in Aboriginal thought. Ecological forces uniquely gift each person. The process of recognizing and affirming one's gifts or talents is the essence of learning. Each person must decide to develop his or her potential by understanding its relationship to the earth. Any person who sets out on the journey to find his or her gifts will be aided by guardian spirits, guides, teachers, and protectors along the way. This quest is to understand how each individual must actively participate in the ecological system. Each life form must understand and realize his or her unknown and unrealized potential; find the capacity to have and respond to dreams, visions, ideals, and teachings; have the courage to express his or her talents; and have the integrity to control his or her gifts in the face of desire, failure, and surprise. Aboriginal thinkers assert that failure is when a person refuses to follow his or her gifts or understandings.

To fulfil their gifts, Aboriginal children are taught to establish close relationships with all the forces of their local ecosystem. The principle of alliance enfolds all the forces in harmony. Enabling or protective relationships, or alliances, are embodied in the concept of *mntu*. *Mntu* contains an English approximation somewhere between dignity, power, and force. United, these English words create a unified Algonquian thought. Aboriginal knowledge is translated in the ideas of "finding one's face, finding one's heart," "seeking life," "becoming complete," and thinking the "highest thoughts," and in the concepts of "orientation" and "pathways."[59]

Learning the existing oral legacy involves intimate and endless listening to stories and dialogue with elders and parents. This process takes time and patience. It is iterative rather than linear. The stories are told in a circular or spiral theme, with each thematic repetition or spiral adding a little. This can be contrasted with the step-by-step, linear progression of an Aristotelian argument.[60]

One of the greatest obstacles to experiencing and understanding is said to be the internal nature of the mind. If one relies on the mind to link ideas to other ideas through logic, or events through time with causation, then one will be blocked from understanding the external world, and the teaching of the ecosystem will be inaccessible. Aboriginal learning is through all the senses and instincts. It requires learning language and the diverse realms and forces contained within and beyond language. Algonquian languages share this knowledge about the overlapping processes within their chosen societies and extended families. These sounds are transformational and relative. They create a realm formed out of spiritual dignity, which they comprehend and act out.

As Gerald Vizenor, an Ojibwa writer, states, "Academic evidence is a euphemism, for linguistic colonization of oral traditions and popular memories."[61] Oral traditions, stories, and memories are a major part Aboriginal teaching. Leslie Silko notes of a person living an Aboriginal life, "Everywhere he looked, he saw a world made of stories."[62] These stories teach of prosperity and joy, of human mistakes and blunders, or of ecological disasters.[63] Not only do stories transmit validated experiences, but they also renew, awaken, and honour life forces. Hence, ancient stories are not generally explanations but focus instead on the processes of knowledge. They discuss how to acquire these relationships on every level, how properly to use them, how to lose them, and the consequences attendant on the relationships. They say that one is lost without allies, and stories about allies are guides to the unseen and the seen.

Only in the past century of contact with modern consciousness have these stories become explanations. Elders say that the new explanations have some *mntu*. They say that any disconnected or fragmented forms of consciousness or explanation can create new animating forces. As represented by the structure of the language, in a connected world the whole is no longer the whole when it is a part of an explanation. A holistic process cannot be explained by first shattering it into its component parts and then assigning local explanations to the segments. If such a process occurs in Aboriginal thought, new forces are unleashed. These forces have always existed and are said in the Algonquian world to have been held in check, contained, by the structure of the language.

While the flux and forces are objective, the rules of inference and perception are viewed as personal. Some people are born with an ability to create relationships with the essential forces in nature; others have to acquire this ability through experience. The vision quest in the forest is one way to make alliances with the *mntu'k*. Alliances with certain forces give dignity to both parties: they are usually intensely private matters and are necessary for ecological harmony. Such acquisitions can also occur by bonds, adoption, or marriages among animals, plants, or families.

A vision creates a personal responsibility to carry out its directive. Often a vision requires the person to organize a group of people to assist in carrying out the directive. Often, but not always, these visions become ceremonies, dances, and rituals. Such manifestations of the vision create special societies among Aboriginal people, societies that share the vision and the means of its manifestation.

One task of decolonization is to replace the sameness of universality with the concepts of diversity, complementarity, flexibility, and equity or fundamental fairness. Eurocentric thought transformed the idea of universality into the idea of assimilation. This worldview regards the questions of what it means to live justly and what it means to think rightly as intimately related. Colonial law made the idea of the universal central to the legal order under the guise of impartiality and equality. Equality was identified with sameness, and difference was identified with deviance or devaluation. These universal norms provided an assimilative template for the denial of the value of Aboriginal people. Such norms not only had to be accepted by Aboriginal people but also adopted and absorbed. Some colonized peoples immersed themselves in the imported culture, denying their origins in an attempt to become "more English than the English."

In Eurocentric thought, there are two origins of knowing: curiosity and control. Both ways of European knowing create the polarities of the self as knower and the world as the known, with training or education as the mediator. This corresponds to the ideal English sentence: subject-verb-object. The self is the subject (agent/character) seeking to know (verb/action) the object (goal). Both of these ways of knowing create a distance between the self and the world. In this distance, the world can become a plaything – a malleable entity to be constructed and deconstructed according to desire or purpose. It often becomes an alienating place.

In the Aboriginal worldview, there are diverse ways of knowing: those of thinking, feeling, and willing. Each is interwoven yet distinct. Thinking is part of the flux, feelings are a particular location in the flux, and willing is using thinking and feelings. In contrast with the Eurocentric model, the Aboriginal ways of knowing are focused on caring about the world. As with the verb-rich structure of Aboriginal languages, the self exists only within a world that is subject to flux and action. The object of knowledge is to reunify the world or at least reconcile the world to itself. Uniting these three modes of knowing is necessary; each can contribute to human development, and each requires its own appropriate expression.

Aboriginal ways of knowing hold caring as the source from which all teaching arises, the feeling that survives the tensions of listening for truth and allowing truth to touch our lives. It is the way of living within a context of flux, paradoxes, and tensions. In the realm of flux, truth is a relationship that enables a person to know the spirit in every relationship. Developing these ways of knowing, which leads to freedom of consciousness and solidarity with the world, is the task of Aboriginal education.

Renewing Aboriginal Order

Ecological sensibilities have also determined the development, movement, and structure of Aboriginal nations. Harmonization with the natural order is the prime ordering principle and goal of Aboriginal societies. Harmonization involves a sacred responsibility, since creating disorder within the natural order creates dire results. Thus, "when Indians talk about restoring or preserving their cultures they talk about restoring their lands in the same breath."[64] This responsibility was based on teachings, rituals, art, education, and honouring the sacred covenants with the life forms of the place.[65]

In contemplating their implicate order, Aboriginal thinkers place faith in experiencing parts of the vast world, in reflecting on the inner space of vision, and in performing rituals and ceremonies for renewing the world's beauty. This form of contemplation is a way of showing respect for the vastness of the unknown. It is often called the state of intelligence. Thus, for example, the Míkmaq talk about "order" through the sound *ta' n tela'sik koqoey* or *tela'skl wistqamoe'l*. The root verb of both sounds is *tela'sikl*, which translates as "the process that is meant to be."

Aboriginal people share an ecological vision of society that is enfolded in a view of interactive harmony. Our elders say that if we are to live in harmony we must accept the beauty and limits of our ecology. We must accept our relationship with the surrounding life forces and ourselves as we are. We must honour diversity as a basic right through respectful behaviours. We must be good and kind to all diversity in the circle of life. We must learn to believe and trust the other life forces, to believe in a life force greater than ourselves that gives everything strength to exist, and to endure through many changes.

In Eurocentric thought, these visions of order can be characterized as lifeworlds without systems, while European society was divided into lifeworlds and systems.[66] In describing German sociologist Jurgen Habermas's concept of lifeworld, American sociologist Robert Bellah stated:

> The characteristic feature of the lifeworld is that it is organized in terms of language. The use of language, in formal and informal ways, is the core of how the lifeworld functions. The lifeworld includes things like family, local community, and religious groups, but in a complex society it also includes the realms of public discourse. It is by no means exclusively private: it is that part of our lives where language, expressing what is important to us, is at the centre. For some of us, what we mean by community is virtually identical with the lifeworld, but for reasons that will become clear later on, Habermas resists such an identification and does not use the term community.[67]

Systems are organized primarily through nonlinguistic media, such as money in the marketplace and power in the administrative state. Habermas has vividly characterized the colonization of the modern Eurocentric lifeworld by the system. He argues that this has reversed the proper relations between lifeworlds and systems.[68]

For a long time, Eurocentric thought saw Aboriginal worldviews and order as a sign of the backwardness of Aboriginal people. Now, however, some Eurocentric scholars are having second thoughts. Aboriginal order has never needed an artificial system. Every member belongs to an extended family that occupies a large part of his or her life. The organic kinship structure stresses relationships among families, clans, communities, and other nations.

Activities that might be connected with a variety of distinct groups in European society are concentrated within a few relationships. These relationships teach Aboriginal people about love and solidarity, about faith and hope, and about respect. Aboriginal worldviews teach that everyone and everything is part of a whole, and each is interdependent with all the others. Each person has a right to a personal identity as a member of a community but also has a responsibility to other life forms and to the ecology of the whole. It is inconceivable that a human being can exist without a relationship with the keepers of the life forces (totems), an extended family, or his or her wider kin.

While Eurocentric literature creates a sharp contrast between insiders and strangers in Aboriginal societies, Aboriginal languages have no concept of "strangers." "Guests" within their territory are typically assigned to local families or clans for education and responsibilities. Such kinship is a necessary part of Aboriginal peace and good order. The diplomacy and treaties with the Crown dramatically illustrate this point because they used kinship as their model. Within the vast fabric of energies, life forms, families, clans, and confederacies, every person stands in a specific, personal relationship to all the others. Thus, Aboriginal thought values the group over the individual and the extended family over the immediate or biological family.

Kinship Order

The Aboriginal order of kinship implies a distinct form of responsibilities or "rights." Everyone strives to live in harmony not only with all the forces of the circle of life but also with one another. This creates a sense of belonging to a place and to a people. Everyone has the right to give and receive according to his or her choices. Those who give the most freely and generously enjoy the strongest claims to sharing, and these claims are directed to their relations. Aboriginal thought, therefore, recognizes a matrix of reciprocal relationships.

In the Aboriginal order, enjoying individual rights means having the freedom to be what one was created to be. Because no person knows what that path is for another, each person has the independence and security to discover that path without interference. From infancy, children are born into families and surrounded by relatives and friends who are considered to be uncles and aunts. The actual blood kinship may be worked out in time, but everyone appears related. Children are constantly reminded to respect and respond to the feelings of all their kin. They are praised for showing sensitivity and generosity to others, teased for being self-centred, rude, or acquisitive, but rarely punished.

Childhood experiences of intense collective support and attention combine with self-discipline and responsibilities to create a personality that is cooperative and independent, self-restrained yet individualistic, attuned to the feelings of others but nonintrusive. Sharing is learned through the extended family structure by helping, then spiritually by respectfully living with an ecosystem. At the same time, individuals are left free to discover their gifts and talents and to select their courses of action by personal choice and integrity. This kind of personality is compatible with a certain kind of social order that strives for consensus but tolerates a great deal of diversity and nonconformity.

Order is established where leaders seek to persuade through example but do not command.[69] The behaviour of leaders is a symbol of the resiliency of Aboriginal people. Leaders must live in a way that enables them to inspire hope of a better society. They must learn to be patient in times of trouble and to symbolize endurance and dignity. They must help everyone share difficulties and tragedies. They must be able to show enthusiasm and humour at all ceremonies and rituals. They must teach others the joy of decent thoughts and respectful lives and learn not to inflict "ills" on others.

Within this order, personal safety and economic security are ensured by linguistic solidarity, ritual, socialization, and kinship rather than by external power or law.[70] Members of Aboriginal societies believe themselves to be tied together by deep and lasting communal bonds. A Crow thinker, Shining Arrows, summed up this sensibility: "If you have one hundred people who live together, and if each one cares for the rest, there is One Mind."[71] People understand and trust those who have always loved them. As a Lakota stated, "Love is something that you can leave behind you when you die. It's that powerful."[72]

These values make it possible for Aboriginal thought to tolerate a degree of nonconformity that may distress "civilized" and authoritative societies. A nonintrusive, autonomous personality is inconsistent with the demands of a state, however, whether it is governed by a democratic majority or by an authoritarian minority. Aboriginal thought does not recognize Eurocentric communities, states, or nations, since these entities exist only in the artificial constructs of Eurocentric language. No state or external political authority, separate from your relatives, can exist. This is why most treaties with the British sovereign are grounded in kinship terms.

Aboriginal leaders do not shed their kinship responsibilities but remain tied to their clans. This renders the rights of citizens against the state as meaningless, because there is no state to argue against, only relatives. This situation is now changing as the North American system of education entrenches the notion that states and citizens are essential to society, thus fostering a belief in authoritarian governments. To Aboriginal people, a "state" is a group of strangers who demand obedience through coercive and restrictive measures. This demand is a challenge to Aboriginal order and its intimate realms of relationships.

Aboriginal Law

An understanding of ecosystem also forged Aboriginal laws. In most Aboriginal worldviews and languages, laws are processes that sustain and nourish relationships. The sense of having a worldview whose hold over the members has such gravity that it need never be spelled out creates a communal solidarity that is the foundation of customary laws. This ecological understanding of the flux creates a worldview that identifies what is with what ought to be. This worldview denies its members the experience of moral doubt. Most Aboriginal laws do not have a conception of rights as being something towering above the natural and the social worlds that surround them. Aboriginal law, religion, child rearing, and art all express an ecological unity that is seen as inseparable. This solidarity creates an implicate mechanism by which ecological order presupposes and evokes order in the soul.

No inherent category exists in Aboriginal consciousness to define an independent human law. Aboriginal people perceive their local ecology, contain it in language, and interpret it to generate Aboriginal legal order. What is defined as law is about living with the forces of an ecosystem, which is understood as a sacred realm. The Algonquian concept of dignity thus becomes a model of proper conduct toward nature and humans, which is transmitted as part of the experience of learning to participate in the great flux. As a Mohawk stated, "To forget or ignore basic Indian values, traditional values, human values, natural law – is a crime."[73]

Aboriginal order was originally formulated as a series of anecdotes or stories rather than as a catalogue of explicit rules. In most models, stories of the trickster symbolically represent the great flux and possible sources of transformations. Explicit black-letter rules or commands are useless in a spontaneous world: no system of rules can do justice to nature's subtle refinements and complex forces.

Rather than being an established system of rules and principles, Aboriginal law is a highly integrated communion of values and processes. The Cree "rules" for picking plants are a good example of this form of legal consciousness. These rules disclose the fundamental processes of all Aboriginal law, most of which are unknown to Eurocentric law. The Cree rules provide for seven procedures.

(1) Learn from others how to identify the specific plants you need through your senses (so that you do not pick other plants unnecessarily).
(2) When you identify the plant you need, place tobacco (the keeper of all the plants) on the earth as an offering to the ecology, say a prayer asking for guidance, and wait in silence for guidance. This is to show respect and to acknowledge the sacred in all the forces of life.
(3) Pick only the amount you need.
(4) Practice the skill of selection. This means to pick "here and there" to prevent stripping the plants from one area.
(5) Be aware that you are a "guest" in this habitat and should not disturb the plants' space unnecessarily.
(6) Watch where you step, leaving the habitat in its natural condition.
(7) Use those plants selected and be "grateful" for the ecology, since it provides for your needs.[74]

Together these rules of process acknowledge the dignity, respect, and solidarity that sustain the relationship with nature. Aboriginal people conceive of this relationship as taught, experienced, and understood. It is not viewed as human-made or artificial.

Individual behaviour accommodates the collective flux. Proper behaviour is always relative to the context. Deference to the forces of nature and alliances is the process by which individual passions are contained. Proper behaviour is a mixture of dignity and protection, requiring exemplary conduct and sensitivities. Improper behaviour violates dignity and most often leads to a loss of protection from spiritual forces. These beliefs create a firm consensus of proper respect toward the inherent dignity of all life forms.

Aboriginal order and law are distinct from Eurocentric order and law. Aboriginal order and law are part of a search for harmony based on an implicate order in the ecology. Aboriginal thinkers believe that ecology preexists the making of laws and can be used as a standard against which to judge them. Aboriginal order and law are not focused on human nature or on how humans ought to behave. They seek to discover how every life form can live together in a respectful way rather than looking to assign rights or wrongs. They assert that there are keepers of intelligible essences in the ecology that create order and with whom humans can have a relationship. In contrast, Eurocentric natural rights theorists seek to discover an intrinsic order in social relations rather than in ecology. These theorists believe that human consciousness is independent of ecological forces rather than interrelated. Yet these theorists still search for rules or laws as if they had an autonomous logic of their own that survives in all their transmutations.

Aboriginal order and law are based on shared values. Since most Aboriginal orders never had centralized leaders above the families, they never had the task of creating artificial rules to control resources and individuals; instead, they adjusted to the cycles or seasons of the ecology. Consensual ceremonies and processes create harmony by allowing for the renewal of resources and sharing. Most Aboriginal orders do not impose order on relationships by establishing rules that govern general categories of acts and persons and then using these rules to decide particular disputes. Instead, they determine that harmony, trust, sharing, and kindness are the shared ends of the circle of life and then make choices that contribute to these goals.

Aboriginal order and law are about sustaining relationships through ecological understanding, shared worldviews and languages, and ceremonies.[75] Aboriginal laws are more about respect for every process in an ecosystem than about power over them. Aboriginal law is the law of being in a sacred space: speaking softly, walking humbly, and acting compassionately. Aboriginal order and law are not about a quibbling noun-subject discourse between humans; they are about the rituals or processes that create peace of mind and harmonious lives. As a Kwakiutl stated, "It is a strict law that binds us to distribute our property among our friends and neighbors. It is a good law. Let the white man observe his law, we shall observe ours."[76]

Conclusion

As the Seventh Fire teachings say, in rekindling the old flame of the Seventh Fire, the new people will emerge. They will have to retrace their steps to find what was left by the trail: the task will not be easy.[77] As Aboriginal people, we must reclaim our worldviews, knowledge, languages, and order to find the path ahead. We must sustain our relationship with our environment and follow our elders' advice. We must rebuild our nations on our worldviews and our good values. We must be patient and thorough, because there are no shortcuts in rebuilding ourselves, our families, our relationships, our spiritual ceremonies, and our solidarity. We must use our abilities to make good choices. To remain rational, all human societies must become more ecologically sustainable.

Notes

1   L. Little Bear, "Relationship of Aboriginal People to the Land and the Aboriginal Perspective on Aboriginal Title," in CD-ROM, *For Seven Generations: An Information Legacy of the Royal Commission on Aboriginal Peoples* (Ottawa: Canada Communications Group, 1996), cited in Royal Commission on Aboriginal Peoples, *Treaty Making in the Spirit of Co-Existence: An Alternative to Extinguishment* (Ottawa: Canada Communications Group, 1994) at 10-1.
2   H. Berman, *Law and Revolution* (Cambridge: Harvard University Press, 1983) at 33–45.
3   "Orphée Noir," in L. Senghor, *Anthologie de la nouvelle poésie nègre et malgache de langue française* [1948] (Paris: Presses universitaires de France, 1972), cited in L. Noël, *Intolerance: A General Survey*, trans. A. Bennett (Montreal: McGill-Queen's University Press, 1994) at 147.
4   Noël, ibid. at 190–1.
5   A. Memmi, *The Colonizer and the Colonized*, trans. Howard Greenfield (New York: Orion Press, 1965) at 104–9.
6   Noël, *supra* note 3 at 148–9.
7   Ibid. at 145.
8   P. Monture-Angus in *Breaking Anonymity: The Chilly Climate for Women Faculty*, ed. The Chilly Collective (Waterloo, ON: Wilfrid Laurier University Press, 1995) at 11–28.
9   P. Monture-Angus, *Thunder in My Soul: A Mohawk Woman Speaks* (Halifax: Fernwood Press, 1995).
10   G.W.F. Hegel, *The Phenomenology of Mind*, trans. J.B. Baillie (London: S. Sonnenschein; New York: Macmillan, 1910).
11   P. Freire, *Pedagogy of the Oppressed* (New York: Seabury, 1970).
12   See Marie Battiste and Jean Barman, eds., *First Nations Education in Canada: The Circle Unfolds* (Vancouver: UBC Press, 1995).
13   L.M. Silko, *Ceremony* (New York: Penguin Books, 1977) at 68–9.
14   L. Hogan, "Creation," *Dwellings: A Spiritual History of the Living World* (New York: W.W. Norton, 1995), at 98. See also L. Hogan, *Power* (New York: W.W. Norton, 1998).
15   The idea of unitary culture is primarily anthropological, while the notion of subcultures is predominantly sociological. Classical European writers such as the objectivist Emile Durkheim believed that social life was fixed and constrained.
16   See, generally, R.L. Barsh, "Are Anthropologists Harmful to Aboriginals?" (1988) 15(4) *Journal of Ethnic Studies* at 1.
17   L. Little Bear, "Concept of Native Title," (1982) 5 *Canadian Legal Aid Bulletin* at 99.
18   R.M. Unger, *Passion: An Essay on Personality* (New York: Free Press, 1984) at 5–6; R.M.

Unger, *Social Theory: Its Situation and Its Task: A Critical Introduction to Politics, a Work in Constructive Social Theory* (Cambridge: Cambridge University Press, 1987).

19 See W. Bevis, "Native American Novels: Homing In," in B. Swann and A. Krupat, eds., *Recovering the Word: Essays on Native American Literature* (Berkeley: University of California Press, 1987) at 601–2.

20 See *Practicing the Law of Circular Interaction: First Nations Environmental and Conservation Principles* (Saskatoon: Saskatchewan Indian Cultural Centre, 1993), principle I, lesson 1, "Mother Earth Is a Living and Viable Entity."

21 This is one language group with three dialects: Dakota, Nakota, Lakota.

22 She is the mother of all living things and is the earth herself. See *supra* note 20, lesson 2 (*Otokahekagapi*: First Beginnings). Spiritual beings who were created to be servants to the spirits, the *pte oyate*, were said to dwell in the regions of the earth, where they grow special foods that spirits *nagi* (powers to be) like to eat. *Iktomi*, the spirit of wisdom (*ksa*), who falls into bad ways and is banished to the earth as a spider or trickster, tricked some of the *pte oyate* to come to the surface of the earth, where they transformed into the Dakota/Nakota/Lakota peoples. In the earth lodge, they did not have their own food sources, so other *pte oyate* were sent to the earth to provide for them. These became the buffalo and *wamaksskan* (animals).

23 This space extends approximately 20,000 square miles. In modern terms, *Mikmaki* described the territory now called Newfoundland, Saint-Pierre et Miquelon, Nova Scotia, New Brunswick, northern Maine, Prince Edward Island, the Magdalene archipelago, and the Gaspé Peninsula of Quebec.

24 C. LeClercq, *The New Relation of Gaspesia with the Customs and Religion of the Gaspesian Indians* [1691], ed. and trans. W.F. Ganong (Toronto: Champlain Society, 1910) at 277.

25 See *Circular Interaction, supra* note 20, principle III.

26 C. Vecsey, "American Indian Environmental Religions," in *American Indian Environments: Ecological Issues in Native American History* (Syracuse, NY: Syracuse University Press, 1980) at 1–45; A. Tanner, *Bringing Home Animals: Religious Ideology and Mode of Production of the Mistassini Cree Hunters* (London: Hurst, 1979); A. Tanner, "Significance of Hunting Territories Today," in B. Cox, ed., *Cultural Ecology: Readings on the Canadian Indians and Eskimos* (Toronto: McClelland and Stewart, 1973) at 101–14; and F. Speck, *Penobscot Man: The Life of a Forest Tribe in Maine* [1940] (New York: Octagon Books, 1970) at 208.

27 This was not the response of British society when Darwin suggested that Europeans and other peoples had evolved out of the animal world and could recognize the terrible and obsolete manlike ape as their distant cousin. His theories revolutionized European mentality, creating scientific racism and a religious battle over creation versus evolution. See J. Highwalker, *The Primal Mind: Vision and Reality in Indian America* (New York: Meridian Books, 1981) at 17-39.

28 In English, this concept is often spelled "Manitou" or called "medicines" by the immigrants.

29 One who understands everything about the known world is called *kaqinestmu'k*; if one knows only a part of the known world, one is called *mukaqinestmu'k*. Common sense is called *nsituo'qn*, while the entire process of understanding is called *nestmnmk*. Thus, these sounds are often used to describe the world or humankind.

30 The deepest part of earth is said to provide sustenance to life on earth. This lodge is also analogized to grandmother, which is often translated as Mother Earth. In the deep earth lodge are sacred caves where seekers may receive and be instructed by the animating forces (*mntu*). These forces work in all the realms but are said to belong or reside in either the deep earth or the sky lodge. The physical forms of rocks, plants, animals, and humans are made possible by the potencies of these forces. These potencies can be known to humans, but only in prayers or appropriate ceremonies. There is an enigmatic side to animating forces that come into existence by the abuse or manipulation of the material resources: often these destructive forces are created by the misuse of gifts by humans. In the deep caves (*wlnusúkek*), such as Klooscap's Cave, the original visions were given to the humans. They are the oldest spirit lodges and provide the models for all other spirit lodges or ceremonies on the surface of the earth. Each force is said to have a keeper or

protector (*nujotekwti*) who can punish or grant privileges to humans for their conduct toward the plant or animal form; these *mntu* can make themselves visible to humans on important occasions.

31 This realm is above the deep earth lodge. It is an unusual zone. Little is currently remembered about it, but people are warned about venturing into it because of the presence of the *wjipiskek*, which can capture and contain the human *mntu*. This region demarcates the space of the roots of trees and grasses, the region where bears hibernate, the space of wolf and coyote dens, where rodents and ants and other insects live. It is a transitional zone to the underwater and earth lodges. The life forms that live in this area are considered sacred because they traverse between the surface of the earth lodge and the depths of the root lodge. The stones, roots, and insects located in the root lodge are often considered to be purer life forms than those on the surface of the earth lodge; they are therefore considered better medicine for surface life forms.

32 This is an unknown realm. It cannot be directly experienced by humans; it can only be known through alliances with the keepers of this realm. It covers the oceans, lakes, rivers, and streams, as well as the fish lodges (*nméjuiókóm*). It is the domain of the ancient spirits, much like the parallel realm of the deep earth lodge.

33 This is the realm of the air, water, and surface that provides substance to life on and above the earth and for all the things that grow out of the earth. Within the realm of the earth lodge are four regions: the region of short grasses and plants and small animals; the region of water; the region of tall grasses, humans, and large animals; and the region of trees and forests (*nipuktuk*). The last region is important because tree roots penetrate into the deep earth and extend into the earth walk. Places where the deep earth is directly accessible – including caves, deserts, bare mountaintops – are considered sacred.

34 This is the realm of guardian forces that exist alongside the earth lodge – the watchers of the keepers of the sacred caves in the deep earth or light lodge. They maintain the balance between life forms.

35 This realm contains the clouds, stars, sun, and moon and is associated with flying beings. The mountains are considered part of this realm and are often considered as sacred places, similar to trees, because they partake of three realms: their peaks appear as part of the deep earth lodge that reaches into the sky lodge. The sky realm, like the deep earth realm, contains unique forces. Through the winds, or breath regions (*júsen*), life is possible through the immortal gift of breath. This realm is also occupied by the forces of thunder (*kaqtuko*), who directs clouds (*alw'k*), and rain (*kispesan*), who assists thunder. In the sky lodge are the keepers of the winds (*wjúsen*). They have personal spirit names because they have often revealed their physical form to the people. The east wind is called *wejipek*. The south winds are called either *wsaqniaq* (the sunny, winter winds) or *putuesk* (the cloudy, warm winds). The west wind is called *ekesnuk*. The north wind is called *oqatlk*. In the highest realm above the sky lodge live the creative forces of the universe (*nákus'set*), which create consciousness and give it order but not stability.

36 From this creative realm come the cosmic forces of light that permeate and maintain the world and immortal spiritual potential. Collectively, these forces and potentials are said to direct all the material and spiritual forces of the universe. This realm contains the sources of all light and darkness: it holds the visible lights – the sun (*nákúset*), moon (*tepknuset*), and stars (*kloqoej*) – as well as the invisible cosmic forces (*wasitpáq*) behind the light and the blue darkness (*qujitpaqtek*).

37 Above the light lodge, this realm is connected to the Milky Way, the spirits' path, and is considered much like the earth lodge, except that the being has much greater magic. Plants, animals, and human souls all travel this realm, called by missionaries the "land of the souls." See P. Antoine Maillard, *An Account of the Customs and Manners of the Mickmacks and Maricheets, Savage Nations* (London: S. Hooper and A. Morley, 1758).

38 My appreciation to David Bohm, David Peat, and Leroy Little Bear for helping me to understand the term and its relation to Aboriginal thought. See D. Bohm, *Wholeness and the Implicate Order* (London: Routledge and Kegan Paul, 1980). Others have suggested names of "ensoulment" or "participation mystique" or "geopsyche" for the same process.

See G. Cajete, *Look to the Mountain: An Ecology of Indigenous Education* (Durango, CO: Kivakí Press, 1994) at 83–4.

39   See W. Bevis, *supra* note 19 at 601–2.

40   L. Hogan, "Creation," *supra* note 14 at 95-6.

41   N.S. Hill, Jr., ed., *Words of Power: Voices from Indian America* (Golden, CO: Fulcrum Publishing, 1994) at v–vii.

42   Ibid. at 28 (Chief Joseph).

43   The Lakota expressed this famous insight as "We are all related" (*mitakuye oyasin*).

44   See *Circular Interaction, supra* note 20.

45   Preliminary report of the Special Rapporteur, "Protection of the Heritage of Indigenous People," E/CN.4/Sub.2/1994/31.UN Sub-Commission on Prevention of Discrimination and Protection of Minorities, Commission on Human Rights, United Nations Economic and Social Council (1994) at para. 8.

46   *Mntu* could better be called a verb than a noun, but over the years missionaries, ethnologists, and even some linguists have twisted the concept into a noun. Even better is to think about *mntu* as an essential part of the ever-transforming flux. Turning an Indigenous verb concept into a noun for English discussions is a complicated and artificial procedure. In the early 1700s, A.S. Maillard, a priest among the Míkmaq, used the word *mienndoo* or *manito* to mean "the great spirit" or "spirit being in general." Some time after him, a priest translated this word to mean the Christian devil (*mundoo*). See Maillard, *supra* note 37.

47   The Algonquians are not unique in this understanding: the South American Guarani call this concept *namandu*, the Melanese say *mana*, the Iroquois say *orenda*, the Lakota say *wakan*. Most Aboriginal people believe *something* gives rise to the living organism that contains it and survives this organism when it perishes.

48   The common side is called *asme'k*.

49   M.R. Haas, *Language, Culture, and History* (Stanford: Stanford University Press, 1978) at 37; see, generally, B. Whorf in J. Carroll, ed., *Language, Thought, and Reality* (Cambridge, MA: MIT Press, 1956) at 147–52.

50   S. Chawla, "Linguistic and Philosophical Roots of Our Environmental Crisis," (1991) 50 *Journal of Philosophy* at 253–62.

51   N. Momaday, "Personal Reflection," in C. Martin, ed., *The American Indian and the Problem of History* (New York: Oxford University Press, 1987) at 160.

52   H.C. Wolfart and F. Anenakew, *kinêhiyâwiwininaw nêhiyawêwin: The Cree Language Is Our Identity* (Winnipeg: University of Manitoba Press, 1993).

53   Kiowi author N. Scott Momaday, in *The Names: A Memoir* (Tucson: University of Arizona Press, 1976) at 59–60, has summarized a familiar process: "When I was three years old my head must have been full of Indian as well as English words. The sounds of both Kiowa and Navajo are quite natural and familiar to me, and even now I can make these sounds easily and accurately with my voice, so well established are they in my ear. I lived very close to these 'foreign' languages, poised at a crucial time in the learning process to enter either or both of them wholly. But my mother was concerned that I should learn English as my 'native' language, and so English is first and foremost of my possession."

54   J. Derrida, "Force of Law: The Mystical Foundation of Authority," in D. Cornell, M. Rosenfeld, and D.G. Carlson, eds., *Deconstruction and the Possibility of Justice* (New York: Routledge, 1992) at 18.

55   Ibid. at 17.

56   In modern thought, this traditional form of knowledge is called the "flow of energy." See, for example, W.B. Kemp, "The Flow of Energy in a Hunting Society," (1971) 224(3) *Scientific American* at 105–15, especially charts at 108–9. Also see R.A. Rappaport, "The Flow of Energy in an Agricultural Society," ibid. at 117–32.

57   Vine Deloria, Jr., in Hill, *supra* note 41 at 31.

58   Ibid. at 4.

59   See G. Cajete, *supra* note 38, chaps. 2 and 3.

60   E. Hampton, "Redefinition of Indian Education," in Battiste and Barman, *supra* note 12 at 6.

61 G. Vizenor, "Socioacupuncture: Mythic Reversals and the Striptease in Four Scenes," in Martin, *supra* note 51.
62 L.M. Silko, "Landscape, History, and the Pueblo Imagination," (1986) 57 *Antaeus* at 93.
63 Ibid., *supra* note 13 at 2, 13, 19, 34, 242, and 246.
64 Ibid. at 85, citing Eugene Linden, "Lost Tribes, Lost Knowledge" *Time* (September 23, 1991) at 46–56.
65 Silko, *supra* note 13 at chap. 4.
66 See Jurgen Habermas, *The Theory of Communicative Action*, vol. II (1st German ed., 1981; rpt. Boston: Beacon Press, 1987).
67 R. Bellah, "Community, Modernity, and Religion," keynote address at the Conference on Community, Modernity, and Religion: Eurocentric/Aboriginal Conversation, Saskatoon, St. Thomas More College, June 26, 1995 at 1.
68 Ibid. at 2.
69 R.L. Barsh, "The Nature and Spirit of North American Political Systems" (1986) 110 *American Indian Quarterly* at 181–98.
70 See, generally, J.Y. Henderson, "First Nations Legal Inheritance" (1996) 23 *Man. L.J.* at 1.
71 Hill, *supra* note 41 at 50.
72 John (Fire) Lame Deer, ibid. at 2.
73 *Karoniaktatie* (Alex Jacobs), ibid. See, generally, J. Borrows, "With or without You: First Nations Law (in Canada)" (1996) 41 *McGill L. J.* at 629.
74 *Circular Interaction, supra* note 20, principle II, lesson 1.
75 Mary Ellen Turpel[-Lafond] (*Ani-Kwe*), "Aboriginal Peoples and the Canadian Charter: Interpretive Monopolies, Cultural Difference" (1989–90) 6 *Canadian Human Rights Yearbook* at 3-45; Henderson, *supra* note 70.
76 Hill, *supra* note 41 at 4.
77 E. Benton-Banai, *The Mishomis Book* (Hayward, WI: Indian Country Communication, 1988) at 91-3.

Appendices

Appendix 1: Principles and Guidelines for the Protection of the Heritage of Indigenous Peoples

UNITED NATIONS

Economic and Social Council

Distr.
GENERAL

E/CN.4/Sub.2/1994/31
8 July 1994

Original: ENGLISH

COMMISSION ON HUMAN RIGHTS

Sub-Commission on Prevention of Discrimination and Protection of
Minorities of the Commission on Human Rights, Economic and Social Council
Forty-sixth session
Item 15 of the provisional agenda

DISCRIMINATION AGAINST INDIGENOUS PEOPLES

Protection of the heritage of indigenous people

Preliminary report of the Special Rapporteur, Mrs. Erica-Irene Daes, submitted in conformity with Sub-Commission resolution 1993/44 and decision 1994/105 of the Commission on Human Rights

PRINCIPLES AND GUIDELINES FOR THE PROTECTION OF THE
HERITAGE OF INDIGENOUS PEOPLE

PRINCIPLES

1. The effective protection of the heritage of the indigenous peoples of the world benefits all humanity. Cultural diversity is essential to the adaptability and creativity of the human species as a whole.
2. To be effective, the protection of indigenous peoples' heritage should be based broadly on the principle of self-determination, which includes the right and the duty of indigenous peoples to develop their own cultures and knowledge systems, and forms of social organization.

3. Indigenous peoples should be recognized as the primary guardians and interpreters of their cultures, arts and sciences, whether created in the past, or developed by them in the future.

4. International recognition and respect for indigenous peoples' own customs, rules and practices for the transmission of their heritage to future generations are essential to these peoples' enjoyment of human rights and human dignity.

5. Indigenous peoples' ownership and custody of their heritage must continue to be collective, permanent and inalienable, as prescribed by the customs, rules and practices of each people.

6. The discovery, use and teaching of indigenous peoples' knowledge, arts and cultures are inextricably connected with the traditional lands and territories of each people. Control over traditional territories and resources is essential to the continued transmission of indigenous peoples' heritage to future generations, and its full protection.

7. To protect their heritage, indigenous peoples must control their own means of cultural transmission and education. This includes their right to the continued use and, wherever necessary, the restoration of their own languages and orthographies.

8. To protect their heritage, indigenous peoples must also exercise control over all research conducted within their territories, or which uses their people as subjects of study.

9. The free and informed consent of the traditional owners should be an essential precondition of any agreements which may be made for the recording, study, use or display of indigenous peoples' heritage.

10. Any agreements which may be made for the recording, study, use or display of indigenous peoples' heritage must be revocable, and ensure that the peoples concerned continue to be the primary beneficiaries of commercial application.

11. The heritage of indigenous peoples is comprised of all objects, sites and knowledge the nature or use of which has been transmitted from generation to generation, and which is regarded as pertaining to a particular people or its territory. The heritage of an indigenous people also includes objects, knowledge and literary or artistic works which may be created in the future based upon its heritage.

12. The heritage of indigenous peoples includes all moveable cultural property as defined by the relevant conventions of UNESCO; all kinds of literary and artistic works such as music, dance, song, ceremonies, symbols and designs, narratives and poetry; all kinds of scientific, agricultural, technical and ecological knowledge, including cultigens, medicines and the rational use of flora and fauna; human remains; immoveable cultural property such as sacred sites, sites of historical significance, and burials; and documentation of indigenous peoples' heritage on film, photographs, videotape, or audiotape.

13. Every element of an indigenous people's heritage has traditional owners, which may be the whole people, a particular family or clan, an association or society, or individuals who have been specially taught or initiated to be its custodians. The traditional owners of heritage must be determined in accordance with indigenous peoples' own customs, laws and practices.

TRANSMISSION OF HERITAGE

14. Indigenous peoples' heritage should continue to be learned by the means customarily employed by its traditional owners for teaching, and each indigenous people's rules and practices for the transmission of heritage and sharing of its use should be incorporated in the national legal system.

15. In the event of a dispute over the custody or use of any element of an indigenous people's heritage, judicial and administrative bodies should be guided by the advice of indigenous elders who are recognized by the indigenous communities or peoples concerned as having specific knowledge of traditional laws.

16. Governments, international organizations and private institutions should support

the development of educational, research, and training centres which are controlled by indigenous communities, and strengthen these communities' capacity to document, protect, teach and apply all aspects of their heritage.

17. Governments, international organizations and private institutions should support the development of regional and global networks for the exchange of information and experience among indigenous peoples in the fields of science, culture, education and the arts, including support for systems of electronic information and mass communication.

18. Governments, with international cooperation, should provide the necessary financial resources and institutional support to ensure that every indigenous child has the opportunity to achieve full fluency and literacy in his/her own language, as well as an official language.

RECOVERY AND RESTITUTION OF HERITAGE

19. Governments, with the assistance of competent international organizations, should assist indigenous peoples and communities in recovering control and possession of their moveable cultural property and other heritage.

20. In cooperation with indigenous peoples, UNESCO should establish a programme to mediate the recovery of moveable cultural property from across international borders, at the request of the traditional owners of the property concerned.

21. Human remains and associated funeral objects must be returned to their descendants and territories in a culturally appropriate manner, as determined by the indigenous peoples concerned. Documentation may be retained, displayed or otherwise used only in such form and manner as may be agreed upon with the peoples concerned.

22. Moveable cultural property should be returned wherever possible to its traditional owners, particularly if shown to be of significant cultural, religious or historical value to them. Moveable cultural property should only be retained by universities, museums, private institutions or individuals in accordance with the terms of a recorded agreement with the traditional owners for the sharing of the custody and interpretation of the property.

23. Under no circumstances should objects or any other elements of an indigenous people's heritage be publicly displayed, except in a manner deemed appropriate by the peoples concerned.

24. In the case of objects or other elements of heritage which were removed or recorded in the past, the traditional owners of which can no longer be identified precisely, the traditional owners are presumed to be the entire people associated with the territory from which these objects were removed or recordings were made.

NATIONAL PROGRAMMES AND LEGISLATION

25. National laws should guarantee that indigenous peoples can obtain prompt, effective and affordable judicial or administrative action in their own languages to prevent, punish and obtain full restitution and just compensation for the acquisition, documentation or use of their heritage without proper authorization of the traditional owners.

26. National laws should deny to any person or corporation the right to obtain patent, copyright or other legal protection for any element of indigenous peoples' heritage without adequate documentation of the free and informed consent of the traditional owners to an arrangement for the sharing of ownership, control, use and benefits.

27. National laws should ensure the labeling and correct attribution of indigenous peoples' artistic, literary and cultural works whenever they are offered for public display or sale. Attribution should be in the form of a trademark or an appellation of origin, authorized by the peoples or communities concerned.

28. National laws for the protection of indigenous peoples' heritage should be adopted following consultations with the peoples concerned, in particular the traditional

owners and teachers of religious, sacred and spiritual knowledge, and, wherever possible, should have the informed consent of the peoples concerned.

29. National laws should ensure that the use of traditional languages in education, arts and the mass media is respected and, to the extent possible, promoted and strengthened.

30. Governments should provide indigenous communities with financial and institutional support for the control of local education, through community-managed programmes, and with use of traditional pedagogy and languages.

31. Governments should take immediate steps, in cooperation with the indigenous peoples concerned, to identify sacred and ceremonial sites, including burials, healing places, and traditional places of teaching, and to protect them from unauthorized entry or use.

RESEARCHERS AND SCHOLARLY INSTITUTIONS

32. All researchers and scholarly institutions should take immediate steps to provide indigenous peoples and communities with comprehensive inventories of the cultural property, and documentation of indigenous peoples' heritage, which they may have in their custody.

33. Researchers and scholarly institutions should return all elements of indigenous peoples' heritage to the traditional owners upon demand, or obtain formal agreements with the traditional owners for the shared custody, use and interpretation of their heritage.

34. Researchers and scholarly institutions should decline any offers for the donation or sale of elements of indigenous peoples' heritage, without first contacting the peoples or communities directly concerned and ascertaining the wishes of the traditional owners.

35. Researchers and scholarly institutions must refrain from engaging in any study of previously undescribed species or cultivated varieties of plants, animals or microbes, or naturally occurring pharmaceuticals, without first obtaining satisfactory documentation that the specimens were acquired with the consent of the traditional owners.

36. Researchers must not publish information obtained from indigenous peoples or the results of research conducted on flora, fauna, microbes or materials discovered through the assistance of indigenous peoples, without identifying the traditional owners and obtaining their consent to publication.

37. Researchers should agree to an immediate moratorium on the Human Genome Diversity Project. Further research on the specific genotypes of indigenous peoples should be suspended unless and until broadly and publicly supported by indigenous peoples to the satisfaction of United Nations human rights bodies.

38. Researchers and scholarly institutions should make every possible effort to increase indigenous peoples' access to all forms of medical, scientific and technical education, and participation in all research activities which may affect them or be of benefit to them.

39. Professional associations of scientists, engineers and scholars, in collaboration with indigenous peoples, should sponsor seminars and disseminate publications to promote ethical conduct in conformity with these guidelines and discipline members who act in contravention.

BUSINESS AND INDUSTRY

40. In dealings with indigenous peoples, business and industry should respect the same guidelines as researchers and scholarly institutions.

41. Business and industry should agree to an immediate moratorium on making contracts with indigenous peoples for the rights to discover, record and use previously undescribed species or cultivated varieties of plants, animals or microbes, or naturally occurring pharmaceuticals. No further contracts should be negotiated until

indigenous peoples and communities themselves are capable of supervising and collaborating in the research process.

42. Business and industry should refrain from offering incentives to any individuals to claim traditional rights of ownership or leadership within an indigenous community, in violation of their trust within the community and the laws of the indigenous peoples concerned.

43. Business and industry should refrain from employing scientists or scholars to acquire and record traditional knowledge or other heritage of indigenous peoples in violation of these guidelines.

44. Business and industry should contribute financially and otherwise to the development of educational and research institutions controlled by indigenous peoples and communities.

45. All forms of tourism based on an indigenous people's heritage must be restricted to activities which have the approval of the peoples and communities concerned, and which are conducted under their supervision and control.

ARTISTS, WRITERS AND PERFORMERS

46. Artists, writers and performers should refrain from incorporating elements derived from indigenous heritage into their works without the informed consent of the traditional owners.

47. Artists, writers and performers should support the full artistic and cultural development of indigenous peoples, and encourage public support for the development and greater recognition of indigenous artists, writers and performers.

48. Artists, writers and performers should contribute, through their individual works and professional organizations, to the greater public understanding and respect for the indigenous heritage associated with the country in which they live.

PUBLIC INFORMATION AND EDUCATION

49. The mass media in all countries should take effective measures to promote understanding of and respect for indigenous peoples' heritage, in particular through special broadcasts and public-service programmes prepared in collaboration with indigenous peoples.

50. Journalists should respect the privacy of indigenous peoples, in particular concerning traditional religious, cultural and ceremonial activities, and refrain from exploiting or sensationalizing indigenous peoples' heritage.

51. Journalists should actively assist indigenous peoples in exposing any activities, public or private, which destroy or degrade indigenous peoples' heritage.

52. Educators should ensure that school curricula and textbooks teach understanding and respect for indigenous peoples' heritage and history and recognize the contribution of indigenous peoples to creativity and cultural diversity.

INTERNATIONAL ORGANIZATIONS

53. The Secretary-General should ensure that the task of coordinating international cooperation in this field is entrusted to appropriate organs and specialized agencies of the United Nations, with adequate means of implementation.

54. In cooperation with indigenous peoples, the United Nations should bring these principles and guidelines to the attention of all Member States through, inter alia, international, regional and national seminars and publications, with a view to promoting the strengthening of national legislation and international conventions in this field.

55. The United Nations should publish a comprehensive annual report, based upon information from all available sources, including indigenous peoples themselves, on the problems experienced and solutions adopted in the protection of indigenous peoples' heritage in all countries.

56. Indigenous peoples and their representative organizations should enjoy direct access

to all intergovernmental negotiations in the field of intellectual property rights, to share their views on the measures needed to protect their heritage through international law.

57. In collaboration with indigenous peoples and Governments concerned, the United Nations should develop a confidential list of sacred and ceremonial sites that require special measures for their protection and conservation, and provide financial and technical assistance to indigenous peoples for these purposes.

58. In collaboration with indigenous peoples and Governments concerned, the United Nations should establish a trust fund with a mandate to act as a global agent for the recovery of compensation for the unconsented or inappropriate use of indigenous peoples' heritage, and to assist indigenous peoples in developing the institutional capacity to defend their own heritage.

59. United Nations operational agencies, as well as the international financial institutions and regional and bilateral development assistance programmes, should give priority to providing financial and technical support to indigenous communities for capacity-building and exchanges of experience focused on local control of research and education.

60. The United Nations should consider the possibility of drafting a convention to establish international jurisdiction for the recovery of indigenous peoples' heritage across national frontiers, before the end of the International Decade of the World's Indigenous People.

Appendix 2: Saskatoon Declaration of Indigenous Cultural Restoration and Policy Recommendations on Cultural Restoration Developed at the Saskatoon Summer Institute

1996 International Summer Institute
Social Sciences and Humanities Research Council

July 8, 1996
Convocation Hall
University of Saskatchewan
Canada

The Assembled Circle of Delegates of the Summer Institute,

Bearing in mind that, for Indigenous peoples to realize fundamental human rights and aspirations and become the architects of our own future, the world community must understand that our experiences with colonialism and its effects verify that colonialism is a disease with many diverse symptoms, which affects the environment, human body, mind, and spirit, as well as exists as a brutal form of intolerance, domination, and oppression.

Affirming the importance of consultation and cooperation with Indigenous peoples in solving the existing problems we face in areas of human rights, environment, development, education, and health; and the importance of the process of such planning and implementing the program of activities for the International Decade of the World's Indigenous People is by partnership in action.

Recognizing the crucial importance of the promotion and protection of the rights of Indigenous peoples in the Decade to eradicate the severe and widespread poverty afflicting Indigenous peoples around the earth that has deprived us of our human rights and fundamental freedoms resulting from colonization and dispossession of our land.

Authenticating the empowerment of Indigenous peoples requires making choices that enable us to retain our cultural identity and voice while participating in political, economic, and social life, with full respect for their cultural values, languages, traditions, and forms of social organization.

Declare:

Eastern Door: Self-Determination

1. Indigenous peoples have the right of self-determination as defined by the United Nations Human Rights Covenants, and as defined by our treaties and agreements concluded with others according to their original spirit and intent.
2. By virtue of our existing right of self-determination, Indigenous peoples have the responsibility to promote, develop, and maintain their order and laws, to determine their political status, to pursue freely their cultural destiny and their social and economic development.
3. By virtue of our existing human right of self-determination, Indigenous peoples have the responsibility to realize and effectuate the provisions of the ILO Convention concerning *Indigenous and Tribal Peoples in Independent Countries, 1989,* the 1995 *Declaration on the Rights of Indigenous Peoples* of the Working Group on Indigenous Populations, the *Programme of Activities for the International Decade of the World's Indigenous Peoples* adopted by General Assembly Resolution 50/157, and the *Principles and Guidelines for the Protection of the Heritage of Indigenous Peoples.*
4. By virtue of our existing human right of self-determination, Indigenous peoples

have fundamental human responsibilities to have the dignity and diversity of their worldviews, languages, traditions, gender, and aspirations appropriately respected and reflected in all aspects of their self-determination.

Southern Door: Renewing Our Earth

1. Indigenous peoples have the responsibility and right to restore, maintain, and strengthen their relationship with the Mother Earth in accordance with the lessons of the medicine wheel and in accordance with their responsibilities to future generations.
2. Indigenous peoples have the responsibility and right to the restoration and protection of the total environment and the productive capacity of their lands, territories, and resources.
3. Indigenous peoples have the responsibility and right to their traditional knowledge, including the right to protect and develop their knowledge of plants, animals, and minerals.
4. Indigenous peoples have the responsibility and right to control, protect, and develop their spiritual, cultural, and intellectual property.

Western Door: Restoring Our Civilization

1. Indigenous peoples have the responsibility to restore, maintain, and strengthen their civilizations and their humanity.
2. Indigenous peoples have the responsibility and right to belong to an Indigenous civilization or nation, in accordance with their traditions and ceremonies.
3. Indigenous peoples have the responsibility and right to restore, manifest, practise, develop, and teach their spiritual and religious consciousness, traditions, customs, and ceremonies.
4. Indigenous peoples have the responsibility for the collective right to restore, maintain, and develop the distinct spiritual standards that inform their language, culture, gender, economic, social, and psychological and political characteristics.
5. Indigenous peoples have the responsibility and right to practise and revitalize their worldviews, languages, traditions, and customs.
6. Indigenous peoples have the responsibility and right to their heritage and knowledge. This includes the capacity to restore, maintain, protect, and strengthen the past, present, and future manifestations of their creativity, knowledge, and skills.
7. Indigenous peoples have the responsibility and right to restore, revitalize, use, develop, and transmit to future generations their languages, oral traditions, songs, philosophy, knowledge, writing system, and literature, and their heritage and visions.
8. Indigenous peoples have the responsibility and right to reform, designate, and retain their own names for the land, knowledge, communities, places, and persons.
9. Indigenous peoples have the responsibility to learn their worldview, language, and consciousness. Included with this responsibility is the right to establish and control their educational systems and learning traditions based on their worldview, language, consciousness, and aspirations.
10. Indigenous peoples have the responsibility and right to restore, maintain, and develop their own civilization in accordance with their own traditions and ceremonies.
11. Indigenous peoples have the responsibility and right to formulate, choose, and implement their priorities and strategies for exercising their rights to safety, comfort, and development.
12. Indigenous peoples are entitled to maintain and reinforce their Indigenous order within the international and national legal system. This includes the observance of Indigenous law and custom, Aboriginal and treaty rights, and the use of Indigenous languages and ceremonies. They must have the right to apply them to matters within and between their communities and in disputes with neighbours to maintain harmony, peace, and good order.

Northern Door: Partnerships in Action

1. To ensure that Indigenous peoples, if they so choose, have the right to effective participation in the political, economic, social, and cultural life of the artificial modern state, the United Nations system, and corporations.
2. The United Nations, states, corporations, bureaucracies, and other entities must respect and affirm that Indigenous peoples have the right to effective participation in all levels of decision making in matters that may affect their responsibilities and rights, lives, and destinies through representatives chosen by themselves in accordance with their own traditions and ceremonies.
3. The United Nations, states, corporations, bureaucracies, churches, and other entities must respect the integrity of the worldviews, languages, traditions, and ceremonies of Indigenous peoples and their right to sustain them in all situations and in all media.
4. The United Nations, states, corporations, churches, and other entities must respect Indigenous peoples' right to liberty of conscience, their freedom of spiritual practices, and sacred worldview. They must take necessary and affirmative measures to ensure that no attempts are made to interfere with this freedom or convert them to other religions or to impose on them other beliefs against the will of the community.
5. The United Nations, states, corporations, bureaucracies, churches, and other entities must take effective and urgent measures to guarantee to Indigenous peoples the right to maintain and strengthen their families, traditions, and ceremonies through both Indigenous and public law in an inclusionary legal system.
6. The United Nations, states, corporations, bureaucracies, churches, and other entities must take effective measures to recognize and affirm that Indigenous legal orders are an integral part of the international and nation legal systems and the framework in which Indigenous development takes place.
7. The United Nations, states, corporations, bureaucracies, churches, and other entities must take effective measures to recognize and affirm Indigenous medicine; pharmacology; health practices; and promotion, including preventative and rehabilitative practices, without limiting access to all other health institutions, services, and medical care that ensures adequate health services.

POLICY RECOMMENDATIONS ON CULTURAL RESTORATION DEVELOPED AT
SASKATOON SUMMER INSTITUTE

A. International Policy Recommendations

1. Adoption of the UN Guidelines

DELEGATES should engage their governments and Aboriginal peoples in a cooperative effort to ensure the speedy consideration, adoption, and implementation of the Draft UN *Principles and Guidelines for the Protection of the Heritage of Indigenous Peoples.*

DELEGATES should promote governmental support for adoption of the relevant provisions of the UN *Draft Declaration on the Rights of Indigenous Peoples* and the draft *Inter-American Declaration on the Rights of Indigenous Peoples.*

2. Create Organizational Teams and Networks for WGIP Theme Year of Education

DELEGATES affirmed that special effort should be made by Indigenous educators to prepare for the 1997 theme of education in the Working Group on Indigenous Populations. This year the Indigenous health educators have not organized such a conference.

3. Consolidation of Indigenous Conferences

DELEGATES agreed that the proliferation of meetings on Indigenous topics, especially on traditional Indigenous knowledge, be consolidated and coordinated through the Working Group on Indigenous Populations and its Indigenous participants. Because of the time, expense, and travel involved in the various meetings, Indigenous peoples are being denied access to these meetings.

4. Strengthen the UN Human Rights Centre

DELEGATES agreed that the existing Human Rights Centre is inefficient and inadequate to meet the cultural restoration needs of Indigenous people. The centre should be strengthened with a new cultural restoration mandate or agency and focus on hiring Indigenous staff and interns.

5. UN Commission on Sustainable Development (UNCSD)

In conjunction with Aboriginal organizations, DELEGATES should play a larger role in preparing their governments' annual reports to the commission and in ensuring that each report contains an explicit audit of measures taken thus far to implement their governments' obligations to Aboriginal peoples under Agenda 21 (in particular, Chapter 26).

DELEGATES should also consider the establishment of a program to increase Aboriginal participation in the work of the commission, including as nongovernmental representatives and as experts seconded to the commission's New York office and to the UN Food and Agriculture Organization (FAO).

6. UNCSD Intergovernmental Panel on Forests (IPF)

Consistent with the UN initiative of placing traditional knowledge on the agenda of this new policy body, Aboriginal people should play a leading technical role in the panel's deliberations. In collaboration with their governments' Forest Service and Foreign Affairs, DELEGATES should facilitate the organizing of an Aboriginal Working Group on Traditional Knowledge for the purpose of preparing and submitting independent scientific reports to the panel.

7. Implementing the Biodiversity Convention

DELEGATES should promote the creation of a special unit of Indigenous experts within the secretariat for the convention, which was relocated to Montreal and, in cooperation with DFAIT, encourage other state parties to contribute voluntarily to the additional cost of such a technical and scientific body.

DELEGATES should also consider creating a special dedicated fellowship fund to encourage Aboriginal scholars and science students to engage in research or training as residents of the secretariat's Montreal office.

8. Ratification of ILO Convention No. 169

DELEGATES should encourage the convening of parliamentary hearings in Canada and in their countries on the desirability of ratifying the ILO Convention and collaborate with the ILO Liaison Offices and Aboriginal educational institutions in raising public awareness of the convention and understanding of ILO provisions, especially within Aboriginal communities. Whether or not the convention is ultimately ratified, the review exercise should help to build political support for domestic legislative action on the issues with which the convention is concerned.

9. Increased Efforts with UNESCO

DELEGATES agreed that Canada continues to play a large and positive role in UNESCO, the lead UN agency in scientific and cultural affairs, and should influence UNESCO's commitment to making its existing programs more accessible to Indigenous peoples. This should include assistance in conserving sites of cultural or ecological importance through the World Heritage Center and Man and Biosphere Programme, recovering cultural material through the mediation of the Committee on Moveable Cultural Property, and the development of information-sharing links between Indigenous peoples in different regions through UNESCO's Chairs in Communications (ORBIQUAM), one site for which is at the University of Quebec at Montreal.

As a first step, DELEGATES should facilitate an exchange of proposals between Aboriginal organizations, Aboriginal educational institutions, and the Canadian Committee for UNESCO. DELEGATES should also consider the possibility of helping to organize eight broadly representative delegations of Aboriginal educators, cultural authorities, and scientists to the next UNESCO General Assembly in September 1997 to help explore these ideas with other countries and UNESCO officials.

10. Canadian Overseas Development Aid

DELEGATES affirmed that many Aboriginal organizations and institutions are interested in participating more actively in exchanges of expertise with Indigenous communities abroad. In particular, it was suggested that the Canadian International Development Agency (CIDA) should be encouraged to make greater use of Aboriginal expertise at all levels and to facilitate direct contacts between Aboriginal institutions in Canada and overseas. Special CIDA funding should be set aside for the establishment of technical networks linking individual experts, communities, and institutions on areas such as ecology and traditional medicine, for the secondment of Aboriginal experts to CIDA projects that involve Indigenous peoples, and for the recruitment of Aboriginal college and university students as trainees to participate in CIDA-supported projects.

DELEGATES should also consider engaging CIDA and relevant Aboriginal institutions in devising procedures to ensure that CIDA projects, and other international development-assistance programs to which Canadians contribute financially, respect the rights of Indigenous peoples and, in particular, take into account the UN guidelines.

11. Wildlife Conservation Treaties

DELEGATES affirmed that Canada and other governments are an active party to a growing web of wildlife management treaties, which increasingly affect the ability of Aboriginal peoples to maintain their traditional uses of living resources. These include regional arrangements on migratory birds, polar bears, Arctic caribou, salmon, halibut, and fur scale, and global ones such as the *Convention on International Trade in Endangered Species* (CITES) and *Convention of Highly Migratory and Straddling Fish Stocks*. Aboriginal peoples have an interest in the equitable application of these treaties, and in the negotiation of the terms of new conservation measures, and can make significant scientific contributions to these arrangements.

As a first step, DELEGATES should consider cooperating with DFAIT and Aboriginal educational institutions in producing a clear guidebook for Aboriginal communities, surveying their governments' treaty commitments in this field, and their relationship to domestic conservation measures. This baseline report should be followed by publication of an annual review of the status of implementation of their governments' obligations and conflicts that have arisen with Aboriginal resource uses. Aboriginal expertise should be included routinely in their governments' delegations to conferences for the negotiation and adjustment of wildlife treaties.

DELEGATES should consider designating at least one Aboriginal institution to serve as a centre for gathering data from Aboriginal communities and coordinating Aboriginal expertise that may bear on their governments' wildlife treaties.

12. Fur Trade Boycott in Europe

DELEGATES were concerned with the European Economic Union banning furs taken from the Arctic by Indigenous peoples. They see this act as a violation of their human rights and as an act of genocide.

13. NAFTA and Regional Trade Liberalization

Many Aboriginal, as well as non-Aboriginal, groups have raised concern for the impact of NAFTA on their government's cultural heritage. The anticipated expansion of NAFTA membership in Latin America will mean a significant growth of Canadian trade with other countries that will have an important impact on Indigenous heritage. This will increase trade in Indigenous peoples' cultures, products, arts, and knowledge and, undoubtedly, lead to trade disputes regarding the protection of Indigenous heritage and intellectual property. Heritage and intellectual property right standards will be targets of legal challenges and of pressure for harmonization.

DELEGATES should consider collaborating with Aboriginal organizations and Aboriginal legal experts in bringing these issues to the attention of Canadian trade officials, ensuring that they are taken into account in ongoing NAFTA negotiations, and supplying relevant expertise to the negotiations as required.

DELEGATES should also consider facilitating the convening of technical meetings between Indigenous legal and cultural affairs experts of the present and anticipated NAFTA member countries to seek a common base of understanding of what measures should be taken to mitigate any adverse effects of trade liberalization. One possible solution would be negotiation of side agreements, like the NAFTA side agreement on the environment, to protect Indigenous heritage.

14. WTO and Global Trade Liberalization

Complementary measures should be considered in relation to global trade liberalization administered by the new World Trade Organization (WTO) at Geneva. New WTO rules on "TRIPs" (trade-related intellectual property rights) will ordinarily supersede any inconsistent provisions of past intellectual property right treaties to which Canada is a party, such as the *Berne* and *Paris Conventions*. Hence, future diplomatic efforts to defend their government's domestic protection of Aboriginal peoples' culture and knowledge will need to focus on WTO rather than on WIPO. The tendency of WTO will be to disallow high national standards of protection, the opposite of WIPO's objectives. Aboriginal participation in Canadian diplomacy at the WTO will therefore become essential, lest their governments' domestic initiatives to protect Aboriginal rights risk being struck down as barriers to trade.

16. Postcolonial Studies

DELEGATES urged the development of a new interdisciplinary graduate program in postcolonial studies in nation-states with more than 50 percent Indigenous population and within the UN University, hence maintaining the momentum and study of cultural restoration in very practical ways.

17. Indigenous Diplomatic Training Institutions

DELEGATES agreed that Indigenous educational institutions should create a centre for training Indigenous peoples in the UN diplomatic and technical skills. A program of financial, technical, and legal assistance should be established to assist individuals to learn how to negotiate within the many levels of the UN system. This program should have many sites, and students should be required to travel to each campus before obtaining their degrees.

18. CD-ROM Archival Project

DELEGATES agree that a major priority of the decade must be a CD-ROM project to collect all the documents and history of the Indigenous Movement in the UN. The CD should be made accessible to all Indigenous peoples and libraries.

B. Canadian and Domestic Recommendations

1. Protecting Aboriginal Languages

DELEGATES should facilitate with Aboriginal peoples the protection of Aboriginal languages that control the knowledge of each Aboriginal people. Within these languages are not only the intellectual and cultural knowledge but also the procedures for maintaining and renewing this knowledge. Conservation of Aboriginal languages should be acknowledged formally as constitutional rights and as an element of the inherent right to self-government under current policy.

2. Protecting Aboriginal Heritage

DELEGATES should facilitate the devolution of the minister's heritage conservation authority under section 91 of the *Indian Act,* through, among other things, special programs of financial and technical assistance. Conservation of knowledge and cultural heritage should be acknowledged formally as an element of the inherent right to self-government.

3. Land-Claims Settlements

DELEGATES should ensure, through participation in the negotiation of unresolved land claims, that heritage conservation is expressly and thoroughly addressed in final settlement agreements. This is the current trend. Final agreements should include, at a minimum, identification of significant ecosystems and important cultural sites and assign responsibility for conserving them as an intrinsic part of the parties' legal obligations.

4. National Park and Heritage Sites

DELEGATES should engage Parks Canada and Heritage Canada in a review, in collaboration with Aboriginal communities, of significant cultural values and traditional uses of existing parks and heritage sites, with a view to assuring their protection through co-management agreements.

DELEGATES should also develop a program to assist Aboriginal organizations and communities with the identification and documentation of important sites and resource uses that should be added to the national parks and heritage site system.

DELEGATES should consider proposing legislation, on the model of Australia, authorizing the minister to designate special Aboriginal heritage sites at the request of Aboriginal people.

5. National Cultural Institutions

DELEGATES should collaborate with Aboriginal educational institutions in an effort to inventory culturally significant materials in museums, both within Canada and abroad, and make this information available to Aboriginal communities. A program of financial, technical, and legal assistance should be established to assist communities in repatriating significant materials, in providing facilities for the conservation of these materials under community control, and in making shared-custody arrangements with museums. Canadian museums and teaching institutions should be encouraged to repeat the UN draft guidelines as a condition of federal financial support.

6. Designation of Aboriginal "Masters"

DELEGATES should consider proposing new legislation to authorize the minister, or a special Aboriginal commission, to designate individuals as masters of traditional knowledge or arts upon the recommendation of Aboriginal communities. The main aim of this designation would be to validate the national importance of these individuals and increase the interest of young people in learning their skills. Financial stipends should ordinarily not be involved. Japan's designation of individuals as "living cultural treasures" may be taken as a model.

7. Designation of "Living Laboratories"

DELEGATES should consider proposing new legislation to authorize the minister, or a special Aboriginal commission, to designate particular traditional resource-use sites as living laboratories to be conserved, under local Aboriginal management, for the study of Aboriginal ecology and resource management, and maintenance of the associated systems of ceremonies and knowledge. This would build on the original objectives of UNESCO's Man and the Biosphere program and might be undertaken in cooperation with the secretariat (UNEP) of the *Biodiversity Convention* and the World Heritage Office of UNESCO.

8. Federal Environmental Assessment

DELEGATES should engage Environment Canada and Aboriginal educational and scientific institutions in developing a protocol for assessing the impact of proposed activities on Aboriginal heritage and knowledge, a routine requirement of FERA. At a minimum, this protocol should aim to ensure the compatibility of any proposed activities with articles 8 and 10 of the *Biodiversity Convention*.

Rapid assessment under FERA would be facilitated by *anticipatory mapping* of Crown lands for heritage sites and cultural sensitivities. DELEGATES should consider programs of financial and technical cooperation with Aboriginal communities and institutions for this purpose.

9. Fisheries and Wildlife Management

In accordance with the *Biodiversity Convention*, DELEGATES should take immediate steps to ensure that the Department of Fisheries and Oceans, the Canadian Wildlife Service, the Canadian Forest Service, and, as far as possible through intergovernmental agreements, relevant provincial forest and wildlife agencies (a) minimize the impact of conservation measures on traditional Aboriginal uses of resources; (b) promote and help to finance the widest possible use of co-management agreements with Aboriginal communities; and (c) tender ecological research on species utilized by Aboriginal peoples to Aboriginal institutions.

10. Patent and Copyright Protection

DELEGATES should consider drafting legislation, in collaboration with Aboriginal organizations and communities, that would specially protect Aboriginal heritage and knowledge, through registration with a special national commission or trustee, on the model of the WIPO model laws on folklore. Special legislation would be needed to overcome limitations in the *Copyright Act* ("originality"), the *Patent Act* ("inventiveness," "novelty"), and the *Seeds Act*, respecting protectability, the duration of the protection, and the holder of the rights. This would include creating a new Indigenous group copyright. Compatibility of the special legislation with NAFTA and GATT requires careful attention. The WIPO model law has a foundation in the *Berne Convention*, which was amended in 1971 to permit registration of "folklore" to a trustee designated by national law. Other restrictions, such as expiry of the protection after a term of years, still apply. Under subsequent trade liberalization treaties, however, cross-boundary differences in scope and duration of protection may be challenged as restrictive in effect.

11. Trademark, Appellations of Origin

DELEGATES should consider developing measures, in collaboration with Aboriginal organizations and communities, to establish a comprehensive and effective program of trademark protection for Aboriginal products and services, building upon their government's previous experience with arts and crafts designations. Aboriginal governments, trade associations, arts organizations, and scientific institutions should be given authority to create and register unique trade names and trademarks that should be deposited in a special national registry.

DELEGATES should also consider a program to heighten public awareness of these trademarks, in Canada and abroad, and to provide financial, technical, and legal assistance to Aboriginal people and organizations to pursue infringements.

12. Import-Export Controls

DELEGATES should recommend amendments to the *Cultural Property Export and Import Act* for the purposes of (a) restricting the export of any moveable cultural property that an Aboriginal community or Aboriginal traditional owner's request be protected, regardless of monetary value; and (b) directing the minister to recover cultural property, on behalf of the traditional Aboriginal owners, within Canada as well as abroad, including the use of administrative procedures in UNESCO.

13. Civil Liability Legislation

DELEGATES should develop legislation, in collaboration with Aboriginal organizations and communities, authorizing the federal courts to hear civil actions brought by traditional Aboriginal owners for recovery of culturally significant objects, for protecting the privacy of holders of traditional Aboriginal knowledge, and for ensuring confidentiality where traditional knowledge has been conditionally shared or licensed. The customary laws of the Aboriginal peoples concerned should be made dispositive in any dispute over ownership or authorized use.

14. Institutional Capacity-Building

Programs of federal funding for Aboriginal primary and secondary education should give higher priority to the maintenance of Aboriginal languages, not only through special language training courses but also through instruction presented in Aboriginal languages. Equal fluency, rather than English or French dominance, should be an explicit policy, and greater efforts should be made to support educational institutions that develop and publish Aboriginal-language instructional materials.

Federal funding for Aboriginal higher education should target the establishment and strengthening of centres for research on traditional knowledge and its applications and the training of younger Aboriginal scholars in this field. Highest priority should be given to colleges and institutes chartered or operated by Aboriginal communities and to university-based programs that are directly accountable to Aboriginal people. A "centre of excellence" should be identified in each of the principal biogeographic regions of Canada in the spirit of UN General Assembly resolutions 49/214 and 50/176 (on the International Decade of the World's Indigenous People).

15. National Research Funding Councils

DELEGATES should engage the National Science and Engineering Research Council and the Social Sciences and Humanities Research Council in the development of strategic initiatives to support capacity-building and research in the field of traditional knowledge, targeting institutes chartered or operated by Aboriginal communities, and university-based programs that are directly accountable to Aboriginal people. Funding councils should be urged to bring their research ethics standards into conformity with the UN draft guidelines.

16. Postcolonial Graduate Studies

DELEGATES urged the development of a new interdisciplinary graduate program in postcolonial studies at the University of Saskatchewan in partnership with the Saskatchewan Indian Federated College, which may inspire similar initiatives at other Canadian universities, hence maintaining the momentum in very practical ways.

[signed by Marie Battiste, Director, 1996 Summer Institute on the Cultural Restoration of Aboriginal Peoples]

Contributors

Marie Battiste is a Mi'kmaq educator from Potlo'tek First Nations in Unama'kik, Nova Scotia, and a professor in the Indian and Northern Education Program at the University of Saskatchewan. She is co-editor of *First Nations Education in Canada: The Circle Unfolds*, co-author with J.Y. Henderson of *Protecting Indigenous Knowledge* (Saskatoon: Purich Publishing, 2000), and a board member of the International Research Institute for Maori and Indigenous Education in New Zealand and of the International Development Research Centre (IDRC) of Canada. With degrees from the University of Maine, Harvard University, and Stanford University, her international publications and lectures on Aboriginal languages, knowledge, and education have earned her honorary doctorate degrees from St. Mary's University and the University of Maine at Farmington.

Gregory Cajete is Tewa from Santa Clara Pueblo in New Mexico. Formerly dean of the Institute of American Indian Arts in Santa Fe, which has produced many fine Indian artists, dancers, and writers, he is currently a faculty member at the University of New Mexico. He received his PhD from William Lion University in San Diego. He is the author of *Look to the Mountain: An Ecology of Indigenous Education* (Skyland, NC: Kivaki Press, 1995), *Ignite the Sparkle: An Indigenous Science Education Model* (Skyland, NC: Kivaki Press, 1999), and *Native Science: Natural Laws of Interdependence* (Santa Fe, NM: Clearlight, 2000). As a consultant for Tewa Consulting, he has spoken widely on the foundations of Indigenous education and has served on many national and international committees and boards.

J. Edward Chamberlin was born in Vancouver and educated at the University of British Columbia, Oxford University, and the University of Toronto. Since 1970, he has been on the faculty of the University of Toronto, where he is now a professor of English and comparative literature. He has been a senior research associate with the Royal Commission on Aboriginal Peoples in Canada and a poetry editor of *Saturday Night*. His books include *The Harrowing of Eden: White Attitudes towards Native Americans* (1975), *Oscar Wilde's London* (1987), and *Come Back to Me My Language: Poetry and the West Indies* (1993). He is currently directing a project on oral and written traditions.

Erica-Irene Daes is a member of a United Nations Sub-Commission to Protect Minorities, the chair of the UN Working Group on Indigenous Populations, and a collaboratrice of the Hellenic Institute of International and Foreign Law. Author of a number of publications dealing with matters such as war crimes, self-determination for minorities and their treatment in Europe, a draft constitution for a new Europe, and an international bill of human rights, she received an honorary doctorate of laws at the 1996 International Summer Institute at the University of Saskatchewan.

Bonnie Duran, Dr. P.H., has been working in the field of public health with Native American populations for twenty years. She is an assistant professor at the Master's of Public Health Program at the University of New Mexico School of Medicine. She conducts health services research and mental health epidemiology research with the Navajos and Pueblos of New Mexico, and she teaches public health intervention theory. She is co-author of *Native American Post-Colonial Psychology* (1996).

Eduardo Duran is Apache/Tewa and currently the director of the Behavioral Services Department, First Nations Community Healthsource, in Albuquerque, New Mexico. His PhD in clinical psychology was awarded by the California School of Professional Psychology in 1983. Among his several books are *Transforming the Soul Wound: A Theoretical and Clinical Approach to American Indian Psychology* (1990); *Native American Post-Colonial Psychology* (co-authored, 1996); *Healing PTSD among Native Americans* (co-edited, in press); and *Domestic Violence in Indian Country: A Post-Colonial Perspective* (co-edited, in press).

L.M. Findlay is a graduate of Aberdeen and Oxford Universities and currently a professor of English and the director of the Humanities Research Unit at the University of Saskatchewan. A former president of ACCUTE, he is now vice-president (External Communications) for the Humanities and Social Sciences Federation of Canada. He was trained as a Victorianist and has published extensively on nineteenth-century thought and culture. In recent years, his interest in cultural theory and disciplinary history led him to edit and contribute to *Value and the University* (1993); *Realizing Community: Multidisciplinary Essays* (1995); and the forthcoming *Authority and Interpretation*.

James (Sákéj) Youngblood Henderson is Chickasaw, born to the Bear Clan of the Chickasaw Nation and Cheyenne Tribe in Oklahoma. Sákéj is one of the leading tribal philosophers, advocates, and strategists for North American Indians. In 1974, he was one of the first American Indians to receive a juris doctorate in law from Harvard Law School. After graduation, he sought through scholarship and litigation to restore Aboriginal culture, institutions, and rights. During the constitutional process in Canada from 1978 to 1993, he served as a constitutional advisor for the Assembly of First Nations and the Mi'kmaq Nation. He is currently a member of the College of Law, University of Saskatchewan, and the senior administrator and research director of the Native Law Centre. He is the author of *Mi'kmaq Concordat* (1997), a co-author of *Aboriginal Tenure in the Constitution of Canada* (Carswell, 2000), and *Protecting Indigenous*

Knowledge (2000), and a co-editor of *Continuing Poundmaker's and Riel's Quest* (1995), and he is widely published in law review journals.

Ian Hingley is a teacher at Churchhill School in La Ronge, in northern Saskatchewan, and was on leave to work on a master's degree in the Educational Foundations Department at the University of Saskatchewan at the time of this writing. He is actively engaged in research and writing in the area of human rights education, in particular, in order to create an activity-based human rights education. His teaching methodology seeks to reflect and incorporate a diversity of educational theories within a hands-on experiential learning environment.

Linda Hogan is a Chickasaw poet, novelist, and essayist. Her *Through the Sun* received the American Book Award from the Before Columbus Foundation. She is also the author of *Calling Myself Home* (1978); *Mean Spirit* (1990); *The Book of Medicines* (1993); and, most recently, *Dwelling: A Spiritual History of the Living World* (1995) and *Solar Storms* (1995). *Mean Spirit* was recognized as the runner-up for a Pulitzer Prize. Currently, she is a professor at the University of Colorado.

Poka Laenui (Hayden F. Burgess) received his juris doctorate in 1976 from William Richardson School of Law, Hawaii. He is currently the executive director of Hale Na'au Pono, a community-based behavioural health agency in his home community of Wai'anae. The agency provides an Indigenous alternative to the Western/clinical model in the provision of behavioural health services. From 1984 to 1990, he was vice-president of the World Council of Indigenous Peoples, where his primary responsibility was as an advocate for international human rights. He has also participated actively in working groups under the United Nations and the International Labor Organization.

Ted Moses is Grand Chief of the Grand Council of Crees of Quebec and their ambassador to the United Nations. Educated at Ryerson and at McGill University, he has been a long-time advocate of Aboriginal human rights. Prior to his election as grand chief in 1984, he played a prominent role in the negotiation of the James Bay and Northern Quebec Agreement and in the James Bay Crees obtaining formal NGO status at the United Nations. He also received an honorary doctorate degree at the 1996 International Summer Institute at the University of Saskatchewan.

Leroy Little Bear is a member of the Blood tribe of the Blackfoot Confederacy. He is the former director of the Native American Program at Harvard University and professor emeritus of Native studies at the University of Lethbridge, where he was formerly department chair. He has served as a legal and constitutional advisor to the Assembly of First Nations and on many influential committees, commissions, and boards dealing with First Nations issues. He has written several articles and co-edited three books: *Pathways to Self-Determination: Canadian Indians and the Canadian State* (1984); *Quest for Justice: Aboriginal Peoples and Aboriginal Rights* (1985); and *Governments in Conflict and Indian Nations in Canada* (1988).

Graham Hingangaroa Smith is currently a professor of Maori education in the School of Education and the pro-vice chancellor (Maori) at the University of Auckland. His academic research is based in critical theory approaches to Indigenous transformation. His PhD dissertation at the same university is entitled "The Development of Kaupapa Maori: Theory and Praxis," in which he examines and theorizes the educational revitalization by Maori in the 1980s. He has worked extensively with Indigenous peoples from around the world, including Asia, the Pacific, and North and South America. He has published extensively on Maori and Indigenous education and is regarded as a leading Indigenous scholar in New Zealand. More significantly, perhaps, he is widely known as an innovator of new ideas within education and has had firsthand involvement in preschool, primary school, secondary school, and tertiary educational interventions for Maori learners. Professor Smith is of Ngati Apa and Ngati Porou tribal descent.

Linda Tuhiwai Te Rina Smith is an associate professor in education and the director of the Research Institute for Maori and Indigenous Education at the University of Auckland. She is a Maori from Ngati Awa and Ngati Porou tribal groups. She has worked as a researcher in areas of health and education for a number of years. Her book *Decolonizing Methodologies: Indigenous Peoples and Research*, stemming from her doctoral dissertation at the University of Auckland, has been recently published by Zed Books and the University of Otago Press (1999).

Asha Varadharajan is an associate professor at Queen's University, having completed her PhD at the University of Saskatchewan in 1993. Her *Exotic Parodies: Subjectivity in Adorno, Said, and Spivak* was published recently by the University of Minnesota Press. She is also the author of "Dissensus, Dissolution, and the Possibility of Community" in the *University of Toronto Quarterly* (fall 1997), and she has several forthcoming publications on cultural politics and postcolonialism, on Adorno, on history and theory, and on David Dabydeen, among others. She is currently at work on a book-length project about the intersections among psychoanalysis, postcolonialism, and historicism.

Robert Yazzie is Navajo and the chief justice of the Navajo Nation. With a law degree from the University of New Mexico, he was appointed to the bench in 1986. He is a strong advocate of the sharing of traditional values and continues to implement the Navajo philosophy in the Navajo Nation courts. He is a formidable leader in the Navajo campaign against the pain of domestic violence and an advocate for victims' rights. Since his appointment as chief justice, he has initiated sentencing commissions, expanded the Navajo Nation Peacemaker Division, and promulgated domestic violence court rules that integrate Navajo common law and American common law concepts.

The following pages contain photographs of participants at the 1996 International Summer Institute at the University of Saskatchewan.

Group photo of the delegates and participants of the 1996 Summer Institute at the University of Saskatchewan

Sákéj Henderson confers with delegates from Greece: Erica-Irene Daes and Kalliopi Kouffa

Eduardo Duran speaking about
postcolonial psychology built on
Aboriginal thought

Vice-Provost of the University of
Auckland Graham Hingangaroa Smith

Animator Leroy Little Bear kept the delegates entertained with his quips; at the
table are Danny Alford and Linda Smith

Linda Tuhiwai Te Rina Smith explains a process for decolonizing methodologies in Maori research

Eber Hampton, president of the Saskatchewan Indian Federated College, provides opening remarks

Gregory Cajete listens in the talking circle to Eric Tootoosis

Augusto Williemson Díaz provides an overview of the events leading to the United Nations Indigenous Human Rights agenda

Asha Varadharajan delivering her thoughts on repressive tolerance and exotic parodies

Participants convene in the Great Hall at the University of Saskatchewan

Gregory Cajete explaining
Indigenous knowledge

Dr. Ted Moses delivered the
convocation address upon receiving
an honorary degree

Delegates Giulia Scarpa, of Florence, Italy; Augusto Williemson Díaz, of
Guatemala; and author/poet Linda Hogan wait for convocation ceremonies
to begin

Animator Leroy Little Bear and other participants of the institute listen to a presentation

Honorary degree recipients Ted Moses and Erica-Irene Daes lead an honouring round dance during convocation ceremonies at the University of Saskatchewan

Editor Marie Battiste and Sákéj Henderson congratulate Erica-Irene Daes on receiving an honorary doctorate degree

Index

Plains Indians, 77, 78, 79
Plants: protocols for picking, 272. *See also* Corn; Natural world
Poems: Clay Pots and Bones, 9; Forest of Europe, 126; Heritage, 55; Listen to the Bones, ix; Our Nation World, 179; The Rose of Hope, 113; The Teachings of My Grandmother, 119
Polarities, 251-2, 267
Political correctness, 143, 147-8
Positive law concept, 20-2, 32
Postcolonial theory, 125, 130, 131, 132, 144-5; acknowledgement of contradictions, 132, 137-8; difficulties within, 132; revision of anthropological analyses, 255
Postcolonialism, xix, xvi, 31-3; healing process, xviii; postcolonial Indigenous thought, xix; role of Indigenous languages, 264; spiritual independence, xix, 47; synthesis of worldviews, 250; transformation of colonial mindset, 31-3, 101; valuing of all worldviews, 87; views of colonized writers, 87, 250-1. *See also* Postcolonial theory
Postmodern analysis, 213
Pottery, 185
Power: decisionmaking structures, 46; imbalances, 46-7; triangle of power, 43. *See also* Domination; Empowerment; Oppression
Prerogative treaties. *See* Treaty commonwealth
Primitive mind theory, 103
Principles and Guidelines for the Protection of the Heritage of Indigenous Peoples, 279-84
Privilege, xxvi, 70-1, 110; control of the rules, 103, 104-5; effects of Canadian constitutional reform on, 167-8; role of Canadian educational system in maintaining, 196; role of free-market economy in maintaining, 216
Pro-active initiatives, 210-11; Maori education, 220-4
The Problem of Indian Administration (report), 128
Psychology: cross-cultural approaches, xvii, 86-7; effects of colonialism on Indigenous psyches, 4-6, 71-2, 84-5, 186-7, 189; need for historical truth, 88; new paradigms, xxvi, 89; of oppression, 4-6; soul wounds, 98. *See also* Decolonization process; Western psychology
Psychometric assessment, 93

Pueblo peoples: dances, 184, 185-6; history, 182-3; Kokopelli, 182; metaphors of education, 181-7; pottery, 185
Pulawa, Wilford: *State of Hawai'i v. Wilford N. Pulawa*, 153, 159, 160n

Quebec: James Bay and Northern Quebec Agreement, 173; sovereignty, 176, 177

Racism: attitudes internalized by children, 102-3; institutional, xxvii, 93; negative valuing of Aboriginal differences, 67-71, 139-40, 253; psychometric assessment, 93; strategies, 66, 67. *See also* Cognitive imperialism; Oppression
Rangatiratanga concept, 239
Religious imperialism, 151
Research: Western research models, 95-6. *See also* Kaupapa Maori research; Scholarship; Universities
Reservation allotments, 40
Riddles, 124-5
Rights: children, 198; civil rights laws, 42; natural rights, 23; recognition of Aboriginal rights in Canada, 173, 174, 175-6. *See also* Indigenous rights
Royal Commission on Aboriginal Peoples, 1996 (Canada), 193

Saskatoon Declaration of Indigenous Cultural Restoration and Policy Recommendations on Cultural Restoration, 285-94
Savagery concept, 28-9, 68, 73n, 97
Scarcity, 15
Scarpa, Giulia, *303*
Scholarship: Indigenous, x-xiii, xx-xxi, 213-14; postmodern analysis, 213. *See also* Research; Universities
Science, 211-12
Self-determination: Declaration on Indigenous Rights, 169-70; Hawaiian people, xxv, 50-3, 152-3, 155-8, 159; imposition of Eurocentric models, 155; Saskatoon Declaration, 285-7; United Nations resolution, 51-2; voters, 53. *See also* Pro-active initiatives; Sovereignty
Sharing (as a value), 79
Slave trade, 71-2
Smith, Graham Hingangaroa, xxix, 298, *300*
Smith, Linda Tuhiwai Te Rina, xxix, 226, 244n, 298, *300, 301*
Social control: in Indigenous societies, 79, 83-4, 85, 271; Navajo peacemaking, 44-6

Indigenous Peoples (1996), University of Saskatchewan
United States: Civil War, 40; establishment of colonies, 41; Hawaiian statehood, xxi, 50-3, 152-3, 155-8, 159; Indian wars, 39; invasion of Hawaii, 51, 152, 160n; laws, 40; occupation of Aboriginal land, 39-40; *The Problem of Indian Administration* (report), 128; reservation period, 39; suppression of Indian culture, 40. *See also* entries beginning with North American
Universalism, 63-5, 69-70, 264-5
Universities: Eurocentrism, xix-xx, 59, 95-6, 164; need for Aboriginal presence, x-xiii

Varadharajan, Asha, xxvii, 298, *302*
Violence: domestic, 43-6, 47; healing response to, 47; postcolonial theory, 132. *See also* Oppression; War
Visions, 267
Von Thater, Rose, xxii

Walcott, Derek: Forest of Europe (poem), 126
Wapachee, Tommy, 173
War: related to Eurocentric thought, 31; state of nature theory, 15-16, 17; treaty commonwealth, 22-3, 24. *See also* Wars
Wars; American Civil War, 40; Indian Wars (United States), 39; Northwest Rebellion, 41; World War I, 41
Ways of knowing, 267-8. *See also* Eurocentric thought; Worldviews
Welfare, 109

Western psychology, 92-3, 95-6; diagnostic inadequacy, 99; effects of colonial ideology, 71-2; failure to meet needs of North American Indians, 89; historical roots, 88-9; possible integration with Indigenous worldviews, 93, 96, 97, 98-9
Western research models, 95-6
Western subjectivity. *See* Eurocentric thought
Western traditions, 145
Whakapapa concept, 234-5
Whanau concept, 221, 224, 230, 240-1
White Bear Indian Reserve, 102-3
WHO. *See* World Health Organization
Wholeness (as a value), 79-80
Williams, Betty, 119-20
Williemson Díaz, Augusto, 177-8, *302, 303*
Women: Maori, 231, 240, 245n, 247n; marginalized in Eurocentric history, 107-8; place in Indigenous societies, 108
World Conference on Indigenous People (1978), 194
World Health Organization, 178
World War I, 41
Worldviews: competition between, 77, 84-5; effects of dissonance between, 186-7; multicultural, 142-9, 187. *See also* Contexts; Eurocentric thought; Indigenous worldviews; Paradigms
Written traditions, 138

Yazzie, Robert, xxv, 47, 298
Young, Iris, 29-30, 32